AMERICAN SLANG

CULTURAL LANGUAGE GUIDE
TO
Living in the USA

Joseph Melillo and Edward M. Melillo, J.D.

Seattle, Washington
Portland, Oregon
Denver, Colorado
Vancouver, B.C.
Scottsdale, Arizona
Minneapolis, Minnesota

ISBN: 1-59404-017-6
Library of Congress Control Number: 2003115816

Printed in the United States of America

Cover Creation: Edward M. Melillo
Art Direction: David Marty Design
Editors: Edward M. Melillo and Joseph Melillo
Illustrations: Joseph Melillo

Address purchasing and distribution inquiries to:
Kiku Education Institute
P.O. Box 15785
Seattle, Washington 98115

Classic Day Publishing
Houseboat #4
2207 Fairview Avenue East
Seattle, Washington 98102
www.classicdaypublishing.com
Email: info@classicdaypublishing.com

PREFACE

This language guide brings the reader closer to the real world of inter-personal communication in American culture and society. It contains over 5,000 slang terms or idiomatic expressions, along with definitions and sentence examples. These words and phrases, in large part, define the cultural heartbeat of the American tongue.

Today, especially, we see a surprisingly large number of slang expressions in books, magazines and other newsprint, as well as spoken in everyday speech. Slang terms are used so much these days, whether in print or in conversation, that it becomes essential to know and understand their meanings. There is no doubt that formal English is essential if you want to read and speak well. But if you want to read and speak well enough to get along, then you need to understand the non-traditional language of slang that one often does not learn in English class.

Slang originally evolved as a style of informal language. It was a way to speak more casually and to identify with others within a certain societal class or cultural group. It also evolved as a somewhat secret vocabulary by particular classes or groups in society to keep others from understanding what was communicated. Historically, too, it was associated with being the language commonly used by the so-called subclasses in society. Today, all of these notions have completely changed. Slang terms are now commonly accepted. They are readily used throughout most social classes and cultural groups. It is hard to converse with another, or read a magazine or newspaper, without coming across slang terms.

Slang expressions tend to emanate from a range of various subcultures in society. The uniqueness of slang is that it embodies the attitudes and values of group members in a particular subculture. From there, a slang term may stay pooled in the particular subculture, or catch on and grow in popularity throughout mainstream society. It can also disappear in use in a generation or two, or otherwise resurface years later. A good example of the changing tide of slang terms can be seen in the use of the slang word, *groovy*. It means something really nice or wonderful, and was immensely popular in the 1960's. Then, in the 1970's and 1980's, *groovy* started to gradually disappear in place of the slang word, *cool*. Today, although *cool* is still used, it is being supplanted with the slang term, *sweet*, especially among the younger generation.

So, today, we have come to realize the acceptance of slang as a common part of speech by people from all walks in life. Cultural groups are not as cloistered as they once were in the past. Consequently, when a slang expression is created, it can more readily evolve as a commonly accepted term in society, thanks to instant and modern communication.

The great notion about slang is that it transcends most cultural barriers. It does not matter whether a person is rich or poor, college educated or street educated, a laborer, manager, professional, student, or English-speaking foreigner. It is undeniable, today, that slang is heard more often and spoken more freely by more Americans than ever before.

Slang words, by their measure, generally are characterized by extreme informality. Some expressions, more than others, are spoken in particular situations or settings, or in private conversations with close friends or certain parties. The informality of slang sees its opposite in the formality of English grammar. To that end, slang often reveals a full assortment of words, from polite to expressive, to the more vulgar uses of words.

Slang terms generally express what one really wants to say. Some terms, as we might know, are very raw in their vulgarity or offensiveness. The editors have been selective to the extent of choosing not to include excessively vulgar terms, or terms derived from cultural hate or racial inconsideration.

This language guide is your reference to the more common American slang terms seen in print or heard in casual conversations today. It brings a cultural understanding to recognizing what in carnation is read or said. So, venture outside the English class and discover a part of a cultural heritage of American English in the United States.

Edward M. Melillo
December 2003

INTRODUCTION

A) What is Slang?

A slang term or idiom is a phrase, often composed of two or more words, which is defined differently from the actual meaning of the individual words. For instance, the slang term, *drive someone up a wall*, does not mean, in the literal sense, that one drives with another in a car vertically up a wall, but rather means to greatly annoy and get someone angry.

Much of our slang comes from social communication among peers. Whether it is in sports, at work or social events, among close friends, or in any other kind of activity in society, slang is heard. Slang is the instinctive element of language, which comes from the cultural heart to express our moods in everyday activities.

Although most slang words tend to be fleeting in time, others become icon favorites. They are also used in different ways by different generations. Slang is the language of interaction and change. It is a form of transactional art in communication. And whether a particular slang may be good or bad art, slang expressions generally add color and vitality to conversations that help to enrich meanings in our daily speech.

You will find that the more intimate, direct, or even offensive forms of slang are generally spoken in non-public settings, or among friends and peers. Such slang is denoted throughout the book as "expressive."

It is certainly not surprising that many common slang terms are used similarly in all walks in life, from high society to the alleyways and streets. The language of slang is truly an important documentary of culture in motion.

B) When and How to Use Slang or Idiomatic Expressions

Perceptions and appropriateness in usage are culturally bound, and may be tied to several factors, such as type of ethnic group, sense of humor, timeliness, or the position or status for or to whom the expression is used or intended. Most often, we hear slang and idioms spoken generally in more casual situations or informal settings, especially among friends or peers. Remember that slang expressions generally are felt when thought out, not grammatically considered when stated. As an analogy, slang can be compared to being improvised music, compared to formal English being sheet music.

It is probably wise to have a sense when to use certain slang terms. It will depend a lot on the situation or setting, and the individuals involved in the communication. It is difficult to advise which situation or setting is appropriate in using certain verbiage. Many sentence examples are provided, which help to better understand how and when to use them. This language guide certainly will set you into better practice.

C) Informal versus Formal English

Colloquial expressions are words, phrases and idioms characterizing informal speech and writing. Colloquial does not, by any means, indicate sub-standard or illiterate usage of the English language. It also does not mean that colloquial words are old or outdated. Colloquial expressions are commonly derived from local or regional dialects, and are used informally or in conversational style. In fact, colloquial language, much of it considered slang, makes up a major exchange of information in television, movies, radio, newspapers, magazines, and everyday conversations.

Formal English, in contrast, is seen primarily in fine reading, religious sermons, or literary works. Such formal language is generally intended for selected listeners and readers.

Informal English is closer to current everyday speech, and closer to practical experiences. It is familiar with the majority of people. Colloquial speech is short, simple, and more direct in movement as contrasted to the more technical and less flexible sentences of formal English.

USE OF THIS LANGUAGE GUIDE

A) Search for Key Words

In this language guide, the slang terms are identified under key words, which are in **heavy bold**. Simply look for what you believe is the key word in the slang term, and search for it alphabetically. Under each key word, you will find the slang expressions listed in alphabetical order. The alphabetical search for slang terms is more detailed below, under *Search for Slang Terms*.

The key word will most likely be a verb, noun, preposition or an adjective, in this order of frequency:

- Verbs in idiomatic expressions appear in a variety of tenses and aspects. More clearly, the sentence example brings out the variety.

- If the phrase includes an object, it is important to know if it is a person or thing. Again, the example sentence may prove helpful.

If you happen not to see a slang expression listed under a certain key word, you may likely see a cross-reference for it under *another* key word in the expression. For example, the slang term, **Off the hook**, is listed under the key word, **Hook**, and is cross-referenced under the key word, **Off**.

Although there is no certain order how or where a slang term might be listed, you should select the word in the term that best portrays the meaning or nature of the term. If there is no listing under the particular key word, and no cross-reference, then select another key word in the term and do a search. Here and there, you will see slang expressions defined under more than one key word.

Here is another example:

Down

Down in the dumps: *See,* **Dump**.

Dump

Down in the dumps/In the dumps: experiencing sadness or gloom; feeling depressed. *He has been down in the dumps ever since his girlfriend left him.*

B) Search for Slang Terms

Slang terms are alphabetized under each key word. As to order, a space or hyphen between words comes first and ahead of words similarly spelled. For example, **Fire sale** would come before **Fired up**.

Differently worded slang terms that have virtually the same meaning are generally listed together, such as: **Blow by/Blow past**, or, **Running on all cylinders/Hitting on all cylinders**. Occasionally, when these slang terms are worded differently, it may be harder to locate the second, third, or even fourth slang term listed, because only the first slang term is alphabetized, such as: **Live off the fat of the land/Live the life of Riley/Live the high life**. Fortunately, all the terms will have the same key word (in **heavy bold**), so that locating a slang term in this setting will be easier.

Pronouns in slang terms will vary, depending on gender or application (singular or plural). Therefore, the generic pronouns, *one* or *someone*, are used to indicate that the object or possessive pronoun should be used in its place, depending on the context of the situation. For example, the term, **Afraid** of one's shadow, can be either stated in the singular form as, *afraid of her shadow*, *afraid of his shadow*, or *afraid of my shadow*, all dependent as to whom it is applied in the situation. In the sentence example, the possessive pronoun was used: *I've been afraid of my own shadow for years.*

C) Definitions and Sentence Examples

Each slang term is followed by a definition and sentence example. Some slang terms may have different meanings, in which case the definitions would be listed in numbered order. The numbering order, however, denotes no importance of priority. That is, the numbering or order placement of the definitions is arbitrary and random. For example:

Bag: 1) to place things in a bag. *At the store, we asked the clerk to bag the groceries.* 2) To forget about; to give up. *We were supposed to go to a picnic in the park but since it's raining, let's just bag it.* 3) be quiet. *I've heard enough about your complaining, so bag it!* 4) to arrest. *The police finally bagged the suspect who had been hiding in a trash bin in the alley.* 5) one's romantic partner or significant other. *Hey, I thought Frank was your bag; or did you break up with him?* 6) an inquiry in response to one's problem. *Hey, man, you look depressed; what's your bag?* 7) one's job or profession. *My bag is shipping, which allows me to travel around the world.*

Other words or expressions may also have two or even three different sentence examples. For example:

Stop short: to cut off just before the ending. *He was stopped short of the goal line as the defensive players tackled him hard. In any oral argument, it is wise to stop short of punching anyone in the face or otherwise committing* *an assault. The police officer today stopped short of giving me a ticket, in sympathy of seeing two crying babies in the back seat of our car.*

D) Slang Terms and Tense

The wording of slang terms can change depending on the usage and tense. Slang terms in the language guide are *generally* set in the present tense, although a sentence example may show the term in the past tense. For example, one of the definitions for **Buy it** is "to accept as being true." The first sentence example shows the term in the present tense: *They didn't buy his story at the parole board.* The second sentence example, however, shows the term in the past tense: *The police bought her story about the accident and decided not to give her a traffic ticket.*

E) Directory

Expressive: This notation is indicated next to potentially abrasive or offensive slang terms. Such terms are generally communicated among peers and often not heard in open public. Certain expressive terms can be considered fighting words if used in certain contexts or expressed during heavy emotion.

[expressive] vs. (expressive): the use of the brackets [ ] means that *all* the underlined slang can be expressive; the use of parentheses ( ) means that the expressive language is limited to the slang wording right before the parenthetical notation. For example:

Bet your boots/Bet your bottom dollar/Bet your ass (expressive): count on it; completely assured. *Asked if I was going to see the show tonight, I replied, "Bet your boots!"*

Bet your boots and **Bet your bottom dollar** are not expressive terms, but **Bet your ass** is indicated as being potentially abrasive or offensive slang.

Beat the (living) daylights/hell/tar/shit (expressive) **out of**: to pummel; to handle harshly; to physically harm; to beat badly (physically or figuratively). *They beat the hell out of us in tonight's ball game.*

Beat the living daylights, Beat the living hell, and **Beat the living tar** are not generally expressive terms, but **Beat the living shit** is considered an expressive term. The expressive term may be listed last rather than in alphabetical order.

Slash Symbol: The slash symbol (/) is used to show the different words used in a slang term. In the immediate example above, the other sentences would include:

They beat the living daylights out of us in tonight's ball game.

They beat the living tar out of us in tonight's ball game.

They beat the living shit out of us in tonight's ball game.

F) Context and Feedback

The editors understand that slang terms may differ in definition or meaning between different groups, regions or cultures in the United States. Thus, meanings may not always be in exact conformity or be as correct as the reader may view them. Additionally, as much as the editors have tried to include the more common American slang terms, there are likely other terms that should have been included. The editors welcome the considerate feedback of readers. Priority is made in seeking and amending definitions, as well as including additional slang terms, where needed, in future editions of the book. Please address your feedback to: Kiku Education Institute, Attn: Slang Feedback, P.O. Box 15785, Seattle, Washington 98115, or email at: KikuEducation.com.

Disclaimer

Individuals named in the sentence examples in this edition are fictional, and do not refer to any specific person in real life. Any such relation is purely coincidental.

ACKNOWLEDGEMENTS

Heartfelt thanks to the many friends and colleagues who have contributed their time in putting this book together. Special thanks go to Erin Wilson, Laura Corcoran, Susan Bressler and others who assisted in the editing of the book. Particular thanks go to Kristen Morris of Classic Day Publishing in Seattle, Washington, who provided key help in bringing the book to print, and to David Marty Design. Finally, special thanks to Daphne Melillo for her many hours of research and review of source materials and especially for contributing her valuable two cents to the book.

DEDICATION

This book is dedicated to
Matthew Nicolo Melillo,
born June 6, 2002.

A

a: going to. *I'm a do it like this.*

About

About face: sharp turn of events in the opposite direction; go against. *He made an about face on his promise.*

About time: phrase used to indicate lateness or long duration to having arrived at a destination. *It's about time you showed up.*

About to: getting ready to. *He is about to get married.*

Hot about: very passionate or very willing. *I am hot about going dancing. He's hot about her.*

How about/What about: what is your desire, wish, information or thinking? *How about having dinner with me? What about going to the wharf instead?*

Above

Above and beyond: much more than what is expected. *He went above and beyond in saving his comrades in battle.*

Above board: without concealment or deception; honest; open; straightforward. *All the testimony about the incident was above board.*

Above suspicion: someone who is honest enough to where his or her credibility is not in question; to not suspect one of wrongdoing. *He is above suspicion based on the testimony of the witnesses at the scene.*

Above water: being able to maintain expenses in a business operation. *The company was able to operate above water during the economic downturn.*

Absent

Absent-minded: forgetful. *That absent-minded guy left his wallet at the shop.*

Absent without leave (AWOL): absent without leave; away from one's duty without authorization (military terminology). *He was AWOL for two days before returning to work.*

Abroad

Abroad: overseas; outside of your country. *Many Japanese go abroad as tourists during their holiday vacation.*

Accident

Accidentally on purpose: acting as if doing something by accident, but really intending to do it. *He missed the barbeque picnic accidentally on purpose so that he could watch the ball game.*

According to Hoyle

According to Hoyle: follows established rules. Historically, this expression originated from the works of Edmond Hoyle (1672-1769), the English authority on chess and card game rules. *The golf monitor said, in helping a golfer determine how to play his shot, "This is where you play your ball, according to Hoyle."*

Account

Give a good account of oneself: to credibly defend oneself or to do well. *The new hire gave a good account of himself.*

On account of: because of. *He was late on account of the accident.*

Take into account: take into consideration. *You have to take into account that he's slightly disabled.*

Ace

Ace it: 1) to win; successful accomplishment. *He aced the game on the last shot with the ball going through the basket as the time clock expired.* 2) getting an "A" on an exam or in a class course. *I aced the class!*

An ace: 1) a first rate individual. *Andy is an ace salesman.* 2) in golf, a hole in one. *I got an ace on the 10th hole!*

An ace in the hole: an additional advantage; something in reserve; final surprise. *Jack has an ace in the hole because of experience.*

An ace up one's sleeve: a hidden strategy or tool used to try to prevail in victory. *I understand that the visiting team has an ace up its sleeve by way of an awesome pitcher they got from the minor league.*

Achilles

Achilles heel: a weak link or a vulnerable area. *The key to victory is not letting the opponent know your Achilles heel.*

Across

Across the board: all around; through all levels. *Salaries throughout the entire company, from the clerk to the top manager, will be raised equally across the board. The governor will be suggesting across-the-board cuts on spending due to the state's budget deficit.*

Get across/Get the message across/Get the point across: to make something understood. *It was hard to get the message across due to the language barrier.*

Act

Act of God: an unforeseen and catastrophic event of nature, such as a tornado, flood or hurricane. *The mudslide that demolished the town was an act of God.*

Act of war: an extreme and usually violent international event caused by one country on another, thereby provoking conflict and cause for declaring war. *The country declared that the bombing of its main shipping port by the Eastern Alliance was an act of war.*

Act up: misbehave or act rudely. *It's embarrassing when you act up in the department store.*

Act your age: behave according to your age; act more maturely. *Stop crying and act your age.*

Clean up one's act: *See,* **Clean**.

Action

Action: excitement; happenings. *Do you know where the action is tonight?*

Bring action: start a lawsuit. *He brought action against the careless driver.*

Piece of the action: *See,* **Piece**.

Take action: start doing something. *I'll take action on this right away and get it done by this afternoon.*

Add

Add fuel to the fire: making a problem even worse. *Laughing at a bad situation surely adds fuel to the fire.*

Add insult to injury: to make matters worse than they are. *Today, James was advised by his doctor that he had to have a prostate operation and, adding insult to injury, he got a traffic ticket driving home from the doctor's office.*

Add up: to be consistent with; within reason. *The facts of the story just don't add up.*

Ad lib

Ad lib: spoken or done without preparation; freely. *The teleprompter failed and the speaker had to ad lib the rest of the broadcast.*

Afraid

Afraid not: to believe, regrettably, that the answer is in the negative. *Jason: Will you be there to help us? Carl: I'm afraid not.*

Afraid of one's shadow: very timid or fearful; easily frightened. *I've been afraid of my own shadow for years.*

Afraid so: to believe, regrettably, that the answer is in the affirmative. *Carl: Is my son in jail? Jason: I'm afraid so.*

After

After hours: past closing time; after normal hours. *After hours, we usually get together for a snack and a drink.*

After the fact: not important; moot; too late. *It doesn't matter much, now that it's after the fact.*

Against

Against someone's will: without agreement or consent. *You cannot force me to admit something against my will.*

Against the clock: fighting time; in a race with time. *They rushed him to the hospital in a race against the clock.*

Against the grain/tide/wind: not conforming; more difficult than expected. *He tends to go against the grain with company policy.*

Against the odds/Against all odds: slight chance of winning; in a very challenged position. *Many gamblers bet against the odds, but they seldom win.*

Ahead

Ahead of one's time: mature; advanced. *Da Vinci was ahead of his time with his divine creations.*

Ahead of the game: to have an advantage. *Teaching kids to read at the age of three will allow them to be ahead of the game.*

Air

Air dirty laundry: to let others aware of the private problems or bad experiences of another. *Are we being informative or otherwise going too far when we air a family's dirty laundry on television?*

Airhead: empty-headed; dumb; naive. *The bandleader was an airhead, but he had command of his group.*

Clear the air: *See,* **Clear**.

Come up for air: *See,* **Come**.

Dance on air/Float on air: feeling very happy and light on one's feet. *He's been dancing on air ever since he met her.*

Full of hot air: *See,* **Full of beans**.

Nose in the air: *See,* **Nose**.

Up in the air: *See,* **Up**.

Walk on air: very happy or excited. *See also above,* **Dance on air**. *Larry is walking on air after hearing of his promotion.*

All

All in all/All things considered: in consideration of everything else; given the totality of the situation. *All in all, I think the community art auction went very well.*

All balled up: in a mess; in trouble; confused and angry. *She was all balled up after getting a traffic ticket.*

All decked out: *See,* **Deck**.

All ears: *See,* **Ear**.

All for nothing: futile; not successful after trying very hard. *The work we did on the house was all for nothing when the hurricane blew it down the next week.*

All hands: everybody. *All hands took part in putting out the fire.*

All hell broke loose: things turned chaotic, turbulent, threatening, etc. *All hell broke loose when the alligator escaped from its pen.*

All in a day's work: typical of a day's accomplishment. *When congratulated in doing a great job, he replied humbly that it was all in a day's work.*

All in good/due time: at some unspecified time in the future. *I will retire all in good time.*

All in one breath: speaking rapidly while excited. *Steve yelled all in one breath, "Hurry! The robber just went out of the back door!"*

All is fair in love and war: most any conduct is acceptable or permissible in certain situations. *All is fair in love and war at the annual clothing sale.*

All meat and no potatoes: *See,* **Meat**.

All-nighter: studying or working throughout the night. *I pulled an all-nighter to finish the homework assignment.*

All out: with every effort; in full force. *They went all out to arrange this meeting with you.*

All over with: finished. *We can go to the movies after the house cleaning is all over with.*

All right already!: impatient affirmation to a belabored inquiry. *All right already! We'll go as soon as I can put on some clothes and eat.*

All set: ready to begin. *Are we all set to leave?*

All shook up: greatly upset, agitated or depressed. *I was all shook up when I missed the last train leaving out of Cleveland.*

All show, no go: a great deal of talk or display, but no action. *Our new hire proved to be all show and no go.*

All that jazz: 1) including all such things, et cetera. *I like all sports, such as soccer, base-ball, football, and all that jazz.* 2) discussion; rumors; happening. *What is all that jazz I'm hearing about you wanting to climb Mt. Everest?*

All the rage: the thing in fashion. *Mobile phones that come with a camera attachment are all the rage for this gift-giving season.*

All thumbs: *See,* **Thumb**.

All to hell: become ruined; messed up; collapsed. *See also,* **Shot all to hell**. *Our deep-sea fishing expedition was shot all to hell on account of the approaching hurricane.*

All walks (in life): all types; different kinds or groups. *Slang is derived from all walks in life, from high society to the streets.*

All washed up: *See,* **Wash**.

All's well that ends well: things turn out satisfactorily, although the outcome was not so certain. *Although he played a poor game, his team still won the championship; so all's well that ends well.*

All wet: completely wrong or inaccurate. *Your thoughts about an effective energy plan are all wet without considering how it affects the environment.*

With all one's heart: *See,* **Heart**.

Alone

Let alone: stop bothering or interfering with someone. *Why don't you let that little boy alone?*

Let well enough alone: be content with things as they are. *Let well enough alone and there will be no trouble.*

Amscray

Amscray: go away; get lost. *Amscray to the other side of the café and don't bother us.*

Ante

Ante up: put your money down; the amount of money a player must put on the table in a card game before they begin playing. *Ok guys, ante up 10 dollars to start the poker game.*

Ant

Ants in one's pants: restless; cannot sit still. *The kids had ants in their pants waiting for Marty the Magician to begin the show.*

Antsy: nervous; anxious; restless. *We were antsy waiting to hear the results of our exam.*

Apple

Apple of one's eye: most beloved. *My first child is the apple of my eye.*

Apples and oranges: completely different things. *When taking about cars versus trucks, we are talking apples and oranges.*

Sure as God made little green apples: very sure; most affirmatively. *As sure as God made little green apples, it was another warm and sunny day in Palm Springs.*

Upset the apple cart: *See,* **Upset**.

Apron

Cut the apron string: release oneself from someone's control. *He finally cut the apron string from his family and went out on his own.*

Tied to one's apron string: controlled by someone. *He may not like being called a momma's boy, even though he's been tied to his mom's apron strings for the past 35 years.*

Arm

Arm and a leg: an excessive amount of money. *He wants an arm and a leg for that run-down car.*

Arm twisting: *See,* **Twist**.

Armchair general/Armchair quarterback: one who speaks with authority but lacks knowledge in the subject. *Many radio commentators seem to come across as armchair generals today with their own spin on any subject according to either a conservative or liberal viewpoint.*

Armed to the teeth: referring to any group or country that possesses deadly weapons to inflict heavy damage. *The warring factions were armed to the teeth, which foretold a deadly battle was ready to take place.*

Armpit: very unpopular or unwanted place. *The best clubs are located in the armpit of town.*

At arm's length: keep a healthy distance from; to deal professionally rather than intimately with. *Keep at arm's length when dealing with your clients.*

Bear arms: carry a weapon. *We cannot bear arms in peacetime except when authorized.*

Long arm of the law: *See,* **Law**.

One-armed bandit: *See,* **Bandit**.

Shot in the arm: *See,* **Shot**.

Strong-arm: use of hard persuasion to get one's way. *The politician was strong-armed into voting for the defense budget.*

Take up arms: go to war or attempt an uprising. *The citizens took up arms in defense of their lives against the rioters.*

Twist someone's arm: *See,* **Twist**.

Up in arms: offended and visibly angry. *Jane was up in arms about being left out of the party.*

Artist

Con artist/Rip-off artist/Scam artist/Bullshit artist (expressive): one who lies or stretches the truth to allure or persuade; one who exaggerates, or deceives another for selfish gain. *He is such a bullshit artist when he talks that I think he even convinces himself. Tourists can be easy prey for con artists.*

As

As a last resort: the final alternative; without anything better. *As a last resort, we will ask the judge for mercy.*

As far as/As much as: to the degree or amount, given the circumstance. *He did well, as much as he could, although he could not finish the race.*

As hard as nails: *See,* **Hard**.

As if there's no tomorrow: 1) willing to give it your every effort; unwilling to wait; to do it now. *He's working so hard as if there is no tomorrow.* 2) no faith in what tomorrow may bring. *He's selling everything he's got, as if there's no tomorrow.*

As the crow flies: most directly; in a straight line. *It's five miles from here, as the crow flies.*

As usual: the same as before; what the norm is. *As usual, he forgot to clean up after his work.*

As we speak: right now; this very moment. *He is arriving at the airport as we speak.*

As you please: as you want. *We will go to the store for the medicine, as you please.*

Ask

Ask for it: deserving rebuke or punishment. *Don't complain because you asked for it.*

Ask for the moon/world: impossible or unreasonable request. *You are asking for the moon with that proposal.*

Asking for trouble: doing or saying something, which may result in trouble. *You're asking for trouble if you travel through this area again.*

Asleep

Asleep at the wheel/switch: failing to perform one's duties. *The policeman was asleep at the wheel when the robber broke into the bank.*

Ass

Ass backwards [expressive]: all wrong; without understanding. *He's doing the job ass backwards.*

Ass in a sling: be placed at risk; in a jeopardized and uncomfortable position; be in trouble. *He got his ass in a sling when he forgot to pick up his boss at the airport.*

Ass kicker: 1) hard and challenging. *Drill sergeants are ass kickers.* 2) something that operates fast. *The new computer is a real ass kicker.* 3) tough; very harsh; very tiring. *The 30 kilometer race was an ass kicker.*

Ass kisser: *See,* **Kiss** *ass.*

Ass on the line: One who risks or jeopardizes his/her reputation for something or someone. *Just remember that he put his ass on the line for you.*

Ass wipe/Asswipe [expressive]: idiot; fool. *You ass wipe; you bought our plane tickets going in opposite directions. Or are you trying to tell me something?*

Asshole [expressive]: disrespectful fool; idiot. *That apartment manager is a real asshole for evicting that elderly lady just because she missed a month of rent.*

Asshole deep in shit [expressive]: to be involved in serious trouble. *Man, you'll be asshole deep in shit if you're caught in this restricted area.*

Bet your ass [expressive]: count on it; completely assured. *Asked if I was going to see the show tonight, I replied, "Bet your ass!"*

Break one's ass [expressive]: work very hard to accomplish something. *I broke my ass to get you this job.*

Burn someone's ass [expressive]: to beat decisively. *He burned your ass in foosball.* 2) to deal deceptively. *If you burn my ass on this deal, then our business relationship is finished.*

Bust one's ass: *See,* **Bust** *a gut.*

Chicken ass [expressive]: 1) scared. *See also,* **Chicken shit.** *Our dog barks a lot but he is a real chicken ass.* 2) inconsequential; of no use; contemptibly insignificant. *Chicken ass rules that are not followed only get in the way of a productive work force.*

Cover one's ass [expressive]: to protect; protect one's reputation or person; be able to defend oneself. *If you want to cover your ass, you should document your actions. You should document the events that occurred today to cover your ass in case you are asked about it later.*

Crack one's ass up: laugh uncontrollably; very funny. *He cracks my ass up.*

Don't give a rat's ass [expressive]: do not care at all. *I don't give a rat's ass if he leaves.*

Drag one's ass [expressive]: purposely slow down; refusing to cooperate. *Since the workers were denied a pay raise, most of them were dragging their asses on the job.*

Dumb ass: *See,* **Dumb.**

Fall on one's ass [expressive]: to fail miserably. *He'll fall on his ass if he extends himself financially.*

Get one's ass in gear: quickly take action; get organized and moving. *I have to get my ass in gear or I won't make the meeting.*

Get the lead out of one's ass [expressive]: quit being so slow or inept; stop wasting time. *Hey, get the lead out of your ass and pick up the pace around here.*

Half-ass [expressive]: poor performance. *Without any sleep the night before, we were doing a half-ass job with all our chores.*

Haul ass: move fast. *See also,* **Kick ass/Kick butt.** *We hauled ass to get across town in time for the show.*

Horse's ass/Jackass: a very stubborn and disagreeable fool. *He acted like a horse's ass in that meeting.*

Kick ass: *See* **Kick.**

Kick in the ass [expressive]: realization; to spur someone to action. *That accident was a kick in the ass for me to not drive after drinking alcohol.*

Kiss my ass [expressive]: an angry expression of disgust or denial. *When she directed him to get something for her, he replied, "Kiss my ass, get it yourself."*

Lame ass [expressive]: one without diligence or responsibility; lazy person. *He is a lame ass who makes others clean up after him.*

Lay one's ass on the line [expressive]: *See,* **Lay down one's life.**

Make an ass out of: *See,* **Make a fool of.**

My ass [expressive]: no way. *See also,* **Like hell.** *My ass, if you think I'm going to town with you wearing that outfit.*

Not give a horse's ass/Not give a rat's ass [expressive]: to not care. *I don't give a rat's ass what you do.*

Not know one's ass from a hole in the ground [expressive]: very dumb; unknowledgeable. *He doesn't know his ass from a hole in the ground when it comes to fixing a flat tire.*

One's ass is grass: *See,* **Grass.**

Pain in the ass: *See,* **Pain.**

Put one's ass on the line: *See above,* **Ass on the line.**

Ride one's ass: *See,* **Ride.**

Rip ass: *See,* **Rip.**

Sit on one's ass [expressive]: to do nothing; not mindful of responsibility. *We were just sitting on our asses all day. Don't just sit on your ass; do something!*

Smart ass: *See,* **Smart.**

Sorry ass [expressive]: 1) pitiful. *You don't expect me to believe that sorry ass excuse, do you?* 2) shameful being. *You only have your own sorry ass to* *blame for what happened. He yells and complains at his employees in front of others, which makes him one sorry ass.*

Stiff ass [expressive]: rigid; unyielding; rote, or by the rules. *Our drill instructor, Mr. Solstice, is a real stiff ass with our program and scheduling, especially on event days.*

Throw someone out on his ass [expressive]: dismiss with force or intent. *When he was caught stealing on the job, they threw him out on his ass.*

Tight ass: *See,* **Tight**.

Up to one's ass [expressive]: extremely; very much so. *He is up to his ass in debt.*

Work one's ass off: work extraordinarily hard. *I worked my ass off today to demonstrate to the boss that I can do the job.*

At

At a loss for words: speechless; confused. *I was at a loss for words when I was suddenly presented with the winning prize.*

At a premium: something priced higher or very high because of demand or quality. *The new sports cars are priced at a premium because many people want to buy them.*

At a snail's pace: very slowly. *When your job is not interesting, time moves at a snail's pace.*

At all cost: price is not a factor; a desire for something regardless of cost. *We must save the company employees from the sinking oil platform at all costs.*

At arm's length: on a professional level. *We got along just fine, as long as we kept at arm's length with one another at work.*

At close range: very near. *Experts can determine if a gun had been fired at close range by the powder burns given off when it's fired.*

At death's door: euphemism for very close to death. *He was at death's door for a brief scary moment when his car almost skidded off the cliff.*

At first glance/At first blush: an initial impression; to know about something or someone quickly. *Dick could tell at first glance that Amy had aspirations for political office.*

At heart: *See,* **Heart**.

At large: 1) missing; whereabouts unknown. *The escaped prisoner has been at large since last night.* 2) roving. *Mr. Strom is our ambassador at large.*

At last: finally. *We are here at last!*

At loggerheads: cannot agree or settle. *The two sides were at loggerheads over the issue of retirement pensions.*

At odds: in disagreement. *Joe is at odds with his parents on his choice of friends.*

At one's fingertips: readily available. *In case of emergency, I have a first aid kit at my fingertips.*

At one's leisure: at one's convenience. *Please come by at your leisure.*

At stake: at risk; in the process of being won or lost. *Your whole life is at stake when taking a college entrance exam.*

At the bottom of the ladder: at the lowest level of authority or pay status. *Although he is at the bottom of the ladder as a new employee, he is very happy to have a job.*

At the crack of dawn: at the earliest part of the day. *Life on the farm starts at the crack of dawn.*

At the drop of a hat: at once; suddenly and without much agitation. *He tends to argue at the drop of a hat.*

At the end of one's rope: at the end of one's endurance. *I was almost at the end of my rope when they finally rescued us.*

At the end of the day: after all things are considered. *At the end of the day, it still amounts to his word against yours.*

At the top of one's lungs: in the loudest voice. *I yelled at the top of my lungs when I spotted the suspect leaving the scene.*

Ate

Ate it: the worst of a situation. *He ate it when he drove off the embankment.*

Ate up/Ate it up: to accept something willingly if not enthusiastically. *They loved his comedy; yes, they ate it up.*

Attitude

Have an attitude: when one acts or appears to act in an arrogant, disrespecting, or inconsiderate manner. *I would stay away from her today; she has an attitude.*

Away

Carry away/Carried away: *See,* **Carry**.

Do away with: eliminate. *They did away with the manual labor and replaced the production line with robots.*

Piss away: *See,* **Piss**.

Put it away: to eat in large amounts; an insatiable appetite; to consume voraciously. *Look at him; he can really put it away.*

Steal away: *See,* **Steal**.

Ax/Axe

Axe to grind: *See,* **Grind**.

Battle axe: a mean, unfriendly woman. *Our instructor is a real battle axe.*

Give someone the axe: fire an employee; forced separation from one's job. *After she was caught stealing from the company, she was given the axe.*

B

Baby

Baby: 1) one's responsibility. *Let him do it because it's his baby. Don't push this job on me because it's your baby, not mine.* 2) one's possession or thing; a thing of personal concern or interest. *This classic show car is his baby.* 3) a young woman. *Hey, baby, how are you doing today?*

Baby boomer: generally, anyone born after WWII during the years 1946-1964. *This town is full of baby boomers.*

Throw the baby out with the bathwater: to get rid of something valuable while trying to get rid of something not wanted. *To get rid of the warehouse would mean giving up a lucrative sub-tenancy business, which would be like throwing the baby out with the bathwater.*

Back

Back away/up: turn back; move back a short distance; change to a different position. *We had to back away from our proposal due to changed circumstances.*

Back door: 1) suspicious; shady; questionable. *The police closed the tavern because of the back-door dealings in illicit drugs that were occurring on the premises.* 2) a computer password (used as an alternative backup) to easily get into a secure program. *The only way to get into this program is to see if it has a back door.*

Back down: fail to carry through; yield your position. *It's better to cool off and back down than to cause a confrontation.*

Back in the groove: *See,* **Groove**.

Back in the saddle again: in control once again. *The President was singing, "I'm back in the saddle again," after his loyal military commanders overthrew the junta and installed him back into office.*

Back it up: 1) to substantiate. *You would need to back it up with more facts before we can print it in the newspaper.* 2) to cover. *You care to back it up with, say, ten dollars?*

Back off: 1) do not interfere. *Back off or I will be forced to call the police.* 2) move away from. *We backed off from the deal after noting too many discrepancies in the accounting records.*

Back on one's feet: feeling well again, physically or financially. *He was soon back on his feet after the car accident.*

Back out: withdraw from an agreement or enterprise. *Shortage of funds caused us to back out of the agreement.*

Back stabber/Backstabber: someone you cannot trust; someone who, in a place of trust, takes advantage or deceives. *He is such a back stabber, like a smiling face telling lies.*

Back talk: brash counter response; rude or insulting reply. *Don't give me any back talk and get to work.*

Back to square one/Back to the drawing board: start over again. *It was back to square one when our prototype crashed in a practice run.*

Back to the salt mines: return to grueling work or disliked activity. *It's Monday again, and time to go back to the salt mines.*

Back to the wall/Back against the wall: with no other options left; all avenues exhausted; in a tough situation, with no escape. *With insufficient revenue to meet payroll, the executives had their backs against the wall in being forced to file for bankruptcy protection. He is great to have as a business consultant when your back is against the wall.*

Back up: to give support. *You have to back up what you say with firm action.*

Backbone: courage; fortitude; strength. *Our supervisor has no backbone when it comes to disciplining employees.*

Backseat driver: a passenger in a car directing the driver how to drive or what to do. *When I drive my mother to town, she likes to take on the role of a backseat driver.*

Behind one's back: something being done secretly without one's knowledge or consent, and generally done in deceit; underhanded. *I cannot believe he made the purchase behind my back. Making competing deals behind my back is not the sign of a trusted employee.*

Bend over backwards: to try very hard to please or pacify someone. *Jason will always bend over backwards to help a needy friend.*

Break one's back: *See,* **Break**.

Flat on one's back: bedridden; helpless; broke. *He's been flat on his back this past week on account of the flu.*

Get off someone's back: leave someone alone; stop bothering another. *I'm tired of being **hounded** by you, so get off my back.*

Go back on one's word: fail to keep a promise. *Mary Elizabeth went back on her word when she failed to show. Once you commit, you cannot go back on your word.*

No shirt off one's back: one is not incurring the cost (so why worry?). *Hey, it's no shirt off your back if he pays his own way, so why are you complaining?*

On the back burner: *See,* **Burner**.

Piggyback: to hang onto; to carry. *This toll-free line piggybacks the main phone line in the office.*

Scratch someone's back: *See,* **Scratch**.

Shirt off one's back: to give everything; one who is most generous. *I have the utmost respect for him because he is always willing to give the shirt off his back to someone in need.*

Stab in the back: *See,* **Stab**.

Take a backseat: not be controlling; observe rather than direct or control. *The medical professor took a backseat and allowed the medical residents to perform the operation.*

Turn one's back: to ignore; disown. *He turned his back on his own family when they disagreed with his political views.*

Watch one's back: be mindful of the surroundings; be careful and cautious. *Watch your back around here.*

Bacon

Bring home the bacon: one who earns the money to support the family. *She brings home the bacon in the family.*

Bad

Bad/baddest: exceptional; intense. *Michael Jordan in the 1990's was basketball's best and baddest player.*

Bad blood: hatred or anger between persons or groups. *There has been bad blood between those warring nations for years.*

Bad egg/apple: one who causes trouble; one who turns out to be nasty or rotten. *That kid's a bad apple.*

Bad hair day: *See,* **Hair**.

Bad mouth: 1) to unduly criticize someone; malign. *Jim bad mouths his boss to his co-workers almost every morning.* 2) to speak foul language. *You have a bad mouth when you're angry.*

Bad to the bone: corrupted; being fairly unmannered to somewhat offensive. *My little kid is bad to the bone.*

Go bad: to spoil; rot. *The food in the refrigerator will go bad if you don't eat it soon.*

Bag

Bag: 1) to place things in a bag. *At the store, we asked the clerk to bag the groceries.* 2) To forget about; to give up. *We were supposed to go to a picnic in the park but since it's raining, let's just bag it.* 3) be quiet. *I've heard enough about your complaining, so bag it!* 4) to arrest. *The police finally bagged the suspect who had been hiding in a trash bin in the alley.* 5) one's romantic partner or significant other. *Hey, I thought Frank was your bag; or did you break up with him?* 6) an inquiry in response to one's problem. *Hey, man, you look depressed; what's your bag?* 7) one's job or profession. *My bag is shipping, which allows me to travel around the world.*

Bag lady: *See,* **Lady**.

Bag of bones: *See,* **Bone**.

Bag some rays: get a suntan. *I'm going to the beach to bag some rays.*

Brown bag: to bring your own lunch, such as to work or on an outing. *I usually brown bag it to work.*

Doggy bag: *See,* **Dog**.

Holding the bag/Left holding the bag: to be left to face blame for something that others should share or be responsible for; get blamed for bad results. *When an accounting scam hit the company, Jack, the new employee, was left holding the bag for all the company's woes.*

In the bag: confident that all will go one's way. *Being 25 points ahead with only 2 minutes left to play in the basketball game, the win was in the bag.*

Let the cat out of the bag: *See,* **Cat**.

Mixed bag: *See,* **Mix**.

Old bag: rude term for an elderly woman. *The old bag tried to hit me with her purse for no reason.*

What's your bag?: 1) What's your problem? *Hey man, what's your bag?* 2) inquiry into one's interest or occupation. *At the party, someone asked Sam, "So, what's your bag?"*

Bail

Bail: 1) to leave in a hurry. *Let's bail this place.* 2) money or other security, including a bond, to allow an accused to be released from incarceration and insure his later appearances in court and trial. *He was released on bail pending a hearing in front of the judge next week.*

Bail one out: save; rescue. *Jack loaned me some money and bailed me out of financial trouble.*

Bait

Bait and switch: to deceivingly attract a customer into the store with a cheap advertised product, then switch the sale to a more expensive one. *At the store, I was told that the sale-priced item was not in stock, but that I could buy the more expensive model right now. It was a typical bait and switch tactic.*

Fish or cut bait: *See,* **Fish**.

Jailbait: *See,* **Jail**.

Wait with baited breath: *See,* **Breath**.

Bake

Baked: 1) strongly under the influence of drugs or alcohol. *We found Jackson baked and lying under a tree.* 2) burned. *We got baked staying under the sun too long.* 3) ruined. *We're baked if we fail to get additional funding for the business.*

Half-baked: *See,* **Half**.

Ball

Another ball of wax: something else entirely different. *Our problems in engineering are another ball of wax compared to the problems going on in budgeting.*

Ball and chain: 1) a disliked, oppressive activity. *For disorderly conduct, the Sergeant has me on ball and chain detail cleaning out the restrooms on the military base.* 2) a crude term for one's spouse or partner. *I cannot stay out late tonight because the ball and chain wants me home early.*

Ball of fire: full of energy. *Albert was a ball of fire when he was a baby.*

Ballpark figure: rough estimate. *Give me a ballpark figure of what the project will cost.*

Ball

Balls: courage. *It takes balls to admit when one is wrong.*

Be on the ball: be efficient and alert. *I eat breakfast every morning so I can be on the ball at work.*

Behind the eight ball: *See,* **Behind**.

By the balls [expressive]: under one's full control; held in a precarious or painful position. *We got them by the balls now.*

Carry the ball: assume responsibility. *The assistant manager had to carry the ball after the manager became ill.*

Get the ball rolling/moving: get back to action; invigorate an undertaking. *Hey fellows, let's get the ball rolling and finish this job!*

Have a ball: enjoy oneself. *I was having such a ball at the party that I didn't get home until after midnight.*

Have someone by the balls: *See,* **Have**.

Keep the ball rolling/moving: maintain uninterrupted action. *We must keep the ball rolling to meet the deadline tomorrow.*

Put English on the ball: *See,* **English**.

That's the way the ball bounces: *See,* **That**.

The ball is in your court: it's your turn to act. *What do you say? The ball is in your court now.*

Whole ball of wax: *See,* **Whole**.

Whole new ball game: new approach; reorganized plan. *With this new wireless technology, it's a whole new ball game in the world of espionage.*

Balloon

Balloon: blossom rapidly; grow significantly; fatten. *He ballooned to 300 pounds before he got serious about losing weight.*

Lead balloon: unable to perform; dismal failure; doomed from the beginning. *The meeting between the warring factions was expected to go over like a lead balloon but instead turned out to be a great success.*

Trial balloon: a proposal, idea or plan disseminated in experimental form to see how it works. *The politicians leaked news on the funding proposal for the defense bill as a trial balloon to garner reactions from the public.*

Baloney

Baloney: nonsense; untruth. *The rumor about Jacobs leaving the firm for a seat in politics is a bunch of baloney.*

Banana

Go Bananas: go crazy; to react with extreme emotion. *We went bananas when our team won the game in the final seconds. He went bananas when he saw her. I'm going to go bananas if I don't get a vacation soon.*

Top banana: *See,* **Top**.

Bandit

Make out like a bandit: to come upon riches quickly. *Many original investors made out like bandits investing in a small Seattle company called Microsoft.*

One-armed bandit: a gambling slot machine (called a bandit because it usually takes your money away). *Did you know that Las Vegas International Airport has one-armed bandits in virtually every passenger terminal?*

One-armed bandit

Bang

Bang one's head against the wall: *See,* **Head**.

Bang-up job: excellent; outstanding. *Sam did a bang-up job on his final report.*

Go out with a bang: don't leave a job or situation quietly; doing something significant before leaving. *Babe Ruth went out with a bang as a ball player, hitting 3 home runs in his final game.*

More bang for one's buck: to get more for your money. *You get more bang for your buck shopping at the wholesale store.*

Bank

Bank on: depend on; rely; trust. *You can bank on the fact that we will deliver the goods on time.*

Break the bank: bring on failure; go bankrupt. *It will break the bank if we have to pay for higher fuel prices for our transportation operation.*

You can take that to the bank: one can rely on the information; a trusted matter to be believed; very credible or believable. *Whatever he recommends, you can take that to the bank.*

Barf

Barf: to vomit. *Riding the waves on the fishing boat made me sick enough to barf.*

Barge

Barge in: to enter some place, uninvited or in a rude fashion; intrude upon. *I put a lock on the door to keep him from barging into my office.*

Bark

All bark and no bite: to look mean or intimidating but have no power of enforcement; really pretending to seem what one is not; all talk and no substance. *Politicians who break their promises to their people are seen as having all bark and no bite. You shouldn't fear him because in reality he's all bark and no bite.*

Bark up the wrong tree: going the wrong way; doing the wrong thing. *You're barking up the wrong tree with your proposal.*

Barrel

Barrel down: to come on with full force; come down hard and fast. *They were barreling down the road at a high rate of speed.*

Barrel of fun: a lot of excitement. *Our weekend picnic was a barrel of fun.*

Barrel of laughs: very funny and entertaining. *The comedy show tonight was a barrel of laughs and well worth the cost of admission.*

Bottom of the barrel: *See,* **Bottom**.

Like shooting fish in a barrel: *See,* **Fish**.

Over a barrel: have someone under control or at your mercy. *We had him over a barrel for spying, but he escaped before he could be tried.*

Pork barrel: *See,* **Pork**.

Base

Off base: incorrect or wrong. *That argument is way off base.*

Touch base with: consult or talk matters over with. *Touch base with dad to see if you can get a ride to school tomorrow.*

Bash

Bash: 1) to hit or clobber; to impact. *The vehicle skidded on the ice and bashed into the wall.* 2) a get-together or party. *Our company bash will start at 5 p.m. tomorrow.*

Basket

Basket case: 1) one who cannot function because of emotional disturbance; crazy; mentally too impaired to function normally. *The greatest casualty of war is the large number of people so mentally scarred and wounded that they become basket cases for years to come. The lady who talks to the trees in the park is a real basket case.* 2) economic bankruptcy or chaos. *Bad planning and currency devaluations have turned many countries into economic basket cases.*

Put all one's eggs into one basket: risk everything into one resource or venture. *Don't put all your eggs into one basket, or else you risk losing everything.*

Bat

Bat around: to casually discuss or analyze a matter. *The staff batted around ideas about setting up the exhibit with a limited budget.*

Bats in the belfry: possessing crazy ideas; not of the right mind; mentally imbalanced. *He always acted in public as if he had bats in the belfry, but he really was a nice, personable fellow.*

Batting a thousand: maintaining a perfect score (from baseball terminology of holding a perfect batting average of 1.000); succeeding in perfect order. *So far, we are batting a thousand on the successful store openings this year.*

Batty: crazy. *That old batty woman is much smarter than you realize.*

Blind as a bat: *See,* **Blind**.

Go to bat for: uphold or protect someone. *I'd go to bat for my best friend any day.*

Like a bat out of hell: suddenly. *Spike, our dog, took off like a bat out of hell when he saw the bear come into the yard.*

Not bat an eye: without emotion or conscience. *Having been in the military, Jane takes orders in her civilian job without batting an eye. He greedily took the candy from the young child and consumed it without batting an eye.*

Right off the bat: to happen instantly. *Our stock started making money right off the bat.*

Bawl

Bawl: cry uncontrollably loud. *The babies were bawling and I didn't know what to do; I started to have a conniption fit, so I called out for Mom.*

Bawl someone out: scold someone harshly. *Teachers should not bawl out students, especially in front of the class.*

Be

Be a drag: be a burden or something disliked. *Don't be a drag and come to the party.*

Be a steal: a bargain. *The suit is a steal at $30!*

Be caught dead: to be seen in public in a certain fashion or way (generally used in the negative). *I wouldn't be caught dead wearing that polyester outfit.*

Be had: cheated. *Those are not real jewels; I was had!*

Be my guest: do as one desires (generally stated ironically in response to something ill advised). *If you want to go to the protest march, be my guest; I just don't have the funds this time to bail you out of jail if you get arrested.*

Be one's bag: something one enjoys or specializes in. *Mary threw the best parties in town; entertaining was her bag.*

Be poles apart: be far away from reaching an agreement; be very different in thinking or in personality. *Their viewpoints on the subject were poles apart.*

Be taken in: be deceived or swindled. *The old lady was taken in by his smooth talk.*

Be the in-thing: be in demand; fashionable. *Bell bottoms were the in-thing in the 1970's.*

Bean

Bean: to hit or be hit. *He was beaned in the arm by the pitcher.*

Bean counter: an employee who works with numbers, surveys, and statistics to analyze and tabulate facts and other data. *As an economist, he wanted to do field work rather than become a bean counter in some factory operation.*

Full of beans: *See,* **Full**.

Not know beans: *See,* **Know**.

Spill the beans: *See,* **Spill**.

Bear

Bear market: a general financial condition where the market of stocks are in a downtrend. *The financial bear market of the 1930's is eclipsed by the bear market of technology stocks in 2000.*

Bear trap: to unknowingly fall into a snare. *He fell into a bear trap when he attempted to sell stolen goods in a police sting operation.*

Does a bear shit in the woods? [expressive]: a phrase emphasizing an obvious, affirmative response to an inquiry. *Bob: Are you really going to the Cubs game tomorrow? Jack: Does a bear shit in the woods?*

It's a bear: to be in a tough or unfortunate situation. *It would be a real bear to miss your flight on account of traffic congestion; so leave early.*

Loaded for bear: *See,* **Load**.

Beat

Beat: real tired; exhausted. *I am beat after a hard day's work.*

Beat a dead horse: further effort is fruitless. *Don't bother anymore trying to convince them to change their minds; it's like trying to beat a dead horse.*

Beat around: 1) to discuss or talk about something. *Let's beat this around with the staff for more ideas.* 2) to loaf or idle. *We were just beating around and not doing much.* 3) inquire; checking things out. *He's been beating around the place and asking questions of the employees.*

Beat around the bush: to talk around a subject; not give a direct answer. *Stop beating around the bush and tell me what you bought Jake for his birthday.*

Beat it: to be forced to leave; go away. *Beat it before I have to call the police.*

Beat into one's head: *See,* **Head**.

Beat one's brains (out): try extremely hard. *We published the journal on time, but we beat our brains out doing it.*

Beat one's chest: express greatness or self-gratification. *A great job, Bob; you can beat your chest on this one.*

Beat one's head against a wall: *See,* **Head**.

Beat one's pants off/Beat the pants off: to outscore or win by a large margin; win decisively. *They beat the pants off us at the softball game last night.*

Beat the bushes: diligent attempt to obtain or find something. *We were beating the bushes for clues to the stolen artifacts.*

Beat the clock: *See,* **Clock**.

Beat the living daylights/hell/tar/shit out of (expressive)**:** to pummel; to handle harshly; to physically harm; to beat badly (physically or figuratively). *They beat the hell out of us in tonight's ball game.*

Beat the rap: escape criminal conviction; get away from legal penalty. *He applied to law school, inspired after beating the rap on a murder charge.*

Beat to the punch: accomplishing something before another has a chance to do it; do something before anyone else. *Harold beat Mark to the punch in finding the hidden treasure.*

Beats me: to not know. *Beats me where the museum is located.*

Beef

Beef up: to make stronger; to improve upon. *I want you to beef up the report before we publish it tomorrow.*

Bring home the beef: work to bring home enough money to pay the expenses. *I have to work two jobs in order to bring home the beef these days.*

Don't give me any beef: to not complain. *Please don't give me any beef about failing the exam.*

What's the beef?: what is the matter? Why are you in dispute? *What's the beef that caused the fight between you and your friend today?*

Where's the beef?: Where's the substance? *Where's the beef to this plan that you talk about with so much encouragement?*

Been

Been around: have experience. *No worries about these guys; they've been around.*

Been had: been cheated; treated in a harsh manner. *You've been had.*

Been through the mill: gone through a lot and worn out. *Barney's been through the mill working 12 hours a day this week.*

Has been: someone who was once in the limelight or famous but is no longer important, either due to time or deeds done. *James was well-known in his time as a local loan shark, but is considered a has been in this time of modern banking.*

Beer

Beer belly: one with a bulging stomach or belly. *The owner is the person with the beer belly.*

Behind

Behind closed doors/Behind the doors: in secret. *The board meeting today was held behind closed doors to discuss future plans.*

Behind him/her/them: out of consideration or thought. *She put the sad memories behind her.*

Behind on strikes/Behind on the count: when a pitcher in baseball is in a situation of having thrown more balls than strikes to a batter. *The pitcher was behind on strikes to the worst batter on the opposing team.*

Behind on the count: going too slowly or not fast enough. *Due to the high demand, the company was behind on the count in making enough dolls for Christmas.*

Behind one's back: surreptitious action, generally negative, without the other's knowledge. *He tried to instigate a coup behind the backs of the current leaders of the government. He unsuccessfully tried to work a business deal for personal gain behind his partner's back.*

Behind the curve: slower than or behind others, and needing to catch up. *We are behind the curve in our research to find a cheap and safe fuel source.*

Behind the eight (8) ball: in a difficult situation; awkward position. *No thanks to you, your actions placed me behind the eight ball with the boss.*

Behind the scene(s): private actions not revealed. *There was concern behind the scenes that the annual event would be discontinued in order to cut corporate expenses.*

Behind the times: slow in relation to; still adhering to old ways. *Although the school is very old, its computer networking program is certainly not behind the times.*

Behind the wheel: in control of; guiding; regulating. *Who's behind the wheel running this company? Grandma Gaye was behind the wheel of the big-rig trailer.*

Come from behind: an underdog who prevails in victory; to move ahead of others against the odds to win. *He came from behind and won the governor's race.*

Bell

Bells and whistles: fully loaded; containing all the needed options. *This car has all the bells and whistles for modern convenience.*

Clear as a bell: fully understood (derived from the pure sounds of a bell, which are clearly heard). *Although he was deep inside the cave, he could be heard clear as a bell.*

It rings a bell: when something reminds one of something else; to remember something. *Yeah, that name rings a bell, but I can't put a face to it.*

Saved by the bell: luckily rescued from a difficult situation or setting (derived from the boxing ring when the bell rings at the end of a round, at times saving a knocked down boxer from being counted out). *Our facility was ready to be shut down, but we were saved by the bell when the state legislature agreed to fund the project for another year.*

With bells on: very eager; in a celebratory mood. *I've waited for this celebration all year so I'll be over tonight with bells on.*

Belly

Beer belly: *See,* **Beer**.

Belly ache/bellyache: complain constantly. *Stop your belly aching and finish your homework. Sid always seems to bellyache about his pay.*

Belly-land: to crash an aircraft with the landing gears retracted. *The aircraft had to belly-land in the cornfield after it lost all power.*

Belly up: 1) bankrupt. *The company went belly up after it failed to meet expenses.* 2) upside down. *Our vehicle skidded on the ice and landed belly up along the shoulder of the freeway.*

Belly up to the bar: get together at the bar for a drink. *Let's belly up to the bar and have a cold one.*

Bellyful: a lot of; full amount. *This one customer at the store gave us a bellyful of his complaining about the poor customer service.*

Yellow belly: coward; scared. *The once mighty leader became a retreating yellow belly when he escaped into exile as the people overpowered the corrupt government.*

Belt

Below the belt: dirty way of dealing; not according to standard procedure; unfair. *That tactic was below the belt.*

Belt: 1) a portion of liquor, usually whiskey, which is poured into small, one-ounce glass known as a shot glass, and drunk all at once. *When we ate in certain countries, we would have a belt before each meal as a preventive measure against food poisoning.* 2) to hit another (squarely in the face). *He belted him with a solid right hook to the chin.* 3) to hit something hard. *He belted a homerun out of the ballpark.*

Belt down: drink heavily and often. *He belted down a six-pack of beer at the picnic.*

Belt tightening/Tighten the belt: to reduce spending or expenses. *We have to do some belt tightening if we are to survive the economic downturn this year.*

Hit below the belt: *See,* **Hit**.

Tighten one's belt: *See,* **Tight**.

Under one's belt: *See,* **Under**.

Bench

Bench: the judge's seat (of authority); from the judge. *The order to bring in the witness came straight from the bench.*

Bench trial: a trial without a jury (so the judge serves as the trier of fact in place of a jury of one's peers). Often times, the parties to the lawsuit elect to opt for a bench trial versus a jury trial. *Our bench trial is scheduled for next month, so let's review the case next week.*

Bench warmer: one who does not have an assigned position in a particular game or setting, and who is on the sidelines waiting for the opportunity to substitute and participate. *Sawyer moved from being a bench warmer to becoming a star player when he replaced the injured quarterback.*

Bench warrant: an order by the court that directs law enforcement to forcibly compel a person to make his appearance before the judge. *They issued a bench warrant on him for his failure to show at a court hearing last week.*

Bend/Bent

Around the bend: the other side of the corner; close by. *The gas station is just around the bend.*

Bend one's ear: *See,* **Ear**.

Bend over backwards: to do more than is expected; to go out of the way to help. *The clerics bent over backwards to ensure that the women and children were safely transported from the flooded area.*

Bent out of shape: angry. *He really got bent out of shape when the whaling ship harpooned the mother sperm whale.*

Fender bender: *See,* **Fender**.

Nose bent out of shape: *See,* **Nose** out of joint.

Beside

Beside oneself: very surprised; greatly agitated. *I would be beside myself if anyone would suggest instituting corporal punishment in school.*

Beside the point: not relevant or important. *Your idea is beside the point.*

Bet

Bet on/Bet on it (*See also,* **bank** on): depend on it; guarantee it. *You can bank on Paul getting the job done. You can bet on it that Henry will be one of the top runners in the marathon.*

Bet the farm/Bet the ranch: risk all you have. *I would bet the farm that this invention will be a financial success.*

Bet your ass/Bet your bottom dollar/Bet your boots: *See,* **Ass**.

Better

Better half: one's significant other, such as spouse or partner. *If it were not for my better half, I would not be so successful today.*

Better off: the more favorable option, given a comparison. *You are better off if you do not go to the political rally tonight.*

For the better: a more desirable condition or situation. *It's for the better to leave Chicago for LA during the winter months.*

Had better: ought to; discretion toward wiser judgment. *You had better go now or be stuck in heavy traffic later.*

You better believe it: *See,* **You**.

Between

Between a rock and a hard place: facing a very tough situation or decision. *President Kennedy was between a rock and a hard place during the Cuban missile crisis in 1962.*

Between the lines: what is intimated but not revealed. *Mary learned how to read between the lines in understanding the rules of the game.*

Big

Big Apple: New York City. *We are going to visit the Big Apple in the autumn, then drive up to New Hampshire.*

Big cheese/Big enchilada/Big wheel: the boss; the head honcho. *The big cheese is coming to review the operations today.*

Big daddy: most important; biggest of everything. *I believe the Cadillac was the big daddy of all cars in the 1950's.*

Big deal: *See,* **Deal**.

Big for one's britches: displaying mannerisms of overconfidence and arrogance. *Mike is getting too big for his britches; if he doesn't watch out, someone will cut him down to size.*

Big gun: powerful; most influential. *John Wayne was a big gun during his time.*

Big league: with the best; tough competition. *You're in the big leagues now, so don't mess up.*

Big leaguer: in with the best of players. *Johnny quickly became a big leaguer in the international banking field when he secured the merger of the two largest oil companies in the world.*

Big mouth: loud and obnoxious. *Walter becomes a big mouth at every soccer game.*

Big picture: the totality of the situation or event. *It is hard to vision the plan without looking at the big picture.*

Big shot/wheel: a person of importance. *Whose the big shot around here?*

Big stink: *See,* **Stink**.

Big time: 1) real serious. *It's big time for James, now that he has been elected to political office.* 2) very successfully; really well. *He made it big time with his software company.*

Big wig/bigwig: an important person; high-ranking individual. *Jerry is now some bigwig working overseas for the U.S. State Department.*

Bigheaded: *See,* **Head**.

Talk big: *See,* **Talk**.

Bill

Clean bill of health: *See,* **Clean**.

Fill the bill: to meet the requirements; just what is required. *This gadget seems to fill the bill. The items on the list fill the bill to complete the project.*

Fit the bill: *See,* **Fit**.

Foot the bill: *See,* **Foot**.

Pad the bill: *See,* **Pad**.

Bird

Bird brain/Birdbrain: stupid; dumb; someone who exhibits little or no intelligence. *I'm a birdbrain for forgetting to arrange for a babysitter tonight.*

Bird dog/Birddog: to diligently and persistently search; to not give up. *Everyone had to bird dog for clues to find the missing child.*

Bird in hand: something that is for sure since you already have it. *A bird in hand is better than two in the bush, which means that a sure thing is better than two possibilities.*

Bird in the bush: something unknown. *Figuring the difficult math problem seemed to be like a bird in the bush.*

Bird of a different feather: one with a different style or manner; to be or become different. *See also,* **Horse of a different color**. *Are you now a bird of a different feather on the issue of gun control?*

Birds of a feather flock together/Birds of the same feather: people attracted to the same tastes, desires or abilities; commonality breeds comfort. *Like birds of the same feather, they do almost everything together.*

Early bird: one who arrives early enough. *There is an early bird special for dinner at the restaurant if we get there before 6 p.m.*

Early bird catches the worm: *See,* **Early**.

Eat like a bird: *See,* **Eat**.

Flip a bird/Flip someone a bird: an obscene gesture with the hand, using the middle finger pointed up and the other fingers folded in, which shows strong distaste or anger about something. *Some in the crowd jeered the politician, and a few flipped him the bird.*

For the birds: not worth much or anything. *This place is for the birds.*

Ghetto bird: *See,* **Ghetto**.

Jailbird: a convict. *He is a great worker, but has trouble finding employment since he used to be a jailbird.*

Kill two birds with one stone: *See,* **Kill**.

Lovebirds: a couple in love. *Those two lovebirds are rarely apart.*

Take off like a bird: go suddenly; depart swiftly. *When he heard the police, he took off like a bird.*

Birthday

Birthday suit: without clothing; naked. *I was in my birthday suit when we had to evacuate the burning building.*

Bitch

Bitch: 1) to complain. *My neighbor often bitches about the crows that crap all over his back yard.* 2) vulgar name for a woman who is obnoxious or bad-tempered. *Her personal verbal attacks against him in public made her look like a bitch.*

Bitch session [expressive]: a gathering where individuals can freely express their opinions and feelings. *We had a bitch session at the town hall about the hot issue of subsidies to local farmers.*

Bitchin'/bitchen: used to describe something really awesome or terrific. *He has a bitchin' car.*

Bitchy: moody. *When she gets bitchy, stay out of her way.*

Rich bitch: wealthy and unpleasant woman. *She acts like a rich bitch, demanding everything her way.*

Stop your bitching/bitchin': stop your complaining. *Stop your bitchin' because it's not constructive.*

Bit/Bite

Bite off more than one can chew: to assume more than one can handle. *I bit off more than I could chew when I tried to do everything myself rather than delegating the work.*

Bite one's fingernails: be nervous or excited in anticipation. *The father was biting his fingernails waiting for the birth of his first child.*

Bite one's head off: to respond in loud emotion or great anger; attack someone verbally. *Sorry to see that you lost the bet on the game, but that's no reason to bite my head off!*

Bite the bullet: confront a painful situation with expectation and endurance. *We have to bite the bullet until Dad finds another job.*

Bite the dust: to meet with defeat. *The Apollo 13 space mission almost had to bite the dust when its oxygen tanks malfunctioned and exploded on the way to the moon.* 2) die or be killed. *He bit the dust while saving his comrades.*

Bite the hand that feeds you: go against your means of support. *The strikers bit the hand that fed them when their work stoppage forced the company into bankruptcy.*

Bite your lip/Bite your tongue: instructing another to remain silent and not reveal anything further that one would later regret. *Bite your tongue and don't say a word!*

Do one's bit: perform one's share of the work. *Everyone is expected to do his bit in this company.*

Grab a bite: *See,* **Grab**.

He/she won't bite: not be persuaded or convinced; to refuse to accept. *The car salesman tried his best to persuade the customer to purchase that sedan, but she wouldn't bite.*

Put the bite on: to put the pressure on. *The president put the bite on his management staff to find ways to cut company waste and increase productivity.*

Two-bit: cheap; lower class. *If you want to look more important, the first thing you can do is get out of that two-bit outfit and into some finer threads.*

Two bits: cheap advice (an amount equal historically to 25 cents). *Hey, if I had wanted your two bits about the monorail plan, I would have asked for it.*

Bitter

Accept/Take the bitter with the sweet: accept adversity or loss with the good fortune. *He has a great job but it is so far away from home; we just have to accept the bitter with the sweet.*

Bitter pill (to swallow): a big letdown. *The death of the famous musician was a bitter pill to swallow for everyone who knew him.*

Black

Black and blue: beaten up (black and blue is associated with the blood hemorrhaging under the epidural layer, which makes the skin look black and blue). *Although we won the game, we all felt and looked black and blue.*

Black and white: as clear as can be; very certain. *The facts are black and white that all the witnesses saw the suspect hit the victim while his back was turned.*

Black as coal: dark heart; evil. *She has a heart that is black as coal.*

Black ball: to deny access, generally in a deliberate and harsh way. *Marvin was blackballed from the union because of his association with management.*

Black book: a covert list of names. *When the Russian agents discovered his black book, it was all over for him as a spy.*

Black market: illegal trading of contraband or stolen goods. *Many families in war-torn areas deal in black market goods to survive.*

Black out: *See also below,* **Blackout.** 1) to faint; become unconscious. *He blacked out for several minutes after hitting his head against the wall.* 2) lose one's memory on a certain subject. *I studied so hard, but blacked out when I had to take the exam.*

Black sheep: the outcast or unpopular member of the family. *The family treated Marty like the black sheep in the family, yet he grew up to become a very successful suicide counselor.*

Blacklist: negative listing of an individual; historically known as a list of individuals who were associated with threatening or revolutionary organizations, the dissemination of which smeared the reputation of the individuals identified. *See also above,* **Black** *ball. He lost his job in Hollywood after he was placed on a blacklist.*

Blackout: *See also above,* **Black** *out.* 1) exclusion of television coverage for a certain area. *There will be a local blackout of the football game today since it was not a sellout.* 2) complete shutdown of utilities. *The entire city experienced a severe blackout for several hours due to the stormy weather.*

In the black: in a positive or profitable position. *After losing its major contract, the company failed to stay in the black for many years.*

Blessing

Blessing in disguise: something that may look bad on its face, but really holds a positive outlook. *Although I resented Sheila getting the promotion, her transfer to another office turned out to be a blessing in disguise.*

Mixed blessing: *See,* **Mix.**

Blind

Blind as a bat: 1) unable to see. *I was as blind as a bat in the thick fog.* 2) unable to sense what is ahead; when one cannot view or understand something; be unaware. *I'm blind as a bat when it comes to flower arrangement. Without his good leadership, I think we would be blind as a bat.*

Blind date: going out with a person without knowing who he or she is (generally arranged by friends or relatives); a meeting, such as for dinner or a movie, between two persons unknown to each other. *Hank set me up with a blind date for tonight's party.*

Blinds: venetian blinds, which are generally horizontal slats in a vertical arrangement designed as a window covering (used in place of curtains). *Could you close the blinds so that we can watch a movie?*

Color blind: *See,* **Color**.

Rob someone blind: *See,* **Rob**.

Turn a blind eye: look the other way (so as to purposely avoid); allow something questionable to occur; not interfere with. *The city cannot continue to turn a blind eye to the growing number of homeless people in the area.*

Bling

Bling/Bling bling: flashy accessories; shiny; sparkling with gold or gems; nice. *Hey, that jewelry is really bling bling.*

Blink

Blinkers: eyes. *See also,* **Peep** (Peepers). *I need shades to cover my blinkers in a bright sun.*

In a blink: very fast; in very little time. *When we fed the hungry and homeless dogs, the food disappeared in a blink.*

On the blink: not functioning well or at all; out of order; inoperative. *My appliances seem to go on the blink soon after their warranties expire.*

Blivit

Blivit: an impossible task; needless or useless item. *Trying to get that mission done by tomorrow sounds like a blivit to me.*

Block

Been around the block: been there, done that; having already experienced it. *Hey, I've been around the block, so you don't have to lecture me about it.*

Blockhead: a person lacking normal intelligence; slow or failing to recognize. *He was a blockhead to perform those tasks without any skilled training or experience.*

Chip off the old block: *See,* **Chip**.

It's on the block: ready for sale. *Mr. Rogers placed his house on the block after his children left for college.*

Knock one's block off: to decisively beat someone up; (a threat) to scold someone. *Don't take your little brother to that blood and guts movie or I'll knock your block off.*

Blood

Bad blood: bitterness; resentment; ill-will. *Can you imagine that bad blood existed between the neighbors going back to King Louis XVI?!*

Blood: friend; person of the same culture, creed, race or group; family member. *Yo, blood, see ya at the game.*

Blood is thicker than water: family ties hold together better than other relationships. *Out in the country, blood is thicker than water, as families must help each other out.*

Blood on your hands: to be responsible for someone's death or misfortune. *If you do not warn the town of the viral outbreak, you will have blood on your hands.*

Bloodbath: the violent killing of many people. *The battle at Gettysburg between the North and South during the Civil War was a bloodbath on both sides.*

Blue blood: one grown and raised in a high-class or elite setting in life. *Although Michael was considered a blue blood, he always felt comfortable working on the factory floor with the other laborers.*

Cold-blooded: impersonal; raw without feeling; uncaring. *To cause indiscriminate harm is cold-blooded.*

Hot-blooded: *See,* **Hot**.

In cold blood: refers to punishing one severely without cause or hesitation. *They shot the protesters in cold blood.*

Make one's blood boil: make one very furious. *John's senseless remarks made my blood boil.*

Make one's blood run cold: to be terrified. *To be in that abandoned house where the murder occurred would make my blood run cold.*

New blood: *See,* **New**.

Smell blood: to sense impending action, attack or trouble. *The fugitive smelled blood at the sight of the state troopers at the truck stop, and sped back onto the freeway, toward Mexico.*

Warm-blooded: 1) personable; caring; passionate. *Luke has a warm-blooded character and he enjoys being with others.* 2) human. *I would rather speak with someone warm-blooded than to a recording machine.*

Blow/Blew

Blow: leave; depart promptly. *Let's blow this place and go to the club downtown. Jack told his little brother to blow, or else he would throw him out of the room.*

Blow a fuse/Blow a gasket/Blow one's cool/cork/fuse/lid/stack/top: be overcome with anger or frustration; lose one's temper. *She blew her stack when her children continued to disobey her directions. The boss blew a gasket when he heard that management cut his research budget for next year.*

Blow by/Blow past: to move quickly or hurriedly by; to be surpassed in an overwhelming fashion. *If we don't modernize our equipment in the near future, our competitors will blow by us and take our business away.*

Blow by blow: a detailed account of an event. *The police officer requested to hear a blow-by-blow account of the disaster from each witness.*

Blow chunks [expressive]**:** vomit. *We were blowing chunks overboard all during our fishing trip.*

Blow it: 1) to leave; get out. *Let's blow this trail before we get run over by the oncoming caribou herd.* 2) to forget it; to let it go. *Just blow it; staying upset isn't going to make anything better, including with yourself. After being detected, the burglars decided to blow it.* 3) to ruin something; to not get something right that was obvious or easy to do. *He blew it when he missed an easy lay up for the score to win the game.*

Blow it out your ear: *See,* **Ear**.

Blow off/Blow someone off: abandon; disregard; ignore; to dump. *We had to blow off the meeting today on account of nasty weather. She blew him off for another guy.*

Blow off steam: letting out one's pent-up energy or emotion, usually in a loud or otherwise intensive manner. *Sitting at a desk all day at work makes me restless, so I blow off steam by jogging along the lake shore in the evening.*

Blow one's cover: reveal one's secret identity. *You should leave the meeting, now, before someone blows your cover.*

Blow one's horn: proudly advertising one's deeds or pedigree. *That guy is a bore to most everyone because he constantly blows his horn about his accomplishments.*

Blow one's mind: to be completely amazed. *It would blow my mind if we discovered real life on Mars.*

Blow the lid off: to uncover. *The information gained from forensics helped to blow the lid off the theft ring.*

Blow the whistle: to disclose a secret matter. *The employee blew the whistle on the cost overruns.*

Blow up: 1) to make larger. *"Blow up the photograph so that we can see the faces."* 2) lose one's temper. *He blew up when the referee made a bad call that cost the game.*

Blowout: 1) unloading of goods at a very discounted price. *The rug store is having another blowout sale this month.* 2) puncture or bursting of a tire. *We had a blowout on the freeway.*

Come to blows: *See,* **Come**.

Blown

Blown: 1) ruined. *Our plans to hike Mount Rainier tomorrow are blown on account of bad weather.* 2) discovered; found out. *Our cover has been blown.*

Blown away: 1) shocked in awe. *I was blown away to hear about the large anonymous donation that saved our museum and library from closing down.* 2) gunned down. *The suspect was blown away by a hail of gunfire from police.* 3) inebriated; knocked out; out of order; disarray. *He was blown away after five beers.*

Blue

Blue: depressed. *The children were feeling blue because their favorite teacher was leaving to another school.*

Blue book: referring to a popular book guide of values on new and used vehicles. *What is the blue book value on this 1995 Ford Mustang?*

Blue chip: *See,* **Chip**.

Blue collar: laborer; industrial worker. *This is a blue-collar town, made up of factory workers.*

Blue flu: a fraudulent claim of illness for a sick-out, generally made by employees in an attempt to strike against an employer. *The blue flu among the dockworkers kept many ships from being unloaded.*

Blue in the face: to the extreme; to the point of exhaustion. *We kept sandbagging the levee throughout the night until we were blue in the face.*

Once in a blue moon: *See,* **Moon**.

Out of the blue: unexpected; suddenly. *The lion came upon the deer from out of the blue.*

Boat

In the same boat: in a similar situation together. *We are in the same boat after losing our jobs.*

Miss the boat: to fail to take advantage of an opportunity. *I missed the boat on the high-tech bull market.*

Rock the boat: to disturb, upset, or try to change a stable condition. *If you want to be a good team player, then make darn sure not to rock the boat around here. Your angry reaction will only rock the boat with the other members in the group.*

Body

Body English /Body Language: the way a person physically acts, which tends to portray what that person is thinking about. *You can tell by his body language that he is feeling very uncomfortable.*

Busy body: *See,* **Busy**.

Over my dead body: *See,* **Dead**.

Bogart

Bogart: 1) to steal. *Someone bogarted my stuff!* 2) to hog or take over; not share. *He always bogarts the food at the dinner table.*

Boil

Boil over: be considered insignificant. *This matter will all boil over, and we'll be laughing about it tomorrow; so don't worry.*

Boiled down: final version

Boiling point: the moment when one gets very angry or loses control of one's emotions. *I'm reaching my boiling point in this office; the workers are driving me crazy.*

Boils down to: comes to; results in; concludes as. *All this corporate maneuvering boils down to one thing…a company merger or buy-out!*

Bolt

Bolt: leave fast. *We bolted out of the woods at the sight of the grizzly bear.*

Bomb

Bomb: 1) to fail; bad or disappointing. *The concert bombed. The movie was a bomb.*

Bombed: heavily intoxicated. *We got bombed after attending our friend's funeral.*

Drop a bombshell: announce startling or most unexpected news. *She dropped a bombshell when she announced her candidacy for mayor.*

Bone

Bag of bones: 1) very thin or skinny. *When we found him in the forest, he was just a bag of bones.* 2) a body. *You think I'm just a bag of desirable bones.*

Bone of contention: a matter of argument; a subject about which there is disagreement. *Banning alcohol in the mining town was a bone of contention for many of the workers.*

Bone to pick: to have a confronting issue to discuss; to complain about something. *Samuel had a bone to pick with the city after a garbage truck ran through his flowerbed.*

Bone up: to review; study hard and quickly. *You better bone up on these math problems before the exam tomorrow.*

Bone yard: a cemetery. *This area used to be a bone yard about a hundred years ago.*

Bonehead: dim-witted person; one who does not understand; little intelligence; lack in consideration and understanding. *My landlord is a bonehead who ignores the worsening maintenance problems at the apartment complex.*

Dry as a bone: extremely dry. *Farmers have been suffering this past year because the weather has been dry as a bone.*

Jump on one's bones: desire to become physically intimate with another. *He had to fight the urge not to jump on her bones on the first date without first having her feel the same way about him.*

Know it in one's bones/Feel it in one's bones: to have a strong feeling about something but not know exactly why. *I feel it in my bones that we are going to win the game tomorrow.*

Make no bones about it: to hide nothing; admit something freely. *Make no bones about it, that I will hold you responsible for the children's care.*

Rest one's bones: take it easy; relax. *I'm just lying here, resting my bones.*

Skin and bones: *See,* **Skin**.

Bonkers

Bonkers: crazy; emotionally out of control. *I would go bonkers without him.*

Boo

Boo: 1) an exclamation to scare someone. *Standing behind the corner, Billy yelled, "Boo!" and scared Sally.* 2) significant other. *Hey, boo, come over and sit here with me.*

Boo boo: 1) accidental mess. *Little Timmy made a boo boo when he spilled the carton of milk all over the kitchen floor.* 2) a cut; a scrape. *Little Timmy got a boo boo on his right knee when he fell down.*

Boogey

Boogey/Boogie: 1) dance. *We boogied throughout the night after winning the school literary award for our thesis.* 2) to leave; to get going. *Let's boogey* *out of here to escape the rush-hour traffic.* 3) make one's way to. *I'll boogey on over to your place after my soccer practice.* 4) to move fast. *The suspects boogied down the alleyway when they spotted the police.*

Boogey man: ghost. *A lot of folks believe that a boogey man resides in that old mansion.*

Book

Black book: *See,* **Black**.

Blue book: *See,* **Blue**.

Book: leave promptly; take off; flee. *When the suspects spotted the police, they booked down an alleyway. Hey, it's time to book or we'll be late.*

Bookworm: one who enjoys reading. *We were bookworms in junior high.*

By the book: operate strictly according to set rules or regulations. *In playing golf, you have to go by the book.*

Cook the books: *See,* **Cook**.

Crack (open) the books: *See,* **Crack**.

Hit the books: study. *I have a biology exam tomorrow so I need to hit the books tonight.*

Judge a book by its cover: outward appearances can be deceiving; used generally as an analogy. *Buying the vehicle without checking its mechanical functioning or test driving it is like judging a book by its cover.*

Know like a book: to understand thoroughly; a full knowledge of. *He knows the complex machinery like a book.*

Nose in a book: to be intently or constantly reading something. *He always has his nose in a book, and rarely socializes with the other students.*

One for the books: an event that marks an unusual or uncommon achievement. *That hole-in-one golf shot on the 3rd hole was one for the books!*

Pound the books: *See above,* **Hit** the books.

Read like a book: *See,* **Read**.

Throw the book at: *See,* **Throw**.

Boom

Lower the boom: 1) attack with great strength. *The bartender lowered the boom on the rowdy drunkard, and tossed him out of the bar.* 2) forcibly capture. *The police finally lowered the boom on the crooks.*

Boon

Boondocks/Boonies: an isolated area in the country; jungle or unimproved area. *He lives in the boondocks, and has to commute far to get to downtown.*

Boondoggle

Boondoggle: a big wasted project. *The construction of the business center away from commerce was a boondoggle.*

Boot

Bet your boots: it's for sure; guaranteed. *You can bet your boots that he will return.*

Boot camp: the initial training period of a recruit, such as in the army or police academy. *After passing his physical exam, Hector went straight to boot camp.*

Booted out: to get expelled or disqualified. *He was booted out of the game for making bad gestures to players on the other team.*

Die with one's boots on: *See,* **Die**.

Give one the boot: kick out. *We gave Bob the boot from our club for being dishonest with the fellow members.*

Lick one's boots: *See,* **Lick**.

Booty

Booty: 1) buttocks; body. *I don't know if she can fit through the door with that booty.* 2) not good. *This music is booty.* 3) not attractive; poorly dressed. *She looks booty in that outfit.* 4) stolen or ill-gotten goods. *This stuff looks like booty to me.* 5) sex. *Rover, my dog, got all excited about Fifi, the poodle, for some booty.*

Booty huggers: very tight clothing around the buttocks. *She couldn't bend down because of her booty huggers.*

Kick booty: *See,* **Kick** ass/Kick booty/Kick butt.

Borderline

Borderline: very marginal; having a questionable determination. *My performance was so borderline that I wasn't able to qualify for the football team.*

Boss

Boss: awesome; totally great. *That new open-air café downtown is really boss!*

Botch

Botch up: mess up; fail to accomplish. *Don't botch up the assignment or you'll be sweeping floors in the mailroom!*

Bottle

Bottleneck: disruption of flow; constriction; no movement; a point in which progress cannot move forward. *The cows crossing the road bottlenecked traffic for hours.*

Bottom

Bet your bottom dollar: a guarantee that an action will be completed or assured. *You can bet your bottom dollar that this project will succeed without much trouble.*

Bottom line: the final determination or answer; the profits or losses in a business. *Tell it to me straight and just give me the bottom line.*

Bottom of the barrel: of the lowest grade or quality; scum; low-class. *He exhibits a character that is bottom of the barrel.*

Bottom of the ladder: lowest grade in the hierarchy. *He started at the bottom of the ladder, and worked his way up to become president of the company.*

Bottom out: to become stable at a point as in prices or value; where values have dropped so much and are ready to rise again. *This stock hasn't bottomed out yet.*

Bottoms up: to drink all the liquor in a glass until the bottom of the glass is pointing up; generally used in a toast to others. *Bottoms up!*

Get to the bottom of something: a zeal to discover the facts, and the cause of an action. *We'll get to the bottom of all this and find out who messed up.*

Bounce

Bounce: to leave; to depart. *I gotta bounce or I'll be late for the meeting.*

Bounce back: take a turn for the better. *He bounced back from his illness.*

Bounce it around: give it thought. *Bounce the idea around and give me a call next week about it.*

Bounced: getting tossed out. *Jason was bounced from the bar after having drunk too much.*

Box

Boxed in: stuck; unable to move; surrounded on all sides. *We got boxed in with the downtown traffic and were unable to get to the annual parade in time.*

Pandora's box: mess of trouble; nothing but problems. *The discovery of a county official embezzling funds opened a Pandora's box of deep-rooted corruption in City Hall.*

Think outside the box: possess creative ideas not ordinary; consider matters outside the norm. *The only way to resolve the dilemma is if we think outside the box.*

Boy

Old boys club/Old boys network: the social connection that holds the prestige or power seats in the community; being well connected with power in the community, originally associated with the white male crowd that kept women and minorities out of positions of power or prestige. *Many things haven't changed in this community for the past 75 years because the old boys network still seems to predominate.*

The boys: the guys; social peers among males. *Honey, I'm going out with the boys this weekend to the drag-racing championship.*

Brain

Beat one's brains/Rack one's brains: trying hard to recall or understand. *We were racking our brains trying to figure out the name of that restaurant in Shinjuku station that served some awesome tempura.*

Birdbrain: *See,* **Bird**.

Brain drain: the emigration of skilled and talented individuals. *We are experiencing a brain drain in this area because of the economic downturn.*

Have half a brain: to possess even a little sense. *If he had half a brain, he would have realized the danger of hiking up Mt. Rainier without proper gear or supplies.*

No brainer: 1) a task or effort that requires little or no use of the mind; something that is very easy to do; without effort. *This task is a no brainer.* 2) an obvious matter. *Getting rid of the bad employees in the company is a no brainer.*

Pea brain/Shit for brains (expressive): a dim wit; someone not so smart. *He's a real pea brain, but he sure can run fast. Do you have shit for brains crossing on a red light?*

Pick someone's brains: getting information from a knowledgeable person on the subject. *You should pick his brains for the answers to the test questions.*

Bread

Bread: money. *I need some bread to pay for next month's rent.*

Bread and butter: the basic source of support. *The bread and butter for many elderly and disabled are their monthly social security or government checks.*

Breadwinner: one who works to earn an income in support of the family. *Emily has always been the breadwinner for the family.*

Break

Break a leg!: a comedic way of saying 'good luck' to someone ready to perform. *When you go on stage tonight, Jack, break a leg!*

Break-in period: time necessary for something to become more flexible, like leather goods. *There is usually a break-in period for a new baseball mitt to fit a player's hand.*

Break it up: stop it; quit. *I want you guys to break it up and shake hands.*

Break one's ass/back/balls/neck: *See,* **Break one's ass**.

Break the bank: to go broke. *If we don't secure this contract, it will break the bank and force us to file for bankruptcy.*

Break the ice: make the effort to initiate friendly conversation; socialize or interact diplomatically when parties are at odds or silent with each other. *Ulysses helped to break the ice between the warring factions by showing his scars from previous war wounds.*

Break the news: be the first to relay new information. *You best break the news to the family about Johnny getting into trouble at school today.*

Break out: 1) escape. *There was a break out from the prison camp.* 2) exposure of a medical symptom, such as a rash or pimples. *Timmy tends to break out in a rash if he eats shellfish.*

Getting all the breaks: to have a run of good luck. *Tom got all the breaks when he walked away from the accident without a scratch.*

Tough break: *See,* **Tough**.

Breath

All in one breath: *See,* **All**.

Catch one's breath: *See,* **Catch**.

Don't hold your breath: waiting for the right result could take a very long time. *After college, don't hold your breath about finding the perfect job.*

In the same breath: from the same conversation. *He came to me asking for a loan, but in the same breath, mentioned that he also applied for a second mortgage, all to try to pay for Aunt Mable's heart operation.*

Save your Breath: don't bother talking about it. *Save your breath if you are going to lecture us about procedure.*

Take one's breath away: sudden thrill or awe. *The magnificence of the ship up close took his breath away.*

Under one's breath: whisper; speak softly. *He muttered under his breath how cold it was, although he stayed out all night with friends.*

Wait with baited breath: wait in anxious anticipation. *The entire city waited with baited breath to see if it would be selected as the next site for the world summer Olympics.*

Breathe

Breathe down one's back/Breathe down one's neck: be constantly present to check up on or criticize someone. *It is hard to do our jobs with the boss always breathing down our backs.*

Breathe easy: be more relaxed. *We can breathe easy, now that the tornado warnings have passed.*

Breathing space: have enough space for comfort. *We moved away from the big city to have more breathing space.*

Don't breathe a word: be secret about something. *Don't breathe a word about the surprise party we are preparing for Mr. Shimizu.*

Live and breathe: *See,* **Live.**

Take a breather: time to relax for a while. *Let's take a breather for 10 minutes before going back to work.*

Breeze

A breeze/Breeze through: very easy; with little or no effort. *The project was a breeze.*

In a breeze: right away. *I'll be back in a breeze.*

Shoot the breeze: to make small talk. *The workers were shooting the breeze with each other during the morning break.*

Brew

Brew: 1) fresh coffee. *Let's go get some brew.* 2) beer. *How about we go and have a brew at Mac's Bar and Grill?*

Brewski/Brewsky: beer. *I could use a brewski about now.*

Brittle

Brittle: uptight. *It's a small matter; don't let it brittle you.*

Broke

Broke: out of money. *He went broke at the very beginning of his venture.*

Broken-hearted: overcome with sorrow or grief. *He was broken-hearted after losing his only daughter.*

Flat broke/Stone broke: completely out of money. *We left the casino stone broke. He was flat broke after shopping for his kids.*

Go for broke: gamble all you have; take all the risks to accomplish a matter. *The soldiers went into battle with a go-for-broke attitude.*

If it ain't broke don't fix it: don't interfere with or fix something that is functioning properly. *Leave the apparatus alone; if it ain't broke don't fix it.*

Bruhaha

Bruhaha/Brouhaha: disturbance; argument. *What was the bruhaha all about?*

Brush

Brush-off: to snub; push away; ignore. *The starlet brushed him off when he asked her for an autograph. He got the brush-off when he tried to meet her.*

Brush up: to refresh one's memory. *He wants to brush up on the reading assignment before class.*

Brush with the law: a past criminal encounter with police or law enforcement. *His prior brush with the law taught him a few good lessons about staying out of trouble.*

Buck

Buck: to shoot for; to attain. *The new hire is already bucking for section chief.*

Buck the system: resist organizational rules. *You cannot expect to buck the system and retain your job for long.*

Feel like a million bucks: *See,* **Million**.

Pass the buck: *See,* **Pass**.

The buck stops here: to take responsibility. *U.S. President Truman was popular for a sign on his desk that said, "The buck stops here." It stressed his motto to maintain a disciplined fiscal policy.*

Young buck: strong, male individual. *This young buck will help haul the supplies to the warehouse.*

Bucket

Drop in the bucket: *See,* **Drop**.

Kick the bucket: *See,* **Kick**.

Bud

Bud: 1) a friend or companion. *Hey, bud, wassup?* 2) marijuana; the fruit of the marijuana plant that is most potent in cannabis or drug content. *Let's kick back and have some bud.*

Buffalo

Buffalo: 1) to baffle or confuse as a means of persuasion. *The crafty sales-man tried to buffalo the young couple into buying a vehicle that was too expensive for their budget.* 2) to intimidate, usually by a show of power. *The bully tried to buffalo the other kids into giving up their lunch money.*

Bug

Bug: 1) to annoy. *Quit bugging the girls.* 2) hidden microphone. *Check this office for bugs.* 3) to leave fast. *Let's bug out of here.* 4) virus, cold. *There's a bug going through town, and it's causing many to call in sick to work.* 5) a defect, problem, or imperfection. *We cannot use the software until we clean out all the bugs. We need to test the prototype some more to work out the bugs.* 6) an enthusiast or devoted fan. *I'm a real soccer bug.*

Bug out: get out fast. *We bugged out in time before the hurricane devastated the town.*

Bugger: someone full of trickery; very mischievous person. *Our two-year old son is a little bugger.*

Cuddlebug: someone so adorable you want to hold and caress. *Your little boy is such a cuddlebug!*

(Put a) bug in one's ear: to casually bring some matter to the attention of someone in order to make that person act upon the information. *Go put a bug in his ear about getting him to vote on expanding the research department. I put a bug in his ear about the importance of tomorrow's meeting; so, I hope he goes to it.*

Snug as a bug: very comfortable. *I was snug as a bug in bed when the earth-quake hit.*

Bull

Bull: to make foolish reference; non-logical or untruthful. *The guys were talking bull about the size of the fish they caught and released.*

Bull in a china shop: one who/that is big and clumsy at the risk of upset-ting other people or things. *He was like a bull in a china shop driving his truck down the crowded bicycle path.*

Bull market: a rising stock market. *The bull market had many people investing in stocks.*

Bull session: any idle discussion among associates, peers or friends. *We were having a bull session about how to increase production at the sawmill.*

Bulldog: 1) an aggressive person. *Our boss is a bulldog on the job, but a real quiet person at home.* 2) to act aggressively. *He bulldogged his way through the crowd, not conscious of the people he was knocking down.*

Bull/Bullshit/B.S. [expressive]: strong emotional expression of denial; response to denote that something is nonsense, false, foolish or illogical. *To believe the suspect's story about the crime over that of three unbiased witnesses is bullshit. It's no bullshit that Bigfoot lives up in the forested mountains of the Northwest.*

Cock and bull (story): ridiculous or unbelievable; exaggerated. *The police did not believe the suspect's cock and bull story. Bill told his friends some cock-and-bull story that he was going on a long trip overseas when in fact he admitted himself into a rehab center to detoxify.*

Shoot the bull: *See,* **Shoot**.

Take the bull by the horns: take on the tough challenge; to directly confront; take the risk or initiative. *In life, you have to take the bull by the horns or else you will miss many good opportunities.*

Bullet

Bite the bullet: *See,* **Bite**.

Dodge the bullet: avoid an unfavorable or disastrous situation by luck or quick maneuvering. *Mark was able to dodge the bullet in the investigation and get away clean.*

Sweat bullets: *See,* **Sweat**.

Bum

Bum: to receive; to get. *Can I bum a cigarette from you?*

Bum around: to idle, loaf or loiter around. *We usually bum around the mall after school.*

Bum leg: injured or weakened leg. *My bum leg kept me from joining the National Guard.*

Bum rap: 1) an unfair deal; to be treated unfairly or without consideration. *That was a bum rap for him to leave his friends stranded without a ride.* 2) a false charge. *He was arrested and jailed on a bum rap.*

Bum steer: the receipt of false guidance or information. *We got a bum steer on this property from the previous realtor.*

Bummed (out): disappointed; depressed. *We're bummed out that our team lost.*

Bummer: disappointment; bad occurrence. *That concert was a bummer.*

Bum's rush: forceful removal of someone. *He was given a bum's rush for his obnoxious behavior.*

Bump

Bump into: to meet without expecting to. *I bumped into Sally at the mall today.*

Bump off: to murder or kill. *The cellmate the convict was bragging to, about how he bumped off someone, was really an undercover police officer.*

Bump on a log: useless; not performing; doing nothing. *Quit lying there like a bump on the log and get your chores done.*

Bump up: 1) to promote; to move up. *The airline bumped us up to first class. He was bumped up to vice-president last week.* 2) to suddenly increase or raise. *Oil prices bumped up on news of decreased inventory.*

Goose bumps: 1) frightened. *I had goose bumps when we spotted a UFO hovering over us.* 2) excited. *Winning the book award gave me goose bumps.*

Bunk

Bunk: of poor quality; worthless. *This watch is bunk.*

Burn

Burn a copy: to reproduce something; make a copy. *Burn a copy for me, will you?*

Burn a hole in one's pocket: to spend a lot of money quickly. *The cost of the beautiful black stallion burned a big hole in Sam's pocket.*

Burn one's bridges: having done something that makes going back not possible. *When he insulted the members, he knew that he burned his bridges, and that he would never be invited to the meetings again.*

Burn rate: the expenditure of funds over time. *How has our burn rate improved in comparison with our cash flow?*

Burn rubber: take off very fast in a vehicle, enough to make the tires screech or smoke. *He enjoyed burning rubber around town in his new sports car until the police impounded it for his reckless driving.*

Burn someone's ass: *See,* **Ass**.

Burn the candle at both ends: to overwork; to use an excessive amount of energy at a fast pace without rest. *Martin was burning the candle at both ends by working two jobs in order to support his family.*

Burn the midnight oil: to work/study until very late at night. *We burned the midnight oil in order to meet the news deadline the next morning.*

Burn to a cinder/Burn to a crisp: completely burn. *The house was burned to a cinder, destroying all personal property and leaving nothing behind.*

Burn up: get very angry. *The delay in receiving the shipment of assembly parts really burned up the boss, didn't it?*

Burned out: run down; overworked. *John was burned out after working 12 hours straight.*

Get burned: to get cheated or swindled. *Paul got burned when he invested money in a get-rich-fast scheme.*

Burner

On the back burner: of low priority. *The plan to extract oil from the wildlife refuge was placed on the back burner by Congress.*

On the front burner: accomplish as soon as possible; high priority. *Due to the world oil crisis, the nation's energy policy was placed on the front burner by the new administration.*

Bury

Bury it: forget about it. *You need to bury the idea that you want to seek revenge.*

Bury one's head in the sand: *See,* **Sand**.

Bury the hatchet: make peace with a quarreling party. *After many years of conflict, the parties decided to bury the hatchet.*

Bush

Beat around the bush: *See,* **Beat**.

Bush league: 1) small time; second rate. *I felt like a bush leaguer playing with those young kids.* 2) minor league. *His extraordinary talent as a pitcher helped move him up quickly from the bush league and into the majors.*

Bushed: exhausted. *The players on both sides were bushed after 14 innings of baseball.*

Bust

Bust: failure; no go. *The development project at this site was a bust due to the strong environmental responses not to cut down the forested area.*

Bust a gut/Bust a nut/Bust one's ass/Bust one's butt/Bust one's balls (expressive): exert extreme effort; work very hard on something. *I had to bust a gut getting here; so, what's the problem?*

Bust your ass: penalize harshly. *If you can't follow the rules, I'll bust your ass.*

Busted: 1) caught doing something improper. *The child was busted when his mother caught him reaching into the cookie jar.* 2) to be broken. *Mickey got his nose busted up in the fight.* 3) to be without money. *By the end of our vacation, we were flat busted.* 4) demoted. *The soldier was busted in rank for fighting.*

Busy

Busy as a bee/Busy as a beaver: diligently working. *He is busy as a beaver landscaping the backyard.*

Busy body: nosy; someone checking out what others are doing. *She is such a busy body, always asking what you are doing.*

Butt

Bust one's butt: *See,* **Bust** a gut.

Butt: 1) rear end; gluteus maximus. *He slipped on the icy sidewalk and fell on his butt.* 2) remains of a used cigarette. *The kids were watching a homeless person search for butts in the cigarette receptacle.* 3) a foolish person. *He was being a butt in class and an annoyance to everyone's dissatisfaction.* 4) push through. *We had to butt our way through the crowd in order to get to the stage.* 5) to hit. *Rams like to butt heads during the mating season.*

Butt in: to intrude; interrupt or interfere. *He likes to butt in on our conversations.*

Butt ugly: extremely ugly. *The Ford Edsel became a classic car, primarily because many people thought it looked butt ugly.*

Butthead: a dummy; stupid person. *You don't have to be a nerd to be a butthead.*

Haul one's butt: *See,* **Haul** one's ass.

Kick butt: *See,* **Kick** ass/Kick booty/Kick butt.

Scuttlebutt: rumor. *What's the scuttlebutt all about?*

Butter

Bread and butter: *See,* **Bread**.

Butter someone up: to flatter; sweet talk. *The children were trying to butter up their dad so that they could go to the carnival.*

Butterfingers: clumsy or blundering individual; heavy-handed with things. *This guy is butterfingers on the job, and is of no use to me.*

Button

Button one's lip/Button up: be quiet. *Button up and listen to the instructor. Button your lip around here; people are sleeping.*

On the button: 1) right on time; exactly. *He arrived at his job interview at five o'clock on the button.* 2) on the chin. *He tried to break up the fight, but got hit right on the button.*

Buy

Buy a pig in a poke: to purchase something without first seeing or inspecting it. *Buying that car over the internet is like buying a pig in a poke.*

Buy it: 1) to accept as being true. *They didn't buy his story at the parole board. The police bought her story about the accident, and decided not to give her a traffic ticket.* 2) die. *If you're not careful on this winding road, you can buy it real easily. Jack bought it last week when his vehicle slipped into the ravine off Mulholland Boulevard.*

Buy the farm: to die. *I really thought that dog was going to buy the farm when it crossed the freeway.*

Buzz

Buzz: 1) to call someone over the telephone. *Please give me a buzz when you get into town.* 2) to fly low overhead. *The planes buzzed over the spectators at the air show.* 3) a euphoric feeling, generally experienced after having indulged with herb, drink or drugs. *I got a light buzz after drinking the punch.* 4) rumor. *What's the buzz around town?*

Buzz off: direct expression to another to leave one alone. *Sally told Mike to buzz off.*

Buzzard: an old, cranky and likely disagreeable person. *That old buzzard rarely leaves his property.*

Buzzing: an expression meaning "How are you doing?" or "What's happening?" *So, what's buzzing, cousin?*

Buzzing along: doing one's routine smoothly or quickly. *We were buzzing along in our work and getting a lot done.*

Buzzing around: observing or patrolling around; run or dash about quickly. *Who's that guy buzzing around here?*

Buzzword: 1) rumor or gossip. *The buzzword is that Monique is going to quit her job in California and move to Connecticut.* 2) word or phrase identified with a certain subject. *"Cutting edge" is a common buzzword for modern technology.*

By

By and by: in a while; before long. *By and by, they will show up for the meeting.*

By and large: on the whole; for the most part; everything considered; taking the whole situation into account. *By and large, the meeting went very well, with all the parties agreeing to a 10-year trading partnership.*

By far: to a notable degree; by a clear or comfortable margin. *Jones is by far the best candidate. By far, he's the most eligible.*

By the numbers: done by the rules or set procedures. *Ok, let's do it again, by the numbers.*

By the skin of one's teeth: barely. *We survived the disaster by the skin of our teeth.*

By the way: incidentally. *By the way, did you remember to lock the door on the way out of the office?*

C

Cage

Cagey: 1) smart; clever; sharp-witted; shrewd. *Only a few of the new hires will show the cagey qualities that we hope to find.* 2) cautious; wary. *Everyone is feeling a bit cagey after the earthquake.*

Rattle one's cage: to disturb strongly; annoyingly upset. *He rattles my cage with his smug arrogance.*

Cake

Cake walk: something easily done. *Advanced math is a cake walk for Gregory.*

Icing on the cake: 1) something extra and pleasurable. *For icing on the cake, we are going to see a show after dinner.* 2) sarcastic or comedic phrase to indicate what more else could occur, generally in a negative setting. *When I borrowed Angelo's car, I was stopped and ticketed by the police for a broken tail light. For icing on the cake, I was also arrested when they discovered Angelo's handgun in the back seat.*

Piece of cake: very easy to do. *It would be a piece of cake to program this system.*

Take the cake: *See,* **Take.**

Call

Call: 1) prediction. *Hey, that was a good call on the game tonight.* 2) observation. *The umpire made a lousy call on that play.*

Call a halt to something: request or demand something to be stopped. *The teacher called a halt to all the commotion.*

Call a spade a spade: call something by its right name; speak frankly even if not pleasing. *Let's call a spade a spade; your actions are hurting the company.*

Call into question: to be suspicious or express doubt about something. *The report called into question the police action at the carnival.*

Call it a day: to stop what one is doing, generally after a hard day's work, and relax. *Let's call it a day and go out for some cold drinks.*

Call it quits: to end something; to say that one has had enough. *After ten years in the business, they called it quits.*

Call names: to use insulting or profane words about or to another. *The conversation became more confrontational when they started calling each other names.*

Call of nature: the need to go to the bathroom. *Jack had to respond to a call of nature.*

Call one's bluff: insist that one prove his or her statements true. *I called his bluff to prove to me that he was telling the truth about the incident.*

Call the dogs off: stop hounding or going after someone. *Why don't you call the dogs off my client because you have no evidence, no motive, and no body.*

Call the roll: read out the names of people on a list, generally to check for appearance. *Jimmy, please call the roll to see that everyone is back in class.*

Call the shots/Call the tunes: tell others what to do; be in control; give direction. *Coach Stanley calls the shots around here.*

Call to mind: to bring to memory; to remember. *That trip calls to mind the time we ran for cover when the bear entered our campground.*

Called on the carpet: to be in a challenging situation with looming punishment a possibility; to be scolded or reprimanded. *He was called on the carpet by the supervisor for conducting personal business on company time.*

Calling card: something uniquely related to one's identity. *A hacker usually tends to leave his or her calling card behind when breaking into a computer system.*

Close call: *See,* **Close**.

On call: available when contacted. *The doctor is on call after hours.*

Wake-up call: an event or situation that triggers serious attention about something. *The moderate earthquake that hit the region was a wake-up call for the need to prepare and plan for safety measures when the big shake inevitably occurs.*

Can

Can: toilet. *Hey guys, do you know where the can is around here?*

Can of worms: potentially complicated or unpleasant situation; nothing but problems. *Teaching those rowdy seventh graders is a can of worms. It would be a can of worms to take on that job.*

Canned/Shit-canned (expressive): fired from a job or position. *He was canned for using the company vehicle for personal use.*

In the can: 1) in the toilet *I can't make it to the phone; tell them I'm in the can.* 2) completed; done. *Finally, our planning is in the can and we can begin construction tomorrow.*

Can't

Can't fight one's way out of a paper bag: one who is weak or performs poorly. *If you get him flustered and irritated, he gets to where he can't fight his way out of a paper bag.*

Can't hit the side of a barn: unable to hit anything. *When James started out as a pitcher, he couldn't hit the side of a barn.*

Can't hold a candle to someone: unable to measure up to someone. *Jack can't hold a candle to Tim when it comes to chess.*

Can't make heads or tails: unable to understand. *I can't make heads or tails out of the new computer system. I can't make heads or tails about what he said.*

Can't stand/stomach someone or something: unable to like or tolerate. *Drake can't stand the sight of blood, yet he wants to be a doctor.*

Can't walk and chew gum at the same time: *See,* **Walk** and chew gum at the same time.

Carbon

Carbon copy: a copy; just like another; a look alike. *Our new professor in manner and tone is a carbon copy of his mentor, Dr. Zhivago.*

Card

Card: amusing; witty; quick thinker; smooth talker. *He is such a card in front of the ladies. Albert is a real card at parties.*

Card shark: a clever card player. *Some card sharks make good money at the casinos.*

Card up one's sleeve: hold an advantage. *We need a card up our sleeve, like a fast runner, to win the game.*

In the cards: likely to happen. *Jane's success story was in the cards.*

Lay one's cards on the table: show one's intentions; to reveal one's holdings. *Don't lay your cards on the table too soon when negotiating.*

Play one's cards close to the vest: *See,* **Play**.

Cardinal

Cardinal sin: something very strongly disfavored. *It is a cardinal sin in business to undermine the trust of customers or clients.*

Care

Could care less: feel no sympathy or display any care whatsoever. *I could care less about your problems.*

Carpet

Called on the carpet: *See,* **Call**.

Roll out the (red) carpet: a ceremonious welcome for a very important person (V.I.P.). *They rolled out the carpet for the Secretary of State.*

Sweep under the carpet: *See,* **Sweep**.

Carrot

Carrot and stick: reward and punishment (usually an approach used for incentive purposes). *The carrot and stick approach is often used to teach animals to learn tricks.*

Carry

Carry away/Carried away: 1) lose control of one's actions. *He got carried away and started cutting all the trees in the yard.* 2) to be moved emotionally or psychologically. *We got carried away by the great singing of Placido Domingo. The great orator carried away the crowd.* 3) lose concentration. *Sorry, I got carried away and wasn't paying attention.* 4) highly excited by someone or something. *The soccer fans got carried away and streamed onto the field of play just as the game ended.*

Carry a big stick: one who has a lot of power. *The mayor carries a big stick in this town.*

Carry a lot of weight: to be very influential; commanding power. *Even though he is retired, he still carries a lot of weight in City Hall.*

Carry a small stick: doesn't have much power. *Don't talk loudly if you carry a small stick.*

Carry more weight: one who has more authority. *The chief of police carries more weight than the district judge.*

Carry one's load/Carry one's (own) weight: one who responsibly gets his or her job done. *I've got no problem with the new hire, as long as he carries his load around here.*

Carry out: accomplish. *He was directed to carry out everything until completed.*

Carry the ball: be dependable, especially at a crucial point; hold responsibility. *Tom carried the ball at the meeting and helped to secure the big government contract.*

Carry the day: a saving grace; one responsible for an overall success. *He carried the day for the whole team by winning three gold medals at the track meet.*

Carry the load: one who is important to the operation. *Bob carries the load in this department.*

Carry the torch: show of loyalty to a group or cause. *He carried the torch for 10 years in his quest to bring a hospital to this rural part of the country.*

Cart

Put the cart before the horse: doing things the wrong way. *Aren't you putting the cart before the horse by allocating funds to the departments before they are approved by the legislature?*

Upset the apple cart: *See,* **Upset**.

Carve

Carved in stone: permanent; not subject to change. *One's whole life is not carved in stone, but subject to many turns and changes.*

Case

Basket case: See, **Basket**.

Case in point: as an example. *A case in point of someone known not just as an American hero but a humanitarian of the world is Dr. Martin Luther King, Jr.*

Case the joint: to secretly study a surrounding or place that one wishes later to burglarize or attack. *The group had cased the joint for weeks before they burglarized it last weekend.*

Get off one's case: leave things alone; get off someone's back. *Someone should tell the boss to get off Dan's case.*

Get on one's case: criticize; meddle in someone's affairs; bug someone. *He keeps getting on my case for the smallest things.*

Make a federal case out of something: blow up the importance of something; overreact; blow up. *You don't need to make a federal case out of it.*

Showcase: feature or exhibit on unknown work, item, or performer. *I think if you showcase your product at the convention, you will receive a lot of inquiries for orders.*

Worst-case scenario: a plan or prediction to follow if everything turns out worse than planned. *The worst-case scenario would be to stay home if the storm hits.*

Cash

Cash cow: an excellent source of fast or easy revenue. *Our manure-hauling business is a cash cow with all the organic farmers in the area.*

Cash in one's chips: to give up or expire; to die. *I want to enjoy life before I cash in my chips.*

Cash on the barrelhead: pay cash upon the purchase of goods. *We paid cash on the barrelhead for this car.*

Cashed/Cashed out: tired; exhausted. *I'm cashed after hard day's work.* 2) empty. *There's nothing left; we're cashed out.*

Cold cash: *See,* **Cold**.

Strapped for cash: short of cash. *Quite a few large companies are strapped for cash ever since the recession hit.*

Cast

Cast pearls before swine: a pure waste when not appreciated. *Giving that expensive watch to that bar maiden is like casting pearls before swine.*

Cast the first stone: one to make the first accusation or criticism; the first to bear down on someone. *I'm sorry to cast the first stone but the food at that diner wasn't fit to eat.*

Cat

Cat fight: a noisy and squabbling session or fracas, generally seen in reference to two women in physical confrontation. *A cat fight erupted in the school cafeteria between two girls fighting over the same guy.*

Cat got your tongue?/Cat gets one's tongue: Unable to speak. *The cat gets my tongue every time she passes by.*

Cat is out of the bag/Let the cat out of the bag: to accidentally reveal a secret. *He let the cat out of the bag about the party this weekend.*

Catbird seat: a most favorable position. *She's in the catbird seat being five strokes ahead going into the last 9 holes of the golf tournament.*

Catnap: a short sleep or nap taken during the day. *I had a catnap at noon.*

Copycat: a fake; someone who reproduces the original work of another. *That picture is a copycat. He was discovered as a copycat and disqualified.*

Curiosity killed the cat: being too nosy could lead to trouble. *It might be best to mind one's own business; remember that curiosity killed the cat.*

Fat cat: *See,* **Fat**.

Fraidy cat/Scaredy cat: someone who is easily frightened of something (phrase generally stated by children); coward. *Jimmy is a fraidy cat about going into the woods.*

More than one way to skin a cat: there are other ways to accomplish a matter or reach the same result. *He figures things out by improvising and using his head because he believes that there is more than one way to skin a cat.*

Peroxide pussycat: a woman rigid in her actions who becomes very cooperative and agreeable. *After her arrest on conspiracy charges, she broke down and turned into one peroxide pussycat for the prosecution.*

Raining cats and dogs: very heavy, solid. *It's raining cats and dogs.*

Scaredy cat: *See above,* **Fraidy cat.**

Something the cat dragged in: haggard in appearance; unappealing. *Look at you! You look like something the cat dragged in!*

The cat's meow: the best; any person, thing or plan that is remarkable or excellent (coined in the 1920's). *He is the cat's meow in his league in college and is expected to be a top pick for the professional league.*

Catch

A catch: someone very attractive, and whom one would not mind being with. *Wow, she's a catch, isn't she?!*

Catch and release: the environmentally friendly way to fish, by catching the fish, then releasing it back into the water while it is alive. *Most sport fishing encourages catch and release as the standard to better protect the fish species.*

Catch as catch can: the best you can do with whatever is available. *The depression was very tough on us and every day was catch as catch can.*

Catch hell: to face serious consequence; to receive a severe reprimand or punishment. *You will catch hell from the coach if you miss practice today. You're going to catch hell for wrecking your parents' car.*

Catch in the act/Catch (someone) red-handed: to be seen doing something inappropriately; witnessed in the act of wrongdoing. *He caught the car thief red-handed, and took him to the police. The thief was caught in the act by hidden video cameras. We were caught red-handed sneaking into the swimming pool after closing.*

Catch on: Do you understand? *Do you catch on to what I am saying?*

Catch one's breath: rest to regain normal breathing. *Let's stop here for a while so that I can catch my breath.*

Catch one's eye: attract attention. *I tried to catch her eye but she did not notice me.*

Catch some rays: get some sun. *Since the weather was so nice, I was outside catching some rays.*

Catch some Z's: get some sleep. *I'm gonna catch some Z's before dinner.*

Catch someone off guard: to observe someone during a period of lapse or carelessness. *We need a diversion to catch the nurses off guard in order to get into the ward.*

Catch someone with his or her pants down: *See,* **Pants**.

Catch 22: a difficult situation, in which one is unable to get out of or resolve (made popular by Joseph Heller's 1961 novel, *Catch 22,* about the insanity of war). *The police chief faces a catch 22, confronting angry citizens protesting police brutality, and keeping enough police on the streets to protect the very same citizens.*

Catchy: 1) contagious. *The illness going around school is very catchy, so be careful.* 2) attractive. *I like the song because it has a catchy tune.*

Caught

Caught in the middle/Caught in the crossfire: stuck or left between two fighting groups; making it difficult to remain on the sidelines. *Sam and Gil were arguing and Tom got caught in the crossfire.*

Caught red-handed: *See,* **Catch** in the act.

Caught short: not having enough. *We were caught short last month and could not pay rent on time.*

Caught with one's hand in the cookie jar: *Same as,* **Catch** in the act.

Caught with one's pants down: unprepared; not ready at the vital moment. *We were caught with our pants down when the health department came by unannounced and saw our dirty kitchen.*

Not be caught dead: defiantly against. *I wouldn't be caught dead in that purple suit.*

Cave

Cave in: surrender; to agree to go along with the other's wishes. *Mr. Samuels usually caves in to what his wife wants to do.*

Certifiable

Certifiable: crazy. *You are certifiable for taking on that dangerous job.*

Chance

Chance it: take the risk or opportunity. *I'm going to chance it without an appointment and see if the dean is in his office today.*

Chance of a lifetime: a one-time opportunity. *If you have some funds, this is a chance of a lifetime to get into this start-up company before it is publicly traded on the stock exchange.*

Fat chance: *See,* **Fat**.

Outside chance: a remote possibility; a small likelihood. *Jim has an outside chance of getting into UC Berkeley as an economics major.*

Change

Change horses in the middle of a stream: *See,* **Horse**.

Change of mind: decide to do something otherwise. *I had a change of mind about going on vacation in the middle of winter.*

Change of pace: change one's movement faster or slower. *How about a change of pace? Let's turn in our rental cars and take the rest of the trip by horse through the canyons!*

Change one's mind: to have a different opinion or thought about something. *If you change your mind about going with us, you can call me on my cell number.*

Change one's tune: *See,* **Tune**.

Piece of change: *See,* **Piece**.

Chapter

Chapter and verse: in every detail. *I don't want to hear chapter and verse; just summarize your report.*

Charge

Take charge: assume responsibility during someone's absence. *Take charge of this office while I'm out of town.*

Trumped up charge: *See,* **Trump**.

Chat

Chat/Chit Chat: casual, unimportant discussion; talking to pass the time; small talk. *You may not chit chat during exams.*

Chatty: one who talks a lot. *Jane is a chatty individual, isn't she?*

Chawook

Chawook: big and dumb; a domineering, but kind-hearted man who is physically strong but lacking in wisdom. *Compare with,* **Jamoke** and **Jabroney**. *The bouncer was this big chawook who made sure we all got into the club.*

Cheap

Cheap shot: a degrading remark or inconsiderate act; low blow. *I consider it a cheap shot when my boss criticizes me in front of the whole office.*

Cheapskate/Cheap ass (expressive): one who tries to obtain everything for free or for as little as possible. *Tim is a cheapskate as he never pays when his turn comes up.*

Dirt cheap: very inexpensive. *I got this car dirt cheap from a good friend.*

Check

Blank check: grant unlimited use of authority in a particular setting. *The research and planning department was given a blank check to set up the company's overseas operations.*

Bounce a check: a bank check returned based on insufficient funds. *She bounced a check on the joint account because the husband had earlier withdrawn funds from it to purchase a computer.*

Check out: to leave or depart from. *He checked out with no forwarding address.*

Rain check: 1) a ticket stub, which permits the holder to see another game in case of rain or cancellation. *We got a rain check to the baseball game on account of rain.* 2) to cancel and provide for another opportunity. *Sorry, but I'll have to take a rain check to tonight's show because I have to care for my baby boy who took ill suddenly.*

Rubber check: a bank check drawn on insufficient funds. *Writing a rubber check is an infraction of the law.*

Cheese

Cheesy: cheap. *Don't buy it; it looks too cheesy to me.*

Cut the cheese: *See,* **Cut**.

Say cheese: smile. *Ok, kids, say cheese to the photographer.*

Cherry

Cherry on the cake: an added benefit; a freebie. *The unexpected work bonus we received was cherry on the cake for us this holiday season.*

Cherry pick: to be able to select top quality. *The top college basketball teams always get to cherry pick from the best players in the country.*

Chew

Bite off more than one can chew: taking in more than one can handle. *He really bit off more than he could chew when he challenged the champion boxer to a match.*

Chew out someone/Chew someone out/Chew one's ear out/Chew one's ass out (expressive): scold severely; talk too harshly. *We all got chewed out for misbehaving in the classroom.*

Chew something over/Chew on it/Chew on one's ear: to talk about something with another; to get one's opinion or feedback. *I would like to chew on this information tonight before I speak with the staff tomorrow morning. Can I chew on your ear for a moment about how we should go about this situation?*

Chew the fat/cud: talk randomly; converse idly. *Let's take a break and chew the cud.*

Walk and chew gum at the same time: *See,* **Walk**.

Chick

Chick: young woman. *Who's that pretty chick sitting next to Harold?*

Chicken

Chicken: scared; to not do something because of fear. *I would be chicken to walk in there alone.*

Chicken ass: *See,* **Ass**.

Chicken feed: not very much. *What you lost on that deal was chicken feed compared to what the other guys lost.*

Chicken-hearted: to act timidly or cowardly; to be afraid to act. *You're chicken-hearted for not going mountain climbing with me.*

Chicken out: become afraid to act, unwilling to take chances. *Mac chickened out on the deal.*

Chicken scratch: wording that is hard to read. *I can't read the chicken scratch on this medical prescription.*

Chicken shit [expressive]: *See,* **Shit**.

Chickens come home to roost: words or actions come back to cause trouble for the person. *The chickens finally came home to roost for old man Baker for illegally operating a winery in a residential neighborhood.*

Count your chickens before they hatch: to depend on something prematurely, which may otherwise not occur. *Celebrating now while the project is unfinished is like counting your chickens before they hatch.*

Spring chicken: *See,* **Spring**.

Chill

Chill/Chillin'/Chill out: 1) relax; hang out; spend time together. *Let's go chill at your place. We're just chilling before going back to class.* 2) to calm down. *Will you just chill, and wait until they post the grades on the board?*

Chin

Keep one's chin up: remain confident; face trouble with courage or determination; be brave. *We tried to keep our chin up when our beloved dog died.*

Take it (square) on the chin: to get punished or to suffer harshly. *He really took it on the chin when he got fired for being 5 minutes late to work.*

Up to one's chin in something: greatly involved; overwhelmed. *I am up to my chin in work after coming back from vacation.*

Chintzy

Chintzy: cheap, shoddy. *Why are you wearing that chintzy outfit?*

Chip

Bargaining chip: something to be offered during negotiation. *What can we offer as a bargaining chip?*

Blue chip: first rate; have the highest order or value. *Blue-chip stocks have not been doing so well, lately..*

Cash in one's chips: *See,* **Cash**.

Chip in: contribute a share of something. *We all should chip in and get Bob a gift for his retirement.*

Chip off the old block: a child who looks or acts much like his parents; classic resemblance. *His stubborn style is a chip off the old block from his father.*

Chip on one's shoulder: one who is always looking for a fight or argument. *If you want to be with friends tonight, then get rid of the chip on your shoulder.*

In the chips: very rich. *Mr. Smith got in the chips with his new company.*

Let the chips fall where they may: to take whatever consequence might occur. *Invest all the cash and let the chips fall where they may.*

When the chips are down: at the most dangerous or toughest moment; when it counts. *When the chips are down, you can count on him to make the crucial points in the game.*

Chisel

Chisel: 1) take advantage of others by forcing oneself upon them for favors. *Dick always tries to chisel in on our deals.* 2) Crash parties, gatherings, picnics, and etc. without an invitation. *Dick is an old hand at chiseling in on parties.* 2) to sneak. *Once you commit yourself, then don't try to chisel out of the deal later.*

Chiseled in stone/Chiseled out of stone: not subject to change. *Our contract is chiseled in stone and good for life.*

Choice

Choice: very nice; great; awesome. *This cigar is choice. Management thinks you are choice for the job.*

Choke

Choke: unable to win; to lose the competency or ability to win. *The ball team does great during the season, but seems to choke in the playoffs when it counts the most.*

Choke up: 1) unable to speak clearly because of anxiety. *Dick used to choke up every time he had to make a speech.* 2) to well up with emotion or tears. *The sad movie got us all choked up.*

Enough to choke a horse: in a very large amount. *That guy has enough money to choke a horse.*

Chomp

Chomp: to bite or to eat, generally in large amounts. *The sharks took large chomps from the dead whale carcass floating on the sea. Can I have a chomp of your tuna sandwich?*

Chomping at the bit: extremely eager; overly aggressive. *The news reporters were chomping at the bit to interview the new baseball star.*

Chuck

Chuck/Chuck it: get rid of. *We had to chuck all our gear in order to keep the hot air balloon aloft and high enough to get over the valley. The teenagers were seen chucking their beer cans from the swerving vehicle.*

Chump

Chump: 1) a stupid or arrogantly naïve individual; one who simply does not understand. *That guy is such a chump, yet he thinks he is the center of attention.* 2) displeasing; stupid. *This is so chump!*

Chump change: very small amount. *That's chump change compared to the deal he arranged with the big television networks.*

Circle

Circle the wagons: prepare for a confrontation or fight. *If you propose to eliminate medical benefits, the employees will circle the wagons and wage war.*

Full circle: make a complete cycle; return to the original position or situation. *Modern medicine, which for years created drugs synthetically in labs, has come full circle by seeking herbs to make medicines like they did hundreds of years ago.*

Run around in circles: *See,* **Run**.

Vicious circle: a bad situation that doesn't improve; a sequence of events that only worsens. *Mack gets little pay, spends it quickly, and has to borrow money until next payday—It's a vicious circle.*

Clam

Clam up: 1) keep silent; shut up. *Why don't you clam up and get to work?* 2) refuse to talk or respond. *When the teacher asked who hid the books, the children clammed up under giggling breaths.*

Happy as a clam: thrilled; very excited. *The kids are happy as clams to be going to the science center today.*

Clay

Clay pigeon: a person easy to cheat or take advantage of. *I was set up as a clay pigeon by the culprits before I realized what had happened.*

Clean

Clean as a whistle: spotless. *The bathroom was clean as a whistle.*

Clean bill of health: in good (physical) condition. *The doctor gave June a clean bill of health.*

Clean cut: a look of respectability; reliable or honest; straight; not wayward. *I want clean-cut individuals hired for these jobs, so drug testing will be required.*

Clean one's clock: to beat decisively. *That little kid cleaned my clock in chess.*

Clean slate: a record showing no marks of wrongdoing. *It helps to have a clean slate when running for public office.*

Clean sweep: *See,* **Make** a clean sweep.

Clean up one's act: improve one's performance. *You'll be fired if you don't clean up your act.*

Cleaned out: without money; loss of assets; broke. *That last hand of poker cleaned me out until next payday.*

Clean up: take or win in great amounts. *We cleaned up at the racetrack today!*

Come clean: tell the truth. *I want you to come clean on everything.*

Keep one's nose clean: to stay out of trouble. *He's a good worker, if only he would keep his nose clean.*

Sent/Take to the cleaners: 1) take all or a lot of another person's money, whether competitively, deceptively, or dishonorably. *James was taken to the cleaners by that crackpot investment firm.* 2) lose in competition. *They took us to the cleaners when we played them last year.*

Clear

Be in the clear: free from suspicion. *She is in the clear after they found the missing cash.*

Clear as mud: not understandable. *Your explanation of what happened is as clear as mud.*

Clear sailing: easy to finish; facing no problems. *It will be clear sailing on our project after we get our loan approved.*

Clear the air: to erase doubts or hard feelings after an argument. *Let's have a frank discussion and clear the air.*

Click

Click (with someone): to get along or work well with; to become popular with someone. *Pink hair and nose rings never really clicked with me. They clicked with each other the first time they met.*

Clicks: kilometers. *See also,* **Klick**. *My house is about 50 clicks from here.*

Climb

Climb the walls: 1) feeling very nervous or anxious. *We were climbing the walls waiting to hear from mountain rescue about the fate of the missing hikers.* 2) very bored. *I was just climbing the walls until you got here.*

Clip

Clip: to cheat. *Careful, this dealer will try to clip you with hidden extra charges.*

Clip artist: a con man or swindler. *A clip artist took the partygoers.*

Clip joint: any overpriced, low-quality place of business. *I'll get even with Sam for recommending me to this clip joint.*

Clip someone's wings: to penalize someone; put a restraining hold on someone [refers to a bird with clipped wings that restricts it from flying]. *The boss will clip my wings if I don't watch my expenses.*

Cloak

Cloak and dagger: to operate secretly or covertly; undercover work. *Sometimes I wonder how many embassy personnel are really cloak and dagger types.*

Clobber

Clobber: 1) to hit. *He clobbered a home run over center field.* 2) to beat. *We got clobbered today by a bunch of rookies!*

Clock

Around the clock: all the time; constantly. *We are working around the clock to finish the project.*

Beat the clock: to complete something before it is due or the time has expired. *Our boss was very impressed when we beat the clock in publishing and distributing the information to our customers.*

Clock in/Clock out: originally refers to punching a time clock going to and from one's job. *She clocked in here about noon.*

Milk the clock: make good use of the remaining time [frequently used in the last few minutes of a basketball or football game]. *Every person should milk the clock and make good use of the remaining years in life.*

Close

Close but no cigar: so close, but not enough to win; very near perfect but not a winner. *The horse he bet on almost won the race; close, but no cigar.*

Close call/Close shave: very close to meeting with danger; almost losing or missing something; just getting by; narrow escape. *That was a close call when I missed my step and almost fell off the roof. That was a close shave flying through the canyons.*

Close shop: quit working. *It's five o'clock, time to call it quits and close shop.*

Closed shop: a place or business, factory, etc. operating under a contract agreement between business and labor where only union members are authorized to be hired. *It was a closed shop arrangement and I had no choice but to join the union before I could work.*

Close the gap: to catch up with the competition. *We are closing the gap with our competitors due to our new products on the market.*

Cloud

In the clouds: day dreaming; wandering mind. *My head has been in the clouds all day; I just cannot concentrate.*

On cloud nine: be in a joyous trance; in very bright spirits. *He was on cloud nine after winning the big casino jackpot at the slot machines. Sam is on cloud nine after his promotion.*

Under a cloud: 1) under a watchful eye for wrongdoing; suspected of possible wrongdoing. *All the employees handling the funds were under a cloud of suspicion after an in-store investigation discovered that money was missing.* 2) depressed; sad. *He has been under a cloud lately for losing a good friend to diabetes.*

Clunk

Clunker: an item of poor quality, usually a car. *My uncle's clunker is actually quite a rare classic.*

Cock

Cock and bull story: *See,* **Bull**.

Cockamamie: crazy. *That's a cockamamie story if I ever heard one.*

Cockeyed: one who is confused; insane; crazy. *You're cockeyed; why don't you straighten up?*

Go off half cocked/Half cocked: do something (foolishly) without thinking first. *Make sure you don't go off half cocked at the interview; just be yourself, and relax.*

Cold

Blow hot and cold: passionate one time, then indifferent another. *She has a personality that blows hot and cold.*

Cold: cruel; harsh; unfeeling. *That was pretty cold when you failed to show up at the party.*

Cold as ice: *See,* **Ice**.

Cold blooded: without sensitivity or feeling. *Millie was involved in a cold-blooded murder.*

Cold cash: real currency instead of paper checks or promises. *When I sold my car, I requested cold cash.*

Cold cocked: smacked to near unconsciousness. *Dan was cold cocked while coming out of a dark alley.*

Cold day in hell: never. *It will be a cold day in hell when you take over this company.*

Cold feet: to be afraid to take chances; to back out of a deal or situation; not willing to go forward. *Don't get cold feet when you're ahead!*

Cold shoulder: to ignore or be indifferent. *After his arrest, Jim got the cold shoulder at work.*

Cold turkey: 1) take action without notification or preparation; just do it. *The boss walked in cold turkey and laid out his plan.* 2) to stop suddenly. *He went cold turkey with smoking cigarettes 5 years ago, and he has never looked back.*

In the cold: 1) completely left out; totally unaware of. *We were in the cold about any knowledge of the President's arrival.* 2) greatly surpassed. *The Toyota left the other competitors in the cold going into the last leg of the race.*

Knocked out cold: unconscious. *The boxer challenging the welterweight crown was knocked out cold in the second round.*

Stone cold: *See,* **Stone**.

Collar

Blue-collar worker: an industrial worker. *Blue-collar workers make up the majority of our workforce.*

Hot under the collar: angry. *Getting hot under the collar will not improve your disposition.*

White-collar worker: professional, clerical or other workers not specifically identified as manual or hands-on labor. *Dennis is an accountant and is classified as a white-collar worker.*

Color

Call to colors: a notice to serve in the armed forces. *Many eligible men were called to colors in the Vietnam War.*

Change color: become ghost like or sick. *His face changed color after seeing the birth of his son.*

Color blind: unable to distinguish among colors. *It's good to be color blind among all races.*

Show one's true colors: reveal one's real character. *The way he acted showed his true colors.*

With flying colors: *See,* **Fly**.

Comb

Comb/Combing: to thoroughly look for something or someone. *If they find you missing, they will be combing this place for you. I combed through this book and found a number of good passages.*

Come

As good as they come: the very best. *These bing cherries are as good as they come.*

Come again: to have something repeated; Can you say it again? *Come again, I did not hear you.*

Come along: How are you doing? *How are you coming along?*

Come and get it: a calling that it's meal time. *When the food was all prepared, Mom yelled out, "Come and get it."*

Come apart at the seams: to lose control and burst with emotional anger or sadness. *The President came apart at the seams when he saw new photographs of the military build-up along the border.*

Come away empty handed: return without anything. *I went to the bank for a loan, but I came away empty handed.*

Come by: secure or gain. *Easy profits are hard to come by.*

Come clean: be honest and forthright. *We can help you, but only if you come clean with us.*

Come down on: reprimand; attack. *He came down on him too harshly.*

Come forward: 1) volunteer information. *He came forward and identified the culprit.* 2) To provide. *She came forward with the needed cash.*

Come from behind: *See,* **Behind**.

Come full circle: *See,* **Full circle.**

Come hell or high water: *See,* **Hell**.

Come home to roost: *See,* **Home**.

Come into: to receive or to inherit money. *James came into considerable wealth.*

Come into the world: *See,* **World**.

Come off it: to tell another to stop acting or speaking in a foolish manner or pompous way. *Come off it, Helen; he didn't do this all by himself.*

Come on strong/Come on like gangbusters: overly aggressive; being aggressive or assertive to others. *Don't come on too strong in your interview today.*

Come out in the wash: matters will be resolved eventually; problems will go away as dirt in the wash. *Don't worry about all the little things in life; they will all come out in the wash.*

Come out of the closet: reveal one's secret gay interests. *Jack feels very relieved to have come out of the closet.*

Come through in the clutch: to be successful at a critical time. *We can always depend on our employees to come through in the clutch, especially when the workload gets heavy.*

Come to a head: *See,* **Head**.

Come to blows: to reach a point of physical confrontation or verbal abuse. *We came to blows over a little matter.*

Come to grips with: try to cope. *We had to come to grips with our overwhelming debts.*

Come to nothing: all the effort is worthless. *All the work to save the park came to nothing when the county reduced its parks and recreation budget.*

Come to one's senses: to start thinking clearly. *Why don't you come to your senses and attend school full-time?*

Come under fire: be under criticism for neglect or wrongdoing. *The corporation came under fire for miscalculating its finances.*

Come undone/Come unglued: unable to control emotion or physical character; to lose control emotionally. *Jack came undone due to stress and* *overwork. When the baseball umpire called the runner safe at home plate, the manager of the opposing team came unglued.*

Come up for air: to have some free time; to have a break from a very busy schedule. *I have been so busy today that I've had barely any time to come up for air.*

Come up in the world: *See,* **World**.

Come up smelling like a rose: *See,* **Rose**.

Come what may: regardless of what happens; despite troubles. *I'll finish my college courses come what may.*

Comes with the territory: an expected part of something. *Catching hell around here comes with the territory.*

Comedy

Comedy of errors: so many problems occurring that is looks silly; an amusing series of mistakes or problems. *The business failed due to a comedy of errors committed by management.*

Common

Common law: The law of a state or country based on custom. *Courts in America base justice upon common law.*

Common law marriage: a marriage with no religious or civil ceremony but effected by agreement to live together as husband and wife. *Many states recognize common law marriages.*

Company

Keep company: 1) be friends with. *We keep company with the Millers.* 2) go steady with. *He is keeping company with Helen.*

Misery loves company: to suffer together makes unhappiness easier to endure and bear. *She was suffering with the pregnancy and did not want her husband to go to the ball game – yes, misery loves company.*

Con

Con: to deceive. *He was conned out of his food rations for the day.*

Con artist/Con man: one who swindles by first gaining someone's confidence. *Mark was fooled completely by the con man.*

Conniption

Conniption fit: to become very angry or upset. *He had a conniption fit when his son called him from jail.*

Cook

Chief cook and bottle washer: one in charge of most all matters of an operation, including both the important and menial duties. *As a sole legal practitioner, I act as the chief cook and bottle washer in the firm.*

Cook one's goose: to spoil one's chances or hopes. *We cooked his goose when he tried to cheat us.*

Cook (something) up: to improvise something. *We have the best minds in research and development; they cook up ideas around here that are on the cutting edge of technology.*

Cook the books: to plot and fake financial records. *The corporate secretary and operating officer were charged with cooking the books.*

Cook up: 1) to devise; to create. *So what did you cook up for dinner tonight?* 2) to forge. *I will need to cook up a story about being sick so Bobby won't think that I didn't want to go to the party.*

Cooked: ruined. *Upon seeing the torpedo heading directly at the ship, the commander morbidly replied, "Oh my, we're cooked."*

Cooking: to be doing the right thing and doing it well. *"Hey, now we're cooking!"*

What's cooking: What's going on. *Hey, what's cooking around here?*

Cool

Be cool: be calm or quiet. *Just be cool and everything will be all right.*

Cool: 1) something exciting or wonderful. *As a kid, it was cool to see a real-life hero like Martin Luther King, Jr.* 2) not sympathetic; indifferent. *The public was cool to his art.*

Cool as a cucumber/Cool cookie: calm, not excited. *Mr. Simms remained cool as a cucumber while escaping from the big fire.*

Cool down: relax; calm down. *We'll get there in time, so please cool down.*

Cool it: slow down; relax. *Cool it, will you? You're getting too anxious about nothing.*

Cool off: 1) to become cool. *The weather cooled off today.* 2) Lessen someone's excitement or interest. *The Johnson's cooled off on the purchase of a larger home.*

Cool one's heels: stop for a rest; take it easy for a while. *I'm going to take a break and cool my heels.*

Cool one's jets: slow down; calm down. *I realize you're angry now, but it would be best to cool your jets before going into the meeting.*

Cooler: jail. *He got arrested and thrown into the cooler for drunk driving.*

Lose one's cool: *See,* **Lose**.

Play it cool: approach with fashion; poise; composure, avoid trouble or excitement. *Play it cool and you will remain safe.*

Cop

Cop: 1) police. *I'll call the cops if you don't leave.* 2) to steal. *The crows copped our lunch from the table before we knew what happened.*

Cop a feel: to touch someone without their permission; to feel someone surreptitiously. *He tried to cop a feel, but she pushed him away.*

Cop a plea/Cop a guilty plea: accept a criminal charge by pleading guilty, usually in return for a lighter sentence. *He copped a plea on a lesser charge of assault in return for the prosecutor dropping the attempted murder charge.*

Cop an attitude: to get negative or have an irritating and opposing attitude about something. *She cops an attitude on me whenever she dislikes what I have to say.*

Cop out: 1) drop out. *Come on, don't cop out on us now; stay a while longer.* 2) give up; to go back on a promise. *What a cop out for him to back out of the deal.*

Corner

Around the corner: within a short time. *Final exams are right around the corner so everyone has to start studying now.*

Corner/Corner the market: to create a monopoly; take over the whole market. *We will be able to corner the market with this product.*

Crawl into a corner: *See,* **Crawl**.

Cut corners: *See,* **Cut**.

Cotton

Cotton-picking/Cotton-pickin: dreadful; rotten; shabby; miserable; awful. *Those cotton-pickin' spiders always seem to find their way into our home.*

High cotton: *See,* **High**.

Couch

Couch: to state; to interpret. *You need to couch the language in such a way as to not offend, yet show some conviction.*

Couch potato: one who sits for long periods of time watching television. *My kids are no longer couch potatoes after we started taking hikes through the woods of the Cascade Mountains.*

On the couch: undergoing psychiatric treatment. *Janet is on the couch several times a month.*

Cough

Cough up/Cough it up: 1) pay up; hand over. *You will have to cough up some rent money to stay here another week.* 2) confess; reveal. *With a little prodding, he will probably cough up the whole story about the dorm fight last night.*

Cover

Blow one's cover: *See,* **Blow**.

Cover a lot of ground: accomplish much; do a lot. *We covered a lot of ground on this legislation today.*

Cover charge: extra payment over food and drink at a night spot (generally taken at the door). *There's a cover charge now at Jake's on Friday and Saturday nights.*

Cover for: assume responsibility. *I'll cover for Jim while he's on leave.*

Cover one's hide/Cover one's ass: *See,* **Ass**.

Cover up: to stonewall; hide the truth. *There exists a cover up at the highest levels of government.*

Undercover: secret job; hidden force. *Undercover agents were lying in wait for the drug deal to take place.*

Cow

Cash cow: *See,* **Cash**.

Have a cow: to become very emotional; have a tantrum. *Stay out of the way when the coach is having a cow.*

Holy cow: *See,* **Holy**.

Sacred cow: *See,* **Sacred**.

Till the cows come home: *See,* **Till**.

Crack

At the crack of dawn: *See,* **At**.

Crack a smile: forced to smile when one doesn't want to. *My boss has a hard time cracking a smile.*

Crack down: 1) go after. *The police cracked down on the drug agents* 2) become strict. *The teacher cracked down on the troublemaker.*

Crack (open) the books: intensive studying prior to an exam. *Most students crack the books before each test.*

Crack the whip: get tough. *A supervisor has to crack the whip once in a while.*

Crack up: 1) a crash of a vehicle or airplane. *There was a big crack up on the freeway today.* 2) Break down mentally. *Jane cracked up upon hearing the sad news.*

Dirty crack: *See,* **Dirty**.

Fall between the cracks: *See,* **Fall**.

Have a crack at: to try to do or help with something. *If you can't open the lock, then let me have a crack at it.*

Make a crack about someone: make a joke or funny saying; to tease. *Ned is always making cracks about me in front of others.*

Wise crack: a short, humorous criticism; a statement, which is neither complimentary nor clever. *All right, enough of your wise cracks about my new hairdo.*

Cram

Cram: to put a lot into something very small, such as stuffing a bag, or to do a lot in a very short period of time, such as studying for an exam, etc. *We had two days to cram for our chemistry exam.*

Cram it/Cram it up your ass (expressive): no way; defiant refusal. *See also,* **Stick** it. *When the neighbor told him to stop being noisy, he told him to cram it up his ass. Now they no longer speak to each other.*

Cramp

Cramp one's style: hinder one's ability to maintain stability. *Shopping after a hard day's work, cramps my style.*

Crank

Crank: 1) a deranged stubborn, eccentric person. *Mrs. Shipley, although a crank at times, can be real nice and generous.* 2) to hit hard; to slam one out of here. *He cranked a three-run homer to win the game in the 9th inning.*

Crank call/Crank letter: an obscene, fanatical or hostile telephone call or letter. *He began receiving crank calls after arguing at city hall that some of the parks should be turned into business districts.*

Crank it (up): 1) to get started. *Let's crank up the generator in case we need the additional power.* 2) to increase it to a much higher level. *Crank it up! This is a good song!*

Cranking: to get moving. *Alright everyone, let's get cranking; we have a lot to do today.*

Cranky: bothered; agitated; low tolerance. *Stay away from him when he's cranky.*

Crap

Crap/Crapola: 1) falsehood; nonsense; stupidity. *That story about the monster in the lake is a lot of crap.* 2) odorful; foul. *The food smelled like crap.* 3) excrement. *He stepped in some smelly crap.*

Crap around: waste time; fool around. *He finally stopped crapping around and started to get serious with his life.*

Crap out: to give up; fail; quit. *Being out of physical shape, Howard crapped out of the race.*

Crapper: toilet. (Ironically, Thomas A. Crapper was the infamous inventor of the flush toilet, hence from where the name was derived). *If you're looking for him, well, he's on the crapper.*

Crappy: no good; pretty bad. *The new uniforms look crappy.*

Crapshoot: a risky venture; a big chance. *Investing in this new company is going to be a crapshoot.*

Cut the crap: *See,* **Cut**.

Don't give a crap: do not care. *I don't give a crap about it.*

Don't give me any crap: don't give me nonsense, inconsideration, insincere talk, etc. *Please don't give me any of your crap today.*

Crash

Crash: to sleep. *I'm so tired that I could crash anywhere.*

Crash course: a quick education about something; to quickly learn about something. *We took a crash course in cooking outdoors before going on our camping trip.*

Crawl

Crawl into a corner: desire to hide or be unseen due to embarrassment or guilt. *He felt like crawling into a corner after running the wrong way with the football, and scoring for the other team.*

Crawl out from under a hole: a rude or sarcastic inquiry to one's appearance; to suddenly appear without notice. *It's been such a long time since I last saw you, Jake. So what hole did you crawl out from? Ha! Ha!*

Crazy

Crazy: 1) extremely fond of; excited about. *I'm crazy about her.* 2) out of one's mind; wayward thinking. *You're crazy to climb the mountain during a blizzard.*

Stir crazy: to have a sense of frustration for being or feeling confined in an unfavorable setting. *With all the noise and confusion around here, I'm going stir crazy in this office.*

You drive me crazy/Drive one crazy: make someone get excited or angry. *These kids drive me crazy with their antics and loud noise.*

Cream

Cream of the crop/Cream off the top: the best there is. *Washington State cherries are the cream of the crop.*

Cream puff: a male who exhibits more of a feminine demeanor; a male who is not physically apt. *This is a football team, so quit acting like cream puffs out there and kick some ass!*

Cream someone or something: beat up or defeat decisively. *Lexington creamed Southpark in tonight's baseball game.*

Create

Create a stink: to cause trouble; complain. *Why create a stink about such a small thing?*

Create an uproar: cause an outburst (of excitement). *The dog created an uproar when he retrieved a golf ball during the tournament.*

Creep

Creep: a weird or obnoxious individual. *That guy is a real creep.*

The creeps: scary feeling; frightful sensation. *That old mansion gives me the creeps.*

Crib

Crib: a house. *Ok, whose crib we gonna meet at?*

Croak

Croak: die. *When we crash-landed, I thought we were going to croak.*

Crock

Bunch of crock: nonsense; lies. *That's a bunch of crock!*

Crock/Old crock: reference to a bad-tempered, grouchy or ornery person, especially an old one. *The old crock just won't sell!*

Crock of shit [expressive]: nonsense; lies; frivolous or malicious talk. *That is a crock of shit to cut the old-growth forest because business development is more important.*

Crocodile

Crocodile tears: insincere display of grief. *Her display of sadness over the farmer's death was just crocodile tears for the purpose of taking over the estate.*

Crop

Crop up: to appear out of the blue. *Snakes cropped up all around us when we were cutting the tall grass.*

Cross

At a crossroads: undecided and at a point of decision. *The medical team was at a crossroads in the antibody research.*

Cross my heart (and hope to die): promise to tell the truth. *I cross my heart that I went to school today instead of going fishing.*

Cross one's fingers/Keep one's fingers crossed: to hope for something to come true (noted by crossing two fingers on a hand for good luck. *We kept our fingers crossed throughout the contest, hoping that our team would win; it worked! We crossed our fingers hoping that Mickey would win the game.*

Cross one's mind: come to one's attention; briefly appearing in one's mind. *It crossed my mind the other day to give you a call.*

Cross one's path: unplanned meeting with someone. *Dick and I crossed paths at the mall today.*

Cross someone up: make trouble or betray someone. *I trusted Jim, but he crossed me up at the meeting.*

Cross that bridge when it comes: don't worry about something before you need to. *We'll cross that bridge when the time comes for us to ponder that situation.*

In the crosshairs/In one's crosshairs: in target range; being watched. *With the cameras set around the yard with motion detectors, we easily had the raccoons in the crosshairs to film their courtship.*

Crow

As the crow flies: in a straight direction. *As the crow flies, it's about 10 miles from here.*

Crow: to yammer about; annoying talk. *What are you crowing about this time?*

Eat crow: admit to a humiliating mistake. *Mr. James was forced to eat crow about firing the wrong employee for an alleged theft.*

Crud

Crud: 1) a lowdown, worthless person. *Why do you associate with that crud?* 2) mess; garbage. *Clean that crud off the floor.* 3) untruth; lies. *What you heard is a bunch of crud.*

Cruise

Cruising: 1) driving around; scouting around. *I'm just cruising around searching for antique stores in town.* 2) moving real fast. *We cruised through the job and finished ahead of schedule.*

Cruising for a bruising/Cruisin' for a bruisin': asking for trouble or confrontation. *You best watch your words or you'll be cruisin' for a bruisin'.*

Crumb

Crumb: an unproductive, good-for-nothing person. *When are we going to fire that crumb in the supply room?*

Crummy

Crummy: bad; poor; awful. *The apple pie you made tastes crummy.*

Cry

A far cry: a great difference in comparison. *A terrier is a far cry from a bloodhound.*

Cry bloody murder: vociferous disagreement about something; yell in anger as if something serious has taken place. *Our baby son would cry bloody murder if you took his toy from him.*

Cry on one's shoulder: to seek the sympathy or compassion of another. *Now, if you wreck this car, son, don't come crying on my shoulder asking for another one.*

Cry one's eyes out: to weep bitterly. *Jim cried his eyes out when his friend died.*

Cry over spilled/spilt milk: to regret or be bothered about something already done or not able to be changed. *You are crying over spilled milk about the woman who left you for another person.*

Cry Uncle: admit defeat. *Same as,* **Say Uncle** *The painful arm lock caused the wrestler to cry uncle and concede the championship match.*

Cry wolf: to give a false alarm; to not be believed. *He cries wolf so often, most people have come to not believe what he says anymore.*

Crybaby: one who complains when things don't agree with him or her. *That crybaby will never be satisfied.*

For crying out loud: exclamation used in frustrated response. *For crying out loud, we just got here and, now, you want to go home.*

Cuff

Cuffs: handcuffs. *We found the hostages cuffed to the railing, looking tired and ragged from the ordeal.*

Off the cuff: without practice or preparation; impromptu. *He can talk about anything right off the cuff. The off-the-cuff remarks about polygamy by the politician proved to be his undoing.*

Cup

Cup of tea: a favorite. *Playing chess outdoors on a nice sunny day is my cup of tea. Listening and dancing to raucous music is not my cup of tea.*

Curtain

Curtains: the end. *Unfairly criticizing his political party was curtains for him as far as getting nominated for the party's president.*

Drop the curtain: 1) finish or close out. *Let's drop the curtain on this action.* 2) die. *I'll be fighting them until I drop the curtain.*

Raise the curtain: start or begin something. *Let's raise the curtain on the osmosis project.*

Cushy

Cushy: easy. *See also,* **Plum**. *She gets paid a lot for having such a cushy job.*

Cut

Cut: 1) dilute. *The drink was cut with club soda rather than tonic water.* 2) payoff, sometimes stated in percentages. *So, what's the cut on this deal?* 3) bring one into a deal. *Hey, cut me in.*

Cut a deal: make an arrangement with someone; negotiate a workout. *I need to cut a new deal when my lease expires on my apartment next month.*

Cut a rug: to dance (an expression popular in the jitterbug era during and after WWII); one who is very lively and full of life. *Mr. Jackson is 80 years old, but he can still cut a rug.*

Cut and dried: 1) straight-up; to the point; clearly explained. *The directions are cut and dried, so everyone should understand them.* 2) predictable; scripted. *Every morning our boss gives us the usual cut and dried lectures.*

Cut and run: depart in a hurry. *Hey, I'm going to have to cut and run. I'm late for another appointment.*

Cut corners: make shorter routes or tasks in order to finish faster or under budget; shorten the time, money, labor, etc. *Our office has to cut corners in order to make a profit this period. Cutting corners on this project is unacceptable.*

Cut it out: stop it. *Cut it out, kids, or you'll have to play outside.*

Cut no ice: doesn't make sense; has no meaning. *His proposal didn't cut any ice with his boss.*

Cut (one) some slack: be less harsh on; be easier on. *He's a new employee, so cut him some slack.*

Cut one off at the knees: to stop or interrupt something or someone suddenly and without warning; sharp rebuke. *If we don't get further funding to continue operations, the company will be cut off at the knees and we will have to shut down. It was fairly harsh to cut him off at the knees without explaining his job termination.*

Cut one's own throat: an opportunity ruined by oneself. *He cut his own throat when he gambled away the funds he needed to keep his business in operation.*

Cut out: leave. *It's late, so I'll have to cut out now.*

Cut out for something: having a talent for something. *Dick was not cut out for the medical profession.*

Cut-rate: low priced; inexpensive. *Let's go to that cut-rate store downtown.*

Cut someone down to size: to humble someone; to make a person realize his place in a hierarchy. *He was cut down to size when he spoke out against the company.*

Cut the cheese: flatulate; release of intestinal gas. *Ok, who cut the cheese around here?*

Cut the crap: stop the nonsense. *Cut the crap and give me the real story.*

Cut the funny stuff: be serious; stop the comedy and just tell what happened. *Cut the funny stuff and tell me what occurred at the meeting today.*

Cut the ground from under someone: to destroy or unexpectedly withdraw support from one's plans; to quickly undermine. *Mr. Sims cut the ground from under his opponent by presenting his proposal directly to the voters.*

Cut the mustard: work to the required standard; perform satisfactorily. *If you can't cut the mustard around here, you will lose your job.*

Cut the red tape: reduce the regulation of procedure. *We will need to cut the red tape to get the project finished in time for winter.*

Cut to the chase: get to the point; tell it directly. *Cut to the chase and just tell me what happened.*

Cut up: comedian; a funny or silly guy. *That Jack is a real cut up, isn't he?*

Cutthroat: 1) a person who is ruthless or merciless. *That person is a cutthroat businessman.* 2) In business, one who sells at any cost. *It's a cutthroat world out there; you'll have to be careful on the bargains you get.*

Cutting edge: *See,* **Edge.**

You could cut it with a knife: a sensation of thickness or something very strong in the air. *His breath was so bad you could cut it with a knife. The air was so muggy that you could cut it with a knife.*

Daily

Daily grind: *See,* **Grind**.

Damn

Damn right/Damn straight [expressive]: an expression of strong approval or support. *When asked if he would support the protection of old-growth forests, he replied, "You're damn right I will."*

Damned if you do, damned if you don't: no matter what you do, you are likely to receive criticism. *We have to reduce the workforce or close shop; we are damned if we do, and damned if we don't.*

Don't give a damn [expressive]: don't have any interest. *"Frankly, my Dear, I don't give a damn." (Clark Gable in the 1939 movie, "Gone With the Wind")*

Hot damn [expressive]: expression of excitement. *Hot damn! We won the contest!*

I'll be damned [expressive]: an exclamation of astonishment; cursed I should be. *When he heard that his neighbor won the governor's race, he fell into his chair and exclaimed, "I'll be damned!"*

Not worth a damn [expressive]: useless; of no value. *That gadget you bought is not worth a damn.*

Try one's damnedest [expressive]: try the best you know how. *I'll certainly try my damnedest in my new job.*

Damper

Put a damper on: diminish; depress; hold back. *The low sales are putting a damper on our profits.*

Dance

Dance on air: *See,* **Air**.

Dance to another tune/Dance to a different tune: change one's opinion, attitude or behavior. *Mark will be dancing to a different tune tomorrow when he finds out that his company just fired him.*

Dance to the tune of: be at the mercy of someone. *We have to dance to the tune of the ward boss.*

Song and dance: *See,* **Song**.

Dander

Get one's dander up: get one mad or excited. *Those military practice flights over our neighborhood all day long get my dander up.*

Dare

Dare say: expression which means, "I suppose," or "I would venture to guess." (a common expression heard in many British films). *I dare say you've seem to come across a wild streak of good luck.*

Dare someone: challenge someone's courage. *I dare you to jump into the pond to retrieve your golf ball.*

Dark

Dark: hidden; undisclosed. *Companies around the world conduct more dark projects than the military when it comes to product design and development.*

Dark horse: an unknown contestant; an underdog. *He was a dark horse candidate a month ago, and now seems to lead the incumbent in the race for mayor.*

In the dark: have no knowledge. *I'm in the dark about your project. Keep him in the dark about what we spoke about, alright?*

Shot in the dark/Stab in the dark: a wild guess; to attempt something that might have a slight chance of success. *It may be a shot in the dark but why don't you go up to her and ask her to the movies? I know it may be a stab in the dark, but I have a hunch that he may be at the coffee shop.*

Darn

Darn tootin': you bet it is; for sure. *You're darn tootin' right we're angry that the park has to close due to the city's budget shortfall and its poor planning.*

I'll be darned/Darn it: euphemism or polite word for "damn." *I'll be darned if I have to go through that procedure again.*

Date

Blind date: *See,* **Blind**.

Dawg

Dawg: 1) a good friend (usually male, and used in place of a name). *Hey, how you doing, dawg? These guys have been my dawgs since grade school at Mercy Elementary. Hey Dawg, wassup?!* 2) a fan who is named in reference to a canine that represents the school mascot, such as the University of Washington Huskies, the University of Georgia Bulldogs, the University of Connecticut Huskies, etc. *Real dawgs from the University of Washington wear purple.*

Day

At the end of the day: *See,* **At**.

Call it a day: *See,* **Call**.

Carry the day: *See,* **Carry**.

Day in (and) day out: all the time; constantly; every day. *We see Mr. Grandig tending to his garden day in and day out.*

Day in court: get your chance to defend yourself. *Despite the bad press, Dick is satisfied to know that he will have his day in court so that he can tell his story.*

Day late and a dollar short: miss out altogether on something. *The graduation party was yesterday, fellow; you're a day late and a dollar short.*

Days are numbered: one's time on this earth will end soon. *Our cat's days are numbered since we found out that she has a degenerative disease.*

Field day: exploit the predicament of another; a clammer of activity. *The press had a field day with the news of the mayor's arrest for drunk driving.*

Make a day of it: *See,* **Make**.

Make my day: a sarcastic comment inquiring of another to make their moment (day) an interesting one. *"Go ahead...punk...Make my day."* (Clint Eastwood in the 1970 movie, "Dirty Harry").

Save the day: *See,* **Save**.

That will be the day: *See,* **That**.

Won't give someone the time of day: cannot talk to someone at all; doesn't bother to give another any time or respect. *Jim is so busy, he won't give me the time of day.*

Dead

Ad for dead: ragged; sacked; awful looking due to extreme tiredness. *Did you not get any sleep last night because you look like an ad for dead.*

Beat a dead horse: *See,* **Beat**.

Dead: nothing going on; quiet. *It's dead around here. Where has everyone gone?*

Dead as a doornail/Dead as a dodo: certainly dead or lifeless; finished. *With the environmental laws just implemented, our plans to build on the wetland habitat are now dead as a doornail.*

Dead broke: completely without money. *Most of us were dead broke during the 1930's economic depression.*

Dead duck: a goner; a sure loser; one who is doomed to failure. *You're a dead duck if you don't finish high school.*

Dead end: unable to go any further. *We have reached a dead end on the project.*

Dead giveaway: a definite clue. *The thief's fingerprints were a dead giveaway.*

Dead heat: a tie between two or more contestants. *The lead horses were in a dead heat all the way.*

Dead in the water: not functioning; paralyzed. *Without his participation, we are dead in the water.*

Dead meat: to be in a lot of trouble. *You'll be dead meat if you get caught driving his Ferrari.*

Dead ringer: exact likeness; look alike. *His looks are a dead ringer of his Dad.*

Dead set against: totally opposed. *We're dead set against anyone trying to pollute the environment in this town.*

Dead to the world: 1) to be sound asleep. *I was dead to the world when the earthquake hit, and I didn't feel a thing.* 2) intoxicated. *After only 3 beers, he was dead to the world.*

Deadbeat: an able person lacking initiative; one who makes himself not useful; very lazy person. *You will have a hard time getting a job if you're a deadbeat.*

Drop dead: *See,* **Drop**.

Not be caught dead: very much against. *I wouldn't be caught dead in that polyester suit.*

Over my dead body: absolutely not; no way will you be allowed; not without a fierce fight. *If they try to take over this company it will be over my dead body.*

Deal

Big deal: 1) a significant person or thing. *That Senator is a big deal in his state.* 2) An exclamation of ridicule. *Ok, I got a job flipping burgers…Big deal!*

Bum deal/Raw deal: receive unfair treatment; be dealt with unfairly. *Albert got a raw deal on his vehicle purchase when he later discovered it was a stolen car.*

Cut a deal: *See,* **Cut**.

Dirty deal: *See,* **Dirty**.

Double dealing: *See,* **Double**.

Make a big deal of: make a lot of noise about nothing. *Quit making a big deal out of it.*

No big deal: not very important; inconsequential. *It's no big deal, so don't worry about it.*

Shady deal: illegal participation; suspicious interaction. *They were involved in this shady deal to obtain government contracts without making competitive bids.*

Square deal: *See,* **Square**.

Wheeler dealer: *See,* **Wheel**.

Dear

Dear John letter: a letter indicating that a fiancé, partner, or spouse desires to end a relationship (generally a letter from a woman to a man. Likewise, a "Dear Jane letter" is a letter written by a man to a woman, with the same intent of announcing an end to a relationship). *Many soldiers receive Dear John letters during wartime.*

Death

At death's door: approaching death. *We are all going to be at death's door someday, so be sure to take care of your estate planning now.*

Death warrant: something that causes termination or ruin. *The corporation's lack of sufficient funding was its death warrant.*

It worries me to death: overwhelmed with worry. *It worries me to death to see you in that wretched condition.*

Kiss of death: *See,* **Kiss**.

Thrilled to death: overwhelmed with happiness; extremely overjoyed. *We were thrilled to death when we won the hot air balloon race.*

Deck

Clear the decks: be prepared for action. *Clear the decks, here comes the police.*

Deck: to hit or be hit by someone; knocked down, as in boxing. *I went to settle an argument, but I got decked in the process.*

Decked out: dressed up; stylish. *We got all decked out in our best clothes to go to the Sunday picnic.*

Hit the deck: *See,* **Hit**.

Playing with a full deck: with all one's faculties; one's full ability to perform. *Looking at the way he is acting, I don't think he's playing with a full deck.*

Playing with half a deck: not being all there; without all of one's faculties. *Careful working with that guy because I think he plays with half a deck most of the time.*

Deep

Deep: intricate; complicated. *The math professor's lecture about derivative calculus got so deep that most of the students were unable to understand what was said.*

Deep pocket: *See,* **Pocket**.

Deep root/Deep-rooted: well entrenched; established for a very long time; embedded (in tradition). *Our family has deep roots in this area going back to the days of the federal period in the late 1700's.*

Deep shit [expressive]: *See,* **Shit**.

Deep six: 1) to kill; bury someone six feet deep, the standard depth of a grave. *They ought to deep six that murderer.* 2) get rid of; do away with. *It is best that you deep six that idea about going to Las Vegas when the wife is gone.*

Deep water: in a lot of trouble or in a precarious situation. *I think the boys will be in deep water for painting the school bus red.*

Go off the deep end: to lose it mentally and emotionally. *Our little daughter will go off the deep end if we can't find our pet dog.*

Knee deep: *See,* **Knee**.

Skin deep: *See,* **Skin**.

Devil

Between the devil and the deep blue sea: no where to turn to; no relief or recourse. *With no father, mentor or friend, and running from the law, the young man was between the devil and the deep blue sea.*

Give the devil his due: to accept success even from persons whom you dislike. *He is arrogant and rude, but you must give the devil his due.*

Lucky devil: expression that one is fortunate to receive something; a lucky person. *Jack just won a Honda Accord for shooting a hole-in-one at the golf course—that lucky devil!*

Speaking of the devil: referring to the actual individual you may have been speaking of. *Well, speaking of the devil, there he is in the flesh!*

Diamond

Diamond in the rough: unrefined, but precious nonetheless; one who is good on the inside but has a rough demeanor or exterior; a new person or thing with a lot of potential; one with exceptional or stand-out character, but lacking experience, refinement or style. *Some of the entry-level employees hired this year seem to be diamonds in the rough. That Sally is new but talented; she's a diamond in the rough!*

Dibs

Dibs on something: to lay claim to something found. *He claimed dibs on the dollar bill he found on the sidewalk.*

Dice

Dicey: dangerous; perilous; chancy; touchy. *It's pretty dicey going into that cave without proper support gear.*

No dice: no way; positively not. *You want to borrow my new car after crashing yours? No dice.*

Dick

Dick: 1) detective. *There were two dicks here asking for you.* 2) stupid person (expressive). *He is such a dick!* 3) to cheat or deceive. *That soothsayer dicked me for fifty dollars.*

Dick around: goof off; waste time. *How can you dick around when you have final exams next week?*

Dickhead/Dickwad/Dickweed [expressive]: stupid or senseless person. *You have to be a real dickhead to fail this exam.*

Diddle/Diddly

Diddle around: fool around; waste time. *We are just diddlin' around today.*

Diddly/Diddly squat/Diddly shit (expressive): not a thing; hardly anything; hardly enough. *That ain't diddly what you're offering me for the car. He did diddly shit today.*

Die

Die away: become extinct; diminish. *The music played for hours until finally it died away.*

Die for something: have a very strong desire. *I'm dying to get an alligator bag. I could die for a hot turkey dinner right now.*

Die on the vine: die before bearing fruit. *Our venture died on the vine.*

Die with one's boots on: to die in the prime of life. *Poor guy died with his boots on.*

Never say die: *See,* **Never**.

Diesel

Diesel: 1) really strong or tough. *That guy's diesel, so don't mess with him.* 2) beer. *I could go for some cold diesel right about now.*

Dig

Dig: 1) to search. *Detectives dig for clues to solve crimes.* 2) to like something. *Hey, do you dig it?* 3) to understand something. *Yeah, now I dig it.*

Dig in your heels: to not surrender, but to fight harder; take on the challenge and do your best; work as hard as you can. *If we want to survive, we need to dig in our heels and not give up.*

Dig your own grave: to slowly kill yourself. *If you don't stop smoking, you'll be digging your own grave.*

Dilly-dally

Dilly-dally: do nothing; sitting around wasting time. *You will never succeed if you dilly-dally your hours away.*

Dime

Dime: a $10 bill to a gambler or drug purchaser. *He sold dime bags of weed and coke on the streets until he was arrested.*

Dime a dozen: very cheap; easy to get. *Your item is too expensive; I can get them for a dime a dozen in town.*

Dime store: a prison sentence up to 10 years. *He bought a dime store trying to rob a bank last year.*

Get off the dime: move from a stationary position. *Hey guys, get off the dime and start sweeping the floors.*

Nickel and dime: *See,* **Nickel**.

Playing on the dime: when a fielder in baseball fails to cover much ground. *Jackson's a great hitter but is an average right fielder because he plays on the dime.*

Stop on a dime: stop quickly and instantly. *Wow! This car can stop on a dime!*

Turn on a dime: turn quickly and in a small radius. *He's fast and can turn on a dime.*

Ding

Ding: 1) dent. *Someone dinged my car in the parking lot today.*

Dingaling/Dingbat: dummy; idiot; unintelligent person. *Even a dingbat can figure this problem out, so don't give up.*

Dirt

Dig up dirt: to search for damaging or embarrassing information, generally personal in nature. *Were you able to dig up any dirt on that witness?*

Dirt: 1) denigrated; shameful. *The professor made me feel like dirt today.* 2) awful person. *My former roommate was a piece of dirt.*

Dirt bag/Dirtbag: low life; underhanded individual. *Be careful how you deal with that guy; he's a real dirt bag.*

Dirt cheap: *See,* **Cheap**.

Dirty

Dirty: offensive or obscene. *They did not know it was a dirty movie.*

Dirty bastard [expressive]: a conniving, underhanded individual. *That dirty bastard tried to sell us some stolen goods.*

Dirty crack: a rude or offensive remark. *That was a dirty crack you said about me at the meeting.*

Dirty deal: an unfair bargain. *That salesman gave me a dirty deal; what a crook he is.*

Dirty end of the stick: bad portion of a deal or arrangement. *We got the dirty end of the stick in our joint venture.*

Dirty laundry: unfavorable events in personal lives. *The political race exposed the dirty laundry of both candidates in the local news.*

Dirty (low-down) shame: insult to injury; an unfair event. *It was a dirty shame to see honest people blamed for that crooked individual's misdeeds.*

Dirty mind: having malicious or filthy thoughts. *He seems to constantly exhibit such a dirty mind that it is a wonder he gets anything done!*

Dirty money: money made from illicit gains. *He built his empire on dirty money.*

Dirty pool/Dirty trick: underhanded and deceptive practice. *That was a dirty trick Sam played on me at the party. What he did was dirty pool.*

Dirty work: underhanded activity; crooked dealing. *Who does his dirty work for him now?*

Down and dirty: *See,* **Down**.

Dish

Dish out: to provide without restriction or in large amounts; to give or hand out. *They were really dishing out the food at the mission on Thanksgiving! He really dishes out the charm when he sees a pretty lady. The teacher intends to dish out some discipline around here for yesterday's pranks.*

Distance

Go the distance: engage in an activity to the very last moment; to endure to the very end. *Mary never engages in any activity unless she can go the distance.*

Keep one's distance: avoid being friendly; avoid getting too close. *We kept our distance from the rough kids in school.*

Ditch

Ditch: to skip out; to not go. *We got caught ditching school today.*

Last-ditch effort: *See,* **Last**.

Divvy

Divvy up/Divvy out: divide; split up. *The kids divvied up their marbles to play a game during recess.*

Dive

Dive: a dirty or low-class establishment; a cheap drinking place or gambling house. *That place is a dive.*

Do

Do a double take: look twice to make sure that what is seen is correct. *Most of the audience did a double take when they saw a monkey with three legs.*

Do a flip-flop/Do an about face: change one's opinion to exactly the opposite view; to completely change one's view. *The politician did a flip-flop on the tax proposal.*

Do-hickey/Doo-hickey: anonymous reference to a small object when the object's real name cannot readily come to one's mind. *Bob bought some old do-hickey at an antique store to hang up in his office.*

Do one's thing: do what one is capable of or as one pleases. *After you retire, you are free to do your thing.*

Do someone or something in: create a downfall or a loss. *James was done in by his best business partner.*

Do something with one's eyes closed: so easy to perform. *When told about the delicate technique of making sashimi using the poisonous fugu fish (blowfish), he replied, "I can do that with my eyes closed."*

Do the honors: act as host or hostess to serve guests. *Mr. Albert, will you do the honors and slice the roast beef?*

Do the trick: accomplish the exact requirements. *Give me that hammer; I'm sure it will do the trick.*

Do you see horns out of my head?: do I seem weird to you? *Do you see horns out of my head?*

Doing time: in prison. *Jack began doing time when his child was just two years old.*

Done to a "T": just right, perfect. *The boss always likes the jobs done to a "T".*

Doctor

Doctor up: to touch up; make something look good, generally in a deceptive or fraudulent way. *The accounting books were doctored up to look like profits were always rising.*

Head doctor: *See,* **Head**.

Just what the doctor ordered: *See,* **Just** the ticket.

Does

Does it ring a bell: *See,* **Bell**.

That does it: that's the limit, that's the end. *That does it; I've had enough.*

Dog

Bird dog: *See,* **Bird**.

Call the dogs off: *See,* **Call**.

Can't teach an old dog new tricks: one with formed habits is hard to change, especially the experience that old people don't tend to change their ways. *My grandfather will not change; you can't teach an old dog new tricks.*

Dawg: *See,* **Dawg**.

Dog: 1) a good friend. *What's up dog?* 2) an especially unattractive woman. *Your new supervisor is a dog who naively thinks she is pretty.*

Dog and pony show: go through the motions just to please. *We had to do a dog and pony show for the high brass.*

Dog-eat-dog: unmerciful, sadistic competition. *It can be a dog-eat-dog world in the field of big business.*

Dog gone: euphemism for damn or darn; an expression of anger, joy or amazement. *I'll be dog gone! When did you purchase that new car?*

Dog-leg: a hole in golf resembling a dog's leg, with the fairway bending either to the left or right; it could be a dog-leg left or a dog-leg right. *The next hole is a dog-leg left and a bit tricky.*

Dog out: significantly; to the extreme. *He was trippin' dog out.*

Dogged: 1) (pronounced, "dog-ed"): stubborn; tenacious. *You generally need to be dogged to be a good detective.* 2) to be stuck with. *My roommate left without notice and dogged me out of paying the rent and utilities.*

Dogged out: very tired. *I'm dogged out after our shopping spree.*

Doggy bag: a bag to place leftover food from a meal at a restaurant (intended to mean food for the dog at home) to take home to eat later. *Occasionally, we ask for a doggie bag whenever we eat out.*

Every dog has his day: everyone has a chance to get lucky. *I guess every dog has his day because Jackson, our custodian of 15 years, hit the lottery and quit his job.*

Go to the dogs: be run-down and in need of serious repair; go to ruin. *The company next door went to the dogs several months ago after the economy collapsed.*

Hot diggity dog: *See,* **Hot**.

In the doghouse: in trouble. *He is in the doghouse for damaging his father's car last night.*

Lead a dog's life: *See,* **Lead**.

Let sleeping dogs lie: don't disturb anything for fear of worse conditions. *You better let sleeping dogs lie and not mess up the works.*

Put on the dog: show off as being rich or high class; buying expensive; looking flashy. *He puts on the dog at parties. The girl in the next office always puts on the dog.*

Rain cats and dogs: *See,* **Cat**.

Sick as a dog: *See,* **Sick**.

Top dog: *See,* **Top**.

Underdog: *See,* **Under**.

Doll

Doll: 1) pretty woman. *What a doll, isn't she?* 2) a man's sweet nickname for his lady, wife, significant other, etc. *Hey, doll, would you like to go to the Space Needle for dinner?*

Dolled up: fancifully dressed, generally for a special occasion or gathering. *Look at him, all dolled up for once!*

Dollar

Bet your bottom dollar: an expression to mean that one feels sure of a matter and would risk all of his or her resources; pretty sure of the outcome. *Do you think you will have a good crop this year? Bet your bottom dollar I will.*

Don't

Don't breathe a word: *See,* **Breathe**.

Don't cry over spilled milk: *See,* **Cry**.

Don't give me any crap/static/lip: don't interfere with me or give me any backtalk. *I don't want to hear any more static about your justification for a pay raise.*

Don't have a leg to stand on: one who is in a very weak position. *If the economy continues in the doldrums, my business won't have a leg to stand on.*

Don't hold your breath: *See,* **Breath**.

Don't move a muscle: stay completely still; don't move at all. *Don't move a muscle; there's a rattlesnake at your feet.*

Don't press your luck: don't ask for too much or take silly chances. *Don't press your luck or you'll lose everything.*

Don't rub it in: don't maliciously talk of someone's error or mistake. *I know I messed up, so don't rub it in.*

Door

At death's door: *See,* **Death**.

Back door: *See,* **Back**.

Dead as a doornail: *See,* **Dead**.

Get one's foot in the door: *See,* **Get**.

Lay at one's door: blame someone. *Please don't lay this mishap at my door; I had nothing to do with it.*

Open doors: *See,* **Open**.

Show someone the door: tell or direct someone to leave. *I showed the loan applicant the door after I reviewed his credit record.*

Doozy

Doozy: 1) a startling or special surprise. *It was a real doozy when the boss announced his resignation at the meeting.* 2) Very interesting or enriching. *If you want to win that contract, your presentation has to be a doozy. The company had a doozy of a year.* 3) A strong challenge (to contend with); something tough to do, get through, or to accomplish. *The flu season this year will be a real doozy. Fighting to protect your rights in many countries is still a real doozy. Trying to pick up that heavy box was a doozy!* 4) Strange or bizarre. *He is one doozy dude!* 5) A Duesenberg luxury vehicle of the late 1920's and 1930's. *From a distance, I couldn't tell whether it was a Packard or a Doozy.*

Dope

Dope: 1) real nice. *Hey, the new wheels you got is really dope, man!* 2) contraband, illegal drugs, or narcotics. *He got arrested for possession of dope, and was sentenced to community service.*

Dork

Dork: stupid or foolish person. *He's a real dork.*

Dorky: strange; peculiar. *I saw this dorky guy trying to direct traffic at the intersection like he was a police officer.*

Double

Double cross: to trick or betray; to renege on a promise that another has relied on. *He double crossed me when he failed to pay me his portion of the rent when he left.*

Double dealing: scam-ridden; untrustworthy and faithless. *That's the last time I'll do business with that double dealing dirt bag.*

Double standard: unequal application of law or regulation, usually noted against gender, race or age. *The company seems to follow a double standard of allowing men to do the more responsible tasks, but allowing women little opportunity to take on higher positions.*

Double talk: vague, misleading or deceptive talk; deliberately confuse someone. *He always seems to double talk his way out of trouble.*

Double trouble: two challenging and difficult moments at the same time. *He has double trouble in having to defend against both state and federal authorities about the incident.*

Double whammy: two unfortunate events appearing one after another. *John was hit with a double whammy today when he was first diagnosed with a hernia at the hospital, then got a traffic ticket on his way home.*

On the double: move in double time; move faster. *The first thing a soldier learns is to accomplish tasks on the double.*

Dough

Dough: money. *That guy is loaded with dough.*

In the dough/Raking in the dough: wealthy; surrounded with riches. *Being in the dough is the opposite of down and out. He's been raking in the dough, but he works hard for it.*

Down

Boils down to: *See,* **Boil**.

Down: 1) to drink quickly. *We downed a whole quart of orange juice after working in the garden all afternoon.* 2) in agreement with; in favor of. *Ok, mark me down for that. Hey, I'm down with that.*

Down and dirty: 1) to get involved; take on the challenge. *Ok, it's time to get down and dirty in the final round for the Poker champion of the year.* 2) underhanded or backhanded; nasty; do-anything-to-win behavior. *The politicians conducted a down and dirty campaign.*

Down and out: in a state of being without money; unable to recover. *Mr. Jones has been down and out for the past year.*

Down for the count: virtually out of luck and money. *Our company will be down for the count without the new loan commitment from investors.*

Down in the dumps: *See,* **Dump**.

Down pat: with certainty. *Rest assured, I have everything down pat.*

Down the drain/ Down the tubes: wasted; spoiled carelessly. *All of our efforts went down the drain when we didn't get the contract.*

Down to a "T": to the last detail. *Our boss likes to have everything down to a "T".*

Down to earth: realistic; practical; sensible. *His down-to-earth approach in resolving matters makes him a very popular leader with his constituents.*

Down to the wire: *See,* **Wire**.

Downhill: 1) things are easy to do. *The hard work is behind us, so everything is downhill from here.* 2) to get worse. *Our aunt's health started to go downhill after she broke her hip.*

Lay down the law: *See,* **Lay**.

Shoot/Shot down: to disagree with or veto. *We all shot down his idea, but later agreed that it was the way to go.*

Step down: to resign. *The founder is stepping down as president of the company after 50 years. He stepped down after news of the scandal broke.*

Drag

Drag: 1) unhappy situation. *It's a drag to be out of a job.* 2) to inhale. *The wounded soldier took a heavy drag from the cigarette, smiled for a brief moment, then **expired** on the battlefield.* 3) a cigarette. *Let's step outside and have a drag.* 4) tired; exhausted. *I'm dragged out after working overtime this past week.*

Drag it out/Drag on: to extend, seemingly to the point of delay; prolong. *The case dragged on for months without a determination.*

Drag one's feet/heels/tail/ass (expressive): *See,* **Drag one's Ass**.

Drain

Brain drain: *See,* **Brain**.

Down the drain: gone in a wasteful manner. *Our investment in the biotech project went down the drain when floods destroyed our research plant.*

Drained: tired. *We were drained after the long trip.*

Draw

Draw a blank: come up empty; experience a sudden loss of memory. *I drew a blank when I met my college classmate after almost fifteen years.*

Draw and quarter: to reprimand harshly; severe punishment, including physical torture, hangings, whippings, etc. *In colonial times, it was often the case that prison inmates were regularly drawn and quartered.*

Beat the draw: be quicker that your adversary in a confrontation (Derived from the Wild West when you had to be fast to draw your gun from your holster or be shot). *You have to be real fast to beat Jack to the draw.*

Draw an inference: get an idea from. *Given his excited reaction, we can draw an inference that he is happy to be going to Disneyland.*

Draw fire: attract harsh criticism; encounter strong disagreement. *His remarks are sure to draw fire from all sides.*

Draw out: get someone to talk. *The police tried hard to get the convict to draw out a few words of guilt.*

Draw something up: prepare a written paper (mostly pertaining to legal documents). *Draw up the case sequence for presentation to the court.*

Draw the line: 1) take a position one way or another. *We have to draw the line in keeping our environment clean.* 2) to distinguish where the limits are. *The parents had to draw the line with their teenage children where they could go and when they had to return home on Saturday night.*

Draw to a close: something coming to an end. *The game drew to a close at sunset.*

Quick on the draw: *See,* **Quick.**

Dream

Dream up: think creatively. *When did you dream up that idea?*

Pipe dream: unreal vision or hope; no chance of becoming true. *Most of Mike's visions have been pipe dreams.*

Dress

Dress down: 1) to reprimand or scold. *The coach dressed down his players for their bad conduct on the field.* 2) to wear informal rather than formal clothing; casual wear. *You're requested to dress down for the company picnic.*

Dress up: 1) wear more elegant clothing; improve your appearance. *You'll have to dress up for this occasion; a suit and tie will be required.* 2) improve a plan or presentation. *Your plan needs a little more dressing up on the sales features.*

Dressed to kill: wearing very elaborate or attractive attire; dressed extremely well; dolled up. *Mary was dressed to kill for the charity ball tonight.*

Drip

Drip: boring person. *My date was a drip because we had very little in common to talk about.*

Drive

Backseat driver: *See,* **Back.**

Drive a hard bargain: holding on until the end in getting the highest possible agreement or selling price. *Our real estate salesman drove a hard bargain and obtained a great price for our home.*

Drive in reverse: to do something the wrong way. *The way you are going about this project is like driving in reverse.*

Drive one to drink: the pressure or influence from someone or something that compels one to drink hard liquor (often said sarcastically or in jest). *A strict boss like that, I'm surprised it doesn't drive you to drink.*

Drive someone up a wall: to greatly annoy and get someone angry; an action stressful enough to put one out of ease or out of control emotionally. *His antics drive me up a wall!*

In the driver's seat: *See,* **In**.

What are you driving at: what are you trying to say? *I don't understand what you are driving at.*

Drop

At the drop of a hat: right away; take action immediately. *This dog can respond to your call at the drop of a hat.*

Drop a bombshell: *See,* **Bomb**.

Drop a bundle: to pay a very large amount. *He dropped a bundle on that property, only to see it lose value after the currency devaluation.*

Drop by/Drop in/Drop over: visit someone, generally unplanned or on short notice; to come over. *Feel free to drop by when you are in town. I'll drop in and see you later today.*

Drop by the wayside: give up before the finish. *Many marathon runners were dropping by the wayside under the intense heat of the sun.*

Drop dead [expressive]**:** an exclamation of very sharp disapproval. *After being rudely approached, she told him to drop dead.*

Drop in the bucket: very insignificant in comparison; miniscule; tiny amount; almost nothing. *The limited humanitarian aid was a drop in the bucket compared to how much help the refugees really needed. Your offer is a drop in the bucket. The wages you make working at the cannery is a drop in the bucket compared to what you can earn as a fisherman in a good season.*

Drop out of something: stop being a member; cease to take part or attend something. *Mary had to drop out of her church activities because of her part-time job.*

Drop someone a line: write. *Please drop us a line when you get there.*

Drop the ball: to not do one's job; to mess up; cause failure. *If you drop the ball around here, you'll be looking for another job.*

Dropout: one who quits (a program) prematurely. *The dropout rate is high in astronaut training school because of the physical demands required to qualify.*

Get the drop on someone: have the advantage. *We have the drop on that baseball team; we know some of their signals.*

Drown

Drown one's sorrows: to drink alcohol to forget or to wallow. *We drowned our sorrows last night after losing our jobs.*

Drown out: so much noise being made so that one cannot hear something. *The football quarterback's calls were being drowned out by the noise of fans cheering for the other team.*

Drum

Drum out: get rid of someone, generally because of dishonor. *He was drummed out of the Marine Corps for his pranks.*

Drum something into someone: to make someone learn through constant repetition. *How many times do we have to drum it into young people that smoking tobacco is harmful?*

Drum up: 1) to make something up; create. *He will always drum up some excuse for being late.* 2) come up with an idea; solicit additional business transactions. *We need some fresh ideas on our sales plan; let's see what you can drum up.*

Drummed up charge: false accusation. *The kid was booked on drummed up charges.*

Dry

Dry out: to quit taking drugs, alcohol or other habit-forming intoxicants. *He has been drying out this past month, and you can already see the glow coming back to his face.*

Dry run: a rehearsal. *Let's do a dry run before the show.*

Dry up/Dried up: 1) to gradually stop occurring; to disappear. *The funding dried up quickly on the internet start-up company.* 2) stop talking. *Hey, why don't you just dry up?*

Leave someone high and dry: *See,* **High**.

Duck

Dead duck: a person doomed to failure or death; hopeless; ruined. *If you guys get caught carrying these drugs across the border, you'll all be dead ducks.*

Duck soup: easy assignment or task. *Making good grades in school is duck soup for him.*

Have all one's ducks in a row/Get all one's ducks in order: be organized; be prepared. *Let's have all our ducks in a row before we proceed with the new venture.*

Lame duck: *See,* **Lame**.

Like water off a duck's back: *See,* **Water**.

Sitting duck: a person in great danger; an easy victim. *They were all sitting ducks when the earthquake hit.*

Dude

Dude: friendly nickname for a male person. *Hey, dude, how goes it?*

Duff

Duff: rear end; what you sit on. *Get off your duffs and get to work.*

Dumb

Dumb ass/Dumb bell/Dumb shit (expressive): a stupid or gullible person. *That dumb bell doesn't know much of anything about his job.*

Dumb luck: unfortunate circumstance. *It's just my dumb luck that I locked the car door with the keys in the ignition.*

Dump

Down in the dumps/In the dumps: to be experiencing sadness or gloom; feeling depressed. *He has been down in the dumps ever since his girlfriend left him.*

Dump: to end a close relationship. *He dumped her for another girl.*

Dump on: to ridicule someone. *He dumps on James every chance he gets.*

Dumpy: a feeling of sadness; depression of spirits, gloomy, etc. *Monday is always a dumpy day for me.*

Take a dump [expressive]: have a bowel movement; take care of one's bodily functions. *Excuse me, guys, but I have to take a dump.*

The dumps: a rundown, dirty place. *This place is the dumps.*

Dust

Bite the dust: *See,* **Bite**.

Leave in the dust: outdo; outrun; pull away from with strength. *When he turned on the nitrogen burners, he left the other race cars in the dust.*

To be dust/You're dust: be eliminated or smashed; be in great trouble. *If you screw up, you're dust.*

Dutch

Dutch treat/Go Dutch: each individual pays his or her own way, such as a meal at a restaurant. *Let's go Dutch on this meal.*

In Dutch: in trouble. *I don't want to get in Dutch with the boss.*

Dweeb

Dweeb: nerd; someone interested only in analytical work or computers, with little or no social life; social oddity. *My little brother, the dweeb in the family, owns a software company with 25 employees.*

Eager

Eager Beaver: an extremely diligent, ambitious and dedicated person. *That eager beaver is always on the go.*

Eagle

Eagle eyes: having very sharp sight; good eyes like an eagle. *He has an eagle eye when it comes to spotting phony identification cards.*

Legal eagle: *See,* **Legal**.

Ear

Be all ears/I'm all ears: to listen intently. *The new employees were all ears at their first meeting, eager to learn about the company.*

Bend one's ear: to talk to another to receive some feedback. *Can I bend your ear about something that is on my mind?*

Blow it out your ear [expressive]: an expression of strong disdain or disgust. *Blow it out your ear if you think I'm going to do your dirty work.*

Can't believe my ears: to be surprised to hear something. *I can't believe my ears to hear that Noah quit the firm.*

Chew someone's ear off: to scold harshly; get real mad at someone. *The teacher chewed his ear off for neglecting his homework assignment.*

Coming out of one's ears: so much of something. *We have so much corn this year that it's coming out of our ears!*

Earful: 1) scolding. *He gave his son an earful for staying out too late last night.* 2) to receive a lot of information. *We received an earful about the dangers of our upcoming Amazon jungle trip.*

Fall on deaf ears: *See,* **Fall**.

Get in one's ear: be irritating or annoying. *He can get in your ear when he's in a bad mood.*

In one ear and out the other: to not listen to something. *Compare with,* **Over** one's head. *What he said went in one ear and out the other.*

Keep one's ears open: maintain a lookout for certain information. *We were told to keep our ears open for the first sign of any news from the hospital about the injured workers.*

Music to one's ears: *See,* **Music.**

Pin someone's ears back: *See,* **Pin.**

Play it by ear: 1) take action according to the situation. *Since we can't predict what they will do next, we will just play it by ear.* 2) play without music notes; play by instinct. *Savants are known to play by ear intricate classical music simply by listening to it.*

Prick one's ears: *See,* **Prick.**

Put a bug in someone's ear: *See,* **Bug.**

Turn a deaf ear: have no desire to listen. *The bankruptcy trustee turned a deaf ear to the debtor's proposal.*

Wet behind the ears: *See,* **Wet.**

Early

Early bird catches/gets the worm: the person who gets up early in the morning or gets to something early will have the best chance at success. *We have to get up very early to go shopping because the early bird catches the worm; if we don't, the good clothes will be gone.*

Early to bed early to rise: derived from the proverb "early to bed, early to rise, makes a man healthy, wealthy and wise." *I was asked why I go to bed at 9pm. The best answer I could give was, early to bed early to rise.*

Earn

Disposable earnings: money left over after payment for living expenses. *He is accumulating his disposable earnings toward making a purchase on a home some day.*

Earn one's keep: one who merits his salary by performing the work required. *If you don't earn your keep around here, you better look for another job.*

Earth

Down to earth: practical; realistic. *A down-to-earth attitude in this glamorous job is essential. He is down to earth and very personable.*

Move heaven and earth: *See,* **Heaven**.

What on earth?/What in the world?: of all things (an emphatic phrase used after an interrogative). *What on earth are you doing? What in the world is going on? What on earth is it?*

Easy

Easy as (apple) pie/Easy as duck soup/Easy as falling off a log: requiring no effort; something that is very easy to do. *Assembling computers and understanding software are tasks that are as easy as pie to him.*

Easy come-easy go: what comes easily goes away easily *He spends his money so fast; it's easy come-easy go.*

Easy does it: do it the easy way. *Easy does it; don't strain yourself.*

Easy going: not worried about anything; relaxed. *Melissa is easy going, and hardly gets excited.*

Easy peasy: simple; not difficult. *After a few weeks working around here, things will come by easy peasy for you.*

Easy target: open for attack; sitting duck. *His boasting about winning at the casino made him an easy target for the robbers.*

Easy to come by: readily available. *Good wine is not easy to come by.*

Go easy on: 1) deal leniently with someone. *Go easy on that poor kid.* 2) consume food carefully. *Go easy on the potatoes.*

On easy street: in a state of wealth; having a good life. *He's been on easy street ever since he made those real estate investments.*

Take it easy: relax; don't work hard. *Take it easy and you will live longer.*

Eat

Dog-eat-dog: *See,* **Dog**.

Eat crow/Eat dirt/Eat humble pie: accept humiliation; lose one's pride; admit a mistake. *Sam was forced to eat crow when his get-rich ventures went bankrupt.*

Eat like a bird: to eat very little. *Twiggy eats like a bird but is always very energetic.*

Eat like a horse: to eat a lot. *That guy in front of the line eats like a horse.*

Eat my dust: a sarcastic if not comedic response in telling someone off; responding to another in a playful if not jeering way. *When he got promoted to another department, he told his fellow employees, "Eat my dust."*

Eat nails: one who's very tough and durable. *He's so tough that he can eat nails.*

Eat one's cake and have it too: a desire to have the best of both opportunities or situations. *That greedy person wants to have his cake and eat it too.*

Eat one's heart out: to brood over; to be jealous of; have an urgent desire for something which one does not have. *Harold is going to eat his heart out when he sees Sally in that new Mercedes.*

Eat one's words: to retract what one said; apologize for saying something that isn't true. *He had to eat his words regarding his negative comments about the team.*

Eat out of one's hand: have one at your mercy; have one do what you say. *Give the drivers a good tip in this area and you'll have them eating out of your hand.*

Eat shit [expressive]: *See,* **Shit**.

Eat someone alive: to overcome or defeat thoroughly. *Be careful that your competition doesn't eat you alive.*

Eating away at/Eating someone: bothering and upsetting. *The fact that she has not been able to find her cat, Sammy, a decent home has been eating away at her.*

What's eating you?: *See,* **What**.

Edge

Cutting edge: far advanced; most modern in technology. *This aircraft was built using cutting edge technology.*

Edge/Get the edge/Have the edge: obtain the advantage. *Since we have the edge on our competitor, let's work hard and keep it that way.*

On edge: very anxious; uncomfortably nervous. *The boss has been on edge ever since his wife entered the hospital.*

Set one's hair on edge: *See,* **Hair**.

Take the edge off: reduce the intensity of an action. *Narcotic medication generally can help to take the edge off moderate to severe pain after surgery.*

Egg

Bad egg/Rotten egg: not a good person. *That man hanging around the parking lot is a bad egg.*

Egg in your beer: to want something that is not deserved; something for nothing. *You're asking for more than you deserve; what do you want, egg in your beer?*

Egg on one's face: humiliation due to one's error. *I had egg on my face when I dropped an easy fly ball.*

Egg someone on: to incite or dare someone to do something. *The kids were egging their father to drive faster and faster.*

Egghead: a scholarly individual. *Matt is an egghead when it comes to electronics.*

Go suck an egg: an indignant or repulsive response to an inquiry. *See also,* **Go to hell.** *When the old man told the little boy how much of a pest he was, the little boy told him to go suck an egg.*

Good egg: *See,* **Good**.

Goose egg: *See,* **Goose**.

Have all your eggs in one basket: risk everything in one endeavor. *Play it safe and don't put all your eggs in one basket.*

Lay an egg: total collapse; go up in smoke. *We laid an egg on our new adventure.*

Nest egg: *See,* **Nest**.

Rotten egg: *See above,* **Bad egg.**

Walk on eggs: proceed with great care. *We were walking on eggs when the inspection was underway.*

Eleventh

Eleventh-hour: the last minute; latest possibility. *We were overjoyed to hear of an eleventh hour decision to fund the children's preschool program.*

Elbow

Elbow grease: application of strong physical effort. *Jack's job on the loading pier requires a lot of elbow grease.*

Elbow room/Elbow space: living space; area in which to move around comfortably. *They are moving to a larger home because they need more elbow room with four kids in the family.*

Rub elbows with: *See,* **Rub**.

Up to one's elbows: to have a whole lot of; overwhelmed. *I'm up to my elbows with work, so I can't make it to lunch today.*

End

At the end of the day: *See,* **At**.

End in itself: toward no purpose but it's own. *For Steve, music is an end in itself, regardless of any financial benefit.*

End of one's rope: the end of one's endurance. *Dick is reaching the end of his rope with the new management, and plans to retire next month.*

Hear no end to it: a significant degree of complaining from another in response to something discovered or revealed. *If she ever gets word of what you're doing, you will hear no end to it, you can be sure!*

Jump off the deep end: *See,* **Go off the deep end.**

Keep one's end up: take care of one's portion of the action; be responsible for one's tasks. *Mack is doing a good job keeping his end up in the deal.*

Light at the end of the tunnel: *See,* **Light.**

Make ends meet: to keep expenses within budget. *Many families have difficulties making ends meet.*

Short end of the stick: *See,* **Short.**

English

Body English: *See,* **Body.**

Put English on the ball: make a ball move a certain way, depending how the force strikes the ball. *As a pool player, it's amazing to see how he puts English on the ball in making the most difficult shots.*

Every

Every dog has his/its day: even the least respectful person can be lucky, come into the fore, or come into opportunity. *Sooner or later, even he will get lucky because every dog has his day.*

Every little bit helps: any amount of contribution is useful. *Please give; every little bit helps.*

Every living soul: everyone. *We expect every living soul to be at the ball game today.*

Every man for himself: when each individual looks out foremost for him or herself. *No one helps you out here; it's every man for himself.*

Every now and then/Every once in a while: occasionally, sometimes. *Every now and then we go for a long ride in the country.*

Every Tom, Dick, and Harry: everyone. *Getting into the ballpark was free to every Tom, Dick and Harry.*

Every which way: in all directions. *The cyclone hit us in every which way.*

Everything from A to Z: about everything there is. *This kid understands the programming of the guidance software from A to Z, so listen to him.*

Evil

Evil eye: an angry or a mean look. *She gave him the evil eye.*

Expire

Expire: to die. *He expired on the operating table.*

Eye

An eye for an eye: punishment equaling the injury caused. *We have to exact an eye for an eye in this town to keep the populace under control.*

Black eye: a damaging action to reputation. *The fraudulent action by one employee gave the entire company a black eye.*

Bull's eye: a good shot in the black circle of the target. *He had four bull's eyes out of six shots.*

Catch one's eye: appealing; attractive. *Her warm smile caught my eye.*

Cry one's eyes out: *See,* **Cry**.

Eagle eyes: *See,* **Eagle**.

Eye opener: 1) surprising news. *The story about his resignation was a real eye opener to everyone.* 2) a wake-up tonic or drink. *This black coffee is a real eye opener in the morning.*

Eye-popping: alarming; sudden surprise. *Grandma mistakenly received an eye-popping $5,000 electric bill from the utility company.*

Eyeball: observe closely. *I want you to eyeball this project for any safety violations.*

Eyesore: something unpleasant to look at. *The statue was an eyesore in the center of the square.*

Feast one's eyes on: to be delighted or thrilled at the sight of something. *We were feasting our eyes on all the awesome aircraft, especially at the B2, SR71, and Concorde super jets at the Museum of Flight.*

Four eyes: a person wearing eyeglasses. *Hey four eyes, I'm over here.*

Give someone the eye: to look intently at someone (whether in admiration, anger or otherwise, depends on the body language and situation). *The opponents gave each other the eye in intimidation just prior to the start of the boxing match.*

Goo-goo eyes: eyes expressing attraction or awe; seductive response. *She was all goo-goo eyes over him.*

Have an eye for: have good taste or be a good judge of something. *Jane has an eye for the exact blending of colors.*

Have an eye on/Have an eye out for: To be looking for; to have an interest in. *I have an eye out for a classic Toyota 2000GT roadster.*

Have eyes on/Have eyes for: have a great liking. *He has eyes for you.*

In a pig's eye: *See,* **Pig**.

In the blink of an eye: suddenly. *He was gone in the blink of an eye.*

Jaundiced Eye: a prejudiced view. *He viewed the newcomers with a jaundiced eye.*

Keep an eye out: *See,* **Keep**.

Keep your eyes open: be very watchful or cautious. *Keep your eyes open at the meeting.*

Lay eyes on: *See,* **Lay**.

Make eyes at: *See,* **Make**.

Mud in your eye: *See,* **Mud**.

My eye: an exclamation of emphatic disagreement or dissention; nonsense. *See also,* **Like hell**. *I heard that you made a high jump of eight feet at the track meet. My eye!*

Not bat an eye: show no surprise or reaction. *He didn't bat an eye when she said she was leaving him.*

Open one's eye: notice carefully what's going on. *Open your eyes to the situation, and don't be so naïve.*

Private eye: a private detective or investigator. *The wife didn't buy his story, so she hired a private eye to follow him.*

Pull the wool over one's eyes: *See,* **Pull**.

Raise an eyebrow/Raise one's eyebrows: *See,* **Raise**.

See eye to eye: in full agreement with another. *We see eye to eye on the project in every manner.*

Shut eye: to sleep. *It's midnight already, kids, so let's get some shut eye.*

Sight for sore eyes: *See,* **Sight**.

Face

Egg on one's face: *See,* **Egg**.

Face lift: a new look; remodel; renovate. *We gave the office a face lift by expanding the waiting room and putting in new furniture.*

Face-off: a confrontation. *Government officials had a face-off with residents over the location of a city disposal site in the area.*

Face saving: effort to preserve one's good name. *He needed a lot of face saving after the great blunder he committed.*

Face the music: accept responsibility for wrongdoing. *He had to face the music for misappropriating company funds.*

Face up to: see the facts. *It was difficult for Charles to face up to the fact that he was no longer boss.*

Face value: 1) judging something from its appearance. *Advertisements generally should not be taken at face value since they tend to opinionate statements about a product or service.* 2) actual amount. *The face value of the gold coin is ten dollars, but it's worth $500.00 on the trading market.*

Fall on one's face: *See,* **Fall**.

Have a red face: be embarrassed; have a guilty look. *The boy had a red face when he got caught stealing an apple.*

In your face: up front and direct; in defiant challenge. *The basketball dunk was in your face, which was real excitement for the fans.*

Keep a straight face: *See,* **Keep**.

Let's face it: accept the unhappy truth or turn of events. *Let's face it fellows, we're heading to defeat at this tournament.*

Long face: *See,* **Long**.

Lose face: be humiliated or embarrassed; lose respect. *We will lose face in the industry if we don't make this project a success. The executives lost face when accounting fraud was discovered under their control.*

On the face of it: as it appears. *On the face of it, your report seems to be on the right track.*

Poker face: *See,* **Poker**.

Put a bold face on: display confidence and firmness. *I'll display a bold face on that project until I finish it.*

Save face: keep from losing dignity; avoid humiliation or embarrassment. *They allowed him to save face by resigning from his position rather than firing him.*

Show one's face: show one's presence. *I'll show my face at the party and then go home.*

Slap in the face: *See,* **Slap**.

Stuff one's face: *See,* **Stuff**.

Till one is blue in the face: *See,* **Till**.

Faded

Faded: intoxicated; drunk. *He was faded after just two beers.*

Fair

Fair and square: done with fairness and honesty. *He charges a high price for his services, but he plays fair and square.*

Fair game: an open target for challenge, attack or ridicule. *Every participant in this event is fair game.*

Fair play: competition in good-faith and fair dealing. *We expect fair play in these games, or you will be immediately disqualified.*

Fair shake: to have an equal chance; an equitable bargain. *There are no complaints as we all got a fair shake.*

Fair to midland/Fair to middling: pretty good; mediocre; so-so. *In asking them how they enjoyed the service, they replied, "Fair to midland."*

Fair-weather fan: one who cheers for a team, provided it is winning (opposite to a loyal fan who favors a particular team through thick and thin). *Eddy is a fair-weather fan on his basketball favorites.*

Fair-weather friend: one you can depend on only when all goes well. *Dick is a fair weather friend; I never see him around when I need help.*

Fake

Fake someone out: deceive or bluff someone. *The salesman faked me out with his fancy presentation.*

Fall

Fall (all) over oneself: awkward and eager conduct in an attempt to please. *Tom fell all over himself in his attempt to please his new boss.*

Fall apart: lose control; break down, emotionally or mentally. *He fell apart after his best friend died.*

Fall back on: rely upon; someone whom or something which may be of help at a later time. *It's real nice to know that I have friends to fall back on when I'm in trouble.*

Fall behind: 1) be outdistanced. *We fell behind schedule due to supply problems.* 2) fail to pay one's debts. *I fell behind on my debts when I lost my job.*

Fall by the wayside: give up; quit before finishing something. *The idea to build on the land fell by the wayside after environmental concerns made it too problematic and costly to continue.*

Fall flat: fail. *The whole venture fell flat when the technicians and scientists, the brains on the project, were killed in the plane crash. The negotiations fell flat and the talks broke off.*

Fall for: 1) become infatuated with. *Mary fell for Mark the first time they met.* 2) to believe something. *The story was so good, they all fell for it. I tried to fool him, but he didn't fall for it.*

Fall from grace: go from good to worse; to do bad. *He had a fall from grace when he was arrested for drug possession.*

Fall guy: one who takes the blame when something goes wrong; scapegoat. *He was perceived as the fall guy in the scandal, although he had no involvement in the scheme.*

Fall into a trap: lured into trouble. *You risk falling into a trap with these guys if you're not careful.*

Fall off the wagon: to return to the addictive habit of alcohol consumption or drug use. *He fell off the wagon when he lost his job.*

Fall on deaf ears: to be ignored; to not be heard or understood. *His ideas about vehicles operating on fuel cell energy fell on deaf ears.*

Fall on one's ass: *See,* **Ass**.

Fall on one's face: to blunder; to make an error in judgment. *Most people tend to fall on their face trying to predict the weather around here.*

Fall out of bed: to drop. *The economy is not falling out of bed, but it isn't improving, either.*

Fall out with someone: quarrel; disagree; divorce. *James had a falling out with his boss, and had to look for another job.*

Fall over backwards: to do everything one can to satisfy or please another; to try very hard. *We fell over backwards accommodating our guests during the storm.*

Fall over the edge: go crazy; lose it mentally. *Some soldiers fall over the edge in time of war.*

Fall short: fail to meet a requirement. *We fell short on our sales quota for the third quarter.*

Fall through: fail; not be successful. *Our plans to expand our retail business fell through when the economy worsened and the demand for consumer goods declined.*

Fall through the cracks/Fall between the cracks: to be forgotten, neglected, overlooked, etc. *I got so busy with chores that picking up your dry cleaning fell through the cracks.*

Fall under: 1) come under the authority of. *Who do you fall under in the chain of command?* 2) be listed or classified as. *Biopsy falls under the title of diagnostic procedures.*

Falling out: breaking up or splitting up; a squabble or fight. *The long-time business partners had a falling out, which forced the dissolution of the business.*

Let the chips fall where they may: *See,* **Let**.

Fan

Fan one's tail: 1) to win decisively; overwhelm. *I can fan your tail in any sport we play.* 2) to physically hit one on the buttocks. *Is it right for a father to fan his little kid's tail in public for misbehaving?*

Fan out: 1) engage in something without success. *Jack fanned out after a year in business ventures.* 2) to strike out. *The pitcher was awesome as he fanned out most of the batters.* 3) scatter or spread out. *The detectives fanned out over the field looking for the missing body.*

Fan the flames: to stir up feelings, generally of ill will. *The march by the white supremists only fanned the flames of ill will and hatred in this town.*

Shit hit the fan: *See,* **Shit**.

Fancy

Fancy Dan: a showy person lacking true skill or endurance. *He's just a fancy Dan with very little management skills.*

Fancy footwork: clever distraction in an attempt to confuse, deceive, or undermine. *We had to do some fancy footwork to win over our competitors for the project.*

Fancy that: an expression of soft, pleasant surprise; imagine that. *Well, fancy that; I never knew he was such a smart kid.*

Flight of fancy: an imaginary idea; unrealistic notion. *It's a flight of fancy to expect him to arrive on time since he makes a habit of always being late.*

Take a fancy to: be attracted to. *He immediately took a fancy to flying ultra-light aircraft, and soon became an expert flyer.*

Tickle one's fancy: *See,* **Tickle**.

Far

By far: *See,* **By**.

Far be it for me: not in the position (of authority); something not craved for or wished. *Far be it for me to ask any field worker to risk his life during a lightening storm.*

Far fetched: not liable to happen; not possible. *Your story about the serpent in the lake is too far fetched for me to believe.*

Far gone: very advanced in action or condition; unable to recover physically or mentally. *The injured animal was too far gone to be saved.*

Far out: 1) exciting; real nice. *That new car of yours is far out.* 2) odd; unusual. *You are somewhat far out with that idea.*

So far so good: everything is fine to this point. *So far so good, but we still have a long way to go.*

Farm

Bet the farm: *See,* **Bet**.

Buy the farm: *See,* **Buy**.

Farm out: 1) rent land or other assets for payment. *The Smiths farmed out most of their land.* 2) to contract work to outside sources. *The manufacture of televisions is now farmed out overseas.*

Fart

Fart [expressive]: to pass gas. *My old dog farts a lot.*

Fart around/Fart off: Horse around; goof around; mess around. *I want you young men to do your work today and not fart around.*

Old fart: an elderly person. *Some old fart was driving slowly in the fast lane of the freeway.*

Vanish like a fart in the wind (expressive): to disappear without a trace; to disappear unseen. *The thief seemed to have vanished like a fart in the wind.*

Fast

A fast buck: money gotten quickly and easily, generally without too much concern for ethics. *Watch out for the person or organization that induces you to make a fast buck.*

A fast talker: one who tends to be glib; to mislead under a smooth tongue. *Watch out and don't be deceived by that fast talker.*

Fast food: food served fast and in steady quantities, such as hot dogs, hamburgers, french fries, etc. *Most people eat lunch at a fast food restaurant to save time and money.*

Fast footwork: clever dodging and zigzagging. *You have to do some fast footwork to survive in the garment industry today.*

Faster than you can shake/swing a stick: very quickly; most hurriedly. *When he won the lottery, relatives were appearing faster than you can shake a stick.*

Pull a fast one: gain advantage over another unfairly; try to deceive; trick someone. *He tried to pull a fast one over Bill by hiding his car and saying it was lost; however, Bill had a global positioning system in his car and found it a block away.*

Fat

Chew the fat: converse together in a casual or relaxed manner: *Let's get together soon and chew the fat about old times.*

Fat cat: wealthy individual. *When companies downsize, why is it that the fat cats seem to be the last to exit?*

Fat chance: very little possibility of getting anything. *You'll have a fat chance of succeeding unless you get an education.*

Fat farm: clinic where a person goes to lose weight (many are resort-like locations in the woods). *Our sister Julie is attending a fat farm on the coast for a couple weeks.*

Fat of the land: the best of. *He's living off the fat of the land, and doesn't realize it.*

Feather

Bird of a different feather: *See,* **Bird**.

Bird of the same feather: *See,* **Bird**.

Feather brain: one lacking intelligence; one without knowledge. *Why hire that feather brain when there are better qualified applicants?*

Feather in one's cap/hat: something done that makes one look good to others; a well-deserved accomplishment. *It was a feather in his hat when the community celebrated his work for helping the poor and homeless in the city.*

Feather merchant: person who comes on the job lacking experience. *The new boss is a real feather merchant.*

Feather one's (own) nest: to use power and prestige selfishly, especially when in a trusted position of public office; to help oneself rather than others. *He used the mayor's office to feather his own nest.*

Ruffle one's feathers: get one upset or angry. *He ruffles my feathers when he patronizes the boss.*

Fed

Fed up: have had enough of something. *I'm fed up about all of your nonsense.*

Feds: federal agents. *Our client got arrested by the Feds last night.*

Feed

Bite the hand that feeds you: to turn against or hurt one who really is on your side; return kindness with harm or disrespect. *The sign at the Union Hall read, "To all laborers, you bite the hand that feeds you when you work against the union."*

Chicken feed: *See,* **Chicken**.

Feed the kitty: Put one's contribution down in a card game. *You must feed the kitty if you wish to remain in the game.*

Feel

Feel a person out: find out what one is thinking about. *I can't feel that guy out no matter how hard I try.*

Feel like a million bucks/Feel like a million dollars: *See,* **Million**.

Feel like I died and went to heaven: a wondrous feeling. *When he won the lottery, Jake felt like he died and went to heaven.*

Feel one's oats: 1) feel frisky; in a playful mood; excited; aroused. *The horses were jumping today at the races and feeling their oats.* 2) proceed without fear; be in high spirits. *The young lieutenant was feeling his oats, yelling out orders to the soldiers.*

Feel one's way: take a slower approach on account of a lack of full understanding. *I had to feel my way during the first two years of my job.*

Feel out of place: a sense of not belonging. *I tend to feel out of place at my in-laws.*

Feel put upon: be taken advantage of or exploited. *I felt put upon at the gathering when I found out that the real purpose for the invitation was to sell me commercial products.*

Feel something out: get information on something. *We need to feel our neighbors out about installing a gas line down our street.*

Feel the heat: *See,* **Heat**.

Feel under the weather: *See,* **Under**.

Get the feel of: *See,* **Get**.

Gut feeling: *See,* **Gut**.

Feet

Back on one's feet: *See,* **Back**.

Cold feet: *See,* **Cold**.

Feet of clay: weakness of character. *Former management had feet of clay when it came to dealing with the union.*

Feet on the ground/Keep one's feet on the ground: maintain a steady mental balance; understanding of one's whereabouts. *In these stressful times, it is not easy to always keep your feet on the ground.*

Get one's feet wet: *See,* **Wet**.

Itchy feet: restless or anxious. *When the suspect saw the armed guard at the bank, he got itchy feet and left the scene.*

Jump in with both feet: *See,* **Jump**.

Land on one's feet/Land on both feet: *See,* **Land**.

Six feet under: dead and buried. *I'll be six feet under in this industry if I don't finish this contract on time.*

Stand on one's own two feet: be independent; do things without help or assistance. *In this boarding school, we have no favorites; all of you have to stand on your own two feet.*

Swept one off one's feet: overwhelmed in love or infatuation. *He swept her off her feet and they married three weeks later.*

Think on one's feet: be independently wise; to know what to do without help. *He was hired first because he is witty and can think on his feet.*

Fence

Fence in: to block or interfere; restrict; enclose or confine. *The annual budget of the United States is very difficult to reduce since over 70% of it is fenced in by entitlement programs such as retirement pay.*

Fence mending: attempt to repair strained relations. *I better do some fence mending with the neighbors on account of my dogs barking all night.*

On the fence: undecided. *I'm on the fence about who to vote for in the next election.*

Other side of the fence: the opposing side or position; a different setting. *I used to be a federal prosecutor, but now I'm on the other side of the fence working as a defense attorney.*

Fender

Fender bender: a minor automobile accident. *I got into a fender bender on the freeway today, but luckily no one was hurt.*

Few

Few and far between: very few and wide apart. *Gas stations are few and far between on the way to Las Vegas.*

Fiddle

Fiddle around/Fiddle away: to spend time idly; to not be accomplishing much. *One should not fiddle away his valuable time.*

Fiddle faddle: nonsense; hogwash. *That is a bunch of fiddle faddle that higher taxes will help boost the economy.*

Fiddle with: to play with or work on. *I was fiddling with the motorbike on my lunch hour.*

Fit as a fiddle: *See,* **Fit**.

Play second fiddle: *See,* **Play**.

Fight

Dog fight: 1) a rumpus, uproar, riot, fight or a brawl. *We had a dogfight trying to come up with the new budget.* 2) aerial combat. *Modern aircraft can engage in a dogfight many miles apart due to their sophisticated weaponry. The World War I ace was involved in over 100 dogfights.*

Fight an uphill battle: to face a difficult challenge. *We're fighting an uphill battle driving through two feet of snow.*

Fighting City Hall: tough to get something done when going against the ruling power. *It takes so long to get things done around here, it's like fighting City Hall.*

Fightin' words: irritating words, which are insulting enough to start a fight. *You best watch out, buddy, because those are fightin' words.*

Pick a fight: *See,* **Pick**.

Figure

Figure on: to expect; to depend upon. *We figure on making three trips before nightfall. We are figuring on your support in this upcoming election campaign.*

Go figure: when two incongruent or unexpected factors relate or coincide. *The day after the office building manager goes on vacation, an earthquake destroys the building; go figure.*

Fill

Fill me in: brief me; tell me what's going on. *The boss asked me to fill him in on my last report.*

Fill out: 1) complete the blanks in a form. *When I applied for a job, I was asked to fill out a personal data form.* 2) A young person growing to adulthood and filling out physically. *That next-door girl has filled out pretty well since I last saw her several years ago.*

Fill someone else's shoes: be able to accomplish what someone else has done. *This young kid is so clever that he would be able to fill anyone's shoes.*

Fill the bill: *See,* **Bill**.

Finagle

Finagle: to try to work something out; negotiate wittingly. *He tried to finagle a way out of his dilemma by blaming other colleagues.*

Find

Find myself: to understand where one is in life; know your capabilities and be able to perform to that standard. *College and work study gave me the independence to discover new horizons and find myself.*

Fine

Fine kettle of fish: *See,* **Fish**.

(Go over with a) fine-tooth comb: check in great detail; examine thoroughly. *I went over my presentation with a fine-tooth comb.*

Finger

At one's fingertips: *See,* **At**.

Bite one's fingernails: *See,* **Bit/Bite**.

Butterfingers: clumsy; one who cannot hold onto things well. *Bart is butterfingers with tools.*

Finger in the pie: meddle into someone else's activities. *Whenever we arrange a business venture, it seems that Jason somehow finds out and then wants to get his finger in the pie.*

Give someone the finger: when one raises a hand and extends the middle finger to another, with the back of the hand facing the one being gestured. [It can be a contemptible or hostile gesture, or a sarcastic and contained response.] *Jackson gave the police officer the finger when told to leave the premises; he was promptly arrested for disorderly conduct.*

Keep fingers crossed: hope for the best. *I'll keep my fingers crossed and wait for your test results.*

Light-fingered/Light-fingered Louie: have a temptation to steal. *We caught light-fingered Louie with the stolen goods leaving the store.*

Not lift a finger: to not make any effort or take part in any action. *Tim didn't lift a finger to help his friend change the tire on the car.*

Point the finger at: *See,* **Point**.

Put one's finger on it/You put your finger on it: 1) to remember something from a previous moment in time. *I can't put my finger on it, but I* *seem to remember that person from somewhere.* 2) that is exactly right; that's what it means; you are right about that. *You put your finger on it about the negligence in the way security is handled at the airport.*

Wrapped around one's finger/Twisted around one's finger: under one's complete control; doing as one pleases over another. *She has him twisted around her finger, and makes him do all sorts of errands for her.*

Fink

Fink: to tell on; to inform on. *He finked on the students smoking behind the gym.*

Fire

Add fuel to the fire: increase the intensity of a bad situation. *James added fuel to the fire by arguing with the judge; he was directed to pay the entire fine.*

Ball of fire: a person full of energy. *Your little kid is a ball of fire.*

Come under fire: *See,* **Come**.

Draw fire: *See,* **Draw**.

Fire at will: to freely fire a weapon. *The soldiers fired at will until the enemy was subdued.*

Fire away: 1) go ahead and proceed; start to talk or ask questions. *When the guest speaker finished his lecture, the professor gave us the opportunity to fire away with questions.* 2) to open fire with weapons; fire at will. *The sergeant gave the command to the troops to fire away at the targets.*

Fire in the hole: an expression giving notice to take cover due to weapon(s) ready to fire. *He yelled, "Fire in the hole!" prior to setting off the detonation to blow up the bridge.*

Fire sale: to sell things quickly, generally at much reduced prices; liquidation. *When the project was stopped, we were forced to conduct a fire sale of all the equipment and supplies.*

Fired up: possessed with great energy or fervor. *Calling that big guy a wimp really got him fired up for the football game.*

Fireworks: excitement; spectacular display; strong discussions and arguments. *We had a lot of fireworks at the office when Sam got caught stealing.*

Firing on all cylinders: to be operating very smoothly; at maximum efficiency. *This championship team is firing on all cylinders.*

Go through fire and water: experience difficult times. *Indigenous tribes in the Amazon are going through fire and water seeing their natural jungle surroundings cut down by poor planning, corruption and greed.*

On fire: very mad. *The general was on fire when he heard that the enemy had overrun the border towns.*

Out of the frying pan (and) into the fire: *See,* **Out**.

Putting out fires: taking care of emergency or urgent situations. *I spent all day putting out fires so I was unable to get my regular work done.*

Under fire: open to criticism; under pressure. *The boss has been under fire to finish the job.*

First

First come, first served: people are served in the order they arrive. *It was first come, first served for tickets to tomorrow's big championship ball game.*

First-rate: the very best quality. *The local tailor can really make a first-rate men's suit.*

Fish

Bigger fish to fry: have more important matters to tend to. *I cannot be bothered now as I have bigger fish to fry.*

Drink like a fish: to drink (alcohol) excessively. *He drinks like a fish, but you can hardly tell.*

Fine kettle of fish: a nasty and unpleasant situation. *That's a fine kettle of fish you got yourself into this time.*

Fish or cut bait: take action now or leave it alone. *Let's not waste our time here, so fish or cut bait.*

Fish story: questionable allegation greatly magnified; to stretch the point. *That was the biggest fish story I ever heard.*

Fishy: suspicious. *That proposal sounds fishy to me.*

Like a fish out of water: helpless; unknowledgeable; in strange surroundings. *A cowboy in a big city is like a fish out of water.*

Like a fish to water: so agile, so smooth; excellent in skills. *He performs his job like a fish to water.*

Like shooting fish in a barrel: much too easy; a no-brainer; without effort. *Fishing in the early days was like shooting fish in a barrel; but today, it is hard to catch good stock.*

Plenty of other fish in the sea: many other choices are available. *When Jane snubbed Jim, he said, "Well, there are plenty of other fish in the sea."*

Poor fish: one who is victimized by deviating from right and good. *That poor fish has been hanging around the wrong people and getting into trouble.*

Fit

Fit as a fiddle: in very good shape; feeling fine. *To be fit as a fiddle, you have to watch your diet and exercise. I'm fit as a fiddle and ready to run the marathon.*

Fit like a glove: a perfect fit. *My new jacket fits like a glove.*

Fit the bill: to work out as well as one expected; getting exactly what one desires. *Does the new hire fit the bill?*

Have a fit: emotional tantrum; be heated emotionally. *Little Jessica had a fit when she was told that grandma was unable to make it to her birthday party.*

Keep fit: stay in flexible or physical shape. *I go to yoga class twice weekly to keep fit.*

Fix

A fix: an habitual need for a certain thing so as to feel better. *I need my coffee fix every morning.*

Fix someone up: arrange a date. *Timothy fixed up a date for his friend.*

Fix someone's wagon: punish; plot or get even. *I'll fix his wagon for acting the way he did.*

Fix the outcome of a contest: arrange for a team to win or lose a contest. *The baseball game was fixed.*

Fix to do something: prepare or intend to. *Charles is fixing to go on vacation next month.*

Get a fix on: *See,* **Get**.

In a fix: *See,* **In**.

Flag

Flag down: waive a moving vehicle to stop. *If a law officer flags you down, you must stop.*

Flag waver: a highly visible patriotic person who displays the national flag every chance he gets. *That corner house resident is a dedicated flag waver.*

Run it up the flagpole: *See,* **Run**.

Flake

Flake: unreliable person; a quack or a fake. *That guy is an oddball and a flake.*

Flake out: drop out; to unreliably not show up. *He flaked out at the last minute.*

Flaky: not logical; off-centered. *People who believe that the world is flat are flaky.*

Flap

Flap: disturbance; a fuss. *The show was delayed because of a flap between two of the contestants arguing who should go on stage first.*

Flash

Flash in the pan: a short-lived idea; one who makes a fast start but soon fizzles out. *Mike proved to be a flash in the pan for the baseball team.*

Flashy: showy; pretentious. *That outfit looks pretty flashy.*

In a flash: *See,* **In**.

Flat

Fall flat: to fail; to be ineffective. *We had no idea he would fall flat on his assignments.*

Flat as a pancake: very flat. *After the cyclone, our home looked flat as a pancake.*

Flat broke: *See,* **Broke**.

Flat on one's back: *See,* **Back**.

Flat out: in full speed; all the way. *I did it flat out.*

In nothing flat: very quickly. *He completed his assignment in nothing flat.*

Flea

Flea market: a place, generally in the open air, where vendors sell used, inexpensive, or customized goods. *Let's save and purchase our camping gear at the flea market this weekend.*

Fleece

Fleece: 1) to cheat or swindle. *We got fleeced, because this so-called brand name watch you bought is really a fake.* 2) a warm material used in clothing. *We bought some fleece pullover shirts for winter.*

Flick

Flick: 1) movie. *Seen a good flick lately?* 2) snappy movement with the hands. *You have to flick the lighter to get a flame.*

Flip

Flip flop: 1) to completely change one's decision about something. *Albert flip-flopped on his proposal to buy my car.* 2) slippers; sandals. *Don't forget to take your flip flops to the beach.*

Flip one's lid: lose one's senses due to excitement or madness; to go berserk. *Jason flipped his lid when he heard his car was stolen.*

Flip out: lose control; go wild. *He flipped out when his team lost the championship.*

Flip side: the other side of a question or issue. *The flip side of high gas prices and hotel accommodations is that we stay home and better understand our family.*

Flip someone shit: *See,* **Shit**.

Flop

Flop: failure: *The business was a flop.*

Flop down: go to sleep. *I flop down for about an hour every day.*

Flop house: a cheap place to sleep, such as a shelter for those in need. *When we lost our apartment, we stayed at a flop house for a while.*

Floor

Floor it: 1) to press on a vehicle's gas pedal all the way. *Although I was flooring the gas pedal while driving through the mountain pass, I was barely going 40 klicks.* 2) to speed quickly in a vehicle. *Floor it and let's get out of here.*

Floored/You floor me: 1) overwhelm(ed) with surprise or admiration; very impressed. *You floored me with your outstanding presentation.* 2) knocked down. *The defending champion floored his opponent in the 2nd round with a solid right hook.*

Ground floor: *See,* **Ground**.

Floss

Floss: clean between the teeth. *Did you floss after dinner?*

Flossing/Flossin': showing off; dressed in nice clothing. *Man, she be flossin' today!*

Flossy: clean, excellent. *The baby's room looks really flossy!*

Fly

Fly-by-night: 1) a venture loaded with uncertainty; a business associated with skirting the laws, and having the ability to disappear on short notice, especially when authorities start to investigate. *That fly-by-night outfit was never licensed to do business in this state.* 2) An unreliable person whom you cannot depend on. *That guy is a fly-by-night operator.*

Fly by the seat of one's pants: do something by instinct or wit rather than by set instructions or knowledgeable understanding. *To survive around here, you have to know how to fly by the seat of your pants.*

Fly in the ointment: one to ruin a party or good time; something to slow things down or get in the way. *Who are you? Well, I'm just a fly in the oint-*

ment, Hans. (From the 1983 movie, "Die Hard," the terrorist "Hans" asking about Bruce Willis).

Fly off the handle: lose one's temper; to suddenly become angered. *He flew off the handle when the pitcher hit him in the shoulder with a high ball. Our boss tends to fly off the handle from time to time.*

Fly right: act properly; perform well. *If you fly right, you're bound to succeed.*

Fly the coop: to escape. *He flew the coop but was caught the next day.*

Go fly a kite: *See,* **Go**.

On the fly: in a hurry; on very short notice. *He ate his lunch on the fly.*

Straighten up and fly right: begin to do what is right; clean up your act. *You better straighten up and fly right if you want to hold on to your job.*

With flying colors: in a successful way; outstanding. *Miguel passed with flying colors.*

Fog

In the fog: unaware of things; unable to perform due to restricted conditions or lack of knowledge. *I've been in the fog ever since I began this job.*

Not having the foggiest idea: don't know at all. *I don't have the foggiest idea of what you're talking about.*

Follow

Follow in one's footstep: follow someone's example. *He follows in his mother's footsteps.*

Follow suit: imitate someone else. *We bought a new Buick; then the next-door neighbor followed suit and bought the same model.*

Follow through: bring to full completion. *We lost the contract because Sam failed to follow through as directed.*

Food

Food for thought: an idea or an issue to ponder; something to think about. *Our discussion about paying for child care costs for employees will be food for thought at the next management meeting.*

Junk food: *See,* **Junk**.

Fool

Fool around: to waste time; to have an easy time without accomplishing very much. *There will be no more fooling around from now on.*

Fool hardy: to take risks carelessly. *You can't be fool hardy if you want to succeed around here.*

Fool's paradise: unreal; circumstances of false impressions. *You're in a fool's paradise to think that wealth and happiness will come automatically to you.*

No one's fool: clever; skilled; savvy. *Charles is no one's fool; he knows what he's doing.*

Foot

Foot dragging: to delay or slow down. *To maintain our lead, we must eliminate all the foot dragging.*

Foot in the door: make the initial effort to succeed. *Meeting the director will help you get your foot in the door.*

Foot loose: have no obligations; do as one desires. *Dick became foot loose after his divorce.*

Foot the bill: pay the expenses, usually on a meal. *Let's go and have something to eat; I'll foot the bill.*

My foot: expression of rejection. *My foot, if you think I'll lend you more money.*

On one's feet: alert and in good condition. *Mack is on his feet again after a month in the hospital.*

On the wrong foot: to make a move in the wrong direction; starting the wrong way. *You're starting on the wrong foot if you antagonize your co-workers.*

Put one's best foot forward: *See,* **Put**.

Put one's foot down: get strict. *Do I have to put my foot down to get you to clean your room?*

Put one's foot in one's mouth: make a shameful mistake or commit a careless error. *Albert put his foot in his mouth when he accused the wrong person of the crime.*

Shoe is on the other foot: the situation is reversed. *Now that he's your boss, the shoe is on the other foot.*

For

For a song: very cheaply; for a bargain. *We got this artifact for a song.*

For all I care: to not care. *You can jump in the lake for all I care.*

For all I know: according to what could be. *For all I know, he may be dead by now.*

For all it's worth: for whatever value something might be. *Here's my presentation, for all it's worth. Let me give you my suggestion, for all it's worth.*

For all practical purposes: for all reasonable expectations. *For all practical purposes, you should finish your college before getting a job.*

For all the marbles: for everything; for winning it all. *This race is for all the marbles; winner take all.*

For crying out loud: *See,* **Cry**.

For good measure: adding a little more; something extra. *For good measure, the ice cream parlor always gives the customer an extra scoop.*

For the asking: available free if one asks. *I have an extra set of golf clubs, which is yours for the asking.*

For the birds: totally uninteresting; ridiculous; meaningless. *Swimming in that mud hole is for the birds.*

Fork

Fork over: give up what you have; pay up what is due. *The thief told Jim to fork over his money.*

Forked tongue: to speak with deceitful intent. *Watch out, for he speaks with a forked tongue.*

Fortune

Fortune hunter: 1) one desiring to get rich by marrying into money. *A fortune hunter married the city's richest debutante.* 2) One who travels worldwide looking for riches. *The local professor has been a fortune hunter all his life.*

Foul

Foul mouth: one who uses rude or offensive language. *That guy is a real foul mouth.*

Foul play: from unsafe to treacherous action. *The police determined that there was foul play in the death of the handyman.*

Foul up: 1) to blunder; to mess up. *The ones in charge fouled up the company.* 2) loser; one who cannot get things right. *He's a real foul up in this office.*

Fraidy

Fraidy cat: one who is easily scared. *The little boy was called a fraidy cat because he wouldn't go up the ladder.*

Frame

Frame up: 1) a conviction with falsified evidence or testimony. *Mr. Dickson was framed in a murder conviction.* 2) a dirty, underhanded deal made without one's knowledge. *I was framed into testifying for the convicted slayer.*

Framed: falsely accused of a crime or misdemeanor. *I was wrongly framed for speeding while I was driving through a small southern town.*

Freak

Freak out: 1) panic or lose control. *The operator freaked out when the tractor went downhill.* 2) withdraw from a commitment without prior notification. *We made an agreement by handshake, but the other party freaked out.*

Freaky deaky: very strange; weird. *He started acting freaky deaky after taking his medication.*

Free

Free and easy: 1) live the easy life without obligations. *Everyone dreams of the free and easy life, but it is seldom obtainable.* 2) Accomplish a task without much effort. *Don't go at it full speed; just handle it free and easy.*

Free-for-all: no holds barred; without any restraints; open madness; chaotic crowd. *It was a free-for-all when the doors opened at Barker's Department Store for its annual clothing sale.*

Free-wheeling: joyous, happy, carefree, unlimited indulgence. *That free-wheeling fellow has to settle down to earth sometime.*

Freebee/Freebie: something given without any charge. *Let's go to the football game and get a freebie.*

Freeloader: one who customarily depends on others for free food and other goodies. *Free loaders should work for what they get.*

Scot free: 1) to obtain something for nothing. *I got this antique practically scot free.* 2) get away clean; without any penalty. *He got away scot free.*

Freeze

Freeze: a command given to another directing him or her not to move. *Upon spotting the suspect in the alley, the police officer yelled, "Freeze!"*

Freeze the balls off a brass monkey [expressive]: exceptionally cold. *It was cold enough yesterday to freeze the balls off a brass monkey.*

Freeze up: panic by fear; unable to move, scared stiff. *When deer see the oncoming headlights of vehicles at night, they tend to freeze up.*

'Till hell freezes over: *See,* **Hell**.

Fresh

Fresh: 1) a new and inexperienced person. *James is fresh on the job.* 2) to be rude or sassy. *Don't get fresh with me.* 3) to make a warm pass at. *She tried to get fresh with the doorman in order to get into the club.* 4) great; neat. *That car sure looks fresh!*

Fresh out: just sold out; not available. *Sorry, we're fresh out of bread.*

Friday

A man or girl Friday: a faithful follower; a trustworthy and skillful assistant. *The office clerk typist is our girl Friday.*

TGIF: Thank God it's Friday (An exclamation of joy when Friday approaches). *I'm happy because it's TGIF!*

Frog

Frog in one's throat: 1) having a hoarse voice due to a sore throat or irritation. *I have sinus congestion and a frog in my throat today.* 2) unable to speak well. *I am so smitten with her that I get a frog in my throat when I am near her. I tend to get a frog in my throat when I have to speak in front of a crowd.*

Frogman: a person with SCUBA apparatus. *There were several frogmen at the pier looking for the missing surfer.*

From

From the ground up: from the beginning to the end. *These guys started the business from the ground up.*

From the heart: *See,* **Heart**.

From the hip: *See,* **Hip**.

From the word go: from the start. *We didn't agree with the plan from the word go.*

Straight from the horse's mouth: *See,* **Horse**.

Front

Front: 1) to cover one's position. *Please front for me while I'm on vacation.* 2) a false cover. *The restaurants were really fronts for organized crime syndicates in the area to launder money.* 3) pretend to act tough. *Why do they gotta front?! Hey man, don't front me.*

Frost

Frosted: angry; mad. *He was very frosted when he heard the news.*

Fruit

Fruit (expressive): a male homosexual. *Did you notice that fruit?*

Fruity: acting odd. *He's been acting a bit fruity lately.*

Fry

Out of the frying pan and into the fire: going from bad to worse. *Sam was stopped for speeding today, but that wasn't the end of it. He went from the frying pan and into the fire when he got upset and assaulted the police officer.*

FUBU

FUBU: An acronym, which stands for: *"For Us, By Us."* A brand and style of clothing engaged in encouraging entrepreneurship by African-American owners of products. *We bought several FUBU sports outfits for Theo and Jerry for Christmas.*

Full

Full house: a place filled to capacity by people. *It's a full house at the ball game tonight.*

Full of beans/Full of bull/Full of hot air/Full of it/Full of prunes/Full of shit (expressive): all nonsense or lies. *Don't take her seriously; she's full of beans.*

Full of piss and vinegar: full of vitality. *We like the entry-level employees because most of them are generally full of piss and vinegar.*

Go the full yard: pursue something to the very end. *We went the full yard in making sure we got the job done.*

Funky

Funky: strange; unusual. *Jack is a funky guy. That is one funky outfit. What is that funky smell?*

Funny

Don't get funny: don't be impolite or rude. *Hey, don't get funny with me.*

Funny as a barrel of monkeys: extremely funny. *Red Skelton, an icon among the great comedians of our time, was always as funny as a barrel of monkeys with his down-to-earth humor.*

Funny as shit: *See,* **Shit**.

Funny business: *See,* **Monkey** business.

Funny page(s): the comic section in a newspaper. *When I open the newspaper, I go straight to the funny pages.*

Fur

Make the fur fly: 1) create conflict or trouble. *The big brute made the fur fly when he was offended.* 2) accomplish much in a short time; to do something quickly. *Dick made the fur fly on his last project.*

Fuse

Blow a fuse: become extremely angry. *He blew a fuse when someone splashed water in his face.*

Have a short fuse: have a quick temper. *Our boss is very understanding, but he does have a short fuse when he can't tolerate something.*

Fuss

Fuss: to complain. *She fusses a lot about small things.*

Fuss bucket/Fuss pot: one who complains excessively; a phrase meant tenderly in response to a crying baby or toddler. *Our baby is a real fuss bucket when he doesn't get his way.*

Kick up a fuss/Make a fuss: to quarrel about something. *The kids made a fuss over who got to play with the new toys.*

Ga-ga

Ga-ga/Gaga: extremely infatuated. *Erin went ga-ga when she met the President.*

Gall

Have the gall: to portray no shame; be lacking in good judgment. *He has the gall to say he did it for the group, while having profited from it personally.*

Game

Ahead of the game: ahead of schedule; to be comfortably in front. *The engineers were ahead of the game and within budget on the dam project.*

Blame game: a search for scapegoats; act of laying blame on others and not oneself. *Be aware of the blame game that sometimes occurs in the corporate world.*

I'm game: ready to participate. *I'm game, so count me in.*

Off one's game: not performing as well as before. *Ever since he caught the flu, Steve has been off his game as an acrobatic flyer.*

Gander

Take a gander: view; look at. *Take a gander at this note and tell me what it says.*

What is good for the goose is good for the gander: treat everyone equally, especially not letting select few get away with crimes. *The cabinet officials committed acts punishable as a crime in any court, so they should pay; what is good for the goose is good for the gander.*

Gang

Gang up on: to overcome by force by two or more people. *The young hoodlums ganged up on the homeless man.*

Garage

Garage sale: a display of one's household items for sale in front of one's residence to the public. *Saturday is the best day to check out garage sales in the neighborhood.*

Garden

Garden variety: the ordinary kind; what is commonly seen or available. *This insecticide spray will not only get rid of the garden variety insects that eat your plants, but will also kill the good bugs around the yard like your lady bugs.*

Lead down the garden path: to confuse; take advantage of. *The customers were led down the garden path and swindled out of their hard-earned savings.*

Promise a rose garden: expectation of great riches. *I didn't promise you a rose garden when you joined this company.*

Gas

Full of gas: fully nonsensical; completely wrong. *You are full of gas to believe that animals can't think.*

Gaslight: to pass over; to keep out of the loop or scheme. *We need to gaslight our supervisor and go straight to the director about these accounting errors discovered in the books and records.*

Gassed up: 1) drunk. *You better drive; he's all gassed up.* 2) having a full tank. *We had to gas up before all of us departed on the long cross-country trip.*

It's a gas: very exciting; great enthusiasm. *It was a gas to go up in that hot air balloon!*

Out of gas: without strength; burned out. *The marchers were out of gas after walking for many miles.*

Pass gas: to fart. *Our dog, Cleo, passed gas a lot until we changed her diet.*

Step on the gas: go faster (referring to pressing on the gas pedal of a vehicle in order to accelerate). *You will need to step on the gas or else we will be late for the show.*

Gate

Gate: incoming revenue at the door or entrance. *Certain famous sports players, as part of their contracts, receive a percentage of the gate at their home team's baseball field.*

Gate crasher: attend a function without an invitation or ticket. *The teenagers became gate crashers after they could not get into the show.*

Gatekeeper: one who guards over; one who watches over the entrance as an overseer. *The citizens became their own gatekeepers to rid their neighborhood streets of crime and drugs.*

Gave

Gave out: 1) out of action; not working. *His car just gave out.* 2) to capitulate; to submit to something under pressure. *He gave out when he could not bear to see her cry.*

Gawk

Gawk: gaze with great amazement. *I never fail to gawk in joyful glee when the dolphins and killer whales swim along my kayak.*

Gear

Change gears: to do or talk about something else. *Let's change gears from picking corn to picking pumpkins for Halloween.*

Get one's ass in gear: *See,* **Ass**.

High gear: *See,* **High**.

Low gear: lower rate; slowly. *Operations are in low gear due to the economic recession.*

Out of gear: out of order. *My summer plans to camp in Alaska and climb mountains were thrown out of gear when I decided to stay in Seattle with a wonderful person that I met.*

Strip your gears: problems created by changing matters so suddenly. *You are liable to strip your gears and ruin operations if huge layoffs are made now.*

Geek

Geek: nerd; out of style; not suave; without social grace. *A lot of geeks go to this school.*

Get/Got

Get a break: to receive an opportunity or good deal. *He got a break when he found a buyer for his extra inventory.*

Get a fix on: to locate. *We have to get a fix on the herd before darkness.*

Get a handle on (something): become familiar in or better at doing something. *It took him a while to get a handle on using the night vision goggles.*

Get a life: find more time for oneself socially. *Max works all the time; he needs to get a life.*

Get a rise: tease another to try to excite or anger. *The boys tried to get a rise out of the teacher by hiding the school books.*

Get a word in: to manage to say something when others are talking. *Johnson could not manage to get a word in edgewise during the intense and often volatile discussions about the border dispute.*

Get away with murder: do something very unfair or bad without getting caught or punished. *If you don't punish him, then everyone will think you let him get away with murder.*

Get by: survive on existing means. *He will get by on his own.*

Get down to brass tacks: start discussing the essential matters now. *The parties got down to brass tacks and settled their differences, but only after the leaders took over the negotiations.*

Get even: seek revenge. *The neighborhood children tried to get even with the local bully by filming his assaultive actions and turning the film over to police.*

Get-go: the beginning. *From the get-go, we have to work hard and not make any mistakes.*

Get going/Get a move on: leave now; hurry up. *Mark and Hagos had to get going to pick up the supplies for the trip.*

Get in good: to be in favor with. *He spends much of his time trying to get in good with the boss.*

Get into high gear: *See,* **High**.

Get into the swing of things: to adapt; finding one's smooth rhythm or comfort of operation; working better in an environment or situation. *We got into the swing of things at the country club, and joined in the many social gatherings.*

Get it: 1) to understand. *So, do you get it, or must I explain it again?* 2) to be punished. *Mark was going to get it for hitting the dog.*

Get it out of one's system: to rid or forget; to not dwell upon. *Just get it out of your system and stop worrying about something that is not in your control.*

Get it together: to have full mental control of oneself. *You have to get it together or else you will never be an ace pilot in the sky.*

Get lost: *See,* **Lost**.

Get medieval: to get physically aggressive; to beat or attack someone. *Cool it, or she will get medieval on your ass.*

Get off easy: to escape a worse punishment. *The suspect got off easy because he helped the police locate the other culprits.*

Get off it: a directive to have a matter stopped; to forget it. *After hearing him complain numerous times, he finally told him to get off it.*

Get off one's butt: to stop lazing around. *He needs to get off his butt and find a job.*

Get off someone's back: See, **Back**.

Get on one's nerves: *See,* **Nerve**.

Get one going: get one encouraged. *Don't get him going about baseball; he'll talk with you for hours.*

Get one's act together/Get one's ass in gear (expressive): gain control of one's senses or direction; get promptly organized and ready to go; be serious. *Get your ass in gear now, or you will lose the race. We have to get our act together and think how we are going to get out of this mess.*

Get one's dander up/Get one's goat/Get one's Irish up/Get one pissed off (expressive): to annoy; get one angry or aggravated. *He gets my goat because he complains a lot, but offers no inspiring suggestions about how to improve things.*

Get one's foot in the door: achieve a favorable position. *Talking about getting your foot in the door, Jim is having lunch with the big boss at the country club tomorrow.*

Get one's shit together (expressive): *See,* **Shit**.

Get over it: to overcome one's problem. *Just get over it and move on; you have much more important matters to deal with right now.*

Get real: stop (being foolish). *When Jack thought about going back to the casino to try and win back what he lost in gambling, we told him to get real.*

Get something off one's chest: *See,* **Off** one's chest.

Get the ball rolling: *See,* **Ball**.

Get the drift: to understand; aware of the circumstances. *He got the drift that they did not want him to go on the trip.*

Get the feel of/Get the hang of: become accustomed or experienced with. *The more you get the feel of this new car, the more you'll like it.*

Get the jump on: to gain an advantage. *The car thief got the jump on us when he escaped from the stolen car and disappeared into the neighborhood on foot.*

Get the rap: *See,* **Rap**.

Get the run around: *See,* **Run**.

Get the scoop/Get the poop: derive information, generally non-public or secretive information; obtain the news. *Did you get the scoop on their secret wedding?*

Get the shaft: receive the bad end of something, often unfairly. *He got the shaft when the company fired him for something he was not responsible for.*

Get to the heart of: *See,* **Heart** of the matter.

Get up: how one is dressed in clothing. *That is some get up you have on.*

Get wind of: *See,* **Wind**.

Ghetto

Ghetto: broken down; cheap; of poor quality. *Your car is real ghetto, man.*

Ghetto/Ghetto-fabulous: excellent; great; awesome; outstanding. *That new car she bought is ghetto-fabulous, man!*

Ghetto bird: a police helicopter with a searchlight. *Hey, there's a ghetto bird hovering over the park.*

Ghost

Ghost of a chance: little or no opportunity at hand. *He doesn't have a ghost of a chance to be nominated for the prize.*

Ghost writer: one who writes for someone else. *Many politicians have ghost writers prepare their speeches.*

White as a ghost: *See,* **White**.

Gig

Gig: a job, such as for a music band. *We got a new gig next week at the Spotlight Club downtown.*

Gimme

It's a gimme: a sure bet; a no-lose situation; a free opportunity. *It's a gimme to bet on the number 3 horse in the next race.*

Give

Don't give a damn: *See,* **Damn**.

Give a hoot: *See,* **Hoot**.

Give a little: compromise. *Both of you will need to give a little in order to reach any settlement.*

Give and take: the act of compromise; understanding cooperation. *There is give and take in any relationship if you want to get along.*

Give in: be compelled to settle. *We had to give in and surrender or else face starvation in the hills.*

Give it a go: *See,* **Go**.

Give it one's best shot: try one's best; make one's best attempt. *I gave it my best shot.*

Give me five: a congratulatory hand slap with another. *What a nice shot! Give me five!*

Give someone the eye: *See,* **Eye**.

Glitzy

Glitzy: glamorous; stylish. *That new dress looks glitzy.*

Glutton

Glutton: anyone who has a great capacity for something, i.e., a glutton for food or a glutton for punishment. *He is a glutton for punishment for participating in triathlons.*

Gnaw

Gnaw at: to aggravate. *Quit gnawing at me with your complaints about the neighbor's cats.*

Go

Go/Give it a go: to pursue something; to have a try at something. *Let's give Jason's plan a go and see how it works out. Let me have a go at driving that racing car.*

Go bananas: *See,* **Banana**.

Go belly up: *See,* **Belly**.

Go fly a kite/Go jump in the lake: an expression for someone to go away and stop being annoying (generally used in disagreement with another). *Tired of hearing Tom's complaining, Tim told him to go jump in the lake.*

Go for broke/Go for all the marbles: to risk everything on one big event; use your best effort and skill. *We will need to go for broke to win this race.*

Go full circle: *See,* **Full circle.**

Go-getter: one who works hard to succeed; energetic; ambitious. *The best salesmen are real go-getters; they never seem to quit.*

Go haywire: go crazy; to lose or go out of control. *The machinery went haywire and caught fire. Many of our patients seem to go haywire on the night of a full moon.*

Go like a bastard: See, **Go like a bat out of hell.**

Go nuts: *See,* **Nut**.

Go overboard: to do too much of something. *Putting 18 coats of lacquer paint on his car I think is going overboard.*

Go scot free: *See,* **Free**.

Go through the motions/Go through the paces: to perform mechanically (without thought or feeling); to pretend to do something. *Although we had no work to do at the time, we had to go through the motions in looking busy at our jobs when the chairman came through.*

Go to bat for: to support; to help out. *I would go to bat for him if he were to get in trouble with the law.*

Go to one's head: *See,* **Head**.

Go to pot: to become ruined; deteriorate. *This hot summer has made my lawn go to pot.*

Go to the dogs: *See,* **Dog**.

Go too far: exceed what is acceptable; to overdo something to the point of being defeative. *Do we go too far when we suspend kids from school for bringing an eraser shaped like a small gun?*

Go under: become bankrupt; fail. *The company will go under if it fails to secure additional financing.*

Go under the knife: *See,* **Knife**.

Go with the flow: go forward without resistance; do as others do so not to attract attention to oneself and stand out. *If you want to get along with management, just go with the flow.*

Going down: what is happening. *What's going down at the market today?*

Gofer/gopher

Gofer/gopher: employee or worker who runs errands or caters to others; low-level subordinate. *He serves as a gopher for a Hollywood director.*

Gold

All that glitters isn't gold: not all situations or things are as good as they may seem. *Be careful of those get-rich seminars in real estate; all that glitters isn't gold.*

Goldbrick: one who shirks or avoids duty or work. *He tends to be a goldbrick in the afternoon, and gets very little done.*

Golden touch: one who can make things work or look well. *Guiseppe has the golden touch when he plays the flute.*

Good as gold: comparison of a matter with the highest quality of trust or assurance. *His words are as good as gold.*

Goner

Goner: a person or thing beyond help or assistance. *The structure is so old and the foundation rotted away, that the whole building is practically a goner.*

Good

For the good of: in the best interests of. *For the good of the company, Mr. Jones came out of retirement to rejoin the engineering team.*

Get the goods on someone/Have the goods on someone: discreet and usually damaging information about a certain person. *I want you to get the goods on her about her prior drug use so that we'll have additional evidence for trial.*

Good as gold: *See,* **Gold**.

Good egg/Good Joe: a pleasant, gracious or reliable individual; a well-liked person. *Jack is an all around good egg.*

Good riddance: sarcastic expression of goodbye; very glad to see one leave and not come back. *When our mean neighbor finally moved out, we bid her good riddance. It was good riddance to the baseball pitcher after a poor performance on the mound.*

Good Samaritan: one who helps other people without reward. *John, a good Samaritan, always helps those in need.*

Good shit: *See,* **Shit**.

Good taste: to have qualitative ideas; possess a fashionable sense of selection. *He has good taste in clothing.*

Have a good head on one's shoulder: *See,* **Head**.

Have a good mind to: *See,* **Have**.

Make good: *See,* **Make**.

Make good time: *See,* **Make**.

Not in good taste: *See,* **Taste**.

Goof

Goof/goofball: a fool. *He is such a goofball sometimes, but he seems to always enjoy himself.*

Goof/Goof up: mess up; make a mistake. *I really goofed up when I forgot the tickets to tonight's ball game.*

Goof off: fool around. *I probably will just goof off this weekend.*

Goofy: silly. *He acts goofy in front of the adults.*

Goon

Goon: a dumb or foolish person; one who is out of touch. *The new hire is a real goon.*

Goon squad: an organized group of low-class thugs or tough guys. *Those guys on that street corner is our town's version of the goon squad; they try to seem tough to people who pass by.*

Goose

Cook your goose/Kill your goose: spoil your advantage or desires. *They will cook your goose for not respecting the cultural symbols of the land.*

Goose bumps: *See,* **Bump**.

Goose egg: a score of zero; no go; nothing accomplished. *We came up with a goose egg searching for the fugitive.*

Goose it: to quickly excelerate; step on the gas pedal for quick speed. *I had to goose it to make the lane change and get off the exit.*

Wild goose chase: *See,* **Wild**.

Gouge

Gouged: to be swindled or taken for money. *The tourists were gouged because they did not know the currency exchange rate.*

Grab

Grab a bite: get something to eat. *Let's go grab a bite at the Mexican restaurant today.*

Grab bag: a container holding various articles, which are sold unseen at a fixed price. *Many coin shops sell grab bags of coins to aspiring collectors.*

Grab life by the horns: to energetically take on and face one's challenges in life. *Grab life by the horns now, or you'll regret it later.*

How does that grab you?: How do feel about that? *So, how does that grab you?*

Up for grabs: available to anyone who takes or is available to take; for sale to the first available buyer. *The prize was up for grabs to anyone who first reached the peak of the mountain.*

Grain

Against the grain: going the wrong way or contrary to societal expectations. *To criticize the company is really going against the grain.*

Grain of salt: to hardly notice; to treat very lightly. *We took his advice with a grain of salt because he is rarely correct.*

Grand

Grand/One grand: 1) a thousand dollars. *That car will cost you two grand.* 2) great; wonderful. *That new car is grand.*

Grand Central Station: a very busy place (in reference to the well-known and very busy train station in New York City). *Wow, this place looks like Grand Central Station! It was Grand Central Station at the shopping mall today.*

Grandstand: show off; stressing one's presence. *He used the local meeting to grandstand and posture himself for future political consideration.*

Grass

Grass: marijuana. *We could smell grass being smoked at the concert.*

One's ass is grass [expressive]**:** to be in serious trouble. *Your ass is grass for not appearing at your court hearing.*

Gravy

Gravy: 1) easy money. *Once this product sells, the rest is pure gravy.* 2) extra benefit; a plus. *Every day I can enjoy after I retire will be gravy for me.*

Grease

Elbow grease: *See,* **Elbow**.

Grease lightening: very, very fast; in a flash. *The new test vehicle was fast as grease lightening.*

Grease monkey [expressive]**:** a motor mechanic. *Jim works as a grease monkey at the local gas station.*

Grease one's palm/Grease the palms/Grease the wheels: to pay money in return for a favor. *My grandfather used to grease the palms of the officials with chickens and eggs in return for the authorization to conduct border trading. You will have to grease some wheels if you want anything done around here.*

Greasy spoon: a cheap cafe, which generally serves fatty and greasy food. *There is a greasy spoon named Betsy's on Aurora Avenue in Seattle that serves a 12-egg omelet!*

Green

Green: money (referring to the color green seen on U.S. paper currency). *How much green do you have?*

Green around the gills: inexperienced; novice. *Go easy on him; he's green around the gills.*

Green light: approval or permission to proceed. *We have the green light to begin our river project right away.*

Green mail: business language when a corporate raider accepts payment as settlement for backing off from purchasing additional shares of the corporation. *He is famous for buying large blocks of shares in corporations, then compelling green mail agreements with those same corporations to buy his shares back, but at a significant premium.*

Green with envy: desiring another's possessions or advantages. *All the guys are green with envy over Bob getting to date Cheryl tonight.*

Greenback: U.S. paper currency. *The greenback is accepted almost everywhere around the world today.*

Greenhorn: inexperienced or naïve person; tenderfoot. *Greenhorns are easy targets for swindlers.*

Grind

A grind: laborious and uninteresting. *Working in the hot and humid weather is a grind.*

Axe to grind: a grievance with another. *I have an axe to grind with him since he seems to be spreading false rumors about me.*

Daily grind: the job or work period. *I always get a latte before starting the daily grind. I need to escape from the daily grind and take off to the mountains for a few weeks.*

Keep/Have/Stick one's nose to the grindstone: to keep working hard. *She keeps her nose to the grindstone, working two jobs in order to meet her monthly expenses.*

Grip

Come to grips with: *See,* **Come**.

Get a grip: get control of one's senses. *Calm down and get a grip on yourself.*

Gripping: very; a lot; marvelously. *We had a gripping fine time at the racetracks today.*

Groove

Back in the groove/In one's groove: feeling in rhythm again; feeling back in shape. *After his knee surgery, he seems to be back in the groove again and as good as ever.*

Groovy: real nice or wonderful [1960's & 70's]. *Watching the Grateful Dead in concert was always a groovy scene.*

Off one's groove: not feeling one's rhythm; not doing so well as before; not feeling as strong or confident as before. *He was off his groove and finished fourth in the race.*

Gross

Gross: crude; lacking good taste; unrefined. *Spitting in public is gross.*

Gross me out: to feel disgust about something or someone. *Seeing the oil-laden birds and fauna grossed me out.*

Ground

Cover a lot of ground: *See,* **Cover**.

Gain ground: make progress. *She began to gain ground in her fight against cancer.*

Ground floor: 1) the lowest position. *He started from the ground floor with the company, and eventually became the president 30 years later.* 2) from the start or beginning. *We got into this company from the ground floor.*

Ground up: 1) upward from the bottom. *He worked his way up to top management starting from the ground up.* 2) to mash. *You need to ground up the grain before it is fed to the animals.*

Hold one's ground/Stand one's ground: to keep to one's position; refuse to lose or back down. *We prevailed because we held our ground and didn't give up.*

Lose ground: *See,* **Lose**.

On shaky ground: in a vulnerable position; in a weak stance. *You are on shaky ground if you place all your investment funds in one company.*

Run something into the ground: *See,* **Run**.

Grow

Grow hair on your chest: potent. *This hot sauce will grow hair on your chest!*

Grow like a weed: *See,* **Weed**.

Grow out of it/grow up: don't be illogical or immature, but be more sensible or mature. *He will never grow up as long as he continues to disrespect others. Oh...grow up.*

Grows on you: having both a gradual and positive effect. *Once you start to live in this community, it tends to grow on you.*

Grub

Grub: food. *The grub tastes real good when camping out.*

Grubby: dirty. *Clean those grubby hands. Get your grubby paws off me.*

Grungy

Grungy: dirty; disheveled; unclean and smelly. *He came in looking pretty grungy.*

Gum

Gum up the works: to ruin. *The pilot hoped he would not gum up the works on his first test flight.*

Gun

Gun for: 1) to look to punish or harm. *The bully on the block is gunning for you.* 2) to try with best effort to obtain. *He is gunning for the chance to get on the Olympic team.* 3) encourage on; in support of. *All the students are gunning for their teacher to win the world chess championship.*

Gun shy: timid; afraid; jumpy. *He gets a bit gun shy when it comes to marriage.*

Hired gun: individuals retained to protect others; in business or law, one retained to do a certain job. *Doug was retained as a hired gun to litigate the case at trial.*

Jump the gun: *See,* **Jump**.

Smoking gun: *See,* **Smoke**.

Son of a gun: a saying that expresses surprise. *Seeing 10-year old Sammy parachute from the plane, his grandfather on the ground exclaimed, "Son of a gun!"*

Stick to one's guns: to be firm; to stay on course. *It is hard to stick to your guns without a solid plan of action.*

Top gun/Big gun: the leader. *Who's the top gun in this outfit?*

Under the gun: *See,* **Under**.

Gung-ho

Gung-ho: full of energy; energized in emotion for a certain matter. *I had a gung-ho attitude when Dave was our boss, but then grew uninspired when the new manager took over.*

Gut

Gut/Guts: 1) the stomach or midsection of the body. *He got hit in the gut in the third round and went down grimacing in pain.* 2) basic issue. *The gut of the problem is to preserve corporate credibility rather than to try to save your reputation.* 3) cleared; taken out. *The store was gutted by the burglars.*

Gut feeling/Gut reaction: an instinct; a notion. *I have a gut feeling that the weather will clear up in time for our picnic.*

Guts/Gutsy: courage; stamina; fortitude. *It takes guts to stand up to the boss and wisely persuade him to change policy.*

Spill one's guts: *See,* **Spill**.

Gutter

Get your mind out of the gutter: move away from crude thoughts or profane discussion; to refrain from talking crudely. *Jimmy, get your mind out of the gutter, and quit talking that way!*

Gutter brain: dumb; with crude thought; a character without wit or wisdom. *Jacob is a gutter brain, but he's a hard worker.*

Gutter mouth: one who speaks profanely or with crude thought. *He is a real gutter mouth when he gets frustrated or angry.*

Habit

Creature of habit: predictable in one's ways. *As a creature of habit, Joe goes to the flower shop on Elm Street every Tuesday to buy Joan a bouquet of roses.*

Kick the habit: *See,* **Kick**.

Hack

Hack: mediocre to below-average performer. *The attorney was a hack but he got the job done.*

Hack it: to endure. *If you can't hack it, then leave.*

Hacker: one who penetrates and invades the computer programs or systems of others. *A hacker penetrated our computer network and was able to temporarily disable our system.*

Hair

Bad hair day: a day when one's appearance and hairstyle looks unattractive. *I'm wearing a hat today because of a bad hair day.*

By a hair: by the smallest margin. *Exeter beat Queen's College in the cricket match by a hair.*

Grow hair on one's chest: *See,* **Grow**.

Hair-raising experience: horrifying. *The haunted house was a hair-raising experience for little Matthew.*

Hairpin turn: a sharp, 180 degree turn (similar to the curled end of a hairpin). *He didn't see the hairpin turn, and drove straight off the embankment.*

Hairy: difficult; dangerous. *The journey through the mountains is always hairy during the winter months.*

In someone's hair: annoy someone; to bother and make someone angry. *Get out of my hair; you're bothering me.*

In the crosshairs: *See,* **Cross**.

Make one's hair stand on end/Curl one's hair: extreme fear or terror. *Just the thought of it makes my hair stand on end.*

Set one's hair on edge: very frightening. *I can tell you stories about the haunted mansion that would set your hair on edge.*

Split hairs: to argue in the smallest detail. *Why split hairs over such a minor matter?*

Half

Half ass: *See,* **Ass**.

Half-baked: put together quickly and without due consideration. *Their half-baked plan was shot out of the water by the committee.*

Half-cocked: to speak or act without thinking. *We were going about it half-cocked and confused.*

Half-hearted: lacking enthusiasm or energetic pursuit. *We cannot expect to succeed if we take a half-hearted approach to the matter.*

Half pint: short person; punk. *That half pint is a handful.*

Have half a brain: *See,* **Brain**.

Ham

Ham: one who acts it up in front of others. *He is a real ham in front of the camera.*

Ham actor: actor lacking talent. *You can't expect to get far in Hollywood if you're a ham actor.*

Hammer

Hammer away: work without stopping. *We hammered away on our budget report until midnight.*

Hammer out: to make or produce. *Without the union vote, no deal could be hammered out.*

Hammered: drunk. *We all got pretty hammered at the party last night.*

Under the hammer: 1) under pressure. *Jim is under the hammer by his boss for poor performance.* 2) up for sale at auction. *Everything will be sold under the hammer by next week.*

Hand

At the hands of: through the action of. *He suffered at the hands of the racketeers.*

Bird in hand: *See,* **Bird**.

Bite the hand that feeds you: *See,* **Bite**.

Blood on your hands: *See,* **Blood**.

Change hands: pass ownership over to another. *This car changed hands only twice in 40 years.*

Eat out of one's hands: to completely dominate or control. *We had the prisoners eating out of our hands after we offered them asylum.*

Force one's hand: to compel, generally against one's will. *They forced our hand in giving up after we had no other option.*

Hand-in-hand: doing something well together. *The local police worked hand-in-hand with the FBI in locating the bank robbers.*

Hand-me-down: used clothing or things, generally passed down from older to younger children in the family. *I received a lot of hand-me-downs being the youngest of six children.*

Hand over: surrender the control and possession of. *Hand over the records so that we can review them.*

Hand over fist: very easily; in large amounts. *They were making money hand over fist exporting rare wines to restaurants in Asia.*

Hand-to-mouth: just barely enough to sustain life. *Many children in the world sadly live hand-to-mouth.*

Handpick: to select personally. *He was handpicked by the company president to research the value of the oil discovery.*

Hands are tied: restricted; unable to take action. *Our hands are tied by budget constraints in saving the monuments in the park.*

Hands down: without question. *The fast and smart rookie wrestler beat the reigning champion hands down.*

Hands full: very busy. *The mother had her hands full taking care of three children.*

Hands off: not for the taking. *It was hands off the food until everyone arrived ready to eat.*

Handwriting is on the wall: sense that something is about to happen. *When the company lost several big orders last quarter, we saw the handwriting on the wall that hard times were around the corner.*

Handy dandy: convenient. *It is always handy dandy to have a toolbox in your vehicle in case of an emergency.*

Handyman/Handy person: one who is able to do various household or maintenance jobs in a building or dwelling (such as plumbing, carpentry, moving, hauling, etc.). *Can you call the building handyman to fix our leaky faucet?*

Have a hand in: *See,* **Have**.

Heavy-handed: *See,* **Heavy**.

Lay a hand on: to attack or assault. *He would never lay a hand on that poor kid.*

Off one's hands: no longer one's responsibility. *I have nothing more to worry about, now that it is off my hands.*

Old hand: *See,* **Old**.

One hand washes the other: a favor for a favor. *Around here, if you want anything done, well, one hand washes the other.*

Out of hand: out of control. *The children got out of hand when the teacher left the room.*

Play into one's hands: to operate to the advantage or opportunity of another; to come under someone's control. *You played right into his hands when he convinced you to go along with his scheme.*

Take the law into one's own hands: *See,* **Law**.

Throw up one's hands: to give up. *I throw up my hands and concede the game to you.*

Tie one's hands: *See,* **Tie**.

Wait on hand and foot: *See,* **Wait**.

Wash one's hands of: to absolve or separate oneself from something; to refuse to take blame. *I wash my hands of your actions and will no longer be responsible for you.*

With a heavy hand: with severity or strictness. *The teacher runs his class with a heavy hand.*

Unclean hands: having unfair or unethical experience; not a saint. *A court would not grant equity to one with unclean hands.*

Upper hand: to hold the advantage. *He has the upper hand in this matter since he's the boss around here.*

Handle

Fly off the handle: *See,* **Fly**.

Get a handle on: get control of. *Get a handle on this mess and make sure there are no more problems.*

Handle with kid gloves: treat very gently or with great care. *We handle our clients with kid gloves.*

Hang

Get the hang of: become acclimated; to understand. *As a new employee, he quickly got the hang of the operation.*

Hang: to relax, usually with friends. *We usually hang at the cafeteria after school.*

Hang/Hang around: to loiter or linger. *No one hangs around after class. We decided to hang at the mall for the afternoon.*

Hang a left: take a left turn. *Hang a left at the next intersection.*

Hang a right: take a right turn. *Hang a right at the next light.*

Hang a yoo-ee: make a U-turn. *You can get on the freeway if you hang a yoo-ee at the next light.*

Hang back: stay out of the action; seek the background. *We need to hang back until another opportunity arises.*

Hang by a thread: barely holding on to something. *Diseased and suffering from dysentery in the jungle, his life was hanging by a thread.*

Hang on to your hat: an expression to another about disclosing of a big surprise. *Hang on to your hat—you won't believe this but Henry just asked me to marry him! Hang on to your hats, folks, we're coming in for a rough landing.*

Hang out: a place of leisure and congregation. *Tooki's Bar and Grill is a favorite hang out for many workers from the local steel mill.*

Hang tight: stay in place; remain where you are. *I'll be back soon, so just hang tight.*

Hang time: the number of seconds that a football is in the air from the moment it is kicked until it is either caught or makes contact with the ground. *The ball was kicked only 45 yards, but it had an incredibly long hang time.*

Hang together: to be with others, generally in a social or comradery fashion. *"Yes, we must hang together or, most assuredly, we will all hang separately." (Benjamin Franklin speaking to his fellow members of the Continental Congress in their deliberations on the Declaration of Independence in 1776).*

Hang tough: to stick to one's position; be very determined. *We are going to hang tough and continue to fight for our right to peaceably assemble.*

Hang up one's gloves: to give up; retire. *After twenty years, Mr. Rogers will hang up his gloves as a truck driver.*

Hangover: waking up to a strong headache or nausea, generally in reference to drinking too much alcohol the night before. *I had a hangover from last night's party.*

Hard

Hard: alcoholic. *That cider turned hard, so you best not have the kids take it to school.*

Hard and fast: cannot be changed; fixed. *The teacher laid out a hard and fast rule about tardiness.*

Hard as nails: very stern or tough; unyielding; cold and cruel; unsympathetic. *The guards are as hard as nails with the prisoners. The instructor was hard as nails.*

Hard feelings: ill will; unfriendly thoughts about someone. *There have been hard feelings between the two families for many years.*

Hard going/Hard sledding: filled with difficulty. *It was hard going financially for some time until he got a nice paying job in construction.*

Hard line: rigid rules or system. *The hard-line immigration policy makes everyone uneasy.*

Hard luck: *See,* **Luck**.

Hard-nosed/Hardnosed: uncompromising; rigid. *My boss is hardnosed when it comes to employees misbehaving and not respecting others.*

Hard nut to crack: *See,* **Nut**.

Hard pressed: under strong pressure. *He was hard pressed for ideas to try to save the branch office from closing.*

Hard sell: 1) aggressive tactics in salesmanship to sell a product. *Hard-sell tactics are very evident in telemarketing.* 2) tough to persuade. *Mrs. Hartford is a hard sell; the last car she purchased was twenty-two years ago!*

Hard times: rough period; tough endurance; suffering. *Many families are going through hard times these days.*

Hard to peg: *See,* **Peg**.

Hard up: desperate. *Jim was hard up for a ride to get to work this morning.*

Hardball: be rough; uncompromising. *He plays hardball if you disagree with him.*

Hardcore: rough; no holds barred; uncensored. *The hardcore treatment of the non-violent prisoners has brought on the ire of the community.*

Hardhead: stubborn individual. *He rarely listens to anyone because he is such a hardhead.*

No hard feelings: *See,* **No**.

Has

Has been: out of favor; no longer popular. *Although he used to be a box office attraction, he's a has been now.*

Hash

Hash: concentrated cannabis made into a resiny mixture. *We came across a group of nomads smoking hash.*

Hash it over/Hash out: to work out; to discuss or talk over. *Let's hash out a plan before we begin the journey.*

Hat

At the drop of a hat: immediately; suddenly. *He gets mad at the drop of a hat.*

Feather in one's hat: *See,* **Feather**.

Hang on to your hat: *See,* **Hang**.

Hat trick: performance of an exceptional task. *He can do so many hat tricks on the billiard table.*

Hats off to/I take my hat off to: in recognition of a job well done; in congratulations. *We take our hats off to you for developing a vaccine that is now saving thousands of lives.*

Keep it under one's hat: *See,* **Keep**.

Old hat: *See,* **Old**.

Toss one's hat into the ring: to join a race, usually for political office. *He tossed his hat into the ring, and announced his candidacy for the mayoral race.*

Wear a different hat: *See,* **Wear**.

Haul

Haul ass [expressive]: *See,* **Ass**.

Haul in one's horns: to hold off or retreat from one's more aggressive actions. *Haul in your horns and don't act so aggressively in these sensitive negotiations.*

Haul one's ass/Haul one's butt: to bring someone in very quickly. *The gym teacher hauled Brian's ass into the principal's office for writing dirty slang words on the chalkboard.*

Haul someone over the coals: to admonish strongly; to punish severely. *He was hauled over the coals by the coach for his rough play.*

Have

Can't have one's cake and eat it too: can't have both benefits. *He pushes his employees to work harder and harder, but fails to give them any merit-related pay raises; well, he can't have his cake and eat it too.*

Have a crack at: *See,* **Crack**.

Have a crush on someone: to be enamored or infatuated with another. *Jane has a crush on Jack.*

Have a fling: have a romantic or sexual experience. *James had a fling with her many years ago.*

Have a fit: *See,* **Fit**.

Have a good head on one's shoulder: *See,* **Head**.

Have a good mind to: have an intention or desire to do something. *I have a good mind to call the police on him for leaving his pet dog in the car on such a warm day. I have a good mind to tell my boss to shove this job.*

Have a hand in: be partly responsible; be involved in something. *Mr. Smith had a hand in this office mess.*

Have a (song and a) prayer: have a chance. *Does Millie have a prayer of going to that college?*

Have a say/Have a voice in: have a right to speak about something. *Our boss encourages us to have a say in company matters.*

Have a screw loose/Have a loose screw: *See,* **Screw**.

Have a soft spot in one's heart: be loving and sympathetic to someone. *He gets a lot of breaks from her because she has a real soft spot in her heart for him.*

Have all one's ducks in a row: *See,* **Duck**.

Have an affair: discreet, emotional or physical relationship. *Tom and Jane had an affair and decided to marry soon thereafter.*

Have an attitude: *See,* **Attitude**.

Have an ear for: have a keen understanding; have a talent or desire for. *He has a good ear for foreign languages.*

Have an edge on: 1) to have the advantage. *Let's not fall asleep just because we have the edge on our rival.* 2) to have a few drinks. *Don't try to drive if you have the edge on.*

Have an eye for: *See,* **Eye**.

Have an eye out for: *See,* **Eye**.

Have an itch for: have a strong desire. *I have an itch for a big thick steak.*

Have designs on: have a keen interest in. *He has designs on you, did you notice?*

Have eyes for: *See,* **Eye**.

Have eyes on/Have eyes for: *See,* **Eye**.

Have had it: be completely frustrated. *I've had it with those kids!*

Have half a brain: *See,* **Brain**.

Have in mind: thinking about; intend. *I have in mind to expand my library.*

Have in the palm of one's hand: be completely at the mercy of someone. *He had the president in the palm of his hand for the incriminating information he had on her.*

Have it coming: deserve what's coming to you (good or bad). *He had it coming when he lost his job for his bad attitude and poor work ethic .*

Have it sewed up: confident of a successful completion; assured of success. *Don't worry; we'll have the whole matter sewed up by tomorrow.*

Have money to burn: in possession of a lot of funds. *James had a lot of money to burn after he hit the lottery.*

Have no business: have no right or reason to delve in anyone's affairs or be at a particular place. *You have no business snooping around here, so you'd better leave.*

Have nothing to do with: not involved with. *We have nothing to do with the matter.*

Have one's ass in a sling: *See,* **Ass**.

Have one's fill: to have endured enough. *Dennis says that he has had his fill of this job, and plans to quit soon.*

Have one's hands full: have more work than one can handle. *The backlog of orders should keep your hands full all week.*

Have one's head screwed on backwards: one who does not behave normally or seems strange. *Sometimes he acts like he has his head screwed on backwards.*

Have one's hide: punish someone harshly. *He'll have your hide if you're late to the meeting again.*

Have one's nose to the grindstone: *See,* **Grind**.

Have one's wings clipped: reduced in authority or status. *He had his wings clipped by the boss for creating a hostile atmosphere with the workers.*

Have one's work cut out: have a difficult task or challenging job to do. *With this bad weather, you are going to have your work cut out for you today.*

Have someone by the balls [expressive]: to have a strong upper hand or advantage; have another under one's control. *She had him by the balls with the incriminating pictures.*

Have the courage of one's convictions: be brave enough to stick to one's beliefs. *Mack had the courage of his convictions by refusing to cheat on the job.*

Have the edge: *See,* **Edge**.

Have the heebie-jeebies: nervous fright. *I got the heebie-jeebies when it was our turn to get on the roller-coaster.*

Have the inside track: *See,* **Inside**.

Have the last laugh: to prevail or succeed in the end, despite incurring some earlier setbacks. *We had the last laugh when we took home the prize.*

Have the right of way: have the right to proceed first. *I had the right of way at the intersection, but got clobbered doing so.*

Have the shakes: *See,* **Shake**.

Have the strength of an ox: to possess a lot of physical muscle. *He has the strength of an ox to get the job done.*

Have the time of one's life: *See,* **Time**.

Have two strikes against someone: a tough and challenging position. *Children in poverty already have two strikes against them in life.*

Hawk

Hawk: 1) sharp and focused. *He is in peak physical shape and has the mind of a hawk.* 2) a proponent of a strong military and increased defense spending. *The conservatives in Congress tend to be the military hawks.*

Hay

Ain't hay/That ain't hay: that is not cheap; a great amount. *The cost of living in Tokyo ain't hay. You can tell that what he earns ain't hay.*

Hayride: an easy and fun venture. *Our business partnership was no hayride, but we did great business together.*

Haywire: out of order; out of control. *The machine went haywire and caught on fire.*

Hit the hay: go to bed; get some sleep. *I'm going to hit the hay.*

Make hay while the sun shines: *See,* **Make**.

Needle in a haystack: *See,* **Needle**.

Hazard

Hazard: in golf, a place or thing that can obstruct a ball, such as taller grass and brush. *Jasper sliced his golf ball, which I believe landed in a hazard area on the right side of that bunker over there.*

(If I could) Hazard a guess: an intent to provide a response without insult. *If I could hazard a guess, I would say that a coffee shop would not do well in this location.*

Head

Bang/Beat one's head (against the wall): 1) to try hard, yet be unable to understand or succeed. *No matter how much I beat my head against the wall, I'll never understand business math.* 2) to do nothing fruitful; to be wasting time. *I was just banging my head against the wall waiting for your plane to arrive.*

Beat into one's head: to get one to understand. *How many times must I tell you not to follow too close to other cars on the highway? Do I have to beat it into your head?*

Big-headed/Bigheaded: conceited; arrogant; self-important. *Mallory is smart as a fox, but she's also big-headed.*

Bite one's head off: *See,* **Bite**.

Bring to a head/Come to a head: to reach a crucial point; approach a moment when one must come to a decision. *The whole matter is coming to a head; either we negotiate a new contract or the employees go on strike. The project has come to a head and may have to close operations due to budget problems.*

Bury one's head in the sand: *See,* **Sand**.

Can't make heads or tails: *See,* **Can't**.

Count heads: count the number of people.

From head to foot: the whole body. *Dick was soaked from head to foot getting to his car in the heavy rain.*

Get it through your head: to really understand. *Get it through your head that you cannot visit the mall during your school hours.*

Get your head together: come to your senses; be cognizant. *Get your head together and finish this assignment before the boss arrives next week.*

Go to one's head: become self admiring, arrogant, conceited, etc. *It sure seemed to go to his head about winning the award.*

Good head on one's shoulders: 1) one who is considerate and understanding; someone with good character. *Dick may not be the smartest person, but he has a good head on his shoulders.* 2) one, who thinks well, is educated, experienced, etc. *He has a good head on his shoulders, and is someone who can manage the company.*

Hardhead/Hardheaded: stubborn minded; unyielding. *He is hardheaded and won't leave until he has the chance to speak with her.*

Head: 1) the toilet. *Give me a minute; I need to go to the head.* 2) go to. *Why don't you head over to my place after class and we'll have some coffee.*

Head above water: out of difficulty; not in trouble. *Overwhelmed with debt, and no longer able to keep his head above water, he felt compelled to file for bankruptcy protection.*

Head and shoulders: a whole lot; by a wide margin; without question. *I am head and shoulders in debt. Head and shoulders, he's the best we have.*

Head doctor/Head shrink: psychiatrist. *I have an appointment with my head doctor. She has been seeing a head shrink for the past year.*

Head for the hills: get out right away; go hide someplace. *If you see a tidal wave in this bay, just stop what you're doing and head for the hills.*

Head honcho: the leader; the boss. *Okay, who's the head honcho around here?*

Head in the clouds: the mind is not focused on the subject at hand. *Dick had his head in the clouds after his promotion.*

Head on: with the front facing forward. *Mr. Dickson had a head on collision last week.*

Head out: take off someplace; go to a certain location. *I may head out for the mountains this weekend.*

Head over heels: 1) falling or flipping over; completely off balance. *The children came running all at once into the classroom, head over heels.* 2) overwhelmed with love and affection; completely infatuated with. *See also*, **Stoned in love.** *They are head over heels with one another.*

Head start: to have an initial lead or edge. *We need a good head start in order to keep up with the stiff competition.*

Headhunter: one who finds jobs for others. *The headhunter found me the job in two weeks.*

Heads or tails: a choice between two sides of a coin, generally by the flip of a coin used to select positions in competition such as in sporting events. *On the flip of the coin, I want you to choose heads or tails.*

Heads up: 1) make one aware of some matter. *I wanted to give you a heads up on the situation so that you are well informed before going into the meeting.* 2) an exclamation of impending danger. *Heads up! The neighborhood bullies are coming down our block!* 3) stay on the ball; look alive. *We must always display a heads-up attitude in order to survive in this business.*

Heads will roll: to seek punishment against. *Heads will roll for the company's bad performance this past year.*

Hide one's head in the sand: refuse to face facts; have no desire to see or know. *One cannot hide his head in the sand when it comes to national security.*

Hit the nail on the head: *See,* **Nail**

Hold one's head up: be proud and honorable. *Mr. Jones can hold his head up after educating five children.*

Hole in one's head/Hole in the head: *See,* **Hole**.

Hot head/Hothead: *See,* **Hot**.

Lock heads: to fight or argue over. *Environmentalists and loggers have been locking heads for decades over the cutting down of precious forest land.*

Make heads or tails of something: *See,* **Make**.

Off (the top of) one's head: *See,* **Off**.

On its head: to give opposite meaning to something. *To not allow the group to pursue its own style of lawful domestic living, while not customary, would place the meaning of our constitution concerning 'the pursuit of happiness' on its head.*

Out of one's head: crazy; illogical. *You are out of your head to think I would undermine the trust of my friends.*

Over one's head: 1) beyond understanding or comprehension; not understood. *This complex math problem is over my head.* 2) to skip over the line of authority. *He went over his supervisor's head and spoke with the president.* 3) in a lot of debt. *We were over our heads, financially.*

Price on one's head: *See,* **Price**.

Put our heads together: think well; reason everything out. *Let's put our heads together and try to figure this thing out.*

Scratch one's head: *See,* **Scratch**.

Skinhead: *See,* **Skin**.

Swelled head: one who considers self-importance first; arrogant. *One with a swelled head generally fails to gain popularity among his or her peers.*

Thick-headed: *See,* **Thick**.

Use one's head: make the proper decisions; think well before taking action. *Next time, just use your head rather than make a fool of yourself.*

Yell one's head off: to vocalize extremely loud. *Our voices are hoarse because we were yelling our heads off at the game.*

Heap

Heap: 1) junk vehicle; run-down car. *Where did you get that heap?* 2) to pile on. *Why is the extra work heaped on us all the time?* 3) a great amount. *I have a heap of homework to do tonight.*

Heart

At heart: primarily; naturally. *A natural desire to act free at heart is generally all that a young dog wants to do.*

Break one's heart: create great sadness or emotional disappointment, generally when a love is lost. *He broke her heart when he married another woman.*

By heart: by memory. *Jacob gave his entire speech by heart.*

Change of heart: to have second thoughts or different opinion. *She was having a change of heart about the new job.*

Eat your heart out: *See,* **Eat**.

From the bottom of my heart/From the heart: out of true kindness; sincere intent; free of pretense. *This gift isn't much, but it comes from the heart. From the bottom of his heart, the industrious young individual donated his earnings to the homeless shelter.*

Have a heart: to be kind and considerate. *Have a heart for the homeless families.*

Heart and soul: 1) strong desire; great eagerness. *Quincy's heart and soul is to be a writer.* 2) completely. *If you're trying to improve the team, we're with you heart and soul.*

Heart goes out to: feeling sorry for someone; have pity for. *Our heart goes out to the poor who have no food on the table.*

Heart of gold: good hearted; good natured; kind and trustworthy. *Our next door neighbor has a heart of gold.*

Heart of the matter: the central or significant aspect of something. *If you want to resolve this problem, you have to get to the heart of the matter.*

Heart throb: infatuated feeling of desire for someone. *The famous actor is a heart throb to many female fans.*

Heart-to-heart: a truthful discussion; to discuss freely and openly about a matter. *They had it out heart to heart before parting their ways. The young couple had a heart-to-heart discussion about their future together.*

Heart wrenching: very emotional; full of sadness. *It was heart wrenching to see the whales beach themselves along the shore.*

Heartache: missing of someone who is very much loved. *A mother's heartache for her son going to war is evident around the world.*

Heartbreaker: one who is greatly admired by the opposite sex. *Tim is being chased by several girls, and is known as a heartbreaker.*

Heartless: having no scruples or conscious. *Criminals who hurt others are heartless.*

In a heartbeat: very fast; within the shortest time. *I'll be there in a heartbeat.*

Lose heart: no longer have passion for. *He lost heart in his job after his favorite supervisor retired.*

Stone-hearted: *See,* **Stone**.

With all one's heart: to an extreme degree; with a passion. *With all his heart, he mastered steering the boat through the storm. I love that kid with all my heart.*

Heat

Heat: 1) under pressure or stress. *The heat is on for Bob to complete the project before winter.* 2) an event. *The next heat will be the 100-meter race, featuring the best runners in the world.* 3) law enforcement; police. *Let's get out of here before the heat arrives.* 4) weapon. *What kind of heat are you carrying?*

Feel the heat: to sense or understand the pressure or stress. *You will feel the heat from the boss if the job is not done correctly.*

Stand the heat: to take the pressure or handle the stress. *If you can stand the heat around here, then you will do well in this job.*

Turn on the heat: *See,* **Turn**.

Heaven

Heaven (only) knows: only God knows; unknowing about something or someone. *Heaven only knows where your son is at this time of the night.*

High heaven/Hog heaven: feeling very good; emotionally euphoric. *He's in high heaven after getting accepted to his college of choice.*

Move heaven and earth: to try or do everything one can. *We are moving heaven and earth to search for your missing child.*

Stinks to high heaven: *See,* **Stink**.

Heavy

Heavy: 1) complicated; very detailed or intricate. *That reading material about nuclear propulsion is real heavy and hard to understand.* 2) awesome. *In hearing how the secret rocket formula was made for the special fuel, Poindexter exclaimed, "Wow, that's heavy."*

Heavy duty: extra strong. *The heavy-duty vehicle can go over all types of terrain.*

Heavy-handed: cruel; oppressive. *Guards in prison are generally heavy-handed with the inmates in order to maintain control.*

Heavy hearted: mentally burdened; depressed. *He has remained heavy-hearted ever since she left him.*

Hell

All hell broke loose: things got out of control; chaos. *When you left, all hell broke loose.*

All to hell: *See,* **All**.

Be hell on you: to have punishment or much difficulty come to you. *It will be hell on you if you are caught behind enemy lines.*

Beat the living hell out of: *See,* **Beat** the living daylights/hell/tar/shit out of.

Catch hell: *See,* **Catch**.

Cold day in hell: *See,* **Cold**.

Come hell or high water: notwithstanding disaster or turmoil. *Come hell or high water, we will get through this difficult ordeal.*

Go/drive/run like hell: to be very fast. *We ran like hell when the bull broke out of its holding pen.*

Go through hell: endure the most difficult times. *Many Cambodians during Pol Pot's rule, from 1975 through 1979, went through hell trying to survive.*

Go to hell [expressive]: an emphatic and angry expression of rejection, denial, or disgust in response. *When the coach was asked about the alleged choking of a fan for calling him a "buffoon," he told the reporter to "Go to hell."*

Hell and back: to experience a very serious challenge and be able to survive. *He went to hell and back after returning from the civil war in Africa.*

Hell and high water: great difficulty or trouble. *See also above,* **Come hell** or high water. *The rescuers went through hell and high water to bring supplies to the stranded campers on the mountain.*

Hell bent: extremely or aggressively eager. *He is hell bent in getting rid of his adversary.*

Hell hole: miserable surroundings or situation; very undesirable place, especially in very hot weather; an eyesore. *This place is a hell hole with all the trash and dirty clothing everywhere!*

Hell in a hand basket: ruined; chaotic consequence. *The party went to hell in a hand basket when he showed up.*

Hell of a/Helluva: very much of. *We had a helluva time at your house party last week. The firemen had a hell of a bad week when lightening sparked fires everywhere.*

Hell on wheels: a very fast and awesome vehicle or motorcycle. *Harley-Davidson is well-known to have bikes that are hell on wheels.*

Hell yeah: an expression of strong agreement; of no doubt. *Hell yeah, we will help our good friends.*

Just for the hell of it: for no particular reason; in a fun or comedic manner. *The guys filmed the car wash just for the hell of it.*

Like a bat out of hell: *See,* **Bat**.

Like hell: no way. *Like hell if you want me to go mountain climbing again.*

Looks like hell: very bad. *The backyard looked like hell after the flood.*

Shot (all) to hell/Went to hell in a hand basket: ruined; to fall apart quickly. *The tourist industry went to hell in a hand basket when the country began to suffer under civil disorder and acts of terrorism.*

Snowball's chance in hell: *See,* **Snow**.

'Till hell freezes over: certain not to surrender or give way; take on a challenge to the end. *He won't give up his post 'till hell freezes over.*

What the hell?: a very strong, if not angry, inquiry about something. *What the hell is going on?*

Hella

Hella: extremely; very much; in large quantity. *The sushi at the Japanese restaurant was hella good! That girl is hella fine!*

Helter-skelter

Helter-skelter: chaotic; very disorderly manner; great confusion. *Everything was helter-skelter after the earthquake.*

Hem

Hem and haw: hesitate; delay due to indecision so as to avoid commitment. *The members just hemmed and hawed about the issues and failed to make any decisions.*

Hem in: to constrict or limit; to tie up. *We were hemmed in by the gridlock traffic downtown and could not get to our meeting on time.*

Here

Here and there: in different places. *We looked here and there for the lost pocket book.*

Here goes nothing: an easy-go-lucky expression where one is willing to give something a try, with the understanding that nothing may come from it; an all-or-nothing effort. *In getting ready to kick the game-winning field goal from 40 yards out, he muttered, "Well, here goes nothing."*

Hide

Hideout/Hide-out: a secret place to meet or to keep hidden. *We have several hideouts in town as safe houses for battered women and their children to stay.*

Neither hide nor hare: no trace of something or someone. *There is neither hide nor hare of any rodents since you brought the owls to watch over the place.*

High

High: a euphoric mental state. *Drugs that get you high generally tend to be banned or restricted by law.*

High and low: everyplace; everywhere. *We looked high and low for your cat, but no luck.*

High and mighty: feeling of superiority; arrogant. *Your high and mighty attitude is alienating you from your employees.*

High as a kite: 1) the happiest anyone can possibly be. *Jim was high as a kite after he received his promotion.* 2) intoxicated or under the influence of drugs. *When the police stopped Mack's car, he was as high as a kite.*

High brass: top management. *The high brass will be out here next week to inspect our new prototype.*

High-class: the best quality; of superior status. *The Windy Ridge area is considered a high-class neighborhood.*

High cotton: to be full of happiness or wealth. *He's in high cotton after signing that multi-year sports contract.*

High falutin'/High faluting: pompous; arrogant; boastful. *Mary gets me angry with her high falutin' way of doing things.*

High five: a celebratory greeting when two individuals raise a hand and slap each other on the palm. *The players were giving each other high fives after winning a hard-fought game.*

High flyer: one who acts, talks or believes in an extravagant way. *There are many high flyers in Las Vegas, but very few winners.*

High gear: fast; speedy; furious working motion. *The workers were in high gear preparing the stage for tonight's big show.*

High handed: one who uses the strong-arm method; overbearing; arbitrary. *Using incentives and independent initiatives in getting employees to perform are generally favored over a high-handed approach.*

High-hatted: treating others as lower class; snobbish. *The family is fairly high-hatted when it comes to treating their neighbors.*

High horse: *See,* **Horse**.

High life: experiencing extravagance. *I understand that he is living the high life ever since he won the lottery.*

High on the hog: living laviously. *The Romans lived high on the hog during the peak period of their reign. They have been living the high life after selling their company.*

High roller: one who plays for large sums of money or deals with large assets. *Most high rollers at the casino lose their money quickly unless they are lucky.*

High strung: sensitive; easily excitable; jumpy; emotionally unstable. *Many purebred dogs tend to be high strung.*

High style: the new style or fashion. *The high styles set by the prominent fashion centers are accepted worldwide.*

High tail it out of: to get away quickly. *We had to high tail it out of the warehouse after it caught on fire.*

High-wire act: a risky performance or task. *Cleaning windows outside on tall buildings seems like a high-wire act.*

Highway robbery: charging a very high price. *It is highway robbery for what they charge for a hotdog at the ball park these days.*

Leave someone high and dry: out of touch or contact; stranded; left alone with no help. *I was left high and dry with the restaurant bill when everyone took off to the club. The ice suddenly broke up, and the hunters were left high and dry on a drifting iceberg.*

Hill

Head for the hills: *See,* **Head**.

Over the hill: *See,* **Over**.

What in Sam Hill: a strong inquiry into something, although it is a more polite exclamation to the more expressive phrase, "What the Hell?" *What in Sam Hill are you doing?*

Hip

Hip: real nice; cool. *Yeah, that's hip, man.*

Shoot From the hip: *See,* **Shoot**.

Speak from the hip: to speak unrehearsed; to talk without a script or preparation; ad lib. *A disc jockey's talent is the ability to speak from the hip. Politicians often get in trouble when they speak from the hip and blurt out inflammatory remarks.*

Hit

Hit and miss: unpredictable; unplanned. *Finding good employees for this construction project is hit and miss.*

Hit and run: 1) when a driver involved in an accident leaves without stopping. *The pedestrian was injured by a hit-and-run driver.* 2) to attack without warning and leave the scene quickly. *The army successfully performed a hit-and-run attack on the command center.*

Hit below the belt: unfair attack. *That remark is really hitting below the belt.*

Hit bottom: be in the worst or lowest situation. *Our sales hit bottom for the last six months. He hit bottom after the loss of his job.*

Hit by a ton of bricks: be suddenly surprised or shocked; make a sudden impact. *I felt like I was hit by a ton of bricks when I received a lay-off notice from my company.*

Hit home: successful outcome. *His presentation hit home and made a big impression on the audience.*

Hit it off (with another): positive interaction with another. *The strangers hit it off well because they both have a common interest in mountaineering.*

Hit on: to flirt with; to make a pass at someone. *Jason nervously tried to hit on Patty and ask her to the dance.*

Hit on all cylinders: *See,* **Run** (Running on all cylinders).

Hit one up for a favor: to request a favor of another. *Can I hit you up for a favor about getting two seats to tomorrow's ball game?*

Hit someone between the eyes/Hit someone like a ton of bricks: sudden surprise; a startling occurrence. *The senator was hit between the eyes when his long-time ally suddenly voted against him on the bill.*

Hit the books: *See,* **Book**.

Hit the bull's eye: successfully achieving a specific goal. *Jack hit the bull's eye with the public on his popular report about the plight of the city's homeless shelters.*

Hit the ceiling: become very angry or highly excited. *Mr. James hit the ceiling when he saw his tax bill.*

Hit the deck/Hit the dirt: get out of the way by lying flat on the ground. *The soldiers yelled, "Hit the deck!" to the hostages before spraying the room with gunfire.*

Hit the fan/Hit the ceiling: 1) serious trouble to follow; become chaotic. *The situation will hit the fan when the story becomes public.* 2) become angry or outraged. *If I don't get home right now, the wife will hit the ceiling.*

Hit the hay/Hit the sack: go to sleep. *On trips, the team players have to hit the hay by 10 p.m. or risk suspension.*

Hit the high spots: 1) summarize. *Just hit the high spots and give me a short review of our international project.* 2) visit the better or nicer places of entertainment or attractions in town. *When you visit Seattle sometime, we can hit the high spots around town.*

Hit the jackpot: be very successful or suddenly lucky. *We hit the jackpot when we finally discovered the sunken treasure.*

Hit the nail on the head: to do or say exactly the right thing; to recognize the solution. *You hit the nail on the head with your proposal.*

Hit the road: leave and go elsewhere. *When the river flooded our homes, we had to hit the road toward higher ground.*

Hit the sack: *See above,* **Hit** the hay.

Hit the sauce: to drink alcohol, generally more consistently and in above-average amounts that inebriate. *He began to hit the sauce after he lost his job.*

Hit the skids: reach bottom; reduction of an activity to a crawl or complete stop. *The construction company hit the skids when the economy went into recession.*

Hit the spot: *See,* **Spot**.

It hit me/When it hit me: to suddenly realize something. *I was in the shed cleaning old debris, when it hit me that my childhood toys were in the boxes stored above.*

Shit hit the fan: *See,* **Shit**.

Hob-nob/Hob-knob

Hob-nob/Hob-knob: to socialize with. *He is often seen hob-nobbing with senators and congressional representatives.*

Hocus pocus

Hocus pocus: magical illusion; not real or true. *The rumor about our department closing down is a bunch of hocus pocus.*

Hog

High on the hog: *See,* **High**.

Hog: 1) a Harley-Davidson motorcycle. *He has one nice hog.* 2) to take without cause or charge; inconsiderate; a mooch. *He's not a friend but just a hog who comes here to eat our food and use our things.*

Hog heaven: *See,* **High heaven**/Hog heaven.

Hog wild: ecstatic; crazily excited. *We went hog wild when our college won the NCAA (National Collegiate Athletic Association) basketball tournament.*

Hogwash: nonsense; not the truth. *The rumor about Jack leaving the research team is hogwash.*

Road hog: *See,* **Road**.

Whole hog: go all out; apply all one's energy to go the distance. *The workers went whole hog and completed building the house in five days.*

Hoity

Hoity toity: prudish; pretentious; stuck up. *The more arrogant individuals seem to be the hoity-toity types.*

Hold

Don't hold your breath: *See,* **Breath**.

Hold a grudge: to not forgive; a persistent feeling of ill will or hatred against someone. *He holds a grudge against the company for its refusal to offer the pension he was promised.*

Hold down: keep control or grip on. *The ruthless government held down its people for many years until a people's revolt finally brought it down.*

Hold down the fort: keep temporary watch and guardianship; assume responsibility in another's absence. *I was the only person at the radio station holding down the fort in the early hours of the morning on Sunday. All right son, hold down the fort while I go to the hardware store.*

Hold it: 1) Expression indicating to another to wait a moment. *Hold it a minute; I have to close the shop first before we can leave.* 2) stop moving or doing something. *The police officer instructed the suspect to hold it and not resist.*

Hold it down: quell your anger; make yourself be quiet. *This is a library so hold it down, please.*

Holdin' it down: playing it easy; acting cool. *Yeah, I'm just holdin' it down today.*

Hold off: delay, stop. *We need to hold off the ceremony due to the bad weather.*

Hold one's ground/Stand one's ground: *See,* **Ground**.

Hold one's horses: stop and wait patiently. *Hold your horses until I can get my keys out of my pocket.*

Hold one's own: doing well in defending one's position. *The child is weak but he can hold his own as a survivor very well.*

Hold one's peace: remain silent, usually against temptation for response or reprisal. *We must hold our peace at the conference to avoid any confrontation that will not work to our advantage.*

Hold one's temper: try not to become angry; remain calm. *Jason tried to hold his temper before blasting out.*

Hold one's tongue: keep quiet. *You best hold your tongue about the fight you had in class today.*

Hold one's water: 1) to be patient. *I know you're next so just hold your water.* 2) wait to urinate. *The little boys couldn't hold their water any longer, so they went behind a big tree along the road.*

Hold out: 1) to reach out; extend. *The neighboring countries both held out their hands in friendship after many years of fighting and bloodshed.* 2) one who refuses to conform; to wait and not move forward.. *He was the only hold out on the vote to raise additional funds. The baseball player was holding out for a better offer.* 3) to keep secret; to not reveal certain information. *Are you holding out on us?*

Hold up: 1) robbery. *There was a hold up today at our local bank.* 2) delay. *What's the hold up with the delivery today?* 3) prove to be true. *His version of the accident held up under questioning by police.* 4) to not get worse; remain even. *I hope our sales will hold up this year.*

Hold water: to be sound; to be sensible. *Compare with,* **Doesn't hold water.** *The idea about charging fees for the use of the local parks holds water as a way to help balance the county budget.*

(Left) holding the bag: *See,* **Bag**.

Hole

A square peg in a round hole: the wrong thing or person; a person in a position for which he's unqualified. *I thought we hired the right guy, but we wound up with a square peg in a round hole.*

Crawl out from under a hole: *See,* **Crawl**.

Fire in the hole: *See,* **Fire**.

Hole in one: in golf, to hit the ball from the tee and into the cup on the green in one shot. Also known as an ace in the hole. *On his 15th birthday, he hit a hole in one at the local golf course.*

Hole in one's head/Hole in the head: 1) something completely unwanted or undesired. *I need that thing like a hole in the head.* 2) to be dumb; not understanding. *I don't know how you didn't realize it; you have to have a hole in your head not to see it.*

Hole in the wall: small and unnoticeable; hidden. *The best bread comes from this hole-in-the-wall bakery at the edge of town. There is this hole in the wall I know that serves the best breakfast in town.*

Hole up: to hide. *We found the suspect holed up in the crawl space beneath the warehouse.*

In a hole: in a tough situation, especially when out of money. *With my unemployment insurance soon to expire, I'll be in a hole if I can't find a job by next week.*

Pick holes: *See,* **Pick**.

Holy

Holy cow/ mackerel/Mother of God/Moses/shit (expressive): expression showing strong feelings of awe, astonishment, anger or excitement. *Holy mackerel! He hit that ball out of the ball park! Holy shit! I just saw a car crash into that building!*

Holy roller: an individual who expresses extreme or violent religious feelings during worship. *Our pastor is a holy roller who expresses damnation and suffering to anyone who is sacrilegious.*

Holy smoke(s): exclamation of surprise or disbelief. *Holy smoke, look at that erupting volcano!*

Holy terror: a very disobedient child. *The little boy becomes a holy terror whenever his father leaves on long trips.*

Holier than thou: feeling better than or superior to others in goodness or character. *He has a holier-than-thou attitude that many do not find appealing.*

Home

Come home to roost: all problems will follow you. *Just as I expected, my financial problems came home to roost.*

Hit home: *See,* **Hit**.

Home free: an easy finish or completion, generally after a challenging or tough experience. *We were home free in the sail race after our strongest competitor ripped a sail and had to drop out.*

Homey/Homie: 1) friend; pal; someone from the same neighborhood. *We've been homies for a long time.* 2) a word of greeting to friends. *Hey, homie, how you been?*

Keep the home fires burning: to take care of things while others are gone. *Keep the home fires burning while I'm on this trip.*

Make yourself at home: feel comfortable around here (as if you were in your own home). *Please come in and make yourself at home.*

Nothing to write home about: *See,* **Nothing**.

Honcho

Honcho: boss; supervisor. *The corporate head honcho is coming today to view our new development on the eastside.*

Honey

Honey: one's sweetheart. *I am lucky that my honey is here to care for the children.*

Honey bucket: a portable toilet. *The honey buckets are for the construction workers.*

Honey wagon: a vehicle used to carry away sewage. *You drive behind a honey wagon at your own risk.*

Honeybunch: sweetheart; intimate nickname toward one's love. *Hi, honeybunch; I'm home.*

Honeymoon is over: when the initial bliss or period of happiness between two entities is over. *After a brief holiday peace, the honeymoon was over between the new leader and the old guard.*

Hooch

Hooch: whiskey. *Got any hooch around here?*

Hooch hound: alcoholic. *He had been a hooch hound for many years, but then one day he suddenly stopped drinking.*

Hoochie/Hoochie mama: 1) promiscuous female, usually dressed in revealing or tight clothing, or a lot of make-up; slutty. *She looks like a hoochie mama with the kind of clothes she's wearing.* 2) tacky. *That's a hoochie-lookin' shirt.*

Hook

Get the hook: get discharged from one's job. *It was sad to hear that he got the hook after 20 years with the same company.*

Hook, line and sinker: completely; everything; the whole works; without question or doubt. *We have the opposing team fooled, hook, line and sinker.*

Hook up: to connect with. *I could not hook up with my friends last night on account of the stormy weather.*

Hook-up: a connection. *We lost power when our hook-up to the power source was lost in the storm.*

Hooked: 1) get addicted or habituated. *Many people get hooked on cigarettes and then later find it hard to quit.* 2) get married. *They met, fell in love, and got hooked, all in 3 weeks!* 3) get cheated. *Tourists tend to get hooked by thieves at the local market and bus terminal.*

Hooker: prostitute. *The crime rate went down on Main Street after the police arrested the hookers and drug dealers.*

Off the hook: out of trouble; free of responsibility. *He was off the hook with the prosecutor after his attorney was able to clear him of the charges.*

Hoot

Give a hoot: care for. *Along interstate highways, one will see forest service signs showing an owl that says, "Give a hoot, Don't pollute." He doesn't give a hoot what she says.*

Horn

Blow one's (own) horn: to praise or boast about oneself; self-aggrandizement. *He is the type to blow his own horn without thinking about the achievements and help he received from others.*

Grab life by the horns: *See,* **Grab**.

Horn in: to come in without invitation; to meddle or interfere. *The teacher horned in on the heated discussion between the students before the situation got any worse.*

Horn-swaggled: fooled; deceived. *He was horn-swaggled when he purchased a cheap imitation of a brand-name watch from a street vendor; it stopped working a week later.*

Horny: sexually aroused. *The deer appear horny in springtime because it's the mating season.*

Lock horns: to fight or argue. *She tends to lock horns with him at virtually every meeting.*

Take the bull by the horns: *See,* **Bull**.

Horse

Beat a dead horse: *See,* **Beat**.

Bet on the wrong horse: make the wrong decision. *You are betting on the wrong horse by supporting the river project.*

Change horses in the middle of the stream: significant change or disruption in plans; choosing of a new leader in the middle of an important event, which tends to complicate matters. *Replacing any managers during the peak season is like changing horses in the middle of a stream; it may prove disastrous.*

Dark horse: *See,* **Dark**.

Eat a horse/Eat like a horse: very hungry. *I'm so hungry, I can eat a horse. Make sure you have enough food because he eats like a horse.*

Enough to choke a horse: *See,* **Choke**.

Get back on one's horse: to righteously try again. *I admire one who gets back on his horse and persists in taking on a good challenge.*

High horse: aloof position; on the top looking down, especially in a hierarchical scenario. *Get off your high horse, come down to the assembly line, and see how your workers are really performing under these challenging conditions.*

Hold one's horses: *See,* **Hold**.

Horse around: joke or indulge in rough teasing; playing around. *The boys were horsing around in the backyard before dinner. Stop horsing around and get to work.*

Horse of a different color: something altogether different or separate. *The issue he wants to discuss is a horse of a different color compared to what we are talking about.*

Horse sense: common judgment; wisdom in making decisions. *Your ideas about the organization makes a lot of good horse sense.*

Horse shit [expressive]: complete non-sense; a lie. *For management to ask the unions to take drastic pay cuts while executives are discreetly giving themselves large bonuses is simply horse shit.*

Horse trading: being involved in tough negotiations toward reaching agreement. *A lot of horse trading went on late last night before this agreement was done.*

Horse's ass: *See,* **Ass**.

Hungry as a horse: very hungry. *I'm hungry as a horse after that long hike through the hills.*

Lock the barn door after the horse is gone: *See,* **Lock**.

Put the cart before the horse: *See,* **Cart**.

Straight from the horse's mouth: from the original source; most reliable information. *The orders to evacuate came straight from the horse's mouth, the general himself.*

Hot

Hot: 1) someone or something that is very exciting or attractive. *She is hot, and I can't keep my eyes off her. This story is a hot one, and is bound to get national coverage.* 2) stolen. *When you see someone trying to sell merchandise from the back of a van, it is probably hot.*

Hot about: *See,* **About**.

Hot air: useless talk; exaggeration. *See also,* **Full** of beans. *It is nothing but hot air about those who believe the world is flat.*

Hot and bothered: 1) displeased; excited and worried; confused. *He is hot and bothered about the break-up of the company.* 2) a strong desire toward sexual tendencies. *Quit thinking too much about her or you'll get too hot and bothered.*

Hot and heavy: intensely excited; very enthusiastic. *The tour group is hot and heavy about seeing a live Hollywood show.*

Hot as a pistol: very competitive or productive; cannot be beat. *Our advanced technology division is hot as a pistol in the industry.*

Hot as hell: very hot. *It is hot as hell over here in summer.*

Hot blooded: easily stimulated to react; very emotional. *The loggers received a hot-blooded and charged response from the community when they tried to clear-cut the old growth trees.*

Hot diggity/Hot diggity dog/Hot diggity damn (expressive): an interjection of glee or delight. *Hot diggity dog! We got tickets to the playoffs!*

Hot dish/Hot mama/Hot number/Hot one/Hot tamale: a passionate or sexy woman; a Marilyn Monroe type. *It may be hard to believe, but this hot mama is the mother of 4 children!*

Hot poop: fresh information; most up to date news. *What's the hot poop on the company's latest project?*

Hot potato: a troublesome problem, which nobody wants. *The idea to unionize the workers at the plant is a hot potato with management.*

Hot rod: an automobile renovated to drive at very fast speeds. *He placed a large engine in his car and turned it into a hot rod.*

Hot rodder: a person who drives a car at great speed. *He is a real hot rodder on the road, so I do not ride with him.*

Hot seat: in a difficult or very challenging position. *He's in the hot seat to come up with ideas to save the company from bankruptcy.*

Hot shot: a person who is well regarded in his field as exceptional; very important. *This guy is the hot shot who keeps all of our mainframe computers operating in sync.*

Hot spot: an area of action. *This nightclub is a hot spot that attracts the best dancers in town.*

Hot stuff: 1) someone with exceptional abilities or something sought after or attractive. *With his skills, he is considered hot stuff around here. This information is hot stuff; get it to the editor right now for publication in tomorrow's paper.* 2) one who tries to act superior. *He thinks he's hot stuff.*

Hot tamale: *See above,* **Hot** mama.

Hot to trot: excited and ready for action. *The players are hot to trot and ready for tomorrow's football game.*

Hot under the collar: extremely angered. *He is hot under the collar for missing the publication deadline.*

Hotdog: someone who is a show-off, often associated with doing risky or dangerous stunts. *He is a real hotdog with his new car.*

Hotdogging: fooling around; moving in and out quickly. *The skiers were really hot dogging it on the slopes today.*

Hothead: temperamental individual; one who is easily angered. *This job requires temperament and patient consideration, so that eliminates a hot-head like you. Our secretary is sometimes hotheaded but she is very efficient and time conscious.*

Hotline: a means of instant communication, generally in emergencies. *World leaders have a hotline to one another to discuss matters of crisis.*

In hot water: in a lot of trouble. *He is in hot water for missing the staff meeting today.*

Sell like hotcakes: *See,* **Sell**.

Hound

Hound: invade one's privacy with bothersome surveillance; to always be over one's shoulder. *As a rising new movie star, you constantly will be hounded by the public and the media.*

House

Bring down the house/Bring the house down: receive great applause from the audience. *Your last performance brought down the house!*

Clean house: to win significantly. *Jim cleaned house at the card game.*

Flop house: *See,* **Flop**.

House arrest: under guard or watch in your own home. *She received 90 days of house arrest for driving drunk.*

House-broken: where animals and other pets that live in a house are trained to properly relieve themselves, either in a select location, e.g. a litter box or outside. *Cats are easily house-broken.*

House of cards: something poorly arranged or put together, and easily destroyed; a bad plan or action. *The building collapsed like a house of cards due to its shoddy construction.*

House warming: a party given when you move into a home. *There was a lot of great food at Jim's house warming.*

Keep house: house cleaning and maintaining a tidy household. *I've been keeping house while my parents are on vacation.*

Nut house: a mental hospital or institution. *What nut house did you escape from?*

On the house: free item(s), given by the respective establishment or owner. *The beers are on the house for all winning team members.*

How

How about: *See,* **About**.

How does that grab you?: what do you think about that? *We got tickets to the Raiders and Seahawks game on the 40-yard line. How does that grab you?*

How's that: 1) what did you say? *How's that? I couldn't hear you with the door closed.* 2) inquiring of your opinion. *How's that? Does the picture look straight now?*

Hungry

Hungry: eager to do something. *You have to be hungry in this business to do well.*

Hungry as a horse: *See,* **Horse**.

Hunk

Hunk: a very muscular guy. *Those football players are real hunks.*

Hunker down: to secure oneself; get under shelter or protection. *We hunkered down in our basement while the tornado whirled by the house.*

Hunky dory: all right; things are just fine. *Just stay calm, and everything will be hunky dory.*

Hurl

Hurl: to vomit. *On the deep-sea fishing trip, half of us caught fish and the other half hurled over the side feeding the fish.*

Hush

Hush-hush: something kept quiet or concealed. *The big hush-hush about the project was due to national security reasons.*

Hush up: 1) prevent the dissemination or revelation of something; keep others from knowing. *Governments today are more compelled to be forthright and fair with its public rather than hush up embarrassing matters.* 2) to make or keep quiet. *The ill-behaved little boy was told to hush up when they entered the store.*

Hype

Hype: overblown publicity or rumor. *What's all the hype about?*

Hyped up: 1) overly excited or stimulated. *We are all hyped up about going to the ball game tonight!* 2) inflated; exaggerated. *The movie was hyped up with a lot of advertising in order to get a strong showing at the box office.*

Hyper: to be overly excited. *She gets hyper over the smallest things.*

I

Ice

Break the ice: *See,* **Break**.

Cold as ice: unsympathetic; uncaring. *The soldiers were cold as ice to the prisoners, especially the mercenaries.*

Ice: 1) diamonds. *Oooh, nice ice!* 2) methamphetamine. *He was arrested for possession of ice.*

Ice/Iced: 1) assurance in victory; clinch. *He iced the game with a last-second shot.* 2) kill; murder. *He was iced by a rival gang.* 3) to ban or freeze an internet account or website. *They iced his internet account.* 4) very high on drugs. *Man, I'm so iced.*

Ice up: to take care of; settle. *The elder Mullah helped ice up the plan for nationhood by bringing all the factions together in peace.*

Ice water in one's veins: calm and collected under stress. *He must have ice water in his veins to perform such complicated spinal surgery.*

Icing on the cake: *See,* **Cake**.

On ice: 1) in reserve or readiness. *I want enough inventory on ice in case of emergency.* 2) keep away from notice or scrutiny. *Keep this matter on ice until I can sort things out.*

(Skating) on thin ice: risking loss; taking a chance. *You are skating on thin ice with that sort of strategy.*

Icky

Icky: repulsive; unattractive. *The younger boys in class think girls are icky.*

I.D.

I.D.: abbreviation for identification. *Do you have a picture I.D. to verify payment?*

If

If need be: should the need arise. *You should go to the meeting if need be.*

If only: to be wishful on something. *If only I could forego chocolates forever, I would lose weight.*

If the shoe fits (then wear it): *See,* **Shoe**.

Ill

Ill: to act inappropriately. *I don't want to be around him as long as he's being ill.*

In

Had/Has it in for me/you: to find every fault to blame; to challenge in an adversarial manner. *He had it in for me ever since he became the supervisor.*

In: fashionable. *Those clogs and flared jeans you have on are really in.*

In a bind/fix/jam/tight spot/pickle: stuck with a difficult problem. *I'm in a bind for mistakenly signing that document without an attorney reviewing it first.*

In a flash/In a jiffy/In nothing flat/In no time: very fast; in the shortest time. *I'll be back in a jiffy. When the earthquake hit, we exited the old building in a flash.*

In a hole: *See,* **Hole**.

In a nutshell: simply stated, very summarily. *In a nutshell, your financial statement shows a loss for the year.*

In a pinch: *See,* **Pinch**.

In cahoots with: in questionable association with another or others. *He has been in cahoots with the southern tribal leaders for years in order to ensure continued safe passage for his group.*

In deep water/shit (expressive) **/In Dutch/In for it:** in serious trouble. *You'll be in deep water if you get arrested at the protest march.*

In Dutch: *See above,* **In** deep water.

In hog heaven: very happy and contented. *She was in hog heaven after he proposed to her.*

In kind: barter; trading with other goods rather than money. *In the old days, we traded in kind for our sugar and salt.*

In like Flynn: easy success; in an advantageous and ever-winning position (terminology in reference to the movie star, Errol Flynn, who appeared always looking dapper and successful). *Our wines are in like Flynn after being given the highest rating by the wine experts.*

In limbo: stuck; not moving; on the fence. *The whole project has been in limbo ever since the workers went on strike.*

In one's face: to come up directly and confront, often in intimidation. *As a suspect, the sheriff was in his face about the shooting and what was witnessed.*

In one's Sunday's best: wearing one's best clothes (traditionally, wearing your best clothes to church). *I see Jim in his Sunday's best; it must be a special date he has tonight.*

In orbit: in a euphoric state. *They were in orbit after smoking from the elder's pipe.*

In the air: 1) to leave hanging and unresolved. *The plan to build a second balcony in the concert hall is in the air because of budget costs.* 2) a feeling of. *The sense of the holiday season was in the air.*

In the bag: *See,* **Bag**.

In the black: to be profitable. *Contrast with,* **In** the red. *Our company is finally in the black after five losing quarters.*

In the cards: expected; foreseeable; predictable. *His talent as a leader was in the cards when he was just a little boy.*

In the chips: having financial wealth. *He is in the chips, now that his book made the bestseller list.*

In the dark: ignorant about; not aware of. *Many governments can keep their populace in the dark if they are able to control the news and restrict the freedom of speech.*

In the doghouse/shithouse (expressive)**:** in trouble; in disfavor or dishonor. *I'll be in the doghouse for not giving her flowers on her birthday.*

In the doldrums: depressed; feeling listless. *He's been in the doldrums lately because his friend is ill with pneumonia.*

In the driver's seat: in control; in a position of decision-making power. *Jacque is in the driver's seat, now that he won the mayor's race.*

In the flesh: in person. *There he is, on stage, in the flesh.*

In the groove: in the right position or doing the right thing. *We are in the groove as a team because we practice hard in order to achieve excellence in our work.*

In the hot seat: *See,* **Hot** seat.

In the john: refers to being in the bathroom or on the toilet. *He is unavailable for now because he is in the john.*

In the know: knowing non-public information or secrets others do not know. *Contrast with,* **In** the dark. *He is in the know because he speaks with all the locals about the daily activities of the community.*

In the lap of luxury: living with considerable wealth. *Living in the lap of luxury, he had no worries about getting a job.*

In the line of duty: action done as part of one's job; often associated with heroic action on the job. *He gave his life in the line of duty as a valiant firefighter.*

In the nick of time: just in time; at the last possible moment. *We made it to our plane in the nick of time.*

In the pen: in prison, generally the state prison (short name for penitentiary). *My uncle is in the pen doing five (years) for robbery.*

In the prime of life: in the most productive time of one's life. *It is sad to see any individual stricken with disease in the prime of life.*

In the raw: naked; without covering or addition. *There is a place on the beach where you can swim and tan in the raw.*

In the red: losing money. *Contrast with,* **In the black**. *Our company operation will be in the red next quarter due to the economic slowdown.*

In the saddle: in control. *I'm in the saddle again.*

In the same boat: *See,* **Boat**.

In the short run: in the near or immediate future. *In the short run, we will rent a house, then buy later.*

In the spotlight/limelight: in a noticeable or prominent position, seen by many, generally via the media. *He is in the spotlight after his great performance in his first movie.*

In the works: in preparation; work in progress. *The author has another novel in the works.*

Ins and outs: know what goes on; understand how things operate. *After you've been here a while, you get to know the ins and outs about the place.*

Into orbit: to angrily lose control of oneself. *He went into orbit when the company lost the contract.*

Inside

Have the inside track: to have a favorable advantage due to connections or knowing special information; have an advantage by knowing something others do not. *He has the inside track on the winners since he works for the independent accounting firm that counts the votes.*

Inside job: the help of another, such as an employee, who has inside knowledge of how to sneak or break into a facility (generally involved with crime). *The criminal operation must have required an inside job to break into the company vault.*

Inside scoop/Inside skinny: the secret rumor or news. *The inside scoop is that she is going to be fired next week.*

I.Q.

I.Q.: intelligence quotient (refers to one's mental abilities in accordance with age). *This person has the I.Q. of a ten-year old, but he is only four.*

Iron

Iron horse: a tireless and strong worker, traditionally related to the engine of a railroad train. *He is an iron horse and the reason why we will win the championship this year.*

Iron in the fire: something one is doing or is preoccupied with. *He has a lot of irons in the fire, so he never seems to have time to enjoy the weekends.*

Iron out: to smooth out or come to an agreement. *I want you two to iron out your differences now.*

Pump iron: *See,* **Pump**.

It

It figures: it makes sense or is right. *For being a genius, it figures that he doesn't study much, but gets the highest score in class.*

It gets me: something that annoys or bothers. *It gets me when innocent people are unfairly treated without the balance of the courts to protect their constitutional freedoms.*

It goes without saying: the meaning is very obvious; it is meant to be. *It goes without saying that he will be selected in the first round of the baseball draft.*

It's a cinch: very easy. *For Josh, it's a cinch for him to get everything right on the test.*

It's a deal: it is agreed to. *It's a deal; we will start construction next week.*

It's about time: finally; at long last (an expression stated under a bit of frustration). *It's about time they increased the security around the child care center.*

It's high time: it's long overdue. *It's high time that the county build a traffic light at this dangerous intersection.*

It's your funeral: one risks destruction with one's challenging, if not reckless, action. *If you want to challenge the big boss on this one, well, it's your funeral.*

Itch

Itch: to have a restless desire; a craving. *I'm itching for a vanilla ice cream cone.*

Itchy feet: *See,* **Feet**.

Itchy palm: *See,* **Palm**.

Item

An item: 1) good-looking or admired person. *Jack, the new student, is an item with the girls.* 2) a showpiece; an authentic or rare artifact. *That sculpture you bought is a real item.*

Ivy

Ivy League: of premier quality. Also, the reference to colleges in the eastern United States known as universities of quality education. Originally, the name was in reference to the ivy that grew on and along the walls surrounding the universities. Harvard, Yale and Princeton were the original Ivy League schools, with others such as Columbia, Cornell, Brown, Dartmouth, and the University of Pennsylvania added later to the hallowed list of schools. *Many of the employees here are ivy-league quality. He's good enough to get into any Ivy League school.*

Jabroney

Jabroney/Jabronie: a naive person; a greenhorn or newcomer who is unfamiliar with the culture or area; tenderfoot. *That jabroney is going surfing in the middle of a storm!*

Jack

Ain't jack shit [expressive]: *See,* **Shit**.

Jack: 1) anonymous name wryly referring to the one being spoken to. *Hey! What's up, Jack?* 2) to steal. *The car was jacked last night right in front of our house.* 3) nothing. *He doesn't have jack on us.*

Jack of all trades (and master of none): one who is known to be involved in many different ventures or have many practical skills; a handyman. *Our apartment manager is a jack of all trades because he can repair almost anything.*

Jack shit: *See,* **Doesn't know jack shit**.

Jack someone up: to penalize severely; to rough up. *If you aren't telling me the truth, I'm going to jack you up.*

Jack up: raise the price. *Why do you keep jacking up the rent when the vacancy rates are rising?*

Jack-rabbit start: a sudden move forward from a still position. *He tends to make jack-rabbit starts at traffic lights because he is not used to his new sports car.*

Jacked up: excited, sometimes to the point of over-stimulation; stimulated; feeling charged. *The crowd got jacked up over the team's championship victory, and proceeded to roll over vehicles and become disorderly.*

Jail

Jailbait: a girl below the legal age of consent for sex, which is punishable by law; someone too young to associate with. *She is jailbait, but certainly looks and acts like an adult.*

Jailbird: someone who is in jail or one recently released. *The escorted jailbirds can be seen cutting grass along the highway today.*

Jailbreak: to escape from jail. *There was a jailbreak last night and two prisoners cannot be found.*

Jam

In a jam: *See,* **In**.

Jam: 1) to leave. *I have to jam because I'm already late for my next meeting.* 2) to play music especially well. *Man, this guy can really jam with that guitar. Is he with some rock group?* 3) slam dunk a basketball (to force it through the hoop). *He is only 12 years old, and already is able to leap up and jam a basketball.*

Jammed: 1) very busy. *We are so jammed with back orders to fill that we will need to hire additional personnel.* 2) intoxicated; under the influence of. *After honoring our ancestors, we got jammed on Japanese sake at the bon odori festival.* 3) arrested. *He was jammed for assaulting a police officer.* 4) mad; irritated. *My teacher got jammed when I arrived late to class.*

Jammin': 1) going fast. *They were jammin' out of here when I arrived, so I don't know where they went.* 2) moving in rhythm. *We were jammin' to the music.* 3) playing real well. *We were jammin' on the basketball court today!*

Traffic jam: congestion of vehicles on the road or highway. *There is a traffic jam on the freeway into town, so avoid it for now.*

Jamoke

Jamoke: a dumb-witted or stupid person; fool; jerk. *That jamoke just doesn't get it, does he?*

Jane

Jane Doe: A name used informally to refer to the average unidentified woman. *Who is the Jane Doe in the photograph?*

Jaw

Jaw drop: with astonishment or unexpected surprise. *Our jaws dropped when we won the contest.*

Jawbone: to virtually force your point of view onto another to agree with your wishes. *The politicians were being jawboned by various business lobbyists for greater mineral exploitation of federal lands.*

Jawbone of an ass: one who is just stupid or recklessly ignorant. *You have the jawbone of an ass to believe that you can dive off that cliff!*

Jawbreaker: a word or words hard to pronounce. *That expression, "the big black bug bled black blood on the barnyard floor," is a real jawbreaker.*

Jaws of life: a device used to separate metal, which is generally used at traffic accidents where victims are trapped in crushed vehicles. *They had to use the jaws of life to extract Jack from his overturned and totaled utility vehicle.*

Jazz

(Bunch of) jazz/(Don't give me that) jazz: nonsense; sass or speculate; something not true or unrelated. *That story about Martians coming to earth is a bunch of jazz. Please don't give me any more jazz about the company layoffs because the story is only a rumor.*

Jazz it up: to make something more exciting; to enliven. *We need to jazz the show up in order to attract a bigger audience.*

Jazzed up: 1) having an optimistic or excited state of mind about something. *He is all jazzed up about getting his new product to market.* 2) getting all pretty or nice-looking. *The guys were getting all jazzed up for the dance tonight.*

Jazzy: of animated or flashy character. *Her wardrobe always looks jazzy.*

Jerk

Jerk: 1) foolish, embarrassing person; oddball. *He can act like a jerk after a few beers.* 2) to pull. *For throwing debris onto the field, he was jerked from his seat and thrown out of the ballpark.*

Jerk one's chain: to harass, upset or anger another. *He is just trying to jerk your chain about reporting you to the school principal.*

Jet

Jet/Jet out: to leave in a hurry. *See ya; I gotta jet.*

Jet set: rich, stylish and care-free social group, generally associated with those who travel lavishly in pursuit of adventure and good times. *Humphrey is a worldwide jet setter who is rarely in one place for too long.*

Jib

Jib: to shove or poke. *Jib him in the ribs to get his attention for me.*

Jibbering: mumbling or making incoherent speech. *What are you jibbering about?*

Jitter

Jitters: being very nervous. *I have a case of the jitters; I cannot wait until the school exams are over.*

Jive

Jive: 1) to be evasive or not tell the truth; to lie. *Don't jive me about the event because I was there and saw it myself.* 2) to move quickly from one to side to another. *We were jiving in and out of the traffic lanes in a valiant attempt to quickly get the wounded to the hospital. Muhammad Ali was rarely hit in the face as a boxer because he would constantly jive around his opponents.* 3) to measure up with; to coordinate with; to corroborate with. *That story doesn't jive with what she told me.*

Jive turkey [expressive]: a fool. *You jive turkey; you forgot to fuel the plane before we took off!*

Job

Bang-up job: *See,* **Bang**.

Do a job on: to impose a lot of damage on; to do harm; to make ugly or useless. *The elephant rampage did a job on the landscape.*

Inside job: *See,* **Inside**.

Job hopping: a series of moving from one job to another. *There is a lot of job hopping among attorneys at law firms in this city.*

Lie down on the job: not being productive while working. *The boys were caught lying down on the job and smoking cigarettes.*

Odd jobs: various small, jobs or tasks. *I've have been doing odd jobs around the house while the weather is nice.*

OJT: on-the-job training. *The new employee is doing OJT for the next three weeks.*

On the job: working. *The employees cannot smoke cigarettes while on the job.*

Put-up job: a deceptive arrangement. *The fire alarm was a put-up job to get people out of the building while the thieves burglarized the place.*

Snow job: *See,* **Snow**.

Jock

Jock: 1) someone good in sports. *All the jocks in school have tutors.* 2) to flirt with; to hit on. *He always tries to jock her when she's in class.* 3) to copy from. *Many kids jock the style of their favorite singer or band player.*

Joe

Cup of Joe: a phrase apparently gained from the sarcastic history of sailors in the early 1900's when the Secretary of the Navy, Mr. Josephus Daniels, banned the traditional consumption of "alcoholic liquors on board any naval vessel," which forced sailors to substitute their drinks with a cup of coffee. *I'm going to the coffee shop to get another cup of Joe.*

Good Joe: *See,* **Good**.

Regular Joe: a normal person. *The retired general is just a regular Joe around here.*

John

John: 1) toilet. *Can you tell me where the john is located?* 2) one who does business with a prostitute. *Catching the Johns, as well as arresting the prostitutes, have reduced crime on these streets significantly.*

John Doe: a name used informally to refer to the average unidentified man. *Who is the John Doe in the photograph?*

John Hancock: your name in writing; signature. Originated from John Hancock's large signature on the Declaration of Independence signed in Philadelphia, Pennsylvania on July 4, 1776. *Please place your John Hancock where indicated at the bottom of the page.*

Johnny-come-lately: a new person who takes an active part in group affairs before the group has accepted him; a fast upstart. *We were surprised to see a Johnny-come-lately beat the old favorite in the speed-car race.*

Johnny-on-the-spot: a person who is present at the right time and is alert to the opportunities immediately available. *He seems to be a Johnny-on-the-spot when it comes to financial opportunity.*

Joint

Joint: 1) a cheap bar or restaurant; a nightclub. *He always frequents the local joints near home for a drink after work.* 2) a marijuana cigarette. *While in Vancouver, I visited a café where people were smoking joints while drinking their espresso.* 3) jail. *I was in the joint when I was younger because I didn't know any better.* 4) an enclosed place or setting, such as an apartment, office, etc. *Where do you turn on the heat in this joint?*

Put someone out of joint/Put one's nose out of joint: 1) to make one jealous; to leave one out of favor. *When Martin saw his old girlfriend with Larry, that really put his nose out of joint.* 2) to ruin one's plans; to cause disappointment. *Canceling the trip will really put her nose out of joint.*

Jones

Jones/Jonesing/Jonesin': 1) addiction; a craving for something. *He has such a Jones for warm weather that he leaves Chicago in December to go to Florida. Man, I'm a jonesin' for a caramel latte.* 2) an infatuation for someone. *I've got a Jones for you because I can't keep you out of my mind.*

Keep up with the Joneses: to try to equal your neighbor by purchasing the latest gadgets or fashions. *If you buy that electric appliance just because Harry has one, it is like trying to keep up with the Joneses; will you ever stop being so foolish?*

Juice

Juiced up: energized; invigorated. *The players are juiced up for the big game today.*

The juice ain't worth the squeeze: the effort isn't worth the reward. *We toil so hard and receive so little in return, the juice ain't worth the squeeze anymore.*

Jump

Get a jump on: take an advantage; a step ahead. *With our talent, we will have a jump on any team that plays us.*

Jump: get into. *I'm going to jump into the shower.*

Jump all over/Jump on: to criticize; blame. *Mom jumped all over Johnny for breaking the expensive vase.*

Jump bail: one who fails to appear in court when required by law and subsequently forfeits his bond. *Jason jumped bail and now he is a fugitive from the law.*

Jump down someone's throat/Jump on someone: to scold harshly or with little consideration. *The teacher jumped down his throat when he* *failed to do his homework again. The boss is always jumping on everybody for even minor things.*

Jump from the frying pan and into the fire: when matters go from bad to worse. *Investing in this venture is like jumping from the frying pan and into the fire.*

Jump in the lake [expressive]: expression of harsh refusal or insult. *When the buyer offered only a fraction what the antique was worth, we told him to go jump in the lake.*

Jump in with both feet: enter into something with great enthusiasm and vigor. *We were ready to jump in with both feet to start our new business as organic farmers.*

Jump on the bandwagon: to join a popular cause or movement. *We jumped on the wireless bandwagon early on and profited well from it.*

Jump ship: to abandon or leave hastily from. *He jumped ship to work for a local network as an anchor for the evening news.*

Jump the gun: to do something prematurely or out of turn. *The journalist jumped the gun in publishing the story, which was based on the wrong facts.*

Jump through (a lot of) hoops: trying hard or going out of the way to please another. *I had to jump through a lot of hoops to get this for you.*

Jump to a conclusion: to make a decision prior to hearing all or enough of the facts; deciding too quickly without all the information. *You are jumping to a conclusion in calling the fire an arson before conducting an investigation.*

Jumpstart: 1) a means of getting a start in a challenging situation. *Getting that job for me gave me a real jumpstart in my career.* 2) start another car with another's car battery. *Hey, could you please give me a jumpstart?*

Junk

Junk: cheap or worthless items. *She keeps a lot of junk in her house.*

Junk food: food that is thought not to be so healthy, or of little nutritional value, such as sweets or oily foods. *We eat too much junk food and not enough vegetables and complex carbohydrates.*

Junk mail: unwanted and unsolicited mail generally received from vendors and merchants. *The post office has an address where you can write and request to have your junk mail stopped.*

Junkie: a drug addict. *A lot of junkies tend to frequent our local parks.*

Jury

Hung jury: when the members of a jury in a trial cannot reach a decision as to the guilt, innocence or liability of the defendant. In a criminal trial, most often the jury verdict has to be unanimous, or there is a hung jury. In such case, it is up to the prosecutor whether to re-try the defendant. *There was a hung jury in the murder trial, but the prosecutor wants to re-try the defendant.*

Jury is still out: the decision is unknown. *The jury is still out about the merger.*

Jury-rig: a makeshift assembly or repair. *Given the damage, we will need to jury-rig the aircraft quite a lot to get it back into the air by morning.*

Jury trial: a trial on the issue of fact that is determined by a jury of generally 6 to 12 individuals from the local community who are selected by the parties to serve. In criminal cases, the 6th Amendment to the U.S. Constitution guarantees the accused a jury trial rather than a bench trial. *The jury trial lasted for 3 weeks, and the defendant was found to be not guilty.*

Just

Just a minute/Just a moment: 1) an (interrupting) expression to garner attention to one's explanation. *Just a moment, I was here first.* 2) a very short time. *I'll be back in just a minute.*

Just about: nearly; practically. *We are just about at our destination.*

Just for the fun of it/Just for the hell of it: simply as a matter of amusement. *I'll bring the old golf club to class just for the fun of it.*

Just in time: soon enough. *We arrived just in time to see the beautiful autumn leaves turn color.*

Just the ticket/Just what the doctor ordered: exactly what is needed. *The sound of the oncoming tanks was just the ticket we needed to encourage our commander to retreat. Getting me that cold beer was just what the doctor ordered.*

Justice

Bring to justice: to look for, capture, and punish if required. *The bank robber was finally brought to justice after tips were received from the public.*

Do justice to/Do it justice: to do something as well as one could; to do properly. *Given my busy schedule, I could not do justice to helping you on your assignment.*

Miscarriage of justice: when one's rights are harmed due to an abuse of power under the guise of the law; wrongly accused and convicted; misuse or mishandling of the law. *The best way to avoid any miscarriage of justice in this murder case would be to move the trial to another venue far away.*

No justice, no peace: if there exists no fairness under the law, then there will exist no civility under it. *The crowd outside police headquarters began chanting, "No justice, no peace."*

Kangaroo

Kangaroo Court: a self-appointed group, generally the one yielding the power, who decides the kind of punishment to those who are supposed to have done wrong. *It was admitted years later by prosecutors how the government used the justice system as their own kangaroo court to jail dissidents and keep control over other antagonists.*

Keel

Keel over: 1) to overturn; turn upside down. *While taking sailing lessons in the marina, my sails took more wind that I could control, and the boat keeled over.* 2) To die; to faint or fall down. *Many newcomers to the tropics who overexert themselves, often keel over from the grueling heat and humidity.*

On an even keel: stable; firm; well-balanced. *The company has been operating pretty much on an even keel after emerging from bankruptcy protection last year.*

Keep

Earn one's keep: *See,* **Earn**.

For keeps: 1) possess what you win. *When we play marbles, we play for keeps.* 2) for always; forever. *He left our school for keeps.* 3) it's serious (not funny) and it's real (not a joke). *This is not a drill; it's for keeps.*

Keep a civil tongue: to be polite or respectful when speaking. *He was angry as hell at his boss, but he otherwise kept a civil tongue throughout the meeting.*

Keep a high profile: be in the limelight or in the public eye; be noticed. *He likes to keep a high profile since he savors the attention.*

Keep a low profile: stay discreet or out of sight. *We had to keep a very low profile as there were bandits everywhere in the countryside.*

Keep a stiff upper lip: face trouble or challenges bravely; remain embolden or confident. *The plane lost its hydraulic power and was losing control fast, but the pilot kept a stiff upper lip and landed the aircraft without any serious injuries. She keeps a stiff upper lip when times get rough.*

Keep a straight face: 1) try not to laugh. *We could not keep a straight face when we saw the football players dressed as cheerleaders.* 2) keep the same expression. *Nathan is real good in poker because he can keep a straight face.*

Keep an eye out/Keep a sharp eye: be watchful for; keenly watch out. *Keep an eye out for Bob, and alert us if you see him. Keep an eye out for bad weather when sailing.*

Keep cool: remain calm. *Bob knows how to keep his cool during those contentious corporate meetings.*

Keep house: do the necessary household chores such as cleaning and cooking. *After he broke his hip, he had helpers come in daily to keep house.*

Keep in mind: don't forget. *Keep in mind that the park closes at sundown.*

Keep in step with/Keep up with: maintain progress with another. *The police budget was increased again in order to keep in step with controlling the criminal element.*

Keep in the dark: *See,* **In the dark.**

Keep in touch: a request to continue communicating with another. *We shall keep in touch no matter what happens in the future.*

Keep it under one's hat: maintain secrecy; don't say anything about it. *Let's keep this discussion under our hat, okay? I heard that they are going to lay off employees after the merger, but keep the news under your hat until it's announced publicly.*

Keep it up: 1) continue to try and do well. *We were told to keep it up and not slow down until the next work crew arrived.* 2) just continue to act that way and see what happens. *Keep it up and you will be in big trouble.*

Keep late hours: habitually stay awake into late at night. *I have been keeping late hours since that big project started six months ago.*

Keep on truckin': continue with the effort. *Hey man, I know you'll make it to the Olympics. Keep on truckin'!*

Keep one posted: stay informed or up-to-date. *Please keep me posted on Sadie's medical condition.*

Keep one's chin up: *See,* **Chin.**

Keep one's distance: avoid socializing or establishing intimate contacts. *We kept our distance after the big fight last week, but got together again to make up our differences.*

Keep one's end up: to do one's portion of the work. *If you can't keep your end up in this job, you'll be fired.*

Keep one's eye on the ball: stay focused; be watchful. *If Sedgwick wants to do well at this company, then he'll have to keep his eye on the ball.*

Keep one's feet on the ground: *See,* **Feet**.

Keep one's fingers crossed: *See,* **Cross** one's fingers.

Keep one's head: remain calm; take it easy. *Just keep your head and you'll be fine.*

Keep one's head above water: *See,* **Head**.

Keep one's nose clean: *See,* **Clean**.

Keep one's temper: *See,* **Hold** one's temper.

Keep one's trap shut: don't talk; shut up. *He kept on cutting into the conversation until someone told him to keep his trap shut.*

Keep one's word: commit to a promise. *He kept his word and completed the job.*

Keep pace: to do as well as or go as fast as. *I have to study twice as hard just to keep pace with your I.Q.*

Keep plugging along: to continue to work hard, in the daily road in life. *My parents just keep plugging along, preferring the predictable, conservative lifestyle.*

Keep tabs on/Keep track of: to follow or watch. *We need to keep tabs on the inventory so that we have enough supplies at any time during the event.*

Keep the ball rolling: continue with an activity or action without slowing down or stopping. *We need to keep the ball rolling on this road trip or we will not make our destination in time.*

Keep the faith: to not give up or lose hope; remain always committed. *We kept our faith and survived the long journey through the mountainous war zone.*

Keep the lid on: keep quiet about; do not disclose. *We were told to keep the lid on the situation by not discussing it with anyone until the investigation is finished.*

Keep the pot boiling: sustain an ongoing activity as well as possible. *Just keep the pot boiling on this surveillance action and I will get authority to continue the investigation for another week.*

Keep things humming: to work to maintain smooth and productive operation. *Quality control personnel are needed to keep things humming around here.*

Keep it to yourself: maintain secrecy. *Keep it to yourself that I plan on moving to another job.*

Keep under one's hat: keep confidential. *Please keep this under your hat so that she will not know about the party we are preparing for her.*

Keep up appearances: to maintain an outward showing of well-being. *They no longer could keep up appearances at the country club and had to file for bankruptcy.*

Keep up with the Joneses: *See under,* **Jones**.

Keep up with the times: be up to date or fashionable. *We want to be more nimble so that we can keep up with the times in the technology world today.*

Keep your eyes peeled: be on the lookout; remain on the alert; be watchful. *Keep your eyes peeled for that stolen car.*

Keep your pants on: take it easy; you be calm. *Just keep your pants on; I'll be there real soon.*

Keep your powder dry: stay prepared for action. *We may need you to teach the others how to operate the new machinery, so keep your powder dry.*

Keep your shirt on: don't get excited; relax. *Keep your shirt on; we'll find another flight for you.*

Keeping it real: being cool and collected. *I'm just keepin' it real.*

Kick

For kicks/Get one's kicks: for enjoyment or thrills; for the hell of it. *What do you do for kicks around here?*

Get a kick out of something: an action that brings on enjoyment or thrill in a person. *He got a kick out of going to the ballgame with his father.*

(I can) Kick myself: to be upset for doing or not doing something; to regret. *I can kick myself for not remembering to bring my wallet with me.*

Kick ass/Kick booty/Kick butt: 1) move fast. *This car can kick ass!* 2) take on a challenge with full force and confidence; play hard. *Let's kick butt in today's ballgame!*

Kick back: to take it easy; relax; unstress oneself. *We like to kick back and watch a ball game after work.*

Kick in: to pay one's share. *We each kicked in some money to buy her a birthday gift.*

Kick in the ass/Kick in the pants: 1) realization; to spur someone to action. *That accident was a kick in the pants for me to not drive after drinking alcohol.* 2) very funny; fun to be with. *She's witty and a kick in the pants.*

Kick it around: to have an open discussion about some matter. *I think we should kick this around some more before we decide what to do.*

Kick one around: mistreat another; act in a rude manner. *I got tired of being kicked around at my last job.*

Kick the bucket: to perish; die. *Mrs. Armstrong was 101 years old when she finally kicked the bucket.*

Kick the habit: to stop or break a habit (generally a bad habit). *It is not always easy for a smoker to kick the habit.*

Kick the living daylights/hell/tar/shit (expressive) **out of:** *See,* **Beat** the living daylights/hell/tar/shit (expressive) **out of.**

Kick up a fuss: to be very agitated and reactive. *She is kicking up quite a fuss about the caterer's handling of the banquet.*

Kick up a storm: to cause an uproar. *He kicked up a storm trying to teach the gospel to a group of devout Muslims.*

Kick up one's heels: show spirit; enjoy yourself; have a good time. *I like to kick up my heels at Dewey's Ale House with friends after a hard day's work.*

Kickback: to remit a portion of one's (illegal) profits to another (generally to an agent or facilitator). *He had to apply much of his profits toward kickback payments.*

Kickin': relaxed; taking it easy. *Yeah, we just kickin' and shootin' the breeze.*

Kid

Kid: to joke or fool around. *Quit kidding around and get serious with your work.*

Kid's stuff: a matter that is easy to do; so easy that a kid could do it. *Assembling this computer is kid's stuff.*

Handle with kid gloves: *See,* **Handle.**

No kidding: *See,* **No.**

Kill

A killer: extremely hilarious. *He is a real killer as a comic and usually draws large crowds at clubs in town.*

A killing/Make a killing: an extreme amount in monetary value; a lot of money. *He made a killing in the real estate market, then lost most of it in the stock market.*

Curiosity killed the cat: *See,* **Cat.**

Dressed to kill: *See,* **Dress.**

Kill off: to end completely. *Deforestation of the world's jungles is killing off species we will never see in the wild again.*

Kill the goose that laid the golden egg: to eliminate the source of one's livelihood. *Creating an adversary relationship with the boss is like killing the goose that laid the golden egg.*

Kill time: to let time pass at a leisurely pace; to spend time without accomplishing much. *Let's go to town and kill some time. We decided to kill some time at the arcade center before our train arrived.*

Kill two birds with one stone: to get two things accomplished with one task. *He can kill two birds with one stone by buying both gifts at the same store.*

Kiss

Kiss and make up: when a couple makes matters favorable again between each other; to kiss and be friends again. *After many months, they decided to kiss and make up.*

Kiss ass/Ass kisser: to flatter another to gain their favor. *He really kisses ass each time the boss visits the facility.*

Kiss it goodbye: to accept that something is gone forever; to relent in the understanding that something is now gone. *You can kiss that promotion goodbye if you can't pass the proficiency exam.*

Kiss of death: an action that proves to be fatal in an endeavor; something that is ultimately disastrous or deadly. *Eating the delicious blowfish in Japanese sushi can be the kiss of death if not properly prepared.*

Kiss my ass: *See,* **Ass**.

Kiss off/Kiss-off: 1) to tell someone rudely to go away. *I told that obnoxious and drunk individual to kiss off and not bother us anymore.* 2) the rejection or dismissal of another with little respect. *Sedgwick was surprised and angered at the sudden kiss-off by Mary at the mall.*

Kiss up to someone: to be nice to another to win their affection or confidence. *Jackson seems to be kissing up to the boss during his evaluation period.*

Kisser: lips. *She let him have it right on the kisser; he went out like a light.*

Kit

Kit and caboodle: *See,* **Whole** kit and caboodle.

Klick

Klick: kilometer, which equals about 6/10ths of a mile (also written as **click**). *It's about 50 klicks to the next gas station.*

Klutz

Klutz: very clumsy. *My brother is a real klutz in sports.*

Knee

Bring to one's knees: to force another to give up or surrender. *The great depression of the 1930's brought many families almost to their knees trying to survive.*

Knee deep: very much involved. *I am already knee deep financially in the construction project, so I can't give up now.*

Knee high to a grasshopper: When one was very small or young. *I haven't seen Billy since he was knee high to a grasshopper.*

Knee-jerk reaction/response: an automatic reaction or response. *The stock spiked up $10.00 in a knee-jerk response to the unsubstantiated story, only to settle down days later.*

Knick

Knick: a small cut. *I got a knick going through the doorway this morning.*

Knick knack: small, generally useful or sentimental items. *I packed a few extra knick knacks for the camping trip. You have a lot of knick knacks from the 1920 Yankees on display.*

Knickers: 1) athletic shoes. *You will have to wear your leather shoes instead of your knickers to church.* 2) short pair of pants (or real long shorts). *Baggy knickers are in style with the junior high and high school students.*

Knife

Go under the knife: surgery. *Jim is going under the knife tomorrow to fix his hernia.*

Knife through butter: *See,* **Like** knife through butter.

You could cut it with a knife: *See,* **Cut**.

Knock

Don't knock it: don't criticize it (but otherwise appreciate the value of something). *Don't knock it until you have tried it.*

Knock around: 1) be treated roughly. *The culprit was knocked around by the local citizens before the police arrived to take him to jail.* 2) to discuss. *Let's knock around the idea about buying the company before we commit to it.*

Knock (back) on one's heels/Knock to one's heels: a sudden, unexpected surprise. *Mackey was knocked to his heels to find that he was not selected for the team.*

Knock down: reduce; lower. *We need to knock down the selling price of the house in order to attract interested buyers.*

Knock down, drag out: a heavy fight or challenge; tough situation; unrestrained action. *The animosity between the groups resulted in a knock down, drag out fight after school.*

Knock for a loop/Throw someone for a loop: to suddenly be surprised. *We were knocked for a loop to hear that he decided to live in the mountains. My long-time single friend threw me for a loop when he told me he got married.*

Knock it off: a directive to stop talking or discontinue doing something; shut up. *Knock it off kids; I can't hear Grandma on the phone.*

Knock off: a reproduction or copy; a fake. *This watch is a knock off and not the real thing.*

Knock off one's feet: to surprise and leave one in awe or disbelief; be dumbfounded. *We were knocked off our feet when our dog won best of show at Westminster.*

Knock on wood: a saying or action for good luck (and to prevent bad luck) about a particular matter, accompanied by knocking on some piece of wood. *I knock on wood whenever I tell people that I have never been sick.*

Knock out: 1) a hard blow to the head. *He doesn't remember a thing after being knocked out.* 2) someone stunning in beauty. *From being a little girl with buck teeth, she has grown up to become a knock out. She is such a knock out that my heart races when she is near.* 3) render helpless or inoperable. *The soldiers, behind enemy lines, knocked out the radar site with explosive charges.*

Knock someone off: to murder. *The gang members were convicted of knocking him off.*

Knock someone's block off: to beat or defeat another; to hit one very hard. *The sailor is in jail for knocking his block off last night.*

Knock someone's socks off: 1) to have someone become overly impressed and excited. *Her brilliant scientific discovery on microbes simply knocked my socks off.* 2) to be very attracted emotionally. *She knocked my socks off the first time I saw her.*

Knock the lid off: to mess up a situation; spoil something. *We captured the traitor before he had the chance to knock the lid off our surprise attack on the fort.*

Knock the living daylights/hell/stuffing/tar/shit (expressive) **out of:** to beat someone senseless or render someone unconscious physically (also can be stated metaphorically or in exaggeration). *He knocked the living* *daylights out of Jack, who awoke several minutes later with an enormous headache. They knocked the stuffing out of us in the game.*

Knock yourself out: to make a great effort; to try hard to achieve. *Go knock yourself out, kid, and do good in this world.*

Knocked cold: rendered unconscious. *He was knocked cold when he collided with the other player on the field.*

Knocked up [expressive]: made pregnant. *Our dog apparently got knocked up last month when she escaped from the house for a couple days.*

Know

Know by heart: able to remember by memory. *He knew by heart the names of every person who signed the Declaration of Independence.*

Know it all: one who presumes to know more than others around him, but is generally ignorant to realizing the true situation; an individual who ignorantly thinks he or she knows it all, but really doesn't. *I don't like the guy because he acts like a know-it-all.*

Know like a book: *See,* **Book**.

Know people in high places: to have connections with another in a position of authority or power (comedic slang: to know one in low places). *He can get much done for our community because he knows people in high places who can bring in the funding.*

Know the ropes: *See,* **Rope**.

Not know beans/Not know shit (from shinola) (expressive): a phrase indicating that one has no knowledge about a particular matter; very ignorant or uninformed.

Not know if someone is coming or going: in a shock-like state; not thinking clearly; to not know what to do or where to go. *After the chaos caused by the strong earthquake, most people didn't know whether they were coming or going.*

Not know one's ass from a hole in the ground: *See,* **Ass**.

Not know someone from Adam: a phrase indicating that one does not know a particular individual at all. *I don't know him from Adam.*

Knuckle

Knuckle down: to get serious about doing something; very dedicated to work hard. *We have to knuckle down so that we can keep up with the large work orders.*

Knuckle sandwich: a punch with one's fist. *He gave the neighborhood bully a knuckle sandwich right between the eyes.*

Knuckle under: give in; be beaten. *Never knuckle under to your adversary.*

Knucklebrain/Knucklehead: dummy; fool; ignorant or unwise person. *That knucklehead doesn't know enough to stay out of trouble.*

Kook

Kook: an odd person; someone not ordinary or a little crazy. *I am having a hard time trying to figure out whether this guy is some sort of kook or just an eccentric individual.*

Kooky: weird. *That kid down the block in our neighborhood is sort of kooky. It sounds kooky to me.*

Kosher

Kosher: real fine; of approved quality. *Whatever my children want to become in life is kosher with me.*

Labor

Belabor the point/Labor the point: to explain too much or more than is needed for understanding. *I don't want to belabor the point, but it is important that we must not go over budget on this project.*

Labor of love: something done for personal satisfaction rather than for money or profit. *His skills and knack in inventing things started out from a labor of love because it gave him a feeling of accomplishment.*

Labor under: to endure or be under the strain of. *He is laboring under the false impression that she will return and reconcile with him.*

Lady

Bag lady: homeless woman who carries her possessions in a shopping bag. *The bag lady on this street minds her own business and bothers no one.*

Lady: aside from the true meaning of a person who is a respectable female, the slang reference is used generically by name as a directive to a female individual from someone, likely a male individual, who might feel imposed upon or who intends to be more direct rather than polite. *Listen lady, you have no authority to tell us to leave this building.*

Lady friend: a female friend (connotations vary, from being a platonic acquaintance to a lover. Used according to the context of the conversation). *His lady friend has been seen going to dinner with him after work.*

Lady killer: a man who has a woman fall in love with him, then abandons her and breaks her heart, or a male individual who makes women seriously awestruck or stunned. *John is a lady killer, so I hope you are not serious with him.*

Lady of the house: the woman or wife of the household; hostess. *I have some wallpaper samples to show the lady of the house.*

Lady's man: a male individual quite popular when associating with a woman. *Tom, who was very shy and unbecoming as a child, grew up to be a real lady's man.*

Till the fat lady sings: *See,* **Till**.

Laid

Laid out: arranged. *See also,* **Layout**. *The furniture in her house is very nicely laid out.*

Laid up: bedridden; sick. *I was laid up for a few days with the flu.*

Lame

Lame ass: *See,* **Ass**.

Lame brain: dim-wit; person of low intelligence or standards; one with a lack of knowledge. *We don't need any more lame brains in this office.*

Lame duck: an elected official whose term in office is scheduled to end and therefore is unable to attract enough political backing for his or her initiatives. *As a lame duck, his last year in office was spent more on fishing for trout than garnering political votes.*

Land

Fat of the land: *See,* **Fat**.

Get the lay of the land/Lay of the land: *See,* **Lay**.

Land all over/Land on: *Same as,* **Jump** all over/Jump on: to criticize; scold. *The coach landed all over him for a poor performance at football practice.*

Land on one's feet/Land on both feet: to get out of trouble or be able to gain control; to be successful. *He luckily seems to land on his feet after every disaster.*

Lap

In the lap of the gods: beyond human control. *Natural disasters are in the lap of the gods.*

Lap

Lap up: 1) to take in eagerly. *Ever since he got onto the Olympic team, he has been lapping up the praise and notoriety from adoring fans.* 2) to eat or drink with the tip of the tongue. *The milk disappears from the bowl because the puppies seem to lap it up so quickly.*

Lap of luxury: well cared for; in a very comfortable setting; surrounded with expensive things. *Unlike most of the students at school, he grew up in a lap of luxury.*

Last

At (long) last: after a long wait. *At long last, we finally found our lost dog.*

Last but not least: last to be mentioned but not the least important. *Last but not least, please remember to bring in the houseplants from outside before going to sleep so they won't freeze.*

Last-ditch effort: final and last try. *We searched the flooded plain in a last-ditch effort to rescue any animals.*

Last gasp: literally, one's last moment before death; figuratively, one's final effort. *In his last gasp, he admitted to his fiancée that he was gay.*

Last resort: a final option. *As a last resort, we can mail the merchandise rather than take it with us on the plane.*

Last straw: See, **Straw**.

On its last lap/On one's last lap: See below, **On its last leg**.

On its last leg/On one's last leg: not far from being dead, terminated, or done with. *We were on our last leg when rescuers finally arrived and saved us.*

Laugh

Have the Last laugh: See, **Have**.

Laugh up one's sleeve/Laugh in one's sleeve: to be amused but not reveal it; laugh unnoticed. *We were laughing up our sleeves when the boss fell off his chair at the meeting.*

Laugh (it) away: attempt to laugh to try to forget something or cover an embarrassment. *He tried to laugh away his loss, but when he realized that it included his rent money, he began to cry.*

Laugh up a storm: to laugh out raucously or very hard. *We laughed up a storm when we saw John enter the stage dressed as a sumo wrestler.*

Laughing matter: a joking or silly incident (usually used in the negative context). *Failing the bar exam to become an attorney is no laughing matter.*

LOL: laugh out loud. *We were LOL at the Robin Williams concert last night.*

That's a laugh: something thought to be comically ridiculous. *That's a laugh to think that he can defend his case without good counsel.*

200

Law

Brush with the law: *See,* **Brush**.

Common law: *See,* **Common**.

Common law marriage: *See,* **Common**.

Law and order: strict enforcement of the laws. *The opposite of law and order is chaos and mayhem.*

Law of averages: in the totality of circumstances, probability will influence the outcome of events; in the long run, things will average out. *One should understand the law of averages in the game of blackjack.*

Law of the jungle: survival of the fittest or strongest. *The law of the jungle rules in this part of the country.*

Law unto oneself: one who is independent, and disregards convention or established rules. *You could never tell Old Man Rivers what to do because he was a law unto himself.*

Lay down the law: *See,* **Lay**.

Letter of the law: The exact wording, in contrast to the spirit or intent behind the words. *The spirit of the law, in large part based in equity, is argued in defense to overcome the letter of the law.*

Long arm of the law: the far-reaching authority of law enforcement to catch suspects. *The long arm of the law finally caught up with Old Man Rivers after twenty years undetected, and after fathering five children.*

Possession is nine-tenths of the law: possessing something is more important than making a claim to it. *In the old days, it was tough if you wanted to claim something lost because possession was nine-tenths of the law; the one who held it owned it.*

Take the law into one's (own) hands: Take over or wrest control, generally due to the breakdown or weakness in established authority; to do as one wishes with no regard for the law. *If there is no justice, there will be no peace, because the people will take the law into their own hands. Chaos will reign if the masses are allowed to take the law into their own hands. The laws must be meaningful in an ordered society, or else the populace might rebel and take the law into their own hands.*

Unwritten law: an accepted but informal rule of behavior. *It is an unwritten law that you can smoke cigars with the judge in his chambers.*

Lay

Lay away: to save. *I am trying to lay away some funds for next year's ski vacation.*

Lay down one's life/Lay one's life on the line/Lay one's ass on the line (expressive): to sacrifice one's life for a cause or for another. *Bodyguards often lay down their lives to protect their client.*

Lay down the law: enforce the rules. *New management is serious in laying down the law about how the work schedule will be arranged.*

Lay eyes on: to see and behold. *You won't believe it until you lay your eyes on that beautiful antique. Hey, lay your eyes on that thing.*

Lay hands on (someone): to harm; hurt; to do violence to. *If I ever lay hands on the thief who stole my friend's car, I'll arrest him myself.*

Lay hands on (something): to get hold of or to locate something. *If I can lay my hands on my telescope, I can tell you more about the stars tonight.*

Lay into/Lay on: to pressure; to attack. *The professor laid into him quite harshly for not reading the assignment and being prepared for class.*

Lay it on (someone): 1) to exaggerate. *He really tried to lay it on her about his important job at the plant, hoping that she would be impressed enough to go out with him.* 2) to beat up or to yell at; meet with force, either verbally or physically. *The boss really laid it on the subordinate about his lackluster performance.*

Lay it on the line: to state something clearly and plainly; to speak truthfully. *The supervisor had to lay it on the line with a warning to the employees about eating and drinking while working on the assembly line. Just lay it on the line and tell me what's on your mind.*

Lay it on thick: praise someone too much. *She really began to lay it on thick when she met the new doctor on the hospital staff.*

Lay low: keep out of sight; hide. *We had to lay low until nightfall in order to escape from the bandits.*

Lay of the land: have a good understanding of the surroundings or the local environment. *The Indian scout knows the lay of the land as good as anyone around.*

Lay off: 1) to get rid of workers when business is sour. *When there are lay offs at the mill, the whole town suffers.* 2) stop bothering; leave alone. *Lay off the little kids and challenge others more your size.*

Lay one's cards on the table: be honest; reveal the truth. *He decided to lay the cards on the table and tell his supervisor that he was leaving the company.*

Lay one's life on the line: *See above,* **Lay down one's life.**

Lay oneself open: allowing oneself to be placed in a vulnerable or unfavorable position. *You lay yourself open with such a plan like that; the adversary will discover your strategy in very little time.*

Lay out: to spend or pay out money. *We had to lay out a few extra dollars to get the sports car model.*

Lay rubber: when a car or motorcycle's tire spins on the road surface so fast as to leave a mark on the pavement. *That fast car can lay a lot of rubber on the road!*

Lay someone out: to knock unconscious. *He laid him out with a hard right punch to the face.*

Lay to rest: 1) to bury someone. *Our grandfather was finally laid to rest after 95 years and a full life.* 2) to bring to ease; to be resolved permanently. *The townspeople's fears were laid to rest when the armed fugitive was captured and arrested.*

Lay waste: to cause widespread destruction and damage; to leave in ruins. *The huge flood laid waste to many towns and villages.*

Layover: to arrive and stay in a temporary place before moving on. *We had a layover in Denver for a few hours before connecting on our flight to Washington State.*

Lead

Get the lead out (of your pants): stop wasting time, and get going. *Get the lead out and finish this project now.*

Lead a dog's life: to have a hard life, and be treated unkindly. *You must act wisely and work twice as hard in this world so that you don't end up having to lead a dog's life.*

Lead balloon: *See,* **Balloon**.

Lead foot/Leadfoot: someone who tends to drive fast. *I don't ride with him because he's a lead foot behind the wheel.*

Lead (someone) by the nose: to influence; have control over others. *Don't let any salesperson lead you by the nose when shopping for a new car.*

Leaf

Leaf through: to read over or glance through something, generally papers or some reading material. *The lawyer quickly leafed through his notes before conducting the examination of the witness at trial.*

Turn over a new leaf: to start afresh, using a new method of approach; a new beginning. *John turned over a new leaf when he started his exercise program and lost 25 kilos.*

Lean

Lean on: 1) to pressure another with threats of physical violence, black-mail or withholding of a favor to have the person comply with a demand. *The local gangsters in the early days leaned on the street vendors for a percentage of their earned revenue.* 2) to depend on someone for help. *Everyone needs someone to lean on.*

Lean over backwards: *See,* **Back** (Bend over backwards.)

Leave

Leave a bad taste in one's mouth: to have a bad impression of. *There is something about that person that leaves a bad taste in my mouth.*

Leave at the altar: to decide not to marry someone at the last minute. *He was stunned when she left him at the altar.*

Leave it at that: to not argue or discuss further; to avoid further and more heated disagreement. *We will never agree, so let's just leave it at that.*

Leave no stone unturned: check everything thoroughly. *The police will leave no stone unturned in their search for the missing child.*

Leave someone high and dry: *See,* **High**.

Left

Hang a left: take a left turn. *Hang a left at the next intersection.*

Left-handed compliment: an ambiguous compliment seen as offensive or rude. *He gave them a left-handed compliment about their pierced jewelry and spiked hair.*

Left holding the bag: *See,* **Bag**.

Left in the cold: ignored; neglected. *Many long-time workers were left in the cold when the company suddenly fired them.*

Leftovers: food remaining from a previous meal. *We are going to have left-overs for dinner tonight.*

Left wing: a group or organization of people favoring more radical change in political policies. *The left-wing parties voted unanimously for a general strike.*

Right and left: *See,* **Right**.

Leg

Arm and a leg: *See,* **Arm**.

Have a leg to stand on: factual defense to support a claim. *He doesn't have a leg to stand on, arguing how a racist faction in a diverse community would encourage community cohesion.*

Have a leg up: be ahead. *If you start early in the morning, you'll have a leg up in getting more things done today.*

Legroom: adequate space to feel comfortable. *We had very little legroom on the crowded flight.*

Legwork: anything requiring effort, research, study, etc. *We will need to do a lot of legwork to make this project a success.*

On its last leg/On one's last leg: *See,* **Last.**

Pull someone's leg: try to fool someone with a silly story; make someone try to believe an untrue story just for a joke. *I was just pulling your leg with that story.*

Legal

Legal crook/crookery/Legal trickery: an action that might be within the law but appears deceptive and unfaithful in practice. *It was legal crookery to see how the state insurance commissioner secretly settled with major insurance companies in compromising thousands of consumer claims for earthquake damage.*

Legal eagle: an attorney who is well versed in the law he or she practices; rainmaker. *You can be sure that his wealth can buy the best legal eagles in the country to defend his business and accounting practices.*

Lemon

Lemon: a defective product, generally referred to a vehicle. *This car is a lemon; it broke down a week after I bought it from the dealer.*

Let

Let bygones be bygones: forget about past concerns or problems, with an understanding of forgiveness or openness. *We should let bygones be bygones and not let our past differences divide us any longer.*

Let down: disappointment; failing to do as expected. *Losing to the last-place team was a real let down.*

Let grass grow under one's feet: be lazy or waste time; let time idly go by without doing much if anything. *Knowing her as a very busy person, she is not the type to let grass grow under her feet.*

Let (him) down easy: to refuse or deny someone in a pleasant rather than nasty way. *Knowing that he was a sensitive guy, she was thinking what to say to him to let him down easy.*

Let it all hang out: behave without restraint; let the truth be known; don't disguise anything. *She let it all hang out after getting angry with the used car salesman who sold her the broken-down car.*

Let it ('em) rip/Let it ('em) roll: go forward; proceed ahead; get going; ok to begin. *The dogs were ready to race as the referee shouted, "let 'em rip!"*

Let it slide/Let someone slide: neglect what you were supposed to do. *Sam let his homework slide until test time, then it was too late to study.*

Let it ride: to continue without changing a situation. *"Let it ride," said the player to the dealer about his chips on the craps table.*

Let loose: to take action without restraint or consideration. *He let loose on him and hit him hard for trying to burglarize his residence.*

Let off: discharged; exploded. *The fireworks were let off by an errant spark. The children let off firecrackers on the Fourth of July holiday.*

Let off steam: *See,* **Steam**.

Let off the hook: excuse from responsibility; to not be reprimanded or prosecuted. *The police let him off the hook this time.*

Let someone have it: hit someone hard. *He let him have it in retaliation for harming the innocent dog.*

Let sleeping dogs lie: don't disturb or unsettle the situation; don't make trouble if it can be avoided. *You should let sleeping dogs lie and not worry what he said to you last week.*

Let's split: leave from someplace; go away. *Let's split to another party.*

Let the cat out of the bag: *See,* **Cat**.

Let the chips fall where they may: prepare for any outcome, good or bad; don't worry about results of one's actions. *We cannot worry about the company's tough times, but to only work hard and smart, then let the chips fall where they may.*

Let up: 1) to have stopped or become weaker. *The rain seemed to have let up for now.* 2) to slow down or stop working. *His physician informed him to either let up on his overburdened work schedule or run the risk of sickness in the future.* 3) to not taunt another. *Let up on him, will you?*

Level

Level: to knock out; to immobilize. *The obnoxious bully was leveled by a good punch to the jaw.*

Level best: to do one's best. *We did our level best to get the job done as quickly as possible.*

Levelheaded: even-tempered, especially while under stress. *This job requires a levelheaded person with experience.*

Level with someone/On the level: speak truthfully; be sincere; speak with no tricks or joking involved; straight talk. *On the level, tell me what you know.*

Lick

Lick into shape: work or drill to perfection; to train. *At training camp, the players are licked into shape.*

Lick one's boots: make every effort to please another. *She has her subordinates at work licking her boots.*

Lick one's chops: to selfishly enjoy a pleasant thought; to wait in great anticipation. *We were licking our chops at the thought of winning the big government contract.*

Lick the living daylights/hell/tar/shit (expressive) **out of:** *See,* **Beat** the living daylights/hell/tar/shit (expressive) **out of.**

Licked: beat; defeated soundly. *We got licked in today's ball game.*

Lickety-split: prompt; priority rush; get it done as soon as possible. *We will have the problems resolved lickety-split. The job was done lickety-split, with time to spare.*

Lie (See also, Lying)

Lie down on the job: not work hard; goof off. *We cannot depend on him if he continues to lie down on the job.*

Lie in state: public viewing a corpse in an open coffin, generally in honor of a famous person. *The President will lie in state for the next three days.*

Lie in wait: watch another while hiding, and be poised for attack. *The police decided to lie in wait for the bank robbery suspect.*

Lie like a rug: go to lengths not to tell the truth. *These kids will lie like a rug to get a piece of candy.*

Lie low: stay quietly out of view; try not to attract attention. *We need to lie low until the authorities get here.*

Life

Bring to life: to bring back to consciousness. *The lifeguard was able to bring the child back to life after drowning in the pool.*

Come to life: be active or lively. *Let's show some spunk and come to life around here.*

Facts of life: reality. *We live and die; those are the facts of life.*

For dear life: 1) with desperate effort. *For dear life, he always tried to get off his drug habit.* 2) for fear of one's life. *With the floodwaters breaking the dam, he ran like hell for dear life.*

For the life of me: cannot understand or resolve in one's mind. *For the life of me, I can't understand why she would want to go there.*

High life: *See,* **High**.

Improve one's lot in life: make one's reputation or character look better to others. *Staying in this company will likely not improve your lot in life; there are better opportunities.*

Lay one's life on the line: *See,* **Lay**.

Life is a bed of roses: expressing the comfort or easiness in life. *Life is a bed of roses for him compared to many others who live so marginally.*

Life is not a bed of roses: expressing the difficulties in life. *Life is not a bed of roses for many working families.*

Life of Riley: the easy life. *He seems to be living the life of Riley.*

Life of the party: one who brings enjoyment or excitement. *We invite Jerry to our gatherings because he is the life of the party.*

Low life: *See,* **Low**.

New lease on life: *See,* **New**.

Night life: See, **Night**.

Not on your life: by no means. *I'm not leaving them stranded on the island; not on your life.*

Lift

Lift: 1) get a ride. *Can I have a lift to the grocery store?* 2) to steal. *The little boys tried to lift a few packs of chewing gum from the counter, but were caught by the sharp-eyed employee.* 3) reaction. *We tried to cheer him up, but couldn't get a lift out of him.* 4) a laugh; an exciting moment. *We got a lift watching the teacher scold the bully in the class.*

Light

Came/Come to light: brought to one's knowledge; brought under public scrutiny. *When the political kickbacks came to light, several long-term politicians had to resign in disgrace.*

Caution light: the yellow light in a traffic signal. *Since he passed through the intersection on a caution light, he didn't get a traffic infraction.*

In light of: with the knowledge of. *We should remain calm in light of the terrorist threats.*

Light at the end of the tunnel: despite bad times, the situation will look brighter in the future; expect better times ahead. *Despite the horrors of war, there was light at the end of the tunnel for many of the brave souls who endured.*

Light-fingered/Light-fingered Louie: *See,* **Finger**.

Light of day: come to understand. *The community finally saw the light of day about preserving old-growth forests after witnessing loggers cut down 800 year-old spruce trees in the area.*

Light one's fire: get one excited, either joyfully or sexually. *Elvis in concert would always light the fire of his fans; it was unmatched in his time. "Come on baby, light my fire."* (Song by Jose Feliciano).

Light up: 1) start smoking. *Several of us light up after every work break.* 2) suddenly be pleased and happy. *I cannot wait to see the smiles that will light up the faces of the children at class when the magician arrives.*

Out like a light: *See,* **Out**.

Put one's lights out: to make unconscious, immobile or dead. *She put his lights out with a punch to his face.*

See the light: *See,* **See**.

Shed some light (on the subject): to tell more about something; to better understand or inform. *The news investigation helped to shed some light on the plight of the homeless.*

Like

Like: kind of; in explanation about. *You know, it was like real bad when the cops just pushed everyone around without any warning.*

Like a bat out of hell: *See,* **Bat**.

Like a broken record: *See,* **Record**.

Like a pig in slop/Like a pig in shit (expressive): extreme happiness. *After Albert won the state lottery, he acted for months like a pig in shit.*

Like a sitting duck: being exposed and vulnerable to attack. *We are like sitting ducks out here unless we find some cover.*

Like a three-ring circus: chaotic and full of commotion. *This isn't a work area; it's a three-ring circus.*

Like crazy: something done excitedly and/or excessively. *We spotted Helen buying clothes like crazy at the department store's annual sale. We were looking around like crazy trying to find you!*

Like it or lump it: to either like something or not; to take it or leave it. *I did not like the music, and was told to like it or lump it.*

Like knife through butter: something that is so simple or easy to accomplish. *He got the job done like knife through butter.*

Like pasting jelly to the wall: *See,* **Wall**.

Like shit on goldfish: *See,* **Shit**.

Like shooting fish in a barrel: very easy to accomplish. *He told me that making money in this venture is like shooting fish in a barrel.*

Like water off a duck's back: *See,* **Water**.

Line

Bottom line: the answer in summary. *Skip the explanation and just tell me the bottom line as to what it will cost. Bottom line, it will cost $1,000 to do the work.*

Bring (someone) into line: have one conform to your instruction. *We need to bring the new recruit into line or else he will be discharged.*

Draw the line: *See,* **Draw**.

End of the line: no more; had enough. *We reached the end of the line with his bad attitude, and fired him.*

Hard line: *See,* **Hard**.

Hold the line: to wait, generally while on the phone. *Hold the line while I get a pen to write down your information.*

Lay it on the line/Put it on the line: placing oneself at risk, generally with a wager. *He laid it on the line and bet his entire funds in the championship poker tournament.*

Line one's pockets: to get money the crooked way. *As a politician, he soon lost his noble innocence when big corporate donors began to line his pockets with cash.*

Line something/someone up: to arrange. *Jack's friend tried to line up a date for him.*

On the line: at risk. *Our jobs will be on the line if the company is forced to downsize.*

Out of line: not conforming with instruction. *The students were reprimanded for being out of line for misbehaving during the lunch hour.*

On the line: to stake one's reputation. *He put his reputation on the line when he decided to purchase the local brewery.*

Read between the lines: look for hidden meaning or purpose. *If you read between the lines of the report, it is actually indicating that the financial situation will deteriorate in the coming months.*

Tow the line: carry one's load; follow set rules or orders strictly. *Every employee needs to tow the line around here.*

Lingo

Lingo: language; what is spoken in the area. *Yo, we speak da hip-hop lingo 'round dis place.*

Lion

Lion's share: to obtain or get a large portion of. *Jack got a lion's share of the reward for his great investigative work.*

Lip

Bite one's lip: make an effort not to reveal emotion. *We had to bite our lips to keep from laughing when the toddler pulled off Santa's beard.*

Don't give me any of your lip: don't bother or harass me. *Don't give me any of your lip about the company's poor performance without offering suggestions how it could be improved.*

Keep a stiff upper lip: face tough times with courage or dignity. *We kept a stiff upper lip throughout the unpleasant ordeal.*

Lip: inconsiderate talk. *I was scolded for giving lip to my uncle.*

Lip service: words of support but with no follow-up action. *I sense that they will only pay lip service to your proposal without providing any funding for it.*

My lips are sealed: to promise secrecy. *I won't tell a soul; my lips are sealed.*

Smack one's lips: 1) to hit or slap another. *I'll smack your lip if you don't stop hitting Billy. He smacked my lip when he caught me smoking in the shed.* 2) an expression of pleasure. *He was smacking his lips at the big winnings he made at the blackjack table.*

Tight-lipped: *See,* **Tight.**

Zip your lip: *See,* **Zip.**

Live

Live and breathe: to do or think about something constantly or all the time. *He lives and breathes baseball.*

Live and let live: tolerate others; have respect for others. *If you want others to treat you with respect, you have to live and let live.*

Live beyond one's means: spending more than one earns. *As Jack continues to live beyond his means, his debt grows more out of control.*

Live by one's wits: surviving by being clever. *All these years, she has been living by her wits while most people assumed she was some countess from a foreign land.*

Live down: to make an effort to remove blame or distrust by good conduct, which would provide cause for forgiveness. *He is trying to live down his early days as a drug addict by becoming involved in a number of community service organizations.*

Live (from) hand to mouth: *See,* **Hand.**

Live high on the hog: high-class living; to splurge. *Jack is living high on the hog after coming into wealth suddenly by inheritance.*

Live-in: live where one works, such as a domestic servant. *Our neighbor's housekeeper is a live-in.*

Live in an ivory tower: one who doesn't seem to grasp the real facts of life. *Some politicians seem to live in ivory towers, and do not take the time to understand the average everyday problems of their constituents.*

Live it up: have a joyous or wild time. *Let's live it up on our anniversary.*

Live off the fat of the land/Live the life of Riley/Live the high life: live in luxury or abundance. *He retired when he was 35, and is now living the high life.*

Live out of a suitcase: one who is always on the road or survives without a place to call home. *He has been living out of a suitcase, while desperately searching for a good job.*

Live up to: 1) try to reach a certain standard. *Sam certainly lives up to his goals.* 2) to back one's commitment. *The salesman failed to live up to his promises about the vehicle warranty.*

Living large: maintaining a lifestyle more than one can afford. *Deborah was living large on credit for a while until she found herself a well-paying job.*

Living on borrowed time: flirting with danger. *You are living on borrowed time with a risky job like that.*

Load

Carry the load/Carry a big load: be responsible for most of the work. *We can always depend on her because she carries her load.*

Get a load of: take a look at (presenting a situation of surprise). *Get a load of this; John got married on his trip to Las Vegas.*

Load off one's mind: great relief from worry; to have peace of mind. *It's a load off my mind to know that they finally caught the criminal who assaulted me.*

Loaded: 1) rich; have lots of money. *His uncle is really loaded.* 2) drunk. *We got loaded after our exams.*

Loaded for bear: 1) fully prepared for a headstrong challenge. *The disgruntled shareholders went to the annual meeting loaded for bear about executive compensation.* 2) fully developed; sexually attractive. *Boy, that Larissa is loaded for bear!*

Take a load off (one's feet): rest; relax; stop working. *Take a load off your feet and come have a cup of coffee with me.*

Lock

Lock horns: to fight or skirmish with. *We generally lock horns with our major competitors in business.*

LOCK HORNS

Lock, stock and barrel: everything imaginable. [This idiomatic expression came from the old Kentucky rifle days. A Kentucky rifle of the 1820-30's consisted of a lock, stock and a barrel, just a few parts, but which comprised the entire weapon.] *This carry-on travel case will hold what you need on the trip, lock, stock and barrel.*

Lock the barn door after the horse is gone: try to make good by being diligent or careful when it is already too late. *Securing the website codes after a computer breach is like locking the barn door after the horse is gone.*

Lock up: to be assured of success. *We have the deal all locked up.*

Locked in concrete: not subject to change. *This deal, once it is signed by the parties, will be locked in concrete.*

Long

At long last: *See,* **Last**.

Daddy longlegs: 1) insects or arachnids (such as spiders) with long legs. *There's a daddy longlegs under the bed!* 2) a thin, tall individual. *Everybody on that basketball team is a daddy longlegs.*

In the long run: through it all; overall; when all is said and done. *In the long run, things will turn out well for you.*

Long and short of it: the whole story in a nutshell or in a few words. *The long and short of it is that he always complains and cannot work with others.*

Long face: look of sadness or disappointment; unhappy. *Hey, why the long face? Jason wore a long face after being denied a promotion.*

Long haul: 1) a long trip. *That journey was a long haul through the woods. My uncle is a long-haul trucker in the United States.* 2) something that demands a long or extended period of time. *He is here for the long haul until the oil clean up is certified by the environmental authorities.*

Long row to hoe: a difficult and wearisome task [originated when farmers with horse plows used all their energy to make rows for planting crops]. *A law student has a long row to hoe before he can become a good defense lawyer.*

Long shot: 1) long odds; a risk very likely not to succeed. *Betting on the injured horse to win the race is certainly a long shot.* 2) by a great degree; soundly. *They beat us by a long shot, with runs to spare.*

Long-winded: very extended. *Fidel Castro is well-known for giving long-winded speeches that can last for hours.*

Make a long story short: *See,* **Make**.

Not by a long shot: *See,* **Not**.

Look

Look alive: be lively; work harder. *Ok, you guys, let's look alive around here.*

Look at: to think about something a certain way; having a way of thinking or feeling about something or someone. *Depending how you look at it, the social gathering could be seen as a pleasure or a bore.*

Look down on/Look down upon: condescend; to not treat equally. *You shouldn't look down upon your workers.*

Look for: to expect. *We look for the team to win the baseball tournament this year.*

Look forward to: to expect, generally with pleasure or hope. *Johnny is looking forward to a wonderful evening with Mary at the school dance.*

Look here: a phrase emphasizing the words that follow; a point for notation or focus. *Look here, I had nothing to do with that incident.*

Look in: to check up on or visit someone. *Please look in on him periodically to make sure he is well.*

Look like a million dollars: to look very well in posture and/or in dress. *You look like a million dollars today!*

Look sharp: 1) to be alert or very attentive. *Look sharp when you give your presentation.* 2) to be well dressed or manicured. *Mr. Harvey looks sharp tonight.*

Look (someone) in the face: to assure sincerity or honesty. *Look me in the face and tell me that you didn't do it.*

Look (someone) up: to seek and find. *Look me up when you get to Seattle, and I will show you around the area.*

Look up: 1) to search for information. *It is always a good idea to look up words in the dictionary that you do not understand.* 2) someone referred to as a mentor or good example to follow. *The little kids always look up to the Padre because of his kindness and generosity.* 3) a hope for more success in the future. *Business started to look up after the freeway was built.*

Look who's here! An expression drawing attention to someone who is entering a place. *Well, look who's here...after all these years!*

Loose

Foot loose and fancy-free: free to do what one wants. *Being foot loose and fancy-free, he has little intention now of getting married.*

Have a screw loose/Have a loose screw: *See,* **Screw**.

Loose cannon: someone in the know who is hard to manage or control, and who risks divulging inside knowledge. *We must have a loose cannon in our midst because our secret project is going to be in the news next week.*

Loose ends: Residue of items or things remaining. *Let's tie up the loose ends around here before we leave.*

Loosey goosey: clumsy; slipshod. *Never look or act loosey goosey at a job interview.*

Spring (one) loose: *See,* **Spring**.

Tie up loose ends: *See,* **Tie**.

Lose

Lose face: *See,* **Face**.

Lose ground: to go backward; to fall behind; lose progress. *We are losing ground against the floodwaters. Without reinforcements, we will lose ground and run the risk of capture.*

Lose heart: become discouraged. *She began to lose heart in playing the piano when she gained interest in boys.*

Lose one's cool/Lose one's head/Lose one's temper: to get angry or frustrated, usually triggered by an event. *She began to lose her cool once things did not go the way she planned. He lost his temper when he locked his key in the car.*

Lose one's marbles: go crazy; act irrationally. *He seemed to have lost his marbles after coming back from the war.*

Lose one's nerve: no longer confident; timid or scared; without courage. *Don't look down from the high-dive board or you'll lose your nerve to dive off.*

Lose one's shirt: lose a lot of money. *If you aren't careful, you can lose your shirt on this venture.*

Lose one's touch: not as skillful as before; out of condition. *He began to lose his touch as a ball player after injuring his knees.*

Lose one's way: to become lost. *I lost my way to your house.*

Lose out: fail to win; not make it. *We lost out on the deal.*

Lose touch with: no longer have contact or communication with another. *I lost touch with all my friends in school.*

Lose track: to forget about something; fail to keep up with. *We lost track of the money we spent shopping today.*

Snooze, you lose: if you miss an opportunity in timing, then you lose it. *When we found out that the tickets to the concert were sold out, our friend replied, "Well, you snooze, you lose."*

Lost

Get lost: an inconsiderate expression to tell another to go away. *Get lost and don't bother me anymore.*

Lost cause: no chance of revival; failure. *John is fighting a lost cause trying to replace the computer with a typewriter.*

Lost in space: very confused; the mind being unable to focus; thinking differently from the situation at hand. *Many of the homeless on the streets seem lost in space, and possibly in need of community help.*

Lost in the shuffle: become unaccounted for in the confusion or chaos. *Things got lost in the shuffle due to the storm and electric outage.*

Love

For the love of Pete: an exclamation of astonishment, generally one of disappointment. *For the love of Pete, why did you do such a stupid thing?*

Love at first sight: to be in love at the initial moment of seeing someone. *When I saw her, it was love at first sight.*

Love bucket: full of love. *My cat is a love bucket just prior to feeding time.*

Love handles: the bulging fat that grows around the waistline on a person. *I see that you added on some love handles since I last saw you.*

Lovey-dovey: being very affectionate. *Ever since their first date, John and Sue have been lovey-dovey with each other and always together.*

Make love: to have sexual relations with another. *The newlyweds made love under the oak tree.*

No love lost: no loss of affection for another. *When the crabby neighbor died, there was no love lost for the grief he caused everyone.*

Not for love or money: not under any circumstance. *I would not go to that place again, not for love or money.*

Stoned in love: amorously overwhelmed with another; very much in love. *He is stoned in love with her.*

Low

Lie low: keep out of sight. *Let's lie low until the college provost is gone.*

Low blow: underhanded; devious or unfair; in bad faith. See also, **Below the belt.** *Management was accused of using low-blow tactics against the union employees.*

Low-key: relaxed; easy-going. *John always seems to remain low-key before exams.*

Low life: a bum; one with no style or class. *Jack turned into a low life as the result of drugs and poor association, but the real cause was having a sense of low self-esteem.*

Low man on the totem pole: a subordinate; one with the least rank. *Although he acts like the boss, he really is the low man on the totem pole in the company.*

Lowdown: 1) the true facts; exact information. *What's the lowdown on the suspect?* 2) dishonest; mean; underhanded. *Man, the way you handled that situation was lowdown and nasty.*

Lower forty eight (48): the 48 states of the continental United States located on the mainland of North America and south of Canada, thereby excluding Hawaii and Alaska. *Long-distance telephone calls to the lower forty eight get cheaper and cheaper as time goes by.*

Lower the boom: *See,* **Boom**.

Luck

Don't push/press your luck: you are asking for too much. *Don't press your luck on this deal or you might not get anything.*

Down on one's luck: unlucky streak. *John is down on his luck with his investments.*

Hard luck: unfortunate circumstance. *It was my hard luck that I had to work tonight and miss the ball game.*

Luck of the draw: be the favored winner by chance. *The horse had the luck of the draw in the race.*

Luck out: do better than ever expected. *John somehow lucked out on the exam and passed.*

Potluck: *See,* **Pot**.

Lump

Lump in one's throat: 1) a feeling of grief or happiness so strong that you feel like crying or sobbing. *John's mom had a lump in her throat at his high school graduation.* 2) a feeling of anxiety strong enough that it is hard to speak or articulate. *He suddenly got a lump in his throat when he went up to the podium to speak.*

Lump it/Lump it or leave it: to tolerate something that is disagreeable or unpleasant. *Even though I know you dislike this project, you must lump it and do a good job.*

Lump sum: the complete amount; the total amount due at one time. *He received a significant lump sum payment on his retirement from the company. In case of default on the loan, the lump sum will become due and payable.*

Take one's lumps: to tolerate through the distasteful events. *He took his lumps like everyone else, so he deserves to be a member of the team.*

Lying

Lying through one's teeth: a direct lie; stating an untruth. *He's lying through his teeth about the size of the fish he caught today.*

Take lying down: to be intimidated, insulted or harassed without reaction. *Jackie Robinson had to endure taunts of racism and take it lying down during the early days of his baseball career with the Brooklyn Dodgers.*

Macho

Macho man: male who tends to exhibit masculine actions based more on physique, prowess or confidence. *Jack acts like a macho man when he is with his football friends.*

Macho rhetoric: tough talk. *Your macho rhetoric doesn't impress anyone.*

Mad

Mad as a hornet/Mad as hell: very angry. *He was mad as hell when he couldn't enter the race.*

Made

Got it made: in wealth; comfortable living. *With his inheritance, he's got it made.*

Made in the shade: *See,* **Shade**.

Made in the U.S.A.: a label that can be placed on clothing if more than 95% of the manufacturing is done in the United States or its selected territories. *Levi jeans with the label, "Made in the U.S.A.," are now classic clothes since the jeans are being produced overseas. Hey look, this shirt is made in the U.S.A.!*

Main

Main drag: the major street in town. *Wednesday evening in town is when all the cars cruise up and down the main drag.*

Main squeeze: one's sweetheart or lover. *My main squeeze works the nightshift so I don't see her as often as I would like.*

Make

Make a beeline for something: to hurry straight to somewhere. *When the stadium opened, everyone made a beeline to the front stage.*

Make a (big) hit: be successful. *His antique cars will certainly make a big hit at the show.*

Make a bundle: make lots of money. *My father made a bundle selling Texas prime beef overseas.*

Make a clean sweep: 1) to achieve complete victory with no defeats. *The team made a clean sweep of the series.* 2) to thoroughly cover or completely eliminate. *The soldiers made a clean sweep of the local town searching for bandits.*

Make a crack about someone: tease; ridicule; make fun. *Ned is always making cracks about me in front of everybody.*

Make a day of it: do something the whole day that is pleasurable. *On Saturdays, he grabs a sandwich and coffee, gets on the internet, and makes a day of it.*

Make a dent in: make some progress. *We hardly made a dent in preventing the floodwaters from cresting over the walls.*

Make a federal case (out of it): make a big uproar about something that is of little concern or importance. *The action was already resolved at the meeting, so stop trying to make a federal case out of it.*

Make a fool of/Make a monkey out of/Make an ass out of: to make someone look foolish. *He made a fool of himself about his long-time criticism of drug offenders when he got arrested for possession of illegal prescription drugs.*

Make a fuss (over): *See,* **Fuss**.

Make a go of: to work hard and turn something into a success. *He is so talented I am sure he will make a go of any venture that he pursues.*

Make a killing: *See,* **Kill**.

Make a long story short: to summarize a lengthy story or circumstance. *To make a long story short, they met at a bus stop in Los Angeles, and got married in a cathedral in Rome five weeks later.*

Make a match: when a couple looks like they really belong together. *Jack and Jill really make a match.*

Make a mountain out of a molehill: make a big problem out of a small one; make too much of something that is unimportant or small. *You are making a mountain out of a molehill by worrying about other people's problems.*

Make a name for oneself: become famous or well-known; achieve prominence or distinction. *He made a name for himself by selling products on television.*

Make a pass at: make an amorous advance toward another. *Given the sexual harassment laws, employees have to be careful about making a pass at someone in the office.*

Make a pig of oneself: *See,* **Pig**.

Make a pit stop: go to the bathroom. *Wait a minute for me while I make a pit stop.*

Make a point of/Make it a point: *See,* **Point**.

Make a quick buck: make money the easy way. *You can make a quick buck selling jewelry on the boardwalk at the beach during the summer.*

Make a run for it: quickly dash to safety; make a speedy escape. *If we make a run for it to the hills, we will be able to get away from the bears.*

Make a scene: create unfavorable attention. *So as not to make a scene at the coffee shop, Bob and Mary went outside to discuss their differences.*

Make a splash: *See,* **Splash**.

Make a stink: *See,* **Stink**.

Make an example (out) of: to punish someone publicly to encourage others not to commit the same crime or the wrong action. *The court made an example of the looters by imposing long jail sentences.*

Make an impression: to impress an effect on someone (good or bad). *Courtesy and responsive manners will generally help to make a good impression at a job interview.*

Make away with: to steal or carry away. *The eagle made away with the salmon that the bear just caught.*

Make believe: act as if something were true; to pretend. *Children often play make believe as part of growing up.*

Make do with something: to substitute an alternative. *We ran out of cream so you will have to make do with regular milk for your coffee.*

Make ends meet/Make a living: make enough money to pay living expenses. *I do not enjoy my job but in this tough economy, I have to make a living. Life is tough but we generally seem to make ends meet.*

Make eyes at: flirt; to look at another in a flirtatious or amorous way. *She made eyes at the baseball player. She has been making eyes at him all week long.*

Make fun of: laugh at sarcastically; ridicule. *The boys were making fun of her for her short hair.*

Make good: live up to one's commitment. *He made good on his promise to provide his employees a bonus.*

Make good time: getting to a destination promptly, within a short period, or in better than expected time. *We made good time on the road and arrived before nightfall.*

Make hay while the sun shines: take advantage of a good opportunity. *You should make hay while the sun shines by painting your house while the weather is warm and sunny.*

Make heads or tails of something: to understand. *He could not make heads or tails of anything that was discussed in class today.*

Make it snappy: hurry up. *If you have to go the bathroom now, then make it snappy.*

Make light of: minimize something that is important. *My friend made light of my pilgrimage to South America to study the Amazon jungle.*

Make love: *See,* **Love**.

Make me: a dare; to try to compel one to have to do something. *When told by an older kid to leave, little Timmy bravely replied, "Make me."*

Make my day: *See,* **Day**.

Make no bones about it: *See,* **Bone**.

Make one sick: to feel repulsed or disgusted by another. *It makes me sick to think that he swindled the elderly with his false promises of wealth.*

Make one tick: to motivate; to cause to operate. *John is the brains in the company, but the guy is so eccentric and discreet that we are unable to figure out what makes him tick.*

Make one's blood boil: *See,* **Blood**.

Make one's day: to receive great pleasure, success or satisfaction in something; to feel great. *It makes my day just to see my happy baby each morning.*

Make one's flesh crawl: *Same as,* **Make** one's skin crawl.

Make one's hair stand on end: horrify; frighten. *Last night's horror movie made my hair stand on end.*

Make one's mouth water: *See,* **Mouth**.

Make one's skin crawl: some matter that causes one to shake in fright; shudder in fear. *The sight of rats makes my skin crawl.*

Make oneself at home: an expression of a host to make their guest feel comfortable; feel like as if you are comfortably at your home. *Please have a seat in the living room and make yourself at home.*

Make oneself felt: expose or show one's power or authority. *The senior manager, generally just an observer at meetings, made himself felt by providing advice about reorganizing the sales team; everyone listened.*

Make or break: a crucial event that could cause success or failure. *Getting this contract will be a make or break deal for the company.*

Make out: 1) perform. *How did you make out on the exam?* 2) identify; distinguish; figure out; understand. *I can hardly make out the vehicles in front of us because of the thick fog. Because of the static, we could not make out what she was trying to tell us over the telephone.* 3) to engage in physical caressing. *She told him that she makes out with someone only if she is in love with him.* 4) tell a tale; falsehood; make someone believe. *He tried to make out that he was at the library studying, but someone saw him in the movie theater watching a monster marathon all day.* 5) imply; suggest; indicate. *His testimony tried to make him out as a liar.* 6) prepare; fill out. *I make out the daily reports.*

Make out like a bandit: *See,* **Bandit**.

Make sense: something that seems reasonable. *Does this plan make sense?*

Make something up: invent; create. *He made up the story in order to create sympathy for himself.*

Make the best of: do as well as possible in a tough situation. *There are two minutes before the end of the game, so let's make the best of it in trying to win.*

Make the dust fly/Make the fur fly/Make the feathers fly: an excited fracas; an energetic exchange; fight hard. *The fighting words between the two shoppers really made the fur fly; two security guards had to intervene.*

Make the grade: achieve or satisfy basic requirements. *Don't worry, this equipment will make the grade in getting the job done.*

Make the most of: use to the greatest advantage. *We have limited supplies for our trip, so we will have to make the most of what we have.*

Make the rounds: 1) to follow a routine or procedure; operate along a given route or circuit. *The security guard made his rounds around the premises every hour.* 2) to spread around. *His arrest soon made the rounds in school.*

Make the scene: make an appearance. *I'll be sure to make the scene before the presentations begin.*

Make time: prioritize a matter; do something promptly; find the time to do something. *You will have to make time to take care of the kids.*

Make tracks (now): to leave quickly. *If you want to arrive at the dinner party on time, we better make tracks now.*

Make up: 1) become friends again after a fight or disagreement. *They finally made up after fighting the other day.* 2) construction of. *What is the make up of the vehicle in regard to moving parts?* 3) cosmetics. *The girls were putting on their make up when we arrived at their apartment to meet them.* 4) to do or supply something that is needed or lacking. *We need to make up for lost time that was caused by the bad weather.*

Make up one's mind: decide what to do. *Make up your mind on what you want to do.*

Make waves: cause trouble; create a disturbance. *Please don't make waves at the staff meeting tonight.*

Make way: stand aside; move to allow someone through. *We had to move to the side of the road to make way for the ambulance.*

On the make: forward in one's sexual advances. *She was on the make in order to gain his favor.*

Mama

Mama's boy: a sissy; a boy/man who depends a lot more than usual on his mother. *He must be a real mama's boy because he cannot be depended on to assume any heavy responsibility.*

Man

Man: an explanative toward another. *Man, what a nice day it is.*

Man in the street: the average or ordinary person. *Any man in the street will tell you that we are being taxed too much.*

Man of his word: a man who keeps his promise; a man who can be trusted. *Since he is known as a man of his word, many of his deals are done with a handshake.*

Man-to-man: honest face-to-face discussion without hiding any facts; frank or direct discussion. *Jason had a man-to-man discussion with his Dad about smoking marijuana.*

One-man show: *See,* **One**.

The Man upstairs: *See,* **The**.

Marble

Go for all the marbles: take a big chance; go for the big one; risk it for all you have; go for broke. *At the poker table, John was told by his friends to go for all the marbles and bet all his chips.*

Have all one's marbles: to be competent; mentally sharp. *Many of the street people downtown don't seem to have all their marbles with them.*

Losing one's marbles: losing one's memory or ability to think as before. *He is gradually losing his marbles, unfortunately, to some sort of brain disorder.*

Mark

Easy mark: likely victim; patsy. *Unwitting tourists are often an easy mark for burglars.*

Hit the mark: be just right; the right thing. *A cold beer in the middle of a hot summer hits the mark for me.*

Mark my word(s): a warning to remember what one says. *Mark my words, that if this incident occurs again, we will not take it lying down.*

Make one's mark: achieve success. *Work hard and you will make your mark someday.*

Mark time: 1) be idle; wait for something to happen. *We finished our jobs, and were just marking time until the trucks came for us to load the fruit baskets.* 2) appearing to be working or doing something but really doing nothing at all. *We had to look busy and mark time while the analysts came through our offices to review our work.*

Market

Bear market: a sinking stock market; a business not doing as well over time. *Given the lackluster economy, we can expect our tourist industry to be in a bear market for the next year.*

Black market: *See,* **Black**.

Bull market: a rising stock market; a business or industry doing well over time. *Increased consumer spending will provide for a bull market this year for many appliance stores.*

Flea market: *See,* **Flea**.

In the market for: seeking to buy an item or thing. *I'm in the market for some old golf clubs.*

Priced out of the market: *See,* **Price**.

Matter

For that matter: about that. *He did not call, and for that matter, we won't wait for him.*

Laughing matter: *See,* **Laugh**.

Matter of course: the regular way; habit; something always done. *Police detectives ask questions of witnesses as a matter of course in investigating crimes.*

Matter of fact: an expression of emphasis on a truth. *As a matter of fact, I did go to Bel Air today to have lunch with friends.*

Matter-of-fact: 1) objectively revealing the truth, without emotion. *The commentator on the television news provided viewers with a stark, matter-of-fact account of the murder scene in Brentwood.* 2) showing little caring, feeling or excitement. *She acted in a very matter-of-fact manner at her father's funeral.*

No matter: 1) it makes no difference; regardless of; notwithstanding. *He was going to become a screenwriter, no matter what challenges he will face in Hollywood. No matter what happens, do not leave your post. We had to get the vehicle repaired no matter what the cost.* 2) not anything significant or important. *I wanted to see him before he left, but it's no matter.*

Mean

By all means: of course; certainly; accomplish without fail. *By all means, you must stop smoking.*

By means of: with the aid or use of something. *By means of a loan, we were able to buy our home.*

By no means: in no way; certainly not. *By no means do I want you children anywhere near the rising floodwaters.*

He means business: to be serious about something. *He is the nicest guy, but when he is on the football field during game time, he means business.*

Means to an end: an action which leads to a result or accomplishes a purpose. *He wasn't in love but rather used her as a means to an end in getting a top management job in the company.*

Means well: to have good intentions. *He seems to not care, but he really means well.*

Measure

For good measure: as a bonus; something more than expected. *When I went to the local supermarket, the manager gave me a few extra apples for good measure.*

Measure up to: to be good enough; to regard with higher reference. *None of my teachers ever measure up to Miss. Gilbert, my high school English teacher.*

Meat

All meat and no potatoes: an expression of gratification seeing a well-shaped and nice-looking person; all muscle and no fat. *After losing 20 kilos, Mary looks like all meat and no potatoes.*

Meat and potatoes: the fundamental ingredients or parts of something. *The meat and potatoes of our law firm is the handling of immigration appeals.*

Meat wagon: a police van used to haul those arrested. *The meat wagon came by and picked up the protesters at the logging site.*

Meatball surgery: use of quicker surgical procedures to save lives, applied in very difficult conditions under emergency situations (made well-known with mobile surgical outfits in war, such as MASH units in the U.S. Army). *Wounded soldiers in war generally first undergo meatball surgery to stabilize them before they are shipped to medical hospitals for further medical care.*

Meathead/meatball: slow-witted; slow learner; one who does not understand well. *There are some real meatheads in his family.*

Meet

Meet one's fate: an unfavorable or disastrous ending. *He met his fate on Mulholland Drive, on a wet and slippery, moonlit road.*

Meet one's match: to encounter an equal as a challenger; meet someone as good as oneself. *You will certainly meet your match in this tournament, so do your best.*

Meet someone halfway: compromise with another. *Meet me halfway on the price and we have a deal.*

Meet up with: come together by accident, suddenly and without expectation of meeting. *He met up with an old college friend when visiting the sites in Mozambique.*

Mellow

Mellow: calm. *He is usually a mellow person.*

Mellow out: to relax. *I'm just mellowing out after a hard day's work. You need to mellow out.*

Mend

Mend fences: restore better relations with another; strengthen one's friendship. *The ambassador quickly visited the prime minister of the host country to mend fences in behalf of his country's mistake when its submarine capsized a civilian boat of the host's country.*

Mend one's ways: to reform; positive change in behavior. *You best mend your ways or you'll be arrested again.*

On the mend: getting better; healing. *Jack is on the mend after falling off the roof the other day.*

Metal

Metal: stamina; determination. *Does he have the metal to do it?*

Middle

Middle ground: a compromise between two conflicting arguments. *There has existed no middle ground between the two nations for years.*

Middle of the road: 1) no bias to one extreme side or the other, but favoring a balanced approach. *Presidential candidates tend to favor opinions popular with the majority of voters who tend to be middle-of-the-road.* 2) a type of action balanced between two opposing movements or ideas. *In order for the Constitution to garner favor with the separate colonies, it had to adopt a middle-of-the-road approach in balancing the powers between the federal government and the separate soon-to-be States of the Union.*

Mill

Mill around: to wait while time goes by. *We milled around the studio hoping to meet our favorite movie star.*

Run-of-the-mill: ordinary; satisfactory; mediocre; common kind. *The casinos do not present run-of-the-mill shows but rather do their best to make them expensive and extravagant.*

Through the mill: 1) through real experience of great difficulty of a particular time or way of life; totally worn and beaten down. *It looks like he went through the mill after seeing the boss. He's really gone through the mill with the complications in the surgery.* 2) experienced. *The new manager is well-known for his expertise because he's been through the mill.*

Million

Like a million bucks/Like a million dollars: outstanding; wonderful. *This new car drives like a million bucks. After being accepted for the job, he felt like a million dollars.*

One in a million: *See,* **One**.

Mince

Make mincemeat out of someone: to defeat, destroy, or punish severely. *They made mincemeat out of the opposing team.*

Mince words: to select words carefully in politeness or deception. *People who speak frankly and honestly tend not to mince words much.*

Mind

Bear in mind: bring to memory. *Bear in mind that the safety of the children is your duty to protect while on this trip.*

Blow one's mind: *See,* **Blow**.

Bring to mind: to recall something. *That old wooden staff brings to mind our hikes through the old-growth forests many years ago.*

Change one's mind: *See,* **Change**.

Dirty mind: *See,* **Dirty**.

Enter one's mind: to realize; to discover. *Did it ever enter your mind that I could lose my job for the prank you pulled?*

Give a piece of one's mind: to scold; sharply admonish. *I'll give him a piece of my mind for not showing up on time.*

Half a mind: a desire not yet acted upon. *I have half a mind to drop everything and join the Peace Corps.*

Have a good mind to: *See,* **Have**.

Load off one's mind: *See,* **Load**.

Lot on one's mind: thinking about a lot of matters; very involved or busy mentally. *I've got a lot on my mind right now, so I don't have the time to relax.*

Mind like a steel trap: quick mind; a fast study; very smart. *With a mind like a steel trap, he could have gone to virtually any college.*

Mind one's own business: to not interfere in the affairs of others. *I was told to mind my own business when I inquired about the chemical smell under the ground in the back lot.*

Mind one's p's and q's: to be very mindful of one's words or actions. *Mind your p's and q's when we meet the diplomats at the party.*

Mind-reader: *See,* **Read one's mind**.

Mind the fort/store: watch and take charge of the house or business. *Mind the fort while I'm gone.*

Never mind: do not bother. *Never mind looking for the keys; I found them.*

Out of one's mind: *See,* **Out**.

Read one's mind: to understand what someone is thinking. *I know him so well I can practically read his mind.*

Right-minded: reasonably thinking. *Democracy finds its strength in the power of a right-minded majority.*

Slip one's mind: to temporarily forget to do something. *It got so busy today at work, that it slipped my mind to attend the luncheon.*

Miss

Miss by a mile: fail to achieve something by a significant amount. *He missed the target by a mile.*

Miss out: lose a chance for something; forego opportunity or enjoyment; no venture, no gain. *He's missing out by not going on the camping trip with us to Yellowstone Park.*

Miss the boat: lose out; fail to timely take advantage of an opportunity. *We missed the boat on that investment.*

Miss the point: fail to understand an essential element of something; to overlook an important matter. *You miss the point if you think it's a money issue.*

Mix

Mix up: a confusion; mistake. *There was a mix up at the loading gate, and little Michael could not be found for a while.*

Mixed bag: combination of various items, ideas, people, or circumstances. *The meeting attracted a mixed bag of people from all over the country.*

Mixed blessing: something with good and bad features. *Having him on our team can prove to be a mixed blessing.*

Mixed up: 1) mentally confused; puzzled. *He seemed all mixed up and inaudible after the boxing match.* 2) out of order; messed up. *The papers got all mixed up in the scuffle.* 3) connected with. *Johnny's attitude got worse after getting mixed up with the bad boys in the neighborhood.*

M.O.

M.O.: modus operandi (the method of operation). *What's your M.O. on this project?*

Mob

Mob scene: uncontrolled gathering of people. *It was a mob scene at the year-end clearance sale today.*

Mobbed: overwhelmed by others. *The movie star was mobbed by his fans when he exited the limousine.*

Money

Get one's money's worth: satisfaction in getting what one pays for. *I'm happy that you got your money's worth on this car.*

In the money: making or having a lot of money. *There seems to be less people today who are in the money.*

Launder money/Money laundering: money that is placed in legitimate accounts to clean its ill-gotten source; converting money gained notoriously from theft or contraband sales and transferred into accounts as a way to legitimize the funds. *The pizza parlor was used as a front to* *launder money from illegal drug operations. Money laundering around the world is the knack of drug and weapons dealers, according to international law enforcement.*

Make money hand over fist: to make money easily and in larger than expected amounts. *Trading in gems is risky but you can make money hand over fist if you know what you are doing.*

Money is no object: the price does not matter. *Money is no object when they go shopping.*

Money pit: something that costs a lot of money; a constant cost. *My house is my castle, but it sure is a money pit.*

Money talks: money is power. *You want something? Well, money talks around here.*

Money talks, shit walks [expressive]**:** money gets you everywhere, while words get you nowhere. *In this town, money talks, shit walks.*

Money to burn: to have more than enough money. *I've got money to burn, so let's go shopping today.*

On the money/Right on the money: just right; exactly as planned (*Same as,* **On the nose**). *Most of your bets on the playoff games were right on the money.*

Pour money down the drain: *See,* **Pour**.

Put your money where your mouth is: support or back up one's statements with action or with money to bet. *If you think he will win the race, then put your money where your mouth is and lay some money down. If you think it's so easy, then put your money where your mouth is and try doing it yourself.*

Spend money like water: to expend funds freely and without much concern. *He is unable to save because he spends money like water.*

Time is money: *See,* **Time**.

Monkey

Grease monkey: a person who greases or works on machinery; garage mechanic. *I worked as a grease monkey during college to help pay my expenses.*

Make a monkey out of someone: make one look silly or be laughed at. *She made a monkey out of Adam at the party.*

Monkey around: foolish behavior. *Don't monkey around while on the job.*

Monkey business: 1) unethical, illegal, or deceitful activity. *There have been rumors that a lot of monkey business goes on in that firm.* 2) goofing off; fooling around; comical actions. *Alright, no more monkey business because we have to finish our work.*

Monkey on one's back: a nagging situation; an unsolved matter. *You've been acting like you have a monkey on your back. Care to talk about it?*

Monkey suit: formal wear, especially a coat and tie. *Now that I'm home, let me take this monkey suit off and put on something casual.*

Throw a monkey wrench: to interrupt something that is running smoothly. *When Jackson got arrested at the border, it threw a monkey wrench in our entire operation.*

Mooch

Mooch: be parasitic; to take from others without consideration. *I've been mooching off my parents until I can find a job. You need to pay one half of the rent because I'm not going to let you mooch off me.*

Moon

Ask for the moon: *See,* **Ask**.

Moon: to reveal one's rear-end. *We mooned our friends on the last day of school.*

Once in a blue moon: hardly ever; almost never; rarely. *Once in a blue moon, you can see the spotted owl flying through the old-growth woods. My uncle goes to the doctor once in a blue moon.*

Promise the moon: *See,* **Promise**.

More

More than one bargained for: unexpected, especially as to an unfavorable outcome. *Taking on this case was a nightmare and more than I ever bargained for.*

More than one can chew: overwhelmed in handling or doing something. *When he took on the new assignment, he realized that he took on more than he could chew.*

Mosey

Mosey: 1) to spend idle time; to kill time. *We usually mosey around the water cooler during office breaks.* 2) to visit; to come over. *We decided to mosey over to the gym and play some basketball. Why don't you mosey on over here?*

Mouth

Bad mouth: *See,* **Bad**.

Big mouth: talk too much. *They know everything, now, mainly because you have a big mouth.*

Blabbermouth: one who cannot help but tell stories to others; a loose or constant talker. *She is such a blabbermouth that I can't get anything done when I'm with her.*

Born with a silver spoon in one's mouth: where one received wealth through inheritance rather than by working for it; born into wealth. *His lack of character and appreciation for hard work comes from being born with a silver spoon in his mouth.*

By word of mouth: communication from person to person; information transfer through the spoken word. *Much of our business comes from word of mouth.*

Hand to mouth: *See,* **Hand**.

Leave a bad taste in one's mouth: to have a bad feeling about something; to feel disgusted. *His rude behavior left a bad taste in my mouth.*

Look a gift horse in the mouth: to complain about not liking a gift. (Usually used in the negative). *Be happy about your uncle's gift, and don't look a gift horse in the mouth.*

Make one's mouth water: to look or smell divine; something you see or smell that is very desirous. *The smell of grandma's lasagna makes my mouth water.*

Melt in one's mouth: food so tender and very easy to chew. *The meat was so tender and delicious that it just melted in my mouth.*

Motor mouth: constant talker; to talk and talk. *The new employee is a real motor mouth.*

Mouth off: to talk loudly and with indiscretion; obnoxious talk; complain. *Quit mouthing off and just shut up.*

Mouthful/Say a mouthful: to say a lot, generally with accurate conviction or force. *You said a mouthful at the rally when you condemned the administration for needlessly wasting resources.*

Muck mouth: *See,* **Muck**.

Put one's foot in one's mouth: *See,* **Foot**.

Put words into one's mouth: to speak for or claim feelings by another without authority or basis. *Quit putting words into my mouth about what I saw.*

Put your money where your mouth is: *See,* **Money**.

Run at the mouth: *See above,* Motor **mouth**.

Shoot off one's mouth: *See,* **Shoot**.

Straight from the horse's mouth: *See,* **Horse**.

Take the words out of my mouth: saying something that another is thinking about; anticipate what another is about to say. *You took the words out of my mouth when you asked the boss for a raise at our meeting.*

Move

Get a move on: get going; proceed. *Get a move on; we are behind schedule.*

Move up in the world: improve one's social or financial status. *He has really moved up in the world after the success of his restaurants.*

Movers and shakers: influential people of society; those who get things done. *There will be a lot of movers and shakers at tonight's grand ball.*

On the move: busy; not idle; things to do. *We hardly see Jack any more; he always seems to be on the move.*

Muck

Muck: nonsense; false rumor. *The talk about the plant closing down is a lot of muck.*

Muck (it) up: mess up; ruin. *We are all depending on you, so don't muck it up. We just had the house cleaned, so don't muck it up.*

Muck mouth: one who talks a lot of nonsense or divulges negative tales about others. *I don't enjoy his company because he is such a muck mouth when he talks about others in the office.*

Mud

Clear as mud: *See,* **Clear**.

Mud in your eye: an expression made when toasting a drink. *"Well, here's mud in your eye."*

Name is mud: *See,* **Name**.

Sling mud: say bad things to one another. *A lot of mud slinging occurred at tonight's political debate.*

Stick in the mud: reticent; hard to move; stubborn. *Mrs. O'Reilly is a real stick-in-the-mud about constantly keeping the house clean.*

Mumbo

Mumbo-jumbo: blurry nonsense; confusing talk; rumor. *What is this mumbo-jumbo about you leaving the company?*

Munch

Munchies: craving for food. *Marijuana is an alternative source to help cancer patients get the munchies.*

Muscle

Flex one's muscle: to show strength to another, whether real or imaginary; threaten others by displaying power. *Collection agencies flex their muscle in an attempt to get money from debtors.*

Muscle car: a vehicle equipped with a powerful engine and a lot of horsepower. *The muscle cars of the 1960's, like the Corvette and Ford Cobra, are now high-priced, classic vehicles.*

Muscle in: to force one's way into something. *Don't allow him to muscle in on the deal.*

Music

Face the music: *See,* **Face**.

Musical chairs: a game containing fewer chairs than players; a reference in business when one is uncertain whether he or she is left with a job after a company downsizes. *It has been musical chairs at Bob's firm with the downsizing of the corporation.*

Music to one's ears: something very pleasant to hear. *It was music to my ears to hear of my promotion.*

Nail
Hard as nails: *See,* **Hard**.

Hit the nail on the head: *See,* **Hit**.

Nail down: to firmly secure; to set; make sure. *When can you nail down some time to come out and see our business?*

Nail it: to solidly secure something; to score. *He nailed it at the buzzer, winning the game and the championship.*

Nail one to the cross: punish harshly; make an example of; crucify. *The boss nailed him to the cross for losing the client account to a competitor.*

Nailed: 1) to get caught. *The police nailed the speeding driver by shooting out the tires.* 2) get hit hard. *The challenger was nailed with a sharp right hook and fell hard to the canvas.*

Name

Call one names: offensive or abusive words stated; to swear. *The next time he calls me names, I'll report him to the supervisor. Ok, guys, we can do without the name calling.*

Name is mud: in trouble; one who is blamed or no longer liked. *Please don't mention the car accident to my wife, or my name will be mud.*

Name it: whatever it is; what you want you will have. *Name it and I'll get it for you. You name it and he can cook it.*

Name of the game: the heart of the matter; the central goal. *When time is running out, the name of the game in football is the short pass.*

Nature

Mother nature: the natural environment. *An old-growth tree is a towering gem of Mother Nature, which commands our respect for its ageless beauty of life.*

Nature calls: a remark when one has to go to the bathroom to relieve oneself. *Nature calls...I'll be back in a few minutes.*

Nature lover: one who admires the natural environment. *Jackson decided to live in the hills of the Cascade Mountains in Washington State because he is a real nature lover.*

Neck

Breathe down one's neck: *See,* **Breathe** **down one's back.**

Neck: romantic kissing and cuddling. *Couples go to the top of this hill at night to view the city lights and to neck.*

Neck and neck/Neck to neck: very close contest. *See also,* **Wire to wire**. *The horses ran neck and neck to the finish line.*

Neck of the woods: one's place of residence or familiar surroundings. *Seattle was my neck of the woods where I grew up.*

Pain in the neck: *See,* **Pain**.

Risk one's neck: place one's reputation or life in a risky or dangerous situation. *It was Jerry who risked his neck by pulling you out of the burning vehicle before it burst into flames.*

Save one's neck: *See,* **Save**.

Stick one's neck out/Stick out one's neck: *See,* **Stick**.

Up to one's neck: *See,* **Up** to one's ears.

Wring someone's neck: a threat generally intended to be more psychological in force than physical; to harshly reprimand; to throttle. *If you lose any more of my hard-earned money, I'm going to wring your neck!*

Needle

Needle: to bother. *Please quit needling me and go away.*

Needle in a haystack: something improbable to find or do; against great odds. *Finding grandma's ring in the burned out house will be like looking for a needle in a haystack.*

Thread the needle: *See,* **Thread**.

Neither

Neither fish nor fowl: cannot determine something; something not belonging to any certain classification. *There are a number of boxes in storage with miscellaneous items that are neither fish nor fowl; what shall we do with them?*

Neither here nor there: not relevant to the discussion; unrelated. *Talking about damage to the truck is neither here nor there when we have to worry about Timmy's injuries.*

Nerd

Nerd: often a studious type and generally one who is immaturely out of style in dress; a boring or unpopular person. *What does she see in that nerd?*

Nerve

Get on one's nerve: make one feel edgy, upset or mad. *You get on people's nerves because you are quick to criticize.*

Last nerve: next to one's breaking point; on the verge of getting angry and losing control. *I am on my last nerve, so behave!*

Lose one's nerve: *See,* **Lose**.

Nerve: 1) mental strength to challenge a situation. *Do you have the nerve to endure this rigorous training?* 2) disrespect; inconsideration. *He has* *some nerve cutting into the waiting line ahead of others.* 3) shocking irritation. *He hit a nerve at the executive meeting when he mentioned that the company has been keeping two different accounting records for years.*

Nervous Nellie: a timid individual without courage or stamina. *A nervous Nellie will find it difficult to be a public speaker.*

Of all the nerve/One has some nerve: responsive phrase to an offensive or shocking act by another; how offensive can one be? *Of all the nerve that she slaps her children, and in public. He has some nerve to just get up and leave his job.*

Nest

Feather one's nest: accumulate money for oneself. *Old man Rivers feathered his nest quite well over the years.*

Hornet's nest: the potential for a nasty or strong reaction. *Talking about saving the forests in this logging town may likely stir up a hornet's nest.*

Nest egg: money set aside and saved. *Our nest egg continues to dwindle due to rising medical costs.*

Never

Never had it so good: to have ample opportunities and wealth. *We never had it so good after leaving the trailer park and starting our business in the city.*

Never mind: don't be concerned; forget about it; it is nothing to consider. *Never mind about going to town today because I just want to relax at home.*

Never say die: never quit; don't give up or surrender; don't be discouraged. *John always finishes his marathon race because he is one to never say die.*

New

New blood: to bring fresh energy and vigor; to give new life and spark. *The new international division of the company is composed mostly of new blood.*

New lease on life: a brand new chance to live. *John, who lived in the flat, dry Mojave Desert during his childhood, discovered a new lease on life when he went to college in Hawaii.*

Newfangled: just invented; very complex. *More and more newfangled gadgets with the latest high technology are making it to the market.*

Nickel

Nickel and dime: to charge for every little matter. *I don't like the electrical contractor you hired because he nickel and dimed us at every turn.*

Night

All nighter: throughout the night. *I pulled an all-nighter to study for this exam.*

Fly-by-night: a business that is set up, only to quickly disappear before its disreputable practices are discovered; untrustworthy; unreliable. *What a life; he works as a telemarketer in these fly-by-night operations.*

Night and day: 1) open 24 hours a day. *The grocery market is open night and day.* 2) obvious difference; very clearly evident. *Greta, it is like night and day how the plastic surgery changed the way you look.*

Night life: entertainment at night. *How is the night life in this city?*

Night owl: one who stays awake during the night and into the early morning hours. *Studying and college life has turned me into a night owl.*

Nightcap: a drink, generally alcoholic, taken just before bedtime. *Shall we have a nightcap before we retire to bed?*

One-night stand: *See,* **One**.

Nit

Nitpick: 1) delve into details about something. *The accountant nitpicked through the figures all day.* 2) to unnecessarily harass someone. *Just because he is slower than others in school, the other kids tend to nitpick him.*

Nitpicky: choosy. *He is very nitpicky about his clothing.*

Nitty gritty: small details. *Skip the nitty gritty details and just give me your opinion about whether you like the project.*

Nitwit: a dummy. *He looks like a nitwit, but really is a genius in disguise.*

No

Close but no cigar: *See,* **Close**.

No cigar: unable to make it or do something. *We tried to secure courtside seats to tonight's basketball game but no cigar.*

No deal/No dice/No go/No way: not agreed to; denied; without success; no result. *When asked if the girls could drive the Ferrari, Dad said, "No dice."*

No doubt: 1) certainly; for sure. *The jeweler inspected the watch and said there's no doubt it's a Romex, that is, a fake Rolex.* 2) likely; probably. *Do not doubt the fact that he could surprise us all and arrive on time.*

No end to: to feel continuous or almost endless. *As a child, there was no end to wanting to play. There is no end to the college students playing their loud music at the dorms.*

No frills: just the basic essentials, and no extra service. *You can generally get a no frills ticket on late-night flights and save money.*

No hard feelings: to tell someone you are not angry after a disagreement; without resentment or anger. *I hope there are no hard feelings between us.*

No holds barred: completely without restrictions; going the full force. *I will come at you with no holds barred if you continue to harass my client. They were fighting each other with no holds barred.*

No kidding: not pretending or joking; really; truly. *Jack was not kidding when he said that rats ate his shoes!*

No love lost: to care very little toward another. *There is no love lost between the Army and Navy on game day.*

No matter: *See,* **Matter**.

No pain, no gain: phrase that means if you don't work hard at it, you won't gain or get ahead (originally coined by Benjamin Franklin in the 1700's). *This is the Marines, young man…no pain, no gain, you understand?!*

No picnic: not pleasant at all; very difficult. *It was no picnic driving through the thick fog on the freeway.*

No shit: *See,* **Shit**.

No show: a reservation or appointment where the person fails to honor to come or make it. *There were several no-shows to the court hearings due to the severe snowstorm today.*

No sooner said than done: accomplished swiftly. *No sooner said than done, the head porter at the hotel sent flowers to her room.*

No spring chicken: *See,* **Spring** chicken.

No sweat: no problem. *No sweat about leaving your car in my driveway while you are on vacation to Kashmir.*

No two ways about it: no other choice or alternative. *There are no two ways about it; we have to finish the story by next week or it will not get published in time.*

No use: no purpose; it won't matter; it won't do any good. *It's no use trying to go to town because they blocked all the roads due to the flooding.*

No way: 1) never; not possible. *No way will we be able to get the aircraft ready for flight by tomorrow.* 2) an exclamation of disbelief. *You got the job? No way!*

No wonder: no surprise. *It is no wonder that massive flooding occurred, knowing that the law ignorantly allowed construction on wetlands, and unwise clear-cutting of forests for development.*

Noodle

Noodle head/Noodlehead: a dumb person. *That noodle head just doesn't realize how much they have helped him over the years.*

Use your noodle: think; comprehend; use your head to understand. *Use your noodle and figure it out.*

Nose

Brown nose: patronize; to seek favor. *She is good at brown nosing the boss.*

By a nose: just barely; very marginally. *He won the congressional seat by a nose over his opponent.*

Hard-nosed: *See,* **Hard**.

Have a nose for: to be able to sense

No skin off my nose: *See,* **Skin**.

Nose around: check out; investigate. *Why don't you nose around and see what you can find.*

Nose bent out of shape: *Same as,* **Nose** out of joint.

Nose for: a knowledge and sense for; a keen understanding. *Jack has a nose for understanding the complexities of hydraulic systems.*

Nose in a book: *See,* **Book**.

Nose in the air: to feel that one is too good or better than others around; haughty. *She thinks she is better than others, and walks around with her nose in the air.*

Nose out of joint: be upset or irritated, especially when angered by someone. *He really gets her nose out of joint at the meetings, doesn't he?*

On the nose: exactly; on the mark; perfect. *I got to work at 8 a.m., right on the nose.*

Pay through the nose: *See,* **Pay**.

Not

Not a leg to stand on: no defense; no evidence; no excuse. *Right now, you don't have a leg to stand on because witnesses saw you at the scene with a knife in your hand.*

Not bad: all right; pretty good. *The concert was not bad; we were pleasantly surprised.*

Not by a long shot: something improbable to occur; against all odds. *He is 50 miles behind the first sledder with 120 miles to go; he is not going to win by a long shot.*

Not for the world/Not for all the tea in China/Not for all the coffee in Brazil/Not for love or money: not at any price; not for anything. *Not for the world would I ever hurt her feelings.*

Not in good taste: *See,* **Taste.**

Not know beans about something: have no knowledge about something. *He doesn't know beans about the operation of a car.*

Not know him from Adam: to not know a person; unable to recognize someone. *No, I don't know him from Adam.*

Not know whether one is coming or going: completely perplexed or confused. *John has so many supervisors giving him conflicting directions that he doesn't know whether he is coming or going.*

Not know which way to turn: confused; puzzled; unable to decide. *After losing his job, and needing funds to feed and shelter his family, Bob didn't know which way to turn.*

Not lift a finger: don't help at all. *He didn't lift a finger to help his friend in need.*

Not lift/move a muscle: do not move; freeze (in motion). *Don't move a muscle; there is a rattlesnake at your feet.*

Not on your life: an emphatic expression of refusal; certainly not. *When asked by his 13-year old son if he could drive the new motorcycle, the father stated, "Not on your life!"*

Not show one's face: don't appear; don't come around again. *Don't show your face around here any longer.*

Not up to snuff: not good enough. *His work is not up to snuff.*

Not with a ten-foot pole: not have anything to do with; reject; keep away from. *I would not touch that thing with a ten-foot pole.*

Not worth a dime/Not worth a hill of beans/Not worth a red cent: having no value. *Many high-flying stocks in the year 2000 aren't worth a dime today.*

Nothing

Nothing but skin and bones: very skinny. *After our one-month survival trek out of the mountains, many of us were nothing but skin and bones.*

Nothing doing: certainly not; no way. *When the 12-year old asked to ride the new motorcycle, his father replied, "Nothing doing, son."*

Nothing of the kind: just the opposite; on the contrary. *Asked if he plans to sell his trucking company to a nationwide firm, he replied, "That is nothing of the kind."*

Nothing short of: surely; absolutely; thoroughly. *The test flight was nothing short of spectacular!*

Nothing to sneeze at: do not take lightly; something significant or important. *To be in the top five percent of the graduating class of 1,250 students is nothing to sneeze at.*

Nothing to write home about: nothing to be proud of. *Your poor performance is nothing to write home about.*

Nothing ventured is nothing gained: you have to make an effort in order to succeed. *Once in a while, you have to take a chance and try things in life because nothing ventured is nothing gained.*

Nut

Go nuts: be crazy; become very excited (either angry or happily excited), and react by yelling or losing emotional control. *Our boss went nuts when we lost a big customer to a competitor. We went nuts when our team won the game.*

Hard nut to crack/Tough nut to crack: something quite difficult to do, change or to understand. *Learning to read and write a language like Japanese or Chinese is a tough nut to crack. Bringing both sides together after many years will be a hard nut to crack.*

In a nutshell: in a few words; very briefly stated. *In a nutshell, the project was a bust.*

Nut: 1) odd individual. *Unfortunately, when John fell to the ground and started to shake uncontrollably due to his epilepsy, many of the students wrongly and naively thought he was just a nut case. Some nut is sending me anonymous emails.* 2) crazy about something. *I'm nuts about collecting fossils.*

Nuthouse [expressive]: an institution for the developmentally disabled. *He was a genius in his time; now, he lives in that nuthouse down the street.*

Nuts: 1) an exclamation of disgust, rejection or disappointment. *Oh nuts, I forgot to bring the camera on the trip.* 2) response to another that he or she is wrong or crazy. *You're nuts if you want me to apologize to her.*

Nuts about something: desire or like very much. *Jane is nuts about chocolate candy.*

Nuts and bolts: the pertinent or important details about something. *John deserved to be promoted to executive vice president because he understands the nuts and bolts of the company so well.*

Nutty as a fruitcake/Nuttier than a fruitcake: odd; crazy; mentally unbalanced. *Who hired this guy?! He is nuttier than a fruitcake.*

Oat

Feel one's oats: to act in a proud or important way, openly, and in a way that may look brash; to act influential. *Benito Mussolini was feeling his oats during the peak of his reign in Italy in the 1930's.*

Make oatmeal out of someone: to destroy; to beat (up) decisively. *With such great players on this year's team, we should be able to make oatmeal out of the other teams.*

Sow one's (wild) oats: to mess around; to do wild or silly things, especially while one is young. *We came to America to sow our wild oats.*

Odd

At odds: *See,* **At**.

Odd jobs: temporary jobs without being steady or regular in schedule; various tasks. *He has me doing odd jobs for him all week.*

Oddball: one who acts differently from others, either eccentrically or mentally; a weird person. *This guy may be a genius, but he's an oddball.*

Odds and ends: miscellaneous things; trivial items. *We only need to clean out a few odds and ends in the house before we put it up for sale. I did a few odds and ends around the house over the weekend.*

Odds are against: likelihood of success are slim or less probable. *With the storm coming this way, the odds are against us in getting back home by tomorrow.*

Off

Gloves are off: no more mercy; no more consideration or cooperation; go with full force. *If we cannot agree in mediation, then the gloves come off and we proceed to litigation.*

Go off the deep end: to lose it mentally; to become uncontrollable in emotion. *He will go off the deep end when he finds out he lost his job.*

Off and on: periodically; occasionally; not regularly. *It rains in Seattle off and on throughout the year.*

Off base: wrong; not factual; inappropriate. *The witness was caught off base when his testimony in court contradicted his statements at his deposition. Hey, that story is way off base.*

Off center: odd; inappropriate. *I want to apologize for my off-center remarks to you last night at the meeting.*

Off guard: not prepared; not watching; not alert to approaching danger. *While the second baseman was viewing the crowd, he was caught off guard and missed the baseball that was fielded his way.*

Off one's chest: a relief of one's worries to reveal something that has been repressed. *I was glad to talk about it and get it off my chest.*

Off one's groove: *See,* **Groove**.

Off one's rocker: crazy; not making sense. *You're off your rocker if you think he committed the crime.*

Off the beaten path: *See,* **Path**.

Off-the-cuff: impromptu; unrehearsed; spontaneous. *Her off-the-cuff remarks about the visiting professor being an inciteful orator got her in a lot of hot water.*

Off the hook: *See,* **Hook**.

Off the rack: ready-made; not tailored by hand. *My suits look tailored, but are really off-the-rack.*

Off the record: not for official or legal recording; not for publication. *The coach's off-the-record comment critical of the referees ended up getting published in the next day's sports news.*

Off the top of one's head: speaking without preparation; impromptu thought. *Off the top of my head, I would say that it's going to take an hour to get through this rush-hour traffic.*

Off the wall/Offbeat: strange; unconventional; unusual. *Space law is an offbeat area of law today, but is expected to become a major area of practice in the future.*

Teed off: *See,* **Tee**.

Tell one off: respond to another with disdain or ridicule. *He will tell you off if you get him upset.*

OK

Okey doke/Okey dokey/Oki doki/Okie dokie: yes; all right. *Okidoki, I'll get it for you.*

Old

Old boys network: a system where a group of men either grew up together, went to the same college, or worked together, then later assisted each other in getting ahead in life with good jobs; being favored over others due to connections; promoting or improving one's lot in life through to an established network of friends. *The old boys network makes it harder to get a nice job in the cotton or tobacco industry around here.*

Old geezer: an old man (a phrase generally associated with one being somewhat incapacitated). *That person you called an old geezer beat my ass in tennis last week.*

Old guard: Those who harbor old ideas in comparison to the modern times, and still hold power. *This country has been ruled by the old guard for the longest time.*

Old hand: experienced and skilled; knowledgeable. *Jack is an old hand at fixing virtually anything that plugs into an electrical outlet.*

Old hat: old-fashioned; not new. *That way of thinking is old hat.*

Old maid: spinster; woman who has never married. *My aunt is an old maid, but is my favorite friend because she has taught me much.*

Old school: the thinking of an earlier or older generation. *In the old school, we would say "You look fine," but today, the kids say, "You look hella cool."*

OMG

OMG: The expression, "Oh my God," to indicate great shock or awe. *OMG!!! The Pope has just entered the building!*

On

On a limb: *See,* **Out** **on a limb.**

On a shoestring: survive on very little funds. *We had to survive on a shoestring when we started our business.*

On again, off again: not settled; changeable; uncertain. *The maiden test flight for the secret aircraft has been on again, off again due to suspected security breaches in the systems protocol.*

On an even keel: in an ordered or controlled fashion. *Work at the construction site is finally running at an even keel after yesterday's accident.*

On and on: continually; at no end; at tedious length. *His speech went on and on, which helped to bring a lot of business to the espresso stand nearby.*

On me: an expression to indicate one's intent to pay for the food or drink of others. *Hey, everyone, the drinks are on me.*

On pins and needles: nervous and uneasy; worried. *We were on pins and needles wondering when the rescue team would arrive to save us from the sinking ship.*

On the ball: on the right track; alert; efficient. *Stay on the ball if you want to keep your job.*

On the bandwagon: going with the popular choice; together. *We joined the bandwagon of community assistance and volunteered our time in planting trees and brush along salmon streams in our neighborhood.*

On the button: right on time. *He's right on the button in arriving to work each day.*

On the dot: exactly on time. *I want you here tomorrow at 8 a.m. on the dot.*

On the fence: undecided; in limbo. *The family is on the fence trying to decide where to go for summer vacation. I am still on the fence about my decision in the matter.*

On the house: *See,* **House**.

On the lam: undercover; to hide from; fugitive status. *He's on the lam somewhere in Asia.*

On the level: *See,* **Level**.

On the make: *See,* **Make**.

On the take: *See,* **Take**.

On the mend: becoming better; healing. *He has been on the mend ever since breaking his right arm.*

On the nose: *See,* **Nose**.

On the Q.T.: not to disclose information to others; to be quiet. *The boss said that this matter shall remain on the Q.T.*

On the up and up: to deal honestly: *I really think that he was on the up and up with us.*

On thin ice: *See,* **Ice**.

On top of the world: *See,* **Top**.

Once

Once in a blue moon: *See,* **Moon**.

Once over: a quick examination or review. *He gave the car a once over before paying for it in cash.*

One

One and the same: identical. *The engines in these different cars are one and the same.*

One-armed bandit: *See,* **Bandit**.

One damn thing after another: problems are everywhere. *It was a bad day for me, where it was one damn thing after another.*

One fell swoop: all at once; suddenly. *They took care of all the tasks in one fell swoop, and finished the job overnight.*

One in a million: 1) a very rare thing to happen. *The odds of having survived the volcanic eruption were one in a million.* 2) qualities of something or someone, generally in reference to excellence or positive character. *Grandma Mavis was charming, a great communicator to all, and a very caring person; she was truly one in a million.*

One-man show: an outfit or operation managed solely by one individual. *This business is a one-man show.*

One-night stand: a single performance. *His date was a one-night stand.*

One-track mind: only able to think or dwell on one thing (generally in reference to thinking constantly about sex and the opposite sex). *He has a one-track mind about girls.*

One up: being a step ahead; holding an advantage. *Jack allows his opponents to get one up on him in chess to make them feel good, then he surprises and beats them.*

One upmanship: desire to want to keep ahead of others; trying to show an advantage. *His one-upmanship cost him his friends and his honor.*

Oomph

Oomph: with (physical) emphasis. *Give the wrench some oomph to loosen that bolt.*

Open

Open a can of worms: *See,* **Can** of worms.

Open and aboveboard: honest. *I hired him because he has an open and aboveboard character.*

Open and shut: a certainty; a known conclusion. *Five witnesses saw him rear-end the vehicle, so it seems to me to be an open and shut case as to who was at fault.*

Open-door policy: a welcome entrance to any interested party. *Unlike today, America had an open-door policy on immigration in the early 1900's.*

Open doors: something that will create opportunities. *This book will open doors for you in the publishers market.*

Open-handed: generous; liberal; willing to give or share. *People in the country tend to be much more open-handed than city dwellers.*

Out

Conk out: to stop operating; to collapse. *The runner almost conked out at the end of the race. The car engine conked out at the end of our long trip.*

Out cold: unconscious; fainted. *With one punch to his chin, she knocked him out cold.*

Out like a light: to quickly become unconscious or asleep. *He went out like a light as soon as he lay down on the mattress. Dick was out like a light after two glasses of wine.*

Out of action: not in service due to damage, disruption or malfunction; crippled; useless. *Due to the strike, our faction was out of action for a week. The flu put me out of action for a week.*

Out of circulation: not active; away from the mainstream. *I have been out of circulation with my friends due to my work schedule and overseas assignments.*

Out of gas: run down; having no energy. *We need to take a short break climbing this hill because I'm out of gas.*

Out of hand: 1) uncontrolled; disorderly; chaotic. *The crowd got out of hand at the concert.* 2) quick decision without consultation. *We accepted the coroner's report out of hand.*

Out of here/Outta here: away; gone; over there. *When the Babe hit the ball out of the park, the announcer exclaimed: "That ball is outta here!!"*

Out of kilter/Out of sync/Out of whack: not functioning correctly; broken. *The copier machine is out of kilter after running continuously all week long.*

Out of line: improper behavior. *Jock got out of line when the police tried to arrest him.*

Out of nowhere: appearing without warning; suddenly; unexpectedly. *The number six biker came from out of nowhere and won the desert slalom.*

Out of one's depth: beyond one's understanding, comprehension or ability. *Attempting to climb Mt. Everest as a beginner would be way out of your depth right now.*

Out of one's element: away of one's natural surroundings or knowledge; where one does not feel comfortable or knowledgeable. *Understanding computer programming is out of my element.*

Out of one's hair: to get rid of; move away as a nuisance or a bother. *Get out of my hair and don't bother me.*

Out of one's mind/Out of one's head: illogical; crazy. *Are you out of your mind? You will get in trouble if you miss the appointment.*

Out of one's system: get rid of (usually referred to ridding particular feelings or inclinations in one's mind); flush out. *I had to go outside and yell in order to get the feeling of frustration out of my system.*

Out of place: See, **Feel** out of place.

Out of pocket: 1) money personally spent. *I had to pay for the hotel expenses out of pocket even though I was on a business trip.* 2) having no money. *I found myself out of pocket and unable to pay for my shopping items.*

Out of the blue: unexpected happening; from nowhere. *From out of the blue, a plane came crashing down from the skies.*

Out of the fire: moving away from imminent danger. *John would not have gotten out of the fire on the criminal charge without the assistance of his lawyer in court.*

Out of the frying pan (and) into the fire: to make a bad or tough situation even worse; to go from bad to worse. *His troubles went from out of the frying pan and into the fire when he assaulted the police officer.*

Out of the loop: not involved or connected with; not part of. *We were left out of the loop in the investigation.*

Out of the question: not possible. *That request is out of the question.*

Out of the woods: no longer in harm's way; away from danger. *He is finally out of the woods and beginning to recover from his head injury.*

Out of thin air: 1) appearing from an unknown source; suddenly appearing. *The tiger appeared out of thin air and scared all of us.* 2) without support; coming from nowhere. *Claude could not corroborate his report because his story was made out of thin air.*

Out of this world: wonderful; hard to beat; superior. *He has an immaculate lakefront home that is out of this world!*

Out of touch: not communicating for some time. *I have been out of touch with world events lately because I have been camping in the mountains for the past month.*

Out of turn: 1) not in regular order. *If you proceed with matters out of turn, you will disrupt everyone else's schedule.* 2) hasty response at the wrong time. *Please do not speak out of turn, especially when others are speaking.*

Out of whack: *See above,* **Out** of kilter.

Out on a limb: to openly risk taking an action or stating an opinion; take a risk in order to save something or someone. *Did you know that he went out on a limb for you and covered your missed assignments? He went out on a limb and predicted who would win the race for mayor.*

OUT ON A LIMB

Out on the town: going to clubs or engagements in celebration of an event. *We went out on the town last night in celebration of Bob's promotion.*

Out the window: a futile situation; ruined. *All the time we put into this project is out the window without additional funding from investors.*

Out to lunch: 1) gone for the midday meal. *He's out to lunch and won't return for another hour.* 2) not normal in the head, including being dumb, inattentive, daydreaming, crazy or mad. *That guy is really out to lunch. What's his problem?*

Outfox: to outsmart. *The opponent was literally outfoxed in the last minute of play.*

Pull out all the stops: *See,* **Pull**.

Tuckered out: exhausted. *We're tuckered out from the long hike.*

Over

Head over heels: *See,* **Head**.

Over a barrel: in a helpless or trapped position. *You seem to have the other competitors over a barrel with your unique design, so you should win the contract easily.*

Over my dead body: *See,* **Dead**.

Over one's head: 1) beyond one's understanding. *That matter is over my head.* 2) go to a higher authority. *He went over my head again to the president to ask for additional funding.*

Over the coals: admonish someone harshly. *He was raked over the coals by his boss for losing the big contract to a competitor.*

Over the hill: past one's prime; not able to function as well as before. *I was good, but I'm over the hill now.*

Pack

Pack a wallop/Pack a punch: 1) a big boost; a strong reaction. *This drink really packs a wallop.* 2) able to throw a hard punch. *The new heavyweight can certianly pack a punch!*

Pack rat: one who saves everything. *You should see Mr. Albert's attic; he's a pack rat.*

Packed (in) like sardines: packed very tightly. *During the storm we were packed into the auditorium like sardines.*

Packing: carrying a weapon. *Are you packing today?*

Pace

Change of pace: *See,* **Change**.

Go through the paces: *See,* **Go** through the motions/Go through the paces.

Keep pace: *See,* **Keep**.

Put one through the paces: test what one can do; to take score of one's capabilities. *The team put the new players through the paces at the course to analyze their stamina, character and intelligence.*

Set the pace: act in leadership; establish a standard that others would follow. *He set the pace in the downhill slalom with his unique style, which brought him three gold medals.*

Snail's pace: *See,* **Snail**.

Pad

A pad: a room or apartment. *Dick has a pad on the other side of town.*

Pad one's pocket: pocketing money or assets not belonging to you; embezzle funds. *He padded his own pockets for many years from city funds while he was an accountant; now he has a padded cell in the psychiatric criminal ward of the hospital.*

Pad the bill: to deceptively increase the costs or services to get more money. *The phone company was fined for padding the bills of customers with services they never purchased, such as voicemail and conference calling.*

Paddy wagon: a wagon or a truck used by the police to carry prisoners. *The prisoners were placed in the paddy wagon on their way to court.*

Pain

Pain in the ass/butt/neck: causing agony or anguish. *He is a pain in the neck for leaving us at the meeting without transportation to return to the office.*

No pain, no gain: one cannot succeed without some pain. *In serious exercising to lose weight, they say, "No pain, no gain."*

Under pain of: extremely worried. *He's under pain of losing everything.*

Paint

Paint the town (red): go out for a good time; unrestrained spree. *We painted the town red after our football victory.*

Palm

Grease one's palm: *See,* **Grease**.

Itchy palms: one who desires to get as much money as he can; greed. *He has an itchy palm and will jump at any deal that might make him some money.*

Palm off: pass off by deception. *The gemologist was caught palming off fake gems as real ones.*

Pan

Out of the frying pan and into the fire: *See,* **Out**.

Pan out: to succeed; to work out well. *So, how did your hernia operation pan out?*

Panic

Hit/Push the panic button: overreact; react frantically as if there is a crisis. *That young analyst likes to push the panic button a lot.*

Pants

Ants in one's pants: very restless; jumpy; excited. *You run around the office like you have ants in your pants.*

Catch someone with his or her pants down: catch someone unprepared or unaware. *The opposing debate team caught us with our pants down and defeated us soundly.*

Fly by the seat of one's pants: *See,* **Fly**.

Get the lead out of your pants: *See,* **Lead**.

Kick in the pants: *See,* **Kick** in the ass/Kick in the pants.

Smart pants: *See,* **Smart**.

Paper

Paper over: to cover up. *He tried to paper over the rising costs and delays by laying blame on a shortage of staff to do the job efficiently.*

Paper pusher/Paper shuffler: one who generally works behind a desk handling paperwork. *He had been a paper shuffler for 20 years until, suddenly, he got promoted to field commander in battle.*

Paper tiger: a threat without force; a bluff. *The armed forces of the tiny country are no longer seen as a paper tiger.*

Par

Par for the course: average; that which is acceptable. *Being stuck in traffic around here is par for the course; you best get used to it.*

Up to par: 1) feeling all right; in good health. *Jane is feeling up to par today to play golf on her 90th birthday. Since I'm not feeling up to par today, you will have to go without me.* 2) up to average; getting to normal operation or condition. *You need to bring your school grades up to par or you won't graduate next year.*

Parasite

Parasite: one who grasps onto another for support without consideration. *Although Jack pays rent, he relies on others like a parasite to do his laundry, the dishes, and cleaning around the house.*

Parasite single: a salaried family member who lives with parents without making a useful contribution for his upkeep; a hanger on. *Dick enjoys the free life of a parasite single without a worry in the world. More apartments are for rent because many graduates are living with their parents as parasite singles.*

Pardon

Beg your pardon/pardon me: 1) excuse me. *Pardon me, but could you tell me where the civic center is located?* 2) a request to have someone repeat what was just said. *Sally: She wanted to have you drop it off. Dolly: Pardon me? Sally: Margaret, she wanted you to drop off her scarf at her place today. Dolly: Oh, right.* 3) a declaratory expression in response to a forward or offensive remark (emphasis on the word, "beg"). *I beg your pardon! I never said that!*

Part

Part and parcel: an important aspect; essential element. *Networking is part and parcel of making good business contacts.*

Part company: 1) split up; go separate ways. *I haven't seen her ever since we parted company three years ago.* 2) see things differently; disagree. *We part company on our views of the death penalty.*

Part with: turn or hand over; give something up. *Mary hated to part with her old car on a trade in.*

Parting of the ways: when people or groups split up. *The business partners had a parting of the ways after 22 years together.*

Parting shot: the last word or words, generally sarcastic or insulting, in an argument or discussion. *In leaving the assignment unfinished, he looked toward his boss while walking out, and with a parting shot, stated, "I'm not coming back."*

Party

Party pooper: to leave a gathering or misbehave in one, which tends to spoil the pleasure of others. *Jack is a party pooper by leaving so early. Don't be a party pooper, and stay a while longer.*

Pass

Make a pass at: *See,* **Make**.

Pass away: die. *He passed away in his sleep.*

Pass for: 1) relating to a counterfeit item. *The Gucci handbag was passed for a genuine one.* 2) look like something or someone. *Although he is Eurasian, with a mustache, he can pass for a Latino in this neighborhood.*

Pass muster: meet standard requirements; to qualify; be acceptable. *I doubt that this proposal would pass muster with the committee.*

Pass off: to discontinue. *Sam will pass off drinking beer this summer.*

Pass out: to become unconscious. *He passes out at the first sight of blood.*

Pass over: to give one no consideration or opportunity. *I don't know why Mack was passed over for promotion this year.*

Pass the buck: pass accountability and fault to someone else; avoid responsibility. *The managers were passing the buck on the disaster.*

Pass the hat: request for donations; collection for money. *We all passed the hat to get her a going-away gift.*

Pass water: to urinate. *We all had to pass water after the long lecture.*

Passing fancy: fad; something that is once popular, then fades in fashion. *The hoola hoop was a passing fancy back in the 1950's.*

Paste

Like pasting jelly to the wall: *See,* **Wall**.

Paste: fake or costume jewelry, such as a fake diamond. *Let's have a jeweler determine if this rock is a real diamond or just paste.*

Pasted: 1) beaten up. *He got pasted in the street brawl.* 2) caught. *We got pasted by the principal for smoking in the bathroom.*

Path

Off the beaten path: to stray away from. *When we talk about the Old West, he tends to go off the beaten path and talk about his cowboy buddies of yesteryear.*

On the beaten path: keep disciplined; do not waiver. *Stay on the beaten path with your diet so that your blood sugar level stays within an acceptable range.*

Paw

Paw: hand. *Get your paws off my stuff.*

Pay

It pays: it's rewarding. *It pays to attend college.*

Pay an arm and a leg/Pay through the nose: to pay dearly for something. *I paid an arm and leg for this vacuum cleaner and it doesn't pick up anything. You have to pay through the nose for property around here.*

Pay as you go: pay expenses as they arise. *I'm for pay as you go.*

Pay for: suffer for; undergo reprimand. *You'll pay for your wrongdoing.*

Pay lip service: insincere support. *Jack gave his word to help our cause, but he was only paying lip service.*

Pay off/Payoff: 1) pay all you owe; payment amount to clear a debt. *What is the payoff on the loan?* 2) take revenge. *As pay off for being teased, the little boy filled water balloons to throw at the girls.* 3) bribe. *The city councilman had been receiving pay offs from the casino for the past 5 years.*

Pay through the nose: *See above,* **Pay an arm and a leg.**

Paycheck to paycheck: have barely enough money to keep up with living expenses (where survival is critically dependent in receiving the next paycheck); where one's salary leaves no disposable income. *Many families today live paycheck by paycheck.*

Peanuts

Peanuts: very little money. *I receive peanuts for a salary.*

Pearl

Cast pearls before swine: give a valuable thing to someone who does not appreciate it. *Sam gave a lot of money to one of his relatives, but got very little appreciation in return; it was like casting pearls before swine.*

Peck

Pecking order: person's status or rank in a group; hierarchy of authority or status. *The pecking order in this company is such that the higher up you go, the less they know about company operations.*

P.D.Q.

P.D.Q./PDQ: Pretty darn quick. *Thomas, get those books opened PDQ and finish your homework!*

Pee

Pee [expressive]: to urinate. *The kids have to pee before we depart.*

255

Peep

Peepers: eyes. *My peepers are red today from lack of sleep.*

Peeping Tom: someone who watches others without their knowledge; covert viewer; voyeur. *He was caught as a peeping Tom by the girls at the dorm.*

Peg

Hard (for one) to peg: difficult or unable to figure out. *It's hard for me to peg, but I remember that guy from somewhere.*

Peg leg: a person wearing a wooden leg. *These days, you should say that one wears 'orthotics' or 'prosthetics' rather than call it a 'peg leg.'*

Peg legs: a person wearing pants tapered at the ankle. *Peg legs are getting popular again.*

Round peg in a square hole: a person in the wrong job; does not fit in. *When we hired Sam, we didn't know he would be a round peg in a square hole.*

Take down a peg: reduce one's position or pride. *Mack was brought down a peg due to downsizing.*

Pencil

Pencil pusher: one who performs general office work. *Jack is just a pencil pusher and not a technician.*

Penny

Earn an honest penny: earn money the honest way. *Why don't you go out and earn an honest penny.*

Penniless: very poor. *Some people are penniless all their lives.*

Penny pincher: cheap or stingy individual; one who doesn't like to spend money. *Penny pinchers will very often sponge off other people.*

Penny wise and pound foolish: a proverb meaning that while one is very careful spending money on small things, he or she overspends on large items. *I could name several people I know who are penny wise and pound foolish.*

Pretty penny: a lot of money. *That foreign car of yours must have cost you a pretty penny.*

Pep

Pep pill: any number of tablets or pill containing a stimulant such as amphetamine. *Pep pills speed up physical and mental processes, and energy, but in the long term may lead to mental disorder.*

Pep rally: a meeting where the attendees are aroused to some type of action. *We attend a five-minute pep rally every workday.*

Perk

Perk up: liven up; get more energy; get to feel better. *James perked up pretty well after a long illness.*

Perks: fringe benefits received in addition to one's basic pay, such as insurance coverage, housing, education, vacations, et cetera. *Those in management seem to get all the perks.*

Perky: self confident; lively. *Mr. Samuels is pretty perky after his promotion.*

Pet

Pet peeve: a certain source of irritation or annoyance. *My pet peeve is my girlfriend's cat scratching the corners of my sofa and love seat!*

Teacher's pet: teacher's favored student; one who has favor. *Jack never gets scolded in class because he is the teacher's pet.*

Peter

Peter out: 1) stop functioning or unable to last. *His car petered out on the freeway.* 2) become less crowded or intense. *Let's wait until the traffic peters out a bit before we leave.* 3) become very exhausted. *We were petered out after the race.* 4) die. *His heart couldn't take the strain, and he just petered out.*

Phat

Phat: real nice; awesome (acronym for "pretty hot and tempting"). *Wow, you are looking phat tonight, girl!*

Phooey

Phooey: nonsense. *What you're telling me is a lot of phooey.*

Phony

Phony/Phony baloney: fake; not real; fraudulent. *A lot of phony baloney is going on in this company. That vendor sells phony watches and handbags.*

Pick

Bone to pick: *See,* **Bone**.

Nit-pick: *See,* **Nit**.

Pick a fight: start a confrontation, generally with offensive motions or physical force. *He has a hot temper and is quick to pick a fight with you.*

Pick holes: point out errors or weaknesses; find fault; criticize. *My former boss enjoyed picking holes in everyone's report.*

Pick on: pester; provoke. *They tried to pick on me but I stayed calm.*

Pick one's brain: *See,* **Brain**.

Pick out: single out from a group; to differentiate. *Can you pick out the spoiled ones?*

Pick up the pieces: restore something back to normal. *After the coup attempt, the leaders had to pick up the pieces and restore order in the country.*

Pick up the tab: pay the restaurant bill. *Who's turn is it to pick up the tab for today's lunch?*

Piece

Piece: weapon; gun. *I got a permit to carry a piece.*

Piece of cake: *See,* **Cake**.

Piece of change: a good amount of money. *These old Indian moccasins you have are worth a piece of change.*

Piece of my mind: tough criticism or direct confrontation. *If you come here again, I for sure will give you a piece of my mind.*

Piece of the action/Piece of the pie: a share of the profits; to be part of a venture. *I'll work with you if you give me a piece of the action.*

Piece of work: artifact; a creation (referred to as being wonderful, or sarcastically as an odd thing). *That oil painting of the sand pointers looking for food along the lapping shore is a fine piece of work. That obnoxious woman is a piece of work, isn't she?*

Pig

Guinea pig: when one is made the subject of study or research. *During the war many soldiers were used as guinea pigs without their full knowledge, such as for atomic tests, LSD experiments, and other government projects.*

In a pig's eye: real unlikely; not so. *When airport security inspected and noted the pointed ends on his Congressional Medal of Honor, security personnel stated that it would have to take the medal away from him for security reasons. He replied, "Yeah, in a pig's eye you will."* [A true-to-life story at airport security. And damn right, the veteran was able to keep his medal of honor.]

Like a pig in mud/slop: the height of pleasure. *See also,* **Like a pig in shit** [expressive]. *When Jack plays golf, he is like a pig in mud.*

Make a pig of oneself: to overeat or overindulge. *I am so hungry I am going to make a pig of myself at the buffet.*

Pig-headed: hard to please; difficult to get along with. *No one likes to be with Jack because he is so pig-headed.*

Pig in a poke: something offered as a good deal but really is not; looks good but not worth it. *Many investors bought a pig in a poke when they purchased high flying stocks that later tanked.*

Pig out: to gorge food; to eat starvingly. *I'm hungry and ready to pig out on the chicken you have cooking on the barbeque.*

Piggy bank: a small child's bank in the shape of a pig. *Johnny's piggy bank is full of coins and ready for deposit into the bank.*

Pigeon

Pigeonhole: to classify as or identify with. *I do not want people to pigeonhole me as some two-bit actor but rather as a serious playwright.*

Stool pigeon: an informer, especially for the police. *As a vagabond for years, he earned a good deal of his money as a stool pigeon providing information he heard on the streets to the local sheriff's office.*

Pile

Pile of shit [expressive]: *See,* **Shit**.

Pile up: a wreck involving three or more cars. *Beware of a pile up on the southbound freeway going into the city.*

Rock pile: *See,* **Rock**.

Pin

Pin down: 1) locate and fix. *We need to pin the problem down before the show begins.* 2) to force into revealing information. *The reporters tried to pin him down on his decision to leave college and enter pro ball.* 3) confinement or limited space for escape. *The bombardment forced the soldiers to be pinned down for three days.*

Pin someone's ears back: punish or reprimand harshly. *Dennis got his ears pinned back when he tried to help.*

Pin the blame: focus the accusation on; fix responsibility on. *They tried to pin the blame on Mike but he was nowhere around the scene.*

Pinner: a tightly-rolled marijuana joint. *They would smoke pinners because the weed was so potent.*

Pinch

In a pinch: 1) to be in a bind or difficult situation; in trouble. *I'll be in a pinch if I cannot find a babysitter before going to work.* 2) in an emergency. *I can always count on my friend Amy when I am in a pinch.*

Penny pincher: *See,* **Penny**.

Pink

In the pink: in good physical condition. *Mr. Jackson was found to be in the pink for his last physical.*

Pink slip: a dismissal notice from one's job. *It was very difficult to see people like Mr. Richards get a pink slip after many years of service.*

Tickled pink: *See,* **Tickle**.

Pipe

Pipe down: be quiet. *Pipe down while you're in class.*

Pipe dream: a dream or fantasy. *His idea is only a pipe dream without the financial support.*

Pipe up: speak louder; make yourself heard. *Just pipe up if you need anything.*

Pipeline: a channel of communication and transportation. *Our new product is now in the pipeline.*

Piping hot: boiling hot; very hot. *The coffee is piping hot!*

Pipsqueak

Pipsqueak: a person or a thing low in position, grade or character. *Look at that pipsqueak in the front row trying to act big.*

Piss

A pisser: a difficult undertaking; something that is frustrating or a great annoyance. *That drive through the fog was a real pisser.*

Go piss up a rope [expressive]: a rough expression of denial, rejection, or disgust; response to tell one to go away and leave. *When he asked me for more favors, I told him to go piss up a rope.*

Piss [expressive]: to urinate. *Stop at the next rest stop; I need to take a piss.*

Piss away: to carelessly waste away; squander. *She pissed away her inheritance.*

Piss off/Piss one off [expressive]: 1) go to hell; expression of denial, rejection or disgust. *Piss off and don't tell me what I have to do.* 2) to greatly annoy; to get one very angry *Don't piss him off with a bad attitude. Dave gets pissed off whenever he doesn't get his own way.*

Piss poor: 1) inadequate; unacceptable; low quality. *That's a piss poor way to treat customers. They did a piss poor job laying the bricks on your driveway.* 2) impoverished; penniless. *A positive aspect of capitalism is that it offers many to escape a piss poor life for a fair opportunity to financially excel.*

Piss-poor excuse: lousy or misguided example of. *That's a piss-poor excuse for an answer. That's a piss-poor way to show respect for our foreign guests.*

Pissing contest: an almost needless argument, disagreement, or confrontation that doesn't settle anything. *I was warned by my boss not to get into any silly pissing contests with my co-workers.*

Pit

Pit stop: the need to use the toilet (derived from car racing when a driver must stop occasionally in the pit for emergency maintenance). *One moment before we go—I have to make a pit stop.*

Pitch

In there pitching: working or performing your very best. *James is in there pitching all the time.*

Place

Go places: be successful. *Marie, with her talents, will certainly go places.*

Take place: to happen; come about. *When did the fight take place?*

Plain

Plain as day/Plain as the nose on your face: very obvious; clearly evident. *Given his tired and disheveled look, it was plain as day that he had a rough time at work. It's as plain as the nose on your face that he's lying.*

Plastered

Plastered: 1) drunk. *We got plastered at Jake's party.* 2) beaten decisively. *Our school got plastered in last night's basketball game.*

Play

Make a play for: to seek someone or something out. *Sam made a play for Helen but she turned him away. It won't hurt to make a play for that job.*

Play ball: 1) it's time to get started or begin. *Let's play ball and do the best we can.* 2) cooperate. *Set your differences aside and play ball.*

Play both ends: scheming to get one side against another. *Gary was well-known for scheming and playing both ends with those around him; he only thought what was best for himself.*

Play by ear: take action as it develops. *Let's just play this by ear at each step of the way.*

Play chicken: *See,* **Chicken**.

Play dumb: make people believe you're stupid. *At times, it's good to play dumb.*

Play fast and loose: to operate deceptively; untrusting. *These guys play fast and loose, so watch it.*

Play for keeps: opposite of playing for fun; you keep what you win; there's no giving back what you gain. *In their business world, they play for keeps.*

Play for time: delay play to one's advantage. *Let's play for time until we tire them out.*

Play hard to get: to act coy; act as if uninterested; to not respond so enthusiastically. *In order to keep him interested in her, she had to play hard to get.*

Play hardball: *See,* **Hard** (hardball).

Play hell: 1) bring damage or waste. *The heavy rain played hell with the crops.* 2) play for fun. *Let's go to town and play a little hell.*

Play hooky: skip school or work without permission to be absent. *That big kid plays hooky pretty often.*

Play it by ear: *See,* **Ear.**

Play it close to the chest/Play it close to the vest: be discreet; secretive; watchful of others when accomplishing a task; reveal little or nothing. *We know very little about his business operations because he plays it close to the chest. Given the sensitivity of this information, you have to play your cards close to the vest.*

Play it cool: behave in a shrewd, watchful way. *We played it cool until they gave up.*

Play it safe: operate with caution and without excessive risks. *Play it safe and diversify your investment portfolio.*

Play one's cards right: proceed with great skill in all endeavors; do things correctly. *If you play your cards right, you will do well in life.*

Play one's trump card: the use of a special device, plan, strategy, etc. *John didn't play his trump card until the end.*

Play possum: to pretend to be dead or asleep. *The fox played possum long enough to fool the dogs and escape.*

Play second fiddle: be in a subordinate role to another. *I'm not playing second fiddle to that fool.*

Play the field: to openly search for social contact; an open venture in romance. *After separating, he began to play the field.*

Play the gallery: one who directs his performance to please the audience; one who is very showy. *Playing the gallery is showing off and hot-dogging.*

Play tricks: play jokes, cheat; make a sucker of someone. *It's a shame how they play tricks on the little kids.*

Play up to someone: 1) gain one's favor. *James is constantly playing up to his boss to get a raise in pay.* 2) be affectionate or pleasing. *Janet is playing up to Donald every chance she gets.*

Play with a full deck: be sane and natural; have normal mental power and reasoning. *Given the strange behavior, I don't think he's playing with a full deck.*

Play with half a deck: not all there; when someone is doing something in an illogical or awkward manner; to act without sense; a little crazy. *He seems to be playing with half a deck.*

Playboy: a well-to-do man who seeks enjoyment accompanied by sexual promiscuity. *This club is known to attract the playboy types from uptown.*

Plum

Plum: nice; convenient; cushy; easy. *What a plum job he has working only on weekends.*

Plum forgot: to completely not remember. *I plum forgot to bring the basketball tickets with me to the game.*

Plum out: completely without; nothing left; all gone. *We are plum out of any more good ideas. The stores are plum out of snow shovels due to the demand ahead of the big snow storm.*

Plum-tuckered out: so overly exerted or tired that one feels temporarily incapacitated; burned out. *We were plum-tuckered out after climbing to the top of Mt. Rainier.*

Plunge

Take the plunge: take a big chance; make a significant investment. *He took a plunge into the international freight business covering South Asia and the Middle East.*

Pocket

Deep pocket: a source with a lot of money. *The plaintiffs went after the deep pockets, especially the insurance companies.*

In one's pocket: entirely under one's control. *After this deal, we'll have him in our pocket.*

Line one's pockets: *See,* **Line**.

Out of pocket: *See,* **Out**.

Pad one's pocket: *See,* **Pad**.

Point

Beside the point: not relevant; a deviation from the main matter, therefore not worthy or important. *That matter is beside the point and does not concern us.*

Make a point of/Make it a point: make a practice of. *Make it a point to brush your teeth every day.*

Point blank: directly; without deviation; straight at the mark. *Daniel told them point blank to get off the property.*

Point the finger at: to direct blame. *They pointed the finger at Bob for placing the skunk in the teachers' lounge.*

Pointless: senseless. *It seems pointless sometimes trying to persuade an ignorant mind.*

Pointy head: an intellectual; a learned person. *He is such a pointy head that he doesn't understand many of our jokes or slang words.*

Stretch the point: *See,* **Stretch**.

To the point: without delay; be direct in relaying the information. *Cut out the long explanation and just get to the point.*

Poke

A pig in a poke: *See,* **Pig**.

Poke about/around: to check out or peruse. *The school principal likes to poke around the shopping mall for truant pupils.*

Poke fun at: tease or make fun of. *Dave likes to poke fun at his co-workers.*

Slow poke/Slowpoke: slow person or driver. *A slowpoke has to move to the shoulder if there are more than five vehicles following behind.*

Poker

Poker face: no expression exposed; hard to figure out. *She exhibits such a poker face when interviewing new hires that I'm sure it scares them.*

Pokey/Poky

Pokey: jail. *Dennis landed in the pokey last night for fighting.*

Polish

Polish off: 1) finish a meal or a job quickly. *He polished off five eggs for breakfast.* 2) to eliminate. *Competition is so keen that you can get polished off quickly in this business.*

Pony

Dog and pony show: *See,* **Dog**.

Pony up: 1) tell the truth; confess. *Once he was arrested, he ponied up to his crimes.* 2) to remit on a debt; to pay. *You lost on the bet, so pony up.*

Pooh

Pooh pooh: 1) to stymie; to veto; to deny. *The children wanted to see a late-night movie, but the parents pooh poohed the idea.* 2) stool;

excrement. *See also,* **Poop**. *"Mommy, little Jimmy made some pooh pooh in the back yard."*

Poop

Hot poop: *See,* **Hot**.

Poop: 1) detailed information on something. *Get the poop and report back.* 2) stool; excrement. *"Mommy, the dog pooped in the kitchen."*

Poop out/Pooped: 1) to tire; feel exhausted. *We were too pooped to make another trip.* 2) to withdraw from an activity. *I have to poop out of our meeting due to a family emergency.*

Poop sheet: compilation of information on something. *Let me have the poop sheet on the leave status of our employees.*

Straight poop: the truth. *Give me the straight poop on this guy as to whether he's reliable.*

Too pooped for puzzles: when another tries to explain a story in a mysterious or deductive way, but the listener would rather hear the answer to the inquiry directly. *I'm too pooped for puzzles, so just tell me directly.*

Pop

Pop: 1) one's father. *Pop went to the hardware store.* 2) to punch someone in the face. *I ought to pop you for being such a fool.* 3) to go somewhere. *Let's pop over to the sports bar to watch the football game.* 4) to buy. *Ok, it's my turn to pop for the burgers and fries.* 5) per unit. *If you want some, it's $10.00 a pop.* 6) soda drink. *Let's go to the snack shop for a cold pop.*

Pop one's cork: have a burst of temper; suddenly get angry. *He popped his cork and lashed out at the corporate executives for their questionable accounting schemes.*

Pop the question: to ask someone to join you in marriage. *Mark popped the question to Marilyn after a nice meal at Big Al's restaurant.*

Pork

Pork/Pork barrel: politicians who vote in favor of money projects going to their districts. *There is a lot of pork barrel politics in Washington D.C.*

Pork chop [expressive]: fat person. *Listen, pork chop, who gave you the authority to boss everyone around here?*

Pork out: to eat like a pig; to consume ravenously or in large amounts. *We porked out on pepperoni pizza and garlic bread sticks.*

Porky: very chubby; plump; obese. *Did you see a porky fellow with black-rimmed glasses come through here?*

Possum

Play possum: pretend to be asleep, dead, ill, unaware, etc. *We played possum with our rival company, and then proposed a takeover.*

Pot

Get off the pot: quit wasting time and do it; move to action. *Get off the pot and finish cleaning your room.*

Go to pot: get messed up; go bad. *I can't see how that clean-cut boy went to pot.*

Pot: 1) toilet. *Dad's sitting on the pot so he can't come to the phone right now.* 2) cannabis; marijuana. *Pot smokers proclaim that it is their right and freedom to get high. Drug enforcement authorities arrested him for growing pot plants in his back yard.*

Pot calling the kettle black: one who accuses others is also guilty as well. *Hearing one political opponent accuse another of negative campaigning is like the pot calling the kettle black.*

Pot luck/Potluck: where members of a group bring home-cooked food or meal portions to an informal get-together or party. *We're having a potluck at my place next Friday.*

Potato

All meat and no potatoes: *See,* **Meat**.

Couch potato: *See,* **Couch**.

Hot potato: *See,* **Hot**.

Meat and potatoes: *See,* **Meat**.

Small potatoes: not much; cost very little. *That's small potatoes compared to what he really lost in the deal.*

Pound

Penny wise and pound foolish: *See,* **Penny**.

Pound the books: to study intensely. *I've been pounding the books all day.*

Pound the pavement: to walk the streets, generally to look for work or to find someone. *Sally had to pound the pavement for several months before she finally found a job.*

Pour

Pour it on: give it all you have; speed up fast. *We tried to catch up to his car but he poured it on and disappeared.*

Pour it on thick: *See,* **Thick**.

Pour money down the drain: waste money by spending foolishly. *Investing in this company is like pouring money down the drain.*

Pour oil over troubled waters: diminish the intensity of a serious situation. *The ambassador poured oil over troubled waters and got the warring parties to talk peace.*

Practice

Out of practice: not in condition; not used to doing something that one did better before. *I haven't gone bowling in years, so I know I'll be out of practice.*

Practice makes perfect: do something often enough and you will be very good at it. *Practice makes perfect in winning the spelling bee championship.*

Practice what you preach: follow and do what you talk about; not be a hypocrite. *You will lose credibility if you don't practice what you preach.*

Prayer

Doesn't have a (song and a) prayer: not a chance. *He doesn't have a prayer to make the flight on time.*

Pretty

Pretty: fairly; sort of. *The next gas station on this road is going to be pretty far away.*

Pretty penny: *See,* **Penny**.

Sitting pretty: in a good position; doing very well. *John is sitting pretty with a good job, an excellent house, and lots of money in the bank.*

Price

At any price: regardless of price. *Buy that painting at any price.*

Price on one's head: a wanted person; offer of money in catching someone. *No one knew that the neighbor down the street had a price on his head.*

Priced out of the market: the price is too high for anyone to buy. *Most of the homes in my area are priced out of the market.*

Prick

Prick [expressive]**:** a very disrespectful individual; one who exhibits little or no consideration. *He's a real prick to steal from elderly women.*

Prick one's ears: listen carefully. *We had to prick our ears to hear the speaker over the background noise.*

Program

Get with the program: follow instructions; get along and do your job. *We were all told to get with the program and fly right.*

Promise

Promise the moon: make a promise that cannot be kept. *She left you because you always promised her the moon.*

Psych

Psyched up: mentally and physically ready for any eventuality. *We were focused and psyched up for our final exam.*

Psycho: deranged; mentally ill. *That guy is psycho and belongs in a hospital.*

Pull

Pull a boner: do a dumb and senseless thing. *I pulled a boner when I invested in the wrong stocks.*

Pull a fast one/Pull a trick: See, **Fast**.

Pull for: cheer for. *We're pulling for our high school team.*

Pull in: 1) to arrive. *What time did you pull into Chicago?* 2) to receive. *How much are you going to pull in on this deal?* 3) to arrest or catch someone. *The crook was pulled in right away.*

Pull one's punches: be lenient. *I decided to pull my punches and be nice at the meeting.*

Pull one's weight: 1) do your fair share of the job. *If you don't pull your weight around here, you'll be fired.* 2) exhibit leverage or advantage for opportunity. *Can you pull your weight and get me a job at your company?*

Pull out: 1) go away from a place. *The train pulled out at 3:00 p.m.* 2) withdraw. *We had no choice but to pull out of the agreement.*

Pull out all the stops: to do something without any restriction; go full force all the way. *We pulled out all the stops to get the job done.*

Pull rank: See, **Rank**.

Pull someone's leg: See, **Leg**.

Pull something out of a hat/Pull something out of thin air: without substantiation or factual support; not real. *Rather than be truthful, he pulled a story out of thin air.*

Pull something out of the fire: rescue or save something. *He worked hard and pulled our project out of the fire.*

Pull something together: to get matters organized, usually in a timely manner. *How did you pull everything together so quickly?*

Pull strings: See, **String**.

Pull the plug: 1) discontinue life support for someone terminally ill. *Great grandma wants us to pull the plug if she ever becomes paralyzed due to a* *stroke.* 2) stop (funding) something. *The new highway construction stopped when the government pulled the plug on the program.* 3) reveal information on wrongdoing. *The records clerk pulled the plug on the section chief.*

Pull the wool over one's eyes: fool, deceive; mislead. *He tried to pull the wool over their eyes with his fancy talk. Hey, you can't pull the wool over my eyes.*

Pull through: get through a challenging or painful period; go through a difficult situation. *We lost everything in the storm but, somehow, we will manage to pull through all of this.*

Pull up stakes: move elsewhere. *We pulled up stakes and moved to California.*

Pump

Pump iron: lift weights on your daily exercise. *He pumps iron for one hour each day.*

Pumped/Pumped up: excited; ready for action. *We are pumped about going to the game tonight! The players were pumped up about the big game.*

Punk

Punk: a wild and immature person. *Let's explain to that punk what is right and what is wrong.*

Push

Don't push your luck: don't gamble asking for too much. *You can ask him if you can borrow the car but don't push your luck asking for anything else.*

Pencil pusher: *See,* **Pencil**.

Push comes to shove: when a situation leads to confrontation or hostility. *If push comes to shove, then settle at that time.*

Push on in years: getting older. *When you're pushing on in years you can't be too flashy.*

Push one to the wall: put someone on the defensive. *We pushed our competitors to the wall until we got a chance to buy them out.*

Push the envelope: take a greater risk; go to the extreme. *Humans have an instinctive nature to push the envelope in their quest to discover the universe.*

Push the panic button: *See,* **Panic**.

Pushing up daisies: referring to one who has died and is pushing up flowers from his grave. *That nice old man has been pushing up daisies for five years now.*

Pushover: anything very easy to do; a person or a group easily convinced. *Securing our last contract was a pushover.*

Put

Put a lid on it: shut up. *The teacher told the noisy kids to put a lid on it.*

Put all your eggs in one basket: invest everything in one item; put all one's assets into a single investment. *You are likely to fail if you put all your eggs in one basket.*

Put away: 1) be placed in jail or an institution. *He was put away in a mental hospital.* 2) consume food or drink. *Sam can put away a lot of beer.*

Put away for a rainy day: to save or preserve something for later in time of need. *It's always smart to put something away for a rainy day.*

Put down: 1) reduce one's power of authority. *Mr. Sims was put down one grade.* 2) stop what your doing. *Put down that silly puzzle.* 3) denigrate; find fault with. *He tends to put others down.*

Put English on the ball: *See,* **English**.

Put in: 1) to enter something. *You will need to put in an insurance claim for the damage caused to your car.* 2) spend time doing something. *He puts in a lot of time around the house.* 3) confined. *We were put in by the stormy weather.*

Put in mothballs: stored; set aside; deferred for an indefinite or long duration. *Our plans to go on vacation were put in mothballs due to the children getting sick.*

Put it there: offer of an open palm to receive a slap of a hand of another in expression of joy, agreement, etc. *Put it there, my friend!*

Put off: 1) accomplish something later. *I'll put off doing that project until next month.* 2) be disappointed, upset or mad. *We were put off by his rudeness.*

Put on: deception; ruse; fake cover. *He goes through an elaborate job to look rich; it's all a put on.*

Put on an act: fake the truth. *She often puts on an act to try to impress her friends.*

Put on an event: stage an event. *We're putting on a garage sale.*

Put on the dog: *See,* **Dog**.

Put one's best foot forward: act one's best. *Now that I have a good job, I must put my best foot forward.*

Put one's cards on the table: reveal what one has. *We expect you to put your cards on the table and not hide anything from us.*

Put one's finger on it/You put your finger on it: *See,* **Finger**.

Put one's foot in it/Put one's foot in one's mouth: to blunder. *Dick put his foot in his mouth when he accidentally revealed to friends where the hidden documents were located.*

Put one's hand to the plow: apply maximum effort. *We'll have to put our hands to the plow to get this job done on time.*

Put our heads together: combine the brainpower of a group in discussing and resolving a matter. *Let's put our heads together to figure out what to buy Sally for her birthday.*

Put out to pasture: to lose one's job. *Jack was put out to pasture after the merger.*

Put someone on: to fool or deceive. *Are you putting me on about Jack getting married?*

Put someone on a pedestal: have great respect and admiration for someone. *To please your lady, you have to put her on a pedestal and show her that you care.*

Put someone out: keep one from doing other things. *I hope I'm not putting you out for helping me move out of my apartment today.*

Put someone through the ringer/wringer: give someone a hard time; squeeze someone hard and not make it easy for him or her (an original reference to the old washing machine of the early 1900's that came with a wringer on the top, with rubber rollers to squeeze the excess water from wet clothing). *They really put Jim through the wringer during his on-the-job training.*

Put something over: deceive; confuse. *Don't let them put anything over on you.*

Put that in your pipe and smoke it: take that; a phrase to let another know that you challenge your ground and will not move. *I'm not going to comply with your silly rules, so you can put that in your pipe and smoke it.*

Put the bite on: *See,* **Bit/Bite**.

Put the clamps on: curb or restrict. *Jack's parents put the clamps on his late night driving after he injured a pedestrian.*

Put the heat/screws/squeeze on (someone): to apply pressure; to scare. *The suspect did not say a word until the detectives put the heat on him.*

Put through the mill: be subjected to a tough experience. *Ben was put through the mill at camp, but he survived.*

Put two and two together: figure out the correct solution or gain the proper inference by analyzing the available evidence. *It wasn't hard to put two and two together to understand why he was the prime suspect in the murder.*

Put-up job: a pre-arranged, crooked deal or conspiracy. *The theft of the files was a put-up job arranged by employees sympathetic to the cause of animal rights groups.*

Put up or shut up: a command to take action rather than just talk about it or be in the way. *He couldn't make up his mind about joining the card game, so we told him to put up or shut up.*

Put up with: to live with. *I have to put up with a lot of traffic on my way to work.*

Put words in someone's mouth: to incorrectly state what someone has spoken about. *I never said that; you're putting words in my mouth.*

Put your money where your mouth is: *See,* **Money**.

Put yourself in someone else's shoes: mentally imagine how another feels by a certain action. *If you put yourself in their shoes, you can see how rough they have it.*

Quack

Quack: a fake; an incompetent professional, generally in reference to a doctor. *Much of the malpractice that took place in the hospital was caused by the actions of a few quacks.*

Quantum

Quantum leap: a significant and dramatic advance in knowledge or process. *They have made quantum leaps in aviation technology over the past 20 years.*

Quick

Quick buck: fast and easy money. *It's getting harder to make a quick buck around here.*

Quick on the draw: able to react fast; rapid action or reaction. *You have to be pretty quick on the draw to get good concert seats at this stadium.*

Quickie: 1) anything done in a short duration. *He made a lot of money making videos on quickie exercise workouts for the working person.* 2) fast and impromptu. *They got a quickie divorce in Reno.* 3) sex done hastily and rushed. *We hardly have time for a quickie anymore.*

Quid

Quid pro quo: something for something; fair or equal exchange. *We have a quid pro quo understanding that I keep the area landscaped in return for free rent of the bungalow.*

Rack

Off the rack: factory-made clothing; not individually tailored. *Most men's suits today are purchased off the rack.*

On the rack: in a troublesome situation. *Mason is on the rack for going on leave without notifying his boss.*

Rack [expressive]: female breasts. *The drunkard at the end of the bar said she had a 'nice rack'...and then had a martini thrown in his face.*

Rack one's brains: to strain with great effort. *I racked my brains wondering where I left my wallet; it was right in front of me, mixed in with the junk on the table.*

Rack up: 1) to gain in substance or accomplishment. *He racked up several million dollars last year. They finally racked up a win.* 2) to affect negatively; beat up. *He got racked up in the fourth round.*

Racket

Racket: 1) an uproar or din. *Who's making all that racket?* 2) a fraudulent or dishonest business. *The underground operated a big racket for many years.* 3) the oftentimes monotonous day-to-day routines on the job or in a profession. *I've been in this racket all my life. What's your racket?*

Rad

Rad: radical; awesome; great. *Joshua's new place is really rad.*

Rag

On the rag: [expressive]: a woman's menstrual period; menstruating. *Christine gets so crabby when she's on the rag.*

Rag: 1) to taunt or tease. *Oh, lighten up. I'm just ragging you.* 2) to annoy or put pressure on someone. *Would you quit ragging me,?*

Rag picker: one who makes a living by collecting junk or discarded items. *When I was a kid, we sold junk to the rag-picker.*

Ragged (pronounced: rag-ged): disheveled; overly tired. *He looks so ragged today, I wonder what he did last night.*

Raggedy-ass: 1) disorganized; dirty. *This raggedy-ass old man came into the bank today and deposited a large amount of money.* 2) freakish. *You better change your raggedy-ass attitude or you'll get fired.*

Rags to riches: from poor to wealthy. *Mr. Thompson went from rags to riches in two years.*

Rail

Go off the rails: get off course; go crazy. *If one more misfortune befalls me, I'm likely to go off the rails!*

Rail: to condemn; complain bitterly or abusively. *She railed constantly about her next door neighbor.*

Rain

Rain cats and dogs: rain very hard. *We played our soccer game while it was raining cats and dogs.*

Rain check: 1) free ticket to go to another game because of cancellation on account of rain. *We got a rain check on today's ball game, which was canceled on account of rain.* 2) request to reschedule when one cannot make it at the invited time. *I can't make dinner tomorrow; however, can I have a rain check for next week?*

Rainy day: a time in need; a savings. *I try to keep extra funds in the bank for a rainy day.*

Raise

Raise a rumpus/Raise Cain/Raise hell/Raise the devil/Raise the roof: create a loud disturbance; have a boisterous time. *With the way the party was going, you'd think they had raised the devil himself! After the victory, the students were raising hell well past midnight.*

Raise one's eyebrows: in astonishment or surprise. *Jim's arrest last night for assault caused his coworkers to raise a few eyebrows.*

Raise one's sights: set higher goals, objectives or expectations. *Raise your sights, sister; you're much too good for him!*

Raise the roof: *See,* **Roof**.

Raise the stakes: increase the risk or value of something. *You raise the stakes if you forego the settlement offer, because it's all or nothing if you go to trial.*

Rake

Rake in/Rake up: to take in abundance. *He is raking in a lot of money at the boardwalk as a body piercer and tattoo artist.*

Rake over the coals: to punish harshly. *Jack got raked over the coals for offending the professor.*

Ramble

Ramble: 1) to digress; talk continually without being mindful of the audience. *After about 15 minutes, we all began to wonder what on earth she was rambling about. When he takes his medication, he tends to ramble on about various subject matters for long periods of time.* 2) to walk aimlessly. *For exercise, we just rambled around town all afternoon.*

Range

Out of range: out of reach; an unobtainable goal. *To try to maintain a ten percent growth rate is utterly out of range.*

Within range: within reach; an obtainable goal. *Four per cent growth is within range.*

Rank

Pull rank: to act superior; handling of a subordinate; use one's rank to get desired results. *Don't make me pull rank on you. Mr. Dickson seldom pulls rank, but when he does, he means it.*

Rank and file: ordinary members in a group or organization. *The rank and file approved the new union contract.*

Rap

A rap on the knuckles/wrist: a light punishment. *Dick got a rap on the knuckles for sneaking out to a movie yesterday.*

Beat the rap: *See,* **Beat.**

Bum rap: to receive unfair blame or reprimand. *Poor Joey got the bum's rap, although it wasn't his fault at all.*

Get/Take the rap: to take the blame for an action, regardless of fault. *Our boss took the rap for our poor performance.*

Rap: a casual or down-to-earth conversation. *Lou and I had a rap session about the upcoming holiday party. Let's meet for coffee and rap a bit.*

That's a rap: the matter is adjourned or finished (for the day). *The movie director shouted, "All right, everyone; that's a rap."*

Rat

Don't give a rat's ass: *See,* **Ass**.

Pack rat: *See,* **Pack**.

Rat: a despicable or treacherous person. *I thought for sure we had a rat in our group.*

Rat around: to waste time indeterminately. *When we are bored, Joel and I rat around town.*

Rat fink: 1) an untrustworthy and disrespectful person. *Ron is a rat fink to reveal our secret hiding place.* 2) to reveal someone; to tell on someone; to disclose. *He rat-finked on us, so we have to get away now.*

Rat hole: a poorly kept or otherwise undesirable living space. *John's apartment is a total rat hole.*

Rat on someone: to betray one's comrades. *See also above,* **Rat** fink. *I would not put it past Joe to rat on his co-workers.*

Rat race: reference to the intense competition and struggles that one faces in the modern world. *I tell you, it's hard out there in the day-to-day rat race.*

Rat trap: a dirty, unkempt living area. *See also above,* Rat hole. *Life is tough, which has forced me to live in this rat trap while going to school.*

Rats!: an exclamation of frustration, disgust and/or disbelief. *When Abby didn't get approved on the loan, she screamed, "Rats!!"*

Smell a rat: *See,* **Smell**.

Raunch

Raunch/Raunchy: filthy or grubby; inferior; obscene or vulgar. *That show is all raunch! My lord, that show is really raunchy! He acts like a raunchy person to me.*

Rave

Rave: 1) a dance party that usually doesn't begin until after midnight. *Dude! There's a rave going on tonight, but it doesn't start until 2a.m.* 2) to speak loudly and irrationally. *What are you raving about?*

Stark raving mad: wild and delusional; crazy. *On a full moon, do some people really go stark raving mad?*

Reach

Reach/Reach out to: to connect with. *I failed in not being able to successfully reach out to him prior to his suicide attempt.*

Reach for the sky: 1) one's goals or desires are limitless. *I'm going to reach for the sky after I graduate from college.* 2) a perspective that one's goals or desires are too high. *He has a noble goal but I think he might be reaching for the sky on this one.* 3) a command to another to raise his hands in the air in surrender. *When the armed robber entered the bank, he told everyone to reach for the sky.*

Read

Read between the lines: sense and understand the implied and deeper meaning beyond what is heard. *If you read between the lines about their discussion how well things are going, I feel they are really having problems paying their monthly bills.*

Read into: to understand. *I can't read into these markings; they must be thousands of years old.*

Read like a book: to understand someone or something fully; obvious or transparent. *The salesman tried to sway me with his presentation, but I could read him like a book.*

Read my lips: a phrase used to emphasize one's conviction about something. *Read my lips, Natalie—NO boyfriends over while you're babysitting.*

Read (right) through: able to predict someone's moves. *I can read right through him to know that he is a business politician rather than a compassionate spokesperson for his constituents.*

Read someone's mind: *See,* **Mind**.

Ream

Ream: reprimand intensely. *Mack got reamed by his boss for being late to the staff meeting.*

Rear

Rear: buttocks. *Sam got whacked in the rear with a baseball, and what a bruise it left!*

Rear end: 1) one's buttocks. *My rear end hurts from sitting all day.* 2) the backside of something, such as a vehicle. *Some drunk driver rear-ended my car the other day.*

Record

For the record: an account that transmits or preserves the truth. *For the record, I was never scared.*

Like a broken record: say the same things repeatedly. *He complains about his job like a broken record.*

Off the record: not for publication. *Can this be off the record? Good. What really happened was….*

Red

Caught red-handed: *See,* **Catch**.

In the red: in debt. *We've been in the red for the last year.*

Red-blooded: strong and virile. *That red-blooded boy will do well in college.*

Red carpet (treatment): high-class or special treatment. *The way the Clarks got the red carpet when they entered the party, you'd think they were the relatives of royalty.*

Red eye: 1) strong, cheap whiskey. *Dick got really sick from drinking the red eye.* 2) air flight between midnight and 6a.m. *He caught the red eye back to Chicago after his meetings in L.A. and San Diego.*

Red hot: glowing; very recent or popular; hip. *German cars are red hot right now.*

Red in the face: uncomfortable or embarrassed. *The defendant was looking red in the face while having to testify about the property damage she caused while driving drunk.*

Red light district(s): certain streets in a city dominated generally by prostitutes or porn stores. *The rookie police officers get their training patrolling the red light districts in town.*

Red tape: official forms and bureaucratic procedures, which generally are associated with the delay in processing matters or getting things done; complications or debates that only delay matters. *He knows how to cut through the red tape at City Hall.*

See red: to reach a level of extreme anger. *That dim-witted and rude cashier at the store had me seeing red!*

Reek

Reek: smell awfully bad. *You reek, man!*

Reel

Reel off: to say, write or do something in a quick, competent manner. *The student reeled off President Lincoln's Gettysburg Address from memory.*

Regain

Regain one's composure: to recover one's calmness and well-being. *It took several weeks for Sam to regain his composure after Jenny broke up with him.*

Rein

Free rein: have limitless boundaries. *The babysitter let the kids have free rein of the house.*

Tight rein: to control or limit; forcefully guide. *Mrs. Lewis keeps a tight rein on her finances.*

Ride

Hitch a ride/Thumb a ride: beg a ride from a passing motorist (generally done by extending an arm and using one's thumb to point in the direction desired). *With the money we have left, we can eat but we'll have to thumb a ride to get back home.*

Ride: 1) transportation. *I will need to catch a ride from you today.* 2) to be on; to pressure or criticize. *Ride on him until he agrees to our demands.*

Ride herd on: supervise; keep close watch. *You will need to ride herd on those young kids in class, especially the unruly ones.*

Ride off in all directions: 1) become confused. *James rides off in all directions when he gets flustered.* 2) try to accomplish too much. *Mom has a tendency to ride off in all directions in taking care of things.*

Ride on one's coattails: move up in life on the force of an event or someone's actions. *Everyone at the time rode on the coattails of the economic boom of the 1990's.*

Ride one's ass [expressive]: harass; nag aggressively; give someone a hard time. *He has a tough boss who rides his ass all the time.*

Riding high: at the peak of one's glory. *Tiger Woods was riding high after winning the Masters for the second time.*

Take (one) for a ride: cheat or swindle someone. *Sarah knew she had been taken for a ride by the seller when she discovered that she purchased protected wetland rather than lakefront property.*

Rig

Rig: 1) to set up or put together; to creatively construct. *He rigged a lever using a log and a big rock, and used it to lift the Mini Cooper out of the ditch.* 2) to manipulate to one's favor. *When the boxer fell to the canvas so easily, we suddenly suspected the fight was rigged.* 3) large truck or trailer. *He hauls his classic cars around the country on a big rig.*

Rigamarole/Rigamaroll/Rig-a-ma-roll: a general reference to any matter that is happening. *What sort of rigamarole is going on here?*

Right

In the right: accurate; supported by law. *No matter what you say, he was in the right.*

Right and left: in large numbers or great amounts; from all sides. *The insurance company was getting hit right and left with lawsuits alleging bad faith about its handling of loss claims.*

Right off the bat: directly; instantly. *She knew right off the bat who we were talking about.*

Right on: an affirmative showing in exclamation. *Those who were watching the unruly drunk get a beverage thrown in his face were heard to exclaim, "Right on!"*

Right up one's alley: exactly what one prefers or is able to do. *Drinking a cold beer in the summertime is right up my alley.*

Ring

Ring a bell: to sound familiar. *Does what you promised me five years ago ring a bell?*

Ring up: 1) add and record items on a cash register. *Can you ring these clothes up?* 2) call on the phone. *Please ring me up when you're in town.*

Run rings around: to very easily outperform. *My Fido can run rings around the other dogs at the event.*

Rink

Rinky dink/Rinky dinky: cheap; unsophisticated; low-class. *He owns several rinky-dink nightclubs in the seedy part of town.*

Riot

Read the riot act: to warn harshly, coupled with threat of disciplinary action. *The boss read me the riot act after I disobeyed the company rules.*

Riot: very funny. *That guy is a riot; he makes everyone laugh.*

What a riot!: a phrase to express amazement or excitement. *The show was so funny that we were laughing all night; what a riot!*

Rip

Rip ass: go at high speed. *His new car rips ass!*

Rip into: attack with force, often with words. *That cop ripped into me for jaywalking.*

Rip off: steal or cheat; take advantage of someone. *No one gets my sympathy for ripping off the elderly.*

Rip-off artist: one who steals from unsuspecting individuals. *Tourists are primary candidates for rip-off artists.*

Ripped: under the heavy influence of alcohol or drugs. *When we saw him at the conference, he looked ripped.*

Rise

Get a rise out of: to irritate; to manipulate another's behavior with negative intent. *Ed was purposely being obnoxious to Julie in order to get a rise out of her.*

Rise to the occasion: to meet a challenge directly. *As a troubleshooter, you have to be able to rise to virtually every occasion.*

Roach

Roach coach: a snack truck or van selling ready-made foods of fair or dubious quality, usually near a worksite or other activity. *Hey guys, let's get a coffee and doughnut at the roach coach.*

Road

Middle of the road: *See,* **Middle**.

On the road: traveling. *We received an excellent postcard from John while he was on the road.*

One for the road: a social drink (usually alcohol) before departing. *Before leaving the tavern, they decided to have one for the road.*

Road hog: one who blocks or slows down others while driving on the road, such as an individual who drives slower than the flow of traffic. *On the highway, the road hogs are bad but the tailgaters are even worse.*

Take to the road: to travel or commence traveling. *I can't wait for my vacation! It starts tomorrow, and I'm taking to the road as soon as I wake up!*

Tore the road up: to drive extremely fast. *He tore the road up with his new sports roadster.*

Roar

Roar back: to recover quickly or energetically; to return fast. *John roared back to health after taking a potion from an Amazon tribal doctor.*

Roaring good time: extremely good time; a lot of fun. *We had a roaring good time at Bonnie's party.*

Roaring twenties: reference to the raucous and care-free period in the U.S. during the 1920's. *My grandmother often refers to the roaring twenties as her moment in life.*

Rob

Rob Peter to pay Paul: to settle a matter at another's expense (usually one's own). *The current rate of taxation, I believe, boils down to a matter of robbing Peter to pay Paul.*

Rob someone blind: to deceptively take all of one's money. *He robbed them blind with his business scams.*

Rock

On the rocks: 1) close to ruin. *Their long-term relationship is on the rocks.* 2) a drink served over ice. *I'll have whiskey on the rocks.*

Rock bottom: the very lowest point of something. *Our business hit rock bottom this year.*

Rock pile: a tiresome task. *These monthly reports are nothing but a rock pile for me.*

Rock the boat: *See,* **Boat**.

Rocks: awesome; the best. *Blue Mountain No. 1 coffee from Jamaica rocks.*

Rod

Spare the rod: forego punishment. *He was spared the rod in exchange for staying after school.*

Roger

Roger: response that communication was received or acknowledged. *When asked if he received the message, he responded, "Roger."*

Rogue

Rogue's gallery: 1) collection of photos used by the police to pick out criminals. *We studied the rogue's gallery in the hopes of finding out who nabbed that old lady's purse.* 2) a collection of seemingly shady or untrustworthy characters. *This nightclub is a regular rogue's gallery! Let's get out of here.*

Roll

Roll: to be physically abused; beat up. *Damon got rolled by a bunch of thugs last night.*

Roll out the (red) carpet: give special or royal treatment. *The town rolled out the carpet for the dignitaries in the hopes of winning a bid for big convention business.*

Roll over and play dead: to surrender without a fight. *They never fought back, but just rolled over and played dead.*

Roll up one's sleeves: prepare for hard work. *The next few weeks are going to require all your energy at work, so roll up those sleeves!*

Roll with the punches: to go along with; to go with the flow. *Let's roll with the punches and see how things turn out.*

Rollers: police car. *Oh no, we have some rollers following us.*

Rolling/Rolling in stitches: to laugh in volumes; extremely amused. *That was the funniest film I ever saw! It had me rolling in stitches!*

Rolling in dough: enjoying extreme wealth. *Mason has been rolling in dough ever since he started his international trading company in precious gems.*

Rolly-polly/Roly-poly: fairly overweight; quite fat. *Our French teacher, although a bit rolly-polly, was an agile tennis player.*

Roof

Raise the roof: 1) to be boisterous in celebration; extremely noisy. *For your 21st birthday, let's say we raise the roof a bit and celebrate!* 2) to complain vehemently; get very angry. *She raised the roof when her rival, Bill, walked in.*

Roof fell in: sudden occurrence of misfortune; total collapse. *The roof fell in on our retirement plans when much of our investments were lost in the stock market.*

Root

Root: 1) to cheer for; to support. *We need everyone to come to the game this Saturday to root for the team.* 2) to eliminate; discard. *It is customary for a new administration to root out key appointees from the previous administration.* 3) cause of. *The root of the problem is caused by policy, not personnel.*

Root cause: the primary cause; the main reason. *The root cause of that kid's awful behavior is no discipline at home.*

Rootin' tootin': boisterous; wonderfully adventurous. *We had a rootin' tootin' good time at the party.*

Take root: 1) the time it takes to get established in an area or in an organization; to get settled in; to become more acquainted with. *It took me a while to take root and make friends in this town.* 2) referring to ideas or plans that become effective. *There will be a lot of downsizing when our new policies take root.*

Rope

End of one's rope: *See,* **End**.

Know/Learn the ropes: to gather/to have full knowledge in order to satisfactorily perform a job. *Bobby knows all the ropes around here, and he'll guide you through all the tasks to complete.*

On the ropes: on the verge of losing; helpless; near a breakdown or crackup. *Ever since his divorce, David's been on the ropes. The campaign is on the ropes and there is little hope of victory.*

Rope someone into: to lure or deceive someone, usually into performing an unfavorable task. *I don't know how you roped me into this deal, but you'll pay for this!*

Show one the ropes: *See,* **Show**.

Rose

Come up roses/Come up smelling like a rose/Smell like a rose: come out looking good; have good fortune. *The investor was smelling like a rose after making nice profits with his stock investments.*

Life is a bed of roses: *See,* **Life**.

Life is not a bed of roses: *See,* **Life**.

Rose-colored glasses/See through rose-colored glasses/View the world through rose-colored glasses: to view everything only as pleasurable or nice. *He has little sense of reality because he views the world only through rose-colored glasses.*

Stop and smell the roses: don't rush through moments in life, but rather take the time to enjoy the beauty that is present. *Jake, stop and smell the roses more often or you'll end up in your old age wondering where all the time went.*

Rough

Diamond in the rough: *See,* **Diamond**.

Rough it: exist with minimal comforts. *Jack had to rough it for a few years after graduating college due to financial reasons.*

Rough shod: to treat in an arrogant or inconsiderate manner; reckless. *The Sergeant rode rough shod over the new recruits.*

Rough stuff: rowdy or rude behavior. *Cut this rough stuff out or I will call the cops.*

Rough up: to physically abuse or intimidate someone. *Mack got roughed up in the argument.*

Roughneck: a quarrelsome or noisy person. *That roughneck is always looking for a fight.*

Row

Long/Tough row to hoe: a difficult or tiresome journey or task. *You've got a long row to hoe until retirement.*

Rub

Rub elbows with/Rub shoulders with: to socialize with (usually mixing with a more elite or high-society crowd). *We rubbed elbows with diplomats and movie stars at Jason's wedding party.*

Rub it in: maliciously articulate on someone's error. *I know I messed up; you don't need to rub it in!*

Rub off on: be influenced or affected by. *I hope that all the good traits from the teachers at school will rub off on our misbehaving children.*

Rub someone the wrong way: doing something that irritates or annoys another; to cause friction. *I try to avoid him because his antics and immaturity rub me the wrong way.*

Rub someone's nose in it: bring something directly to another's attention, usually when in error or at fault, in repeated or forceful fashion. *You already lectured me 5 times about my truancy; you don't have to rub my nose in it.*

There's the rub: there's the difficulty or problem. *We would love to go, but our whole family is in town. There's the rub; we can't get away.*

Rubber

Rubber check: *See,* **Check**.

Rubber stamp: to automatically approve something without investigating its merits. *The boss rubber stamps whatever the manager suggests because he has so much trust in him.*

Rug

Cut a rug: *See,* **Cut**.

Rug: a toupee or hairpiece. *He uses a rug to cover that shiny spot on top of his head.*

Rule

Rule of thumb: the usual or unwritten way things are looked at or done. *The rule of thumb is to watch your backside when playing football with that team.*

Rumble

Let's get ready to rumble: an expression, coined and popularized by Michael Buffer, in which he announces at the start of every boxing match or sporting event, to commence some roughhousing. *Before the fight broke out at the roadhouse, I heard someone yell, "Let's get ready to rumble!"*

Rumble: 1) to party; to have some action. *We are going to rumble tonight!* 2) to motor or drive. *I'm going to rumble over to Bob's place for a while.*

Rumbling: 1) rumor. *I heard some rumbling about Sally leaving the firm.* 2) complaining. *What's all the rumbling about?*

Run

Cut and run: *See,* **Cut**.

Dry run: a practice exercise before the real thing; rehearsal. *The new jet fighter made a successful dry run at Edwards Air Force Base.*

Get the run around: to not be told the truth; to detract another by not revealing the truth or telling a direct story. *We got the run around from the doctor about Gina's actual medical condition.*

In the long run: *See,* **Long**.

Make a run for it: *See,* **Make**.

On the run: very busy; constantly occupied. *Jane is always on the run.*

Run a tight ship: control a disciplined and organized institution. *Mr. Rowan is well known for running a tight ship.*

Run amuck (amok)/Run wild: to behave in a wild or unrestrained way; chaotic action. *As soon as we left home, the dogs ran amok in the house and trampled all over the furniture.*

Run around in circles/Run around like a chicken with its head cut off: unproductive; to react wildly to no benefit. *It does you no good if you run around like a chicken with its head cut off. We were running around in circles trying to figure out what went wrong with the reactor.*

Run at the mouth/Run one's mouth off: get carried away in speech. *I would not want her as a neighbor; she really runs her mouth off.*

Run away with: 1) to leave with someone to live together. *She ran away with him and they started a new life together.* 2) to steal. *They ran away with the bank's cash.* 3) to win over the competition; to beat. *He ran away with the victory after beating all the contenders.*

Run circles around/Run rings around: be significantly superior to. *He ran circles around me on the basketball court today.*

Run down/rundown: 1) in poor shape; tired. *I'm run down and in need of some rest. That old house you bought is fairly run down and in need of some work.* 2) a summary or quick account of. *Ok, give me a rundown of the estimated costs to operate this facility for a season.* 3) go for something or someone. *Run down and get Bob for me.* 4) knocked over; hit. *He was run down by a drunk driver.*

Run for one's money: work hard against the keen competition. *The rookie players gave the veteran a real run for his money.*

Run in the family: something that is typical of a group of people, particularly blood relatives. *The greed for money runs in that family.*

Run into a brick/stone wall: 1) to confront a solid barrier, which slows or halts progress. *The construction project ran into a brick wall when the metal workers went on strike.* 2) be suddenly stalled or halted. *We ran into a stone wall trying to get building permits in this area.*

Run into a brick wall

Run it up the flagpole: to test out; to see how others respond. *Senator, we need to run this idea up the flagpole to see what kind of responses we get.*

Run its course: to proceed through in normal fashion; to come to its natural conclusion. *We had to let the fire run its course due to the heavy winds.*

Run like clockwork: operate with perfection. *Our program today ran like clockwork due in large part to a well-trained staff.*

Run of the mill: average; ordinary; nothing unusual. *He lives modestly in a run-of-the-mill home. The prince talks like a run-of-the-mill guy on the street, which I think is great.*

Run one ragged: make another exhausted, generally through hard work or effort. *The new football coach ran us ragged in practice today.*

Run something into the ground: analyze thoroughly, if not excessively. *You can discuss the death penalty until you run it into the ground.*

Run the gauntlet: to be challenged; exposed to adversity. *The new recruits had to run the gauntlet of taunting and criticism during their first year at the academy.*

Run this by someone: to relay information to another for feedback. *Jack, let me run this by you, and let me know what you think about it.*

Running on all cylinders/Hitting on all cylinders: running smoothly and efficiently; going with great speed; utilizing full ability. *We were running on all cylinders tonight when we played magnificently against our cross-town basketball rival.*

Running on empty: without any energy; operating without fuel or funds. *I was exhausted and running on empty when the rescuers found and plucked me from the water.*

Running out of steam: weakening. *The president's proposal for a missile system is running out of steam; no one wants to go for it.*

Running start: an opening advantage or lead. *His experience gave him a running start over the other new employees at his new job.*

The runs: diarrhea. *I got the runs when I traveled overseas.*

Runt

Runt: 1) small and contemptible person (usually used disparagingly). *I'm going to kick that runt out of here if he causes any more trouble.* 2) uncooperative little boy (usually used light-heartedly). *Ok, you little runt. Daddy is going to come after you so you better hide!*

Sack

Sack of shit: *See,* **Pile of Shit.**

Sack out/Hit the sack: go to sleep. *Some people don't sack out until after midnight.*

Sad sack: a pathetic individual. *I used to enjoy hanging out with Mary, but lately she's become such a sad sack.*

Sacred

Sacred cow: something that is immune to attack or criticism. *As the company downsizes, you can be sure it won't touch the sacred cows.*

Safe

Safe and sound: out of harm's way. *We made it back safe and sound.*

Salt

Add salt to the wound: make a bad situation worse; to worsen. *An insensitive remark at this time would only add salt to the wound.*

Back to the salt mines: *See,* **Back.**

Salt away: to lay aside and save. *He accumulated his savings by salting away a small portion of his earnings each pay period for 20 years.*

Salt mine: place of work. *Bye honey, It's time to go back to the salt mines.*

Salt of the earth: the greatest, finest or most honorable person. *My grand-mother was the salt of the earth and very well-liked by everyone.*

With a grain of salt: take little interest in believing something; to not invest too much belief in something until proof is disclosed. *John took Sam's cock-and-bull story with a grain of salt.*

Worth one's salt: one who is trusted for his hard work and honesty; work sufficiently to earn one's wage. *I would recommend him for the job because he is definitely worth his salt.*

Sand

Bury one's head in the sand/Head in the sand: 1) to refuse to face the facts. *He has his head in the sand if he thinks all is well about his financial situation.* 2) to refuse to face challenge or difficulty. *He tends to bury his head in the sand when complicated projects arise.* 3) to not know; to be unaware. *I purposely buried my head in the sand because I could not stand to witness the corruption.*

Sandbag: to deceive a person by initially pretending to lack any ability. *Art sandbagged me out of $300 when we played cards last week!*

Sandbox: toilet. *Excuse me, but I have to go to the sandbox.*

Sashay

Sashay: to walk; to go to. *Sashay over to my office if you want to see the new prototype the engineers developed.*

Save

Save face: *See,* **Face**.

Save one's breath: 1) no need to talk about a certain matter because it was already done or dealt with. *Save your breath; we already spoke at length about it at the meeting.* 2) not worth mentioning; don't waste your words (on an issue). *When Michelle started on the subject for the fifth time in an hour, I finally told her to save her breath.*

Save one's neck/skin: protect one (whether yourself or others) from injury, shame, or penalty. *Thanks for helping me with the loan; you really saved my neck!*

Save the day: to succeed where failure seemed imminent; prevent misfor-tune. *A stroke of luck saved the day for our company.*

Saved by the bell: *See,* **Bell**.

Saving grace: a redeeming quality; something admired in a person. *Her saving grace is her honesty in everything she does at work.*

Say

Goes without saying: it is self-evident. *It goes without saying that you did very well today.*

Say: a positive declaration. *Martin's mom walked into the room and said, "Say, kids! What are you working on?"*

Say a mouthful: to make a significant observation. *You said a mouthful when you indicated that we work our tails off around here!*

Say the word: agree to follow someone's direction when the request is made. *We'll go to a fantastic restaurant whenever you want; just say the word.*

Say Uncle: give up; succumb. *Peter had Billy in a wrestling hold and wouldn't let him go until he was forced to say Uncle.*

That is to say: expression to denote how something is simply stated. *Perry can be very trying on one's patience; that is to say, he can be really annoying.*

To say the least: a most obvious observation. *He's the most qualified, to say the least.*

You can say that again!: in total or unequivocal agreement. *"You can say that again!" chimed Barbara after I explained how difficult I felt the test had been.*

Scalp

Scalp: 1) to angrily seek to penalize someone. *I'll have his scalp if he damages my property.* 2) to beat decisively. *We got scalped real good in tonight's ballgame.*

Scarce

Make oneself scarce: hide; leave quickly; go away. *When the work is being done, he tends to make himself scarce.*

Scarcer than hen's teeth: almost nonexistent. *I've never seen that gadget; it's scarcer than hen's teeth!*

Scare

Scared stiff/Scared half to death/Scared shitless (expressive): terrified; frightened to the extent of immobility. *The hikers were scared stiff when they noticed the large black bear on the trail in front of them.*

Scene

Behind the scene(s): privately; secretly. *There's a lot of crooked business going on behind the scenes at this establishment.*

Create a scene/Make a scene: to cause attraction by one's action; create an uproar. *The child made a scene when his mother told him he could only pick out one toy to take home.*

School

Go to school on someone: study another's activities for example. *I must go to school on that guy to see how he performs so effortlessly.*

Old school: in an older, and presumably more classic fashion or tradition. *Unlike the hip-hoppers, the old musicians were playing old school with their own cool jazz and sipping good old Kentucky whiskey.*

School of hard knocks: an education of experience learning the hard way. *Many of us learn about life from the school of hard knocks.*

Score

Score: 1) to obtain or accomplish, usually in an undercover sort of way. *He scored some weed for the concert tonight.* 2) have sex. *I promise I won't tell anyone that I scored with you.*

What's the score?: what's going on? what's the status? *Coming in 25 minutes late for our professor's lecture, Clara sat down next to us and asked, "what's the score?"*

Scratch

Chicken scratch: *See,* **Chicken**.

From scratch: 1) start from nothing. *Mr. Jones started his bakery business from scratch, and now he's worth millions.* 2) to make something using raw ingredients, such as when cooking. *She made the entire dinner from scratch.*

Scratch someone's back: do a favor for another with the idea of getting the favor returned. *You scratch my back and I'll scratch yours.*

Scratch one's head: to try to figure out; expression of confusion or puzzlement. *They were scratching their heads about the economic downturn that they failed to predict.*

Scratch the surface: to touch upon only superficially; to have covered only a very small portion. *You only scratched the surface about why I quit that job.*

Up to scratch: *See,* **Up to Par**.

Without a scratch: to come through without injury or damage. *He got through the war without a scratch.*

Scream

Scream bloody murder: to express intense dissatisfaction; loud vocal expression of discontent. *Billy screamed bloody murder when he found out he was laid off from his job without any warning. The baby was screaming bloody murder until he received his bottle of milk.*

Screw

Have a loose screw/Have a screw loose: not be fully cognizant; awkward acting; to act unusually out of character; crazy. *Mrs. Gottfried yells at her neighbors and chases kids away with a broom. I'd say she has a screw loose.*

Put the screws on/Tighten the screws: apply force; intimidate. *In order to get the full truth, Chester really had to put the screws on Clyde.*

Screw up: 1) mess up; commit a big mistake. *We cannot afford to screw up the presentation today.* 2) someone who is a loser or cannot accomplish matters. *He is a total screw up.*

Screw you [expressive]: expression of strong disagreement and discontent. *An elderly man cut me off in traffic, and when I honked at him, you know what he did? He shook his fist at me and screamed, "Screw you!"*

Screwed: get cheated; messed up. *We definitely got screwed on that deal.*

Screwy: goofy; odd. *The patients on the psychiatric ward act screwy when a full moon is out.*

Scorch

Scorch: to cheat. *He got scorched on that deal.*

Scorcher: hot and sunny. *It's a real scorcher today!*

Scrooge

Scrooge: a miser. *Don't bother asking him for a donation; he's such a scrooge.*

Scrounge

Scrounge: 1) to search. *Let's scrounge around this junkyard for parts.* 2) collect; pick up; assemble. *What did you scrounge up for dinner tonight?*

Scrounger: a beggar. *There are many scroungers on this street asking for money.*

Scrounging around: looking for something by wandering and aimlessly searching for it. *We were just scrounging around the old battlefield looking for memorabilia that might be buried.*

Scum

Scum/Scumbag/Scum bucket: a person who is low in character; a crooked person. *My wife thinks my business associates are scumbags.*

Scummy: dirty. *Why are you wearing that scummy shirt?*

Search

Search me: I don't know. *Where did the crook escape? Search me!*

Second

Just one second/Just a second here: 1) wait for a very short while. *Just one second, I'll be right back.* 2) an expression of interruption to explain something. *Just a second here; I was first in line.*

Second thought: to reconsider a matter. *On second thought, let's go to the movies instead of watching a video tonight. I'm having second thoughts about this deal.*

Second to none: the very best. *Our fringe benefits with the company are second to none.*

Second wind: *See,* **Wind**.

See

See the handwriting on the wall: *See,* **Hand**.

See the light: to understand. *The neighbors began to see the light about switching from oil to gas furnaces when they noticed significant reductions in their utility bills.*

See through rose-colored glasses: *See,* **Rose**.

Seeing is believing: something is understood to be true by actually viewing it. *I went to Nepal and saw the Buddhist monks meditating in frozen weather—seeing is believing.*

Seedy

Seedy: dirty; filthy; unkempt. *The seedy part of town is where the bars and strip clubs are located.*

Sell

Sell like hotcakes: to sell rapidly and as fast as supply allows. *Our new widget is selling like hotcakes.*

Sell one down the river: betray; dupe; cheat. *In a plea deal with the prosecutor, he decided to sell his criminal buddies down the river in exchange for a lighter prison sentence.*

Sell oneself short: to sell out below market price; undervalue. *Don't sell yourself short; you're a wonderful person, and have a lot to offer.*

Sell one out: deceive; betray; to back out or change one's mind (in negative fashion). *You sold me out just so you could get the promotion!*

Sell someone a bill of goods: to confuse or deceive; trick. *Don't believe that guy; he's just trying to sell you a bill of goods.*

Sense

Come to one's senses: return to a state of sound thinking or reasoning. *She's no good for you! Come to your senses, man!*

Horse sense: *See,* **Horse**.

In a sense: to a restricted degree; in a certain manner. *In a sense, Dick was partly to blame.*

Make sense: reasonable in nature; practical. *What you say doesn't make sense.*

Separate

Separate the men from the boys: indicate differentiation between the mature and the immature; between strength and weakness. *This sport definitely separates the men from the boys.*

Service

At one's service: ready to service or cooperate. *The clerk proudly informed me that he was at my service.*

In (the) service: in the military. *John was in the service for ten years.*

Set

All set: prepared; ready. *Is everyone all set to go to the beach?*

Set about (to): commence an activity. *I set about cleaning the house when the phone rang.*

Set against: in opposition of. *I'm dead set against working on Sundays.*

Set straight: to clarify; correct. *I'm sick of the rumors; I'd like to set everything straight.*

Set the world on fire: achieve great success; become a person of renown. *Some people only desire to set the world on fire; the little things in life are not enough for them.*

Setback: an unanticipated delay or reversal in progress. *The strike proved a setback for our company.*

Shack

Shack up: to cohabitate romantically and/or sexually. *It was only a matter of time before Brad and Brenda would shack up together.*

Shade

Made in the shade: possessing the obvious advantage; easy living. *Working part-time with full-time pay? Man, we have it made in the shade!*

Shades: sunglasses. *You'll need your shades today.*

Shades of: reminiscent of; a reminder. *Wow! That outfit reminds me of the shades of the Sixties.*

Shady: dishonest; unreliable or untrustworthy. *He is one hell of a shady person. To have to pay now without seeing any results seems like a shady deal to me.*

Shady deal: *See,* **Deal**.

Shadow

Five o'clock shadow: in need of a shave (originally due to the facial hair growth making a shadow on a man's face by the end of the day). *Mario easily gets a five o'clock shadow.*

Under (the) shadow of: closely associated with; under inspiration of. *Jameson is under the shadow of Mr. Thompson, his favorite college professor.*

Without a shadow of a doubt: absolutely; most certainly; without question. *He won the race this time, without a shadow of a doubt.*

Shake

Get a fair shake: be treated fairly. *Jason's been working hard, so give him a fair shake.*

Gives me the shakes: discomforting; upsetting. *The memory of that horrible night gives me the shakes.*

Have the shakes: be very nervous. *I have the shakes before I go on stage to perform.*

In two shakes: quickly; real soon. *I'll be back in two shakes.*

More than you can shake a stick at: a whole lot; extreme amount. *She has more shoes than you can shake a stick at.*

Shake: evade; get rid of. *Although we were following closely behind them, they managed to shake us away.*

Shake a leg: get up; get moving (to work). *See also,* **Snap to it**. *Shake a leg and get to work.*

Shake in one's boots/Shake like a leaf: to tremble in fear; very frightened. *We were shaking like a leaf after hearing an awesome howl in the woods that sounded like Bigfoot.*

Shake it/Shake one's booty: move one's body suggestively; dance. *Whoa! She can shake that booty on the dance floor!*

Shakedown: extortion of money; a complete search of a person or place. *The main corporate office did a shakedown of our overseas location, as profits were disappearing for no reason.*

Shallow

Shallow: one with a lack of knowledge or little character. *It's no use talking to that shallow person. If that's all you know, it's pretty shallow.*

Shape

Bent out of shape: *See,* **Bend/Bent**.

Lick into shape: *See,* **Lick**.

Shape of things to come: what is to be expected in the future. *Government austerity will be the shape of things to come to reduce the huge budget deficits.*

Shape up or ship out: perform satisfactorily or else suffer the consequences. *This company doesn't tolerate slackers; you shape up or ship out, you hear?*

Share

Share and share alike: provide to all. *I'm very generous; share and share alike, I say.*

Sharp

Keep a sharp eye/Keep a sharp lookout: be very watchful. *Keep a sharp eye on these gold bars. Keep a sharp lookout for the escaped convicts.*

Look sharp: to appear dapper or clean-cut. *Jack takes the time to look sharp when he goes to town.*

Sharp as a tack/Sharp as a whistle: extremely intelligent; very capable. *That girl is sharp as a whistle; she's going to go places in this profession.*

Sharp practice: crafty work ethic; deceitful dealings. *As a private investigator, he usually has to conduct a sharp practice to get the information he needs for his clients.*

Shatter

Shattered: gone; blasted away; undermined. *Trust in corporate America has been shattered in light of accounting fraud by a number of large public companies.*

Sheesh

Sheesh: polite form of the slang word, "shit." *Sheesh, you don't have to get upset about it.*

Shell

Shell out: to pay. *I had to shell out over $50 just to take my girl to a movie.*

Shellack

Shellack/Shellac: beat overwhelmingly. *We got shellacked by UCLA this week.*

Shine

Shine (it) on: 1) fake it; give a false impression. *He was shining it on as a physician until they discovered that he never graduated from medical school.* 2) quit. *The students decided to shine on the rest of the school day.*

Shine up to: try to please or befriend. *It's tough to shine up to a boss who lacks good management skills.*

Shiner: black eye. *Manuel got a shiner in the baseball game when he played as a catcher without a mask.*

Take a shine to: gain a quick liking to. *She took a shine to him on the first date.*

Ship

Jump ship: *See,* **Jump**.

Run a tight ship: *See,* **Run**.

Waiting for one's ship to come in: awaiting the right opportunity, usually the opportunity to acquire wealth. *Many people wait for their ship to come in, but it never does.*

Shit

Ain't jack shit [expressive]: something said that is of little or no value; not worth it. *When he offered only $100 for rent money, the landlord replied, "That ain't jack shit."*

Apeshit [expressive]: get very excited. *The fans went apeshit when the band took the stage.*

Asshole deep in shit [expressive]: to be involved in serious trouble. *Man, you'll be asshole deep in shit if you're caught in this restricted area.*

Bad shit [expressive]: 1) a significantly menacing or nasty situation. *A lot of bad shit goes on in warfare.* 2) defective, useless or cheap product. *That guy on the street sold you some bad shit; it's worthless.* 3) excellent product or goods (emphasis in tone on the word "bad" in the expression). *Man, this is some real bad shit; can you get some more?*

Beat the shit out of [expressive]: 1) to assault brutally [literal]. *The gang stole their wallets and beat the shit out of them before the police arrived.* 2) defeat overwhelmingly [figurative]. *The Aztecs beat the shit out of the Conquistadors in the soccer championship.*

Big shit [expressive]: 1) a significant matter, event or occurrence. *We knew there was some big shit going on at the Tolbert's residence when limousines* *and police cars showed up.* 2) who cares; of no concern. *When he continued on about his lucrative business deals, she muttered, "big shit."*

Bullshit: *See,* **Bull**.

Bullshit artist: *See,* **Artist**.

Chicken shit [expressive]: 1) fearful. *My dog barks a lot, but he is a real chicken shit when guests enter the premises.* 2) baseless; frivolous; of total nonsense; lowdown. *Squealing to the cops on him without any good reason is pure chicken shit.* 3) not be responsible or to avoid responsibility. *He is a chicken shit for making others do his work.*

Crock of shit: *See,* **Crock**.

Cut the shit: stop the nonsense or lies. *Cut the shit and tell me the truth.*

Cut the shit out: stop it now. *Cut the shit out!*

Deep shit [expressive]: a lot of trouble; very bad or nasty situation. *You'll be in deep shit if you fail to show up at your court hearing tomorrow.*

Dipshit [expressive]: dummy; fool. *What a dipshit!*

Does a bear shit in the woods?: *See,* **Bear**.

Doesn't know jack shit [expressive]: to not know about something, generally due to a lack of intelligence; to not have knowledge about or competence in something. *He doesn't know jack shit about how to run a calibration company.*

Don't shit me [expressive]: don't lie to me. *Don't shit me, man; tell me the truth.*

Dumb shit [expressive]: 1) no good stuff; useless item. *There's a lot of dumb shit that's sold on the online auction sites.* 2) a stupid or ignorant person. *That dumb shit doesn't know his job.* 3) stupid (thing to do). *I did some dumb shit stuff when I was younger.*

Eat shit [expressive]: expression of disgust. *Eat shit; I'm not going to do your dirty work.*

Feel like shit [expressive]: to feel real bad, depressed, sick, etc. *I feel like shit today.*

Flip someone shit [expressive]: to fool someone with mischievous talk; deceptive or untruthful talk. *Don't listen to him; he's just flipping you shit.*

Full of shit [expressive]: completely wrong; of no credibility. *Anyone who says we're not approaching an economic recession is full of shit.*

Funny as shit [expressive]: extremely funny. *It was funny as shit when a crow swooped down and stole his bag lunch from the golf cart.*

Get one's shit together [expressive]: to organize; to be more efficient; to correct oneself. *I better get my shit together, now, or she'll leave me for sure.*

Good shit [expressive]: exceptional item or commodity; high-quality marijuana or drugs. *Hey, this is some really good shit!*

Have/Has the shits [expressive]: to be with diarrhea or difficult bowel movements. *Sparky, my dog, can't run in the park today because he has the shits.*

Holy shit/Oh shit: [expressive]: interjection of surprise. *Holy shit, it's your birthday!*

Horse shit [expressive]: *See*, **Horse**.

Hot shit [expressive]: 1) good stuff; quality goods (not necessarily legal). *This year's crop of marijuana that the police confiscated from that farm was some hot shit.* 2) one who acts like an impressive person; a big shot. *New guys in prison tend to act like hot shit to try to uphold their reputation as being strong.*

Like a pig in shit [expressive]: feeling glorious; very happy. *He felt like a pig in shit after his promotion.*

Like shit on goldfish [expressive]: an analogy about how one tends to follow another around everywhere (originally from a Japanese proverb: "kingyo no unchi"). *Our cat, Cinder, follows Daphne around the house like shit on goldfish.*

Little shit [expressive]: a difficult or annoying person, usually in reference to a little kid; a brat. *I will never babysit for that little shit again!*

Money talks, shit walks [expressive]: *See*, **Money**.

No shit/I shit you not [expressive]: absence of deception or lying; that's the truth. *When asked if her story about the haunted house was true, Sarah replied, "I shit you not!"*

Not know shit (from shinola): *See*, **Not know beans/Not know shit (from shinola)**.

Pile of shit/Sack of shit [expressive]: nonsense; not true. *That story about the ghost in the house is a pile of shit.*

Scare the living shit out of [expressive]: be extremely frightened. *When the possum and I suddenly met eyes in the dark, crawl space underneath the house, it scared the living shit out of both of us!*

Scared shitless [expressive]: extremely terrified. *We were scared shitless when we spotted a bear in our back yard.*

Shit [expressive]: 1) fecal matter; dung. *I wondered what smelled so bad, only to realize that I stepped in some shit.* 2) babble; nonsense. *I don't want to hear any of your shit; you'd better tell me the truth this time.* 3) anything indicating poor or inferior quality. *I just bought this bike, and it's broke; what a piece of shit!* 4) possessions. *Who left their shit in my room?* 5) to lie or deceive. *He's just shittin' you. I shit you not.* 6) small or worthless amount. *He doesn't know shit.*

Shit a brick [expressive]: be very terrified. *He just about shit a brick when he spotted the principal at the shopping mall walking toward him, when he was supposed to be in class.*

Shit-eating grin/smile [expressive]: a rejoicing look of satisfaction; a look of smug satisfaction; gloating look. *On Fridays, Johnny generally seems to exhibit a shit-eating grin on his face in anticipation of weekend fun.*

Shit face/Shitface [expressive]: a very inconsiderate or disrespectful person. *I felt like hitting that shitface for yelling at her.*

Shit-faced/Shitfaced [expressive]: excessively inebriated; very drunk or stoned; under the influence (of something). *We got shit-faced at the party.*

Shit fit/Shitfit [expressive]: angry outburst. *He threw a shitfit when he didn't get his way.*

Shit for brains [expressive]: a dim wit; very unimpressive or unintelligent; stupid. *This guy has shit for brains.*

Shit happens [expressive]: bad things will normally occur (meaning to take the bad things in stride with daily living). *During this past month, I got injured in a car accident, my girlfriend left me, and I got fired from my job; and all you can say is, "shit happens?"*

Shit hit the fan [expressive]: a matter becoming chaotic; a crisis that follows. *Shit will hit the fan in the future if we continue to build on precious wetlands without taking the natural floodwaters into consideration.*

Shit in one's pants [expressive]: 1) be extremely terrified. *We shit in our pants when we came face to face with a black bear in the woods.* 2) very unbelievably surprised. *When he quoted the price on the kitchen remodeling, I just about shit in my pants.*

Shit list [expressive]: names of persons designated with a bad consequence. *You will be placed on a shit list if you don't conform to company policy.*

Shit or get off the pot [expressive]: either do it or don't (*Polite form is,* **Fish or cut bait**). *Shit or get off the pot, and let us know what your decision will be.*

Shit out of luck [expressive]: no chance; politely stated as: S.O.L. *Sorry, Sir, but you're just S.O.L. in getting a flight out of here tonight.*

Shitass/Shithead [expressive]: a blunderer; stupid person. *He is a real shithead to leave his kids in the car on a warm day.*

Shithouse [expressive]: 1) an outhouse. *Just remember, guys, the shithouse will be placed on the southwest corner of the construction site.* 2) a filthy or run-down place. *This house the realtors call charming is a real shithouse.*

Shitload/Shitpot [expressive]: a very large amount. *He won a shitload of money in the state lottery last year.*

Shittin' in high cotton [expressive]: living lavishly. *We had been shittin' in high cotton this past week on our vacation in the Italian Alps.*

Shittin'/Shitting [expressive]: fooling someone; expression similar to "You're kidding." *That Ferrari is yours?! You're shittin' me!*

Shitter [expressive]: 1) toilet. *He's in the shitter.* 2) a contemptible and unreliable person. *He's a real shitter, isn't he?*

Shitty [expressive]: bad; inferior; no good. *The food was shitty.*

Shoot the shit: *See,* **Shoot** the bull.

Talk shit: *See,* **Talk**.

Tough shit [expressive]: that's too bad (generally used ironically and mockingly). *When the wealthy woman complained about the harsh conditions in life, we all thought, "Well, tough shit for her."*

Up shit creek (without a paddle) [expressive]: *See,* Up a **creek** without a paddle.

Weird shit [expressive]: very unusual happenings. *There is some weird shit going on in the cemetery at night that we cannot explain.*

Who gives a shit? [expressive]: who cares? *When told he could not go on the trip, he replied, "Who gives a shit?"*

Shiz

Shiz: a more polite form of the expressive word, "shit," when in need to be publicly discreet. *Oh shiz, we should leave now or we'll be late.*

Shoe

Drop the shoe: not hold up one's responsibility or job. *We can't have anyone drop the shoe around here.*

Fill one's shoes: operate in another's absence; to replace. *She's going to have to fill Anna's shoes, as well as her regular role, until Anna returns from vacation.*

If the shoe fits (then wear it): a proverb that means if what is spoken describes you, then it applies (generally stated in a negative sense). *You neglect to treat your neighbors with respect, then you complain about them ignoring you; well, if the shoe fits....*

In another's shoes: to understand someone in their situation; to feel what another is experiencing. *You can't judge her until you've been in her shoes.*

Shoe is on the other foot: the situation has reversed. *Oh, now you want to make up? I guess the shoe is on the other foot now, isn't it?*

Shoot

Shoot!: exclamation of dismay. *Ahh, Shoot! Can't we stay in New York City for a few more days?*

Shoot from the hip: react impulsively or recklessly with little or no fore-thought. *Tina tends to shoot from the hip when she gets flustered.*

Shoot off one's mouth/Shoot one's mouth off: boast; brag; talk as if one knows everything; give opinions or advice without knowing all the facts. *He hasn't done very well in any business venture, but he is always shooting his mouth off about how business savvy he is.*

Shoot oneself in the foot: to commit a misjudgment or error, resulting in a negative effect or harm to oneself. *Be careful of those with whom you choose to be unfriendly at work; you just might shoot yourself in the foot if any of them in the future becomes your boss.*

Shoot straight: to follow the rules or the law; to not deceive; law abiding. *He has to shoot straight from now on or else he goes back to jail. Shoot straight with me, and I'll be your best business partner.*

Shoot the bull/breeze/shit (expressive)**:** to have casual conversation, usu-ally with friends or acquaintances. *Hey, let's meet after work for a beer and shoot the breeze, okay?*

Short

Fall short: to be incomplete; lacking; possessing barely enough. *Your esti-mate fell short by several thousand dollars.*

Short and sweet: quick and precise. *She laid everything on the line, short and sweet.*

Short end of the stick: the unfavorable part of a deal. *He got the short end of the stick in that deal.*

Short of: lacking. *We're short of sugar and eggs.*

Shot

Call the shots: in control. *Mr. Jacks is the dude who calls the shots around here.*

Cheap shot: *See,* **Cheap**.

Like a shot: suddenly; rapidly. *Upon hearing a scream, he jumped out of bed like a shot and went outside to see what it was.*

Long shot: *See,* **Long**.

Mug shot: a photo or picture of someone. *As a witness to a crime, I was at the police station looking at mug shots of suspects all day.*

Not by a long shot: *See,* **Not**.

Shot: 1) no good anymore. *This car is shot.* 2) an amount of whiskey or alcohol, about one ounce or about 28 grams, placed in a shot glass. *Let me have a shot of whiskey. He drank 4 shots of whiskey before he got into his car and drove through the hurricane.*

Shot down: *See,* **Down**.

Shot full of holes: something that contains many weaknesses. *His story about the incident is shot full of holes.*

Shot in the arm: positive reinforcement; a morale-booster. (Historically, it is written that this phrase came from the early days of Coca-Cola prior to 1905, when the drink was made of gotu-cola and coca leaves. This gave drinkers a "rush" of energy. Customers, as a result, would come up to the counter and ask for "a shot in the arm." Today, modern-day cola drinkers have to settle with caffeine as the modern ingredient). *Having Joe there to cheer me on was like a shot in the arm.*

Shot in the dark: *See,* **Dark**.

Shot in the foot: *See,* **Shoot** oneself in the foot.

Shot out of the water: destroyed; taken apart. *Our plans to travel to Canada were shot out of the water on account of illness.*

Shot to hell: *See,* **Hell**.

Shotgun approach: dealing with matters by going after everything, rather than wisely picking and choosing. *If we deal with this investigation using the shotgun approach, I'm afraid we'll be wasting valuable time.*

Shotgun wedding: a forced wedding. *Many weddings in the old tradition were shotgun weddings with little romance.*

Take a shot at: make an attempt; try. *Have you ever taken a shot at skydiving?*

Should

Should have stayed in bed: revelation of one's dismay over the day's events. *Today I got into an accident, my boyfriend broke up with me, and I lost my job; I should have stayed in bed.*

Shoulder

Chip on one's shoulder: *See,* **Chip**.

Give someone the cold shoulder: to act aloof towards another; snub. *I'm confused; last week you were my friend, but now you give me the cold shoulder.*

Put your shoulder to the wheel: take something on with gusto; put forth great effort. *If you want to meet the deadline, you'd better put your shoulder to the wheel.*

Rub shoulders with: *See,* **Rub** elbows with.

Shoulder the load: take on the weight or responsibility. *The utility engineers had to shoulder the load and keep the electricity operating during the big storm.*

Shoulder to shoulder: together; in strong agreement. *We were shoulder to shoulder with the other neighbors in our dispute about the cable programming in our community.*

Shove

Push comes to shove: *See,* **Push**.

Shove it [expressive]: a phrase indicating disdain; to give no leeway. *You can shove it if you think you can get away with it.*

Shove it up your ass/gazoo/kazoo [expressive]: a more derogatory or forceful saying of **shove** it. *If he thinks he can threaten me to change my mind, then he can shove it up his gazoo.*

Shove off: a direct if not a forceful expression for one to leave or go away. *We told the pesky little kid to shove off.*

Show

For show: having no content; to attract attention only; superficial. *This food is made of cosmetic glaze and is for show only.*

Get the show on the road: to get going and do your thing. *Everyone is ready, so let's get the show on the road!*

Show must go on: proceed despite bad conditions. *The show must go on despite the work slowdown by the striking employees.*

Show off: to try to impress. *He is such a show off.*

Show one the ropes: teach one how to do something; revealing knowledge about a particular trade or activity to someone to allow that person to learn and be able to perform well. *Jack has been my great mentor and the person who showed me the ropes when I was a new recruit with the company.*

Show one's true colors: revelation of one's true nature. *The drill sergeant's true colors were discovered when someone saw him painting on canvas at the beach.*

Showtime: a moment in time for presenting oneself. *A great basketball game is like an event on stage, where the best players act to perfection and grace, which they sometimes call, "Showtime!"*

Steal the show: attract the most attention; preside over. *He stole the show with his magnificent performance.*

Shrink

Shrink: psychiatrist. *She's been seeing a shrink this past year to help her overcome her anxieties and nightmares.*

Sick

Make one sick: *See,* **Make**.

Sick and tired: revolted to excess; annoyed. *I'm sick and tired of hearing the same thing from you everyday!*

Sick as a dog: very ill. *He's been sick as a dog ever since he ate that hamburger.*

Sick 'em/Sic 'em/Sick him: to go after to catch or to win (usually a command to a dog to attack, or a football coach commanding his players in an enthusiastic way). *When the guard spotted the thief escaping through the woods, he commanded his dog to sick him.*

Sight

At first sight: when initially seen or evaluated. *When Jack met Helen, it was love at first sight.*

Lose sight of: to neglect contact with; be absent. *I lost sight of all my cousins.*

Out of sight: great; awesome. *That Boss Hoss V-8 motorcycle is out of sight, man.*

Sight for sore eyes: a person or thing with a pleasant appearance. *Seeing land after 40 days out to sea was a sight for sore eyes.*

Sight unseen: not visible; lacking material substance. *Never purchase anything sight unseen.*

Sign

Sign off: to stop transmission after identifying the broadcasting station; to stop talking. *I'm signing off for now…*

Sign one's own death warrant: to finalize one's misfortune; ensure one's own demise. *Keep away from tripping up your supervisor, as it would be signing your own death warrant.*

Silver

Silver lining: the upside of an apparently bad situation; a positive aspect. *It's not all that bad, you know; I'm sure there's a silver lining to your problem.*

Sing

Sing a different tune: alter one's opinion regarding a situation. *Ever since the police chief became cozy with the mob, he's been singing a different tune regarding those clubs.*

'Till the fat lady sings: *See,* **'Till**.

Sink

Sink in: to sense what has occurred; to have absorbed into the mind. *The news of the disaster took some time to sink in because we could not believe it really happened.*

Sink one's teeth into: 1) something solid to eat. *I want something tonight that I can sink my teeth into, like a thick steak.* 2) to be fully involved or invested in something. *Shirley sunk her teeth into this venture so much, she is not about to give up now.*

Sink or swim: to lose or succeed, no matter what. *All of our money is invested in this store, so we have to do our best, sink or swim.*

Sinking feeling: a sense of dread or loss. *When we arrived at the airport, I had a sinking feeling that I forgot my passport.*

Sit

Sit on one's hands: not take action; be inactive where action is required. *It appears that no matter what I ask of you, you simply sit on your hands.*

Sit out: not take part in; not participate. *He is going to sit out the game due to a sore leg.*

Sit tight: wait; be patient; hold on. *Sit tight while I find out what the delay is all about.*

Sit well with: to be agreeable with or acceptable to; beneficial to. *Your recommendations sit well with the committee.*

Sitting duck: in a precarious or vulnerable position; an easy target. *The soldiers felt like sitting ducks without air support to protect their flanks.*

Sitting on a powder keg: exposed to a potentially volatile situation. *We were sitting on a powder keg and didn't know it.*

Sitting pretty: *See,* **Pretty**.

Size

Cut someone down to size: *See,* **Cut**.

Size up: to figure out; analyze and diagnose; to sense or determine from observation or investigation. *He is a good trouble-shooter because he is able to quickly size up matters.*

Skank

Skank [expressive]: 1) an immoral person; nasty or gross individual. *No one hangs with him 'cause he's a skank.* 2) a slut or whore. *That girl Tim is seeing looks like a skank.* 3) filthy; dirty. *I don't like her skanky looks.*

Skate

Skate: to get by easy; to get away without harm or penalty. *We knew he was guilty, but he skated away thanks to a lack of sufficient evidence.*

Skate on thin ice: risking a potentially dangerous or damaging situation. *You'd better remedy the situation with your parents fast; we're skating on thin ice, here.*

Skeleton

Skeleton in the closet: a secret which would cause embarrassment or shame if made public. *The parties settled the case in order to avoid exposing the skeletons in each other's closet.*

Skid

Skid marks [expressive]: fecal stain on underpants. *Mother said to her little son, "Young man, skid marks on your underpants mean that you must change into a new pair before going out to play."*

Skid row: a squalid urban district where cheap bars and liquor stores are frequented by derelicts and vagrants. *We got lost downtown, and found ourselves in the middle of skid row and the soup kitchen.*

Skin

By the skin of one's teeth: just barely; by the smallest amount. *I got on board the ferry by the skin of my teeth!*

Get under one's skin: make one angry. *With his continuous complaining, he was beginning to get under my skin.*

No skin off my ass/back/nose: of no concern; having little or no effect; having no impact. *It's no skin off my nose whether you stay or leave.*

Save one's skin: 1) avoid injury or death. *We saved our skins by not driving on icy roads during the weekend.* 2) prevent from getting caught; to be saved from a bad situation. *Thanks for saving my skin by giving me this loan.*

Skin [expressive]: a sexy girl. *David never misses to glance at a skin when she passes by.*

Skin alive: punish severely. *If I catch you stealing my peaches again, I'll skin you alive!*

Skin and bones: very skinny. *Johnny is tall but he's all skin and bones.*

Skin deep: superficial or shallow; not real. *Her smiles are skin deep.*

Skin game: a swindling trick. *You should be careful and not get caught in a skin game.*

Skinhead: generally, a person referred as one who follows racist or anarchist politics (many of the followers generally are young and have shaved heads). *Some skinheads in this county are associated with local militia units.*

Skinny: 1) the inside story; the private rumor or information about something. *He has the skinny about what was discussed at the closed-door meeting.* 2) the straight fact; the bottom line. *What's the skinny on the direction of the storm?*

Skinny dip: to swim in the nude. *The toddlers went skinny dipping in the wading pool.*

Thick skin: not easily flustered; emotionally resilient. *If you want to work around here, you have to develop a thick skin.*

Thin skin: easily flustered; more emotional in temperament than with others. *Careful with his feelings because he tends to be thin-skinned.*

Skunk

Skunk: 1) to stink up. *Don't skunk up the place.* 2) to beat decisively and by shut out. *We skunked the other team in foosball 5 to 0.*

Slammer

Slammer: jail; prison. *He was sentenced to 10 years in the slammer.*

Slap

Slap in the face: an unexpected abuse or rudeness; irritating insult; unfairness not expected. *For management to promote less-qualified employees over you is a slap in the face. Refusing to offer me equal treatment was a slap in the face.*

Slap on the wrist: small, almost insignificant punishment for a larger crime or action. *For all the horrible things the street gang committed— setting fires, beating people up—and all they received was a slap on the wrist from the law. Where's the justice?*

Slate

Clean slate: a historical record showing no law violations. *Wow! For once we have a political candidate with a clean slate running for office!*

Wipe one's slate clean: *See,* **Wipe**.

Sleep

Sleep a wink: to sleep only a very short while. *I hardly slept a wink last night.*

Sleep around: promiscuous person. *Some of her friends would sleep around to get an acting job.*

Sleep like a baby/log: sleep very soundly. *I slept like a log last night.*

Sleep on it: to think about something after a good night's sleep. *Let me sleep on it, and I'll give you my answer first thing tomorrow.*

Sleep with: to be sexually intimate with. *Did you sleep with her last night?*

Sleep with the devil: to be exposed to high risks being with another; be in the company of bad influence; risky maneuver or adventure. *Having that person as a business partner is like sleeping with the devil.*

Sleeper: unknown talent or apparatus with much potential in the future. *This guy is a real sleeper for the company; he has a programming mind that knows no bounds.*

Slick

Slick: 1) well-groomed or fashionably dressed; look sharp. *I think you look real slick in those sunglasses.* 2) glib; all show without substance. *Watch out for the slick salesmen at that dealer.*

Slip

Get/Receive a pink slip: receive a dismissal notice from work; to get fired. *Barney got his pink slip early today, so I'll bet he's already at the bar.*

Give someone the slip: to evade; to hide from. *Jack is famous for talking your ear off, so I had to give him the slip so I could get some work done today.*

Let slip: reveal something inadvertently. *I let slip to Bob about the surprise party.*

Slip me five: shake my hand. *Slip me five; I want to thank you for supporting me at the meeting today.*

Slip one over on: deceive; trick or cheat. *You thought you could slip one over on me, but I knew your intentions from the start.*

Slip someone a Mickey: to sneak a sedative or other drug into someone's drink. *Good thing we walked in, right at the time he was about to slip her a Mickey.*

Slippery as an eel: 1) conniving; untrustworthy. *He sarcastically believes that most politicians are slippery as eels. Watch him; he's as slippery as an eel.* 2) very elusive; hard to capture. *The bank robber is so hard to catch with his disguises and various getaway vehicles that he is slippery as an eel.*

Slob

Slob: a bum; a disheveled person; an unclean individual. *I don't want to date a person who looks dapper in public but acts like a slob at home. Mom always gets on my case for being a slob.*

Slobber: spit. *He tends to slobber when he talks excitedly. I'm not going to use that phone after he slobbered on it.*

Slug

Slug: slow, clumsy person. *Who's responsible for hiring that slug?*

Slug head/Slughead: a dumb person. *The unknown hacker emailed a note to the FBI, stating, "You can't catch me, you slugheads!" He was later arrested at the hackers convention.*

Sly

On the sly: operate in a deceptive manner; hidden. *He has been dealing drugs on the sly for years.*

Smack

Smack: 1) a sharp physical blow. *She smacked him across the face for his rude behavior. The car smacked into the wall.* 2) heroin. *Smack is still a problem drug in many communities.*

Smacker: 1) a noisy kiss. *My little kid gave her a smacker on the cheek.* 2) a dollar. *That item will cost you twenty smackers.*

Small

Small fry/Small fish: an insignificant person. *He's just a small fish and not considered a problem.*

Small potatoes: *See,* **Potato**.

Small talk: casual conversation; idle chatter. *We generally stand around the cooler making small talk during our work break.*

Small time: insignificant; not worthy. *Don't worry about that punk; he's small time.*

Smart

Smart as a fox: quick and clever. *That Andrea is as smart as a fox.*

Smart ass/Smart pants/Smarty pants/Smart aleck: one with a forward or abrasive manner. *The boss told that smart ass employee to shut up, which was enjoyable to see.*

Smart cookie: an intelligent person. *That guy in operations is one smart cookie.*

Smash

Smash hit: an outstanding success; very popular. *This movie has been a smash hit for years. His line of clothing is a smash hit with the young urban crowd.*

Smashed: Extremely drunk. *We all got smashed at the party.*

Smashing: great; awesome. *His smashing new sports car was smashed by the garbage truck this morning.*

Smell

Smell a rat: to sense something to be wrong or rotten. *Wait a minute; I smell a rat whenever he is involved.*

Smell blood: hungry and ready for attack; filled with excited spirits in bringing down an opponent or prey. *The group smelled blood after its leader was injured.*

Smell like a rose: *See,* **Rose**.

Stop and smell the roses: *See,* **Rose**.

Smoke

Blowing smoke: saying something that is otherwise not true; portraying something not real; fake. *He acts tough, but most of the time he's just blowing smoke.*

Chain smoke: to smoke constantly, almost in regular procession. *He chain smokes, and consumes about 3 packs a day.*

Holy smoke(s): *See,* **Holy**.

Smoke/Smoked: 1) to win convincingly. *He smoked the opponent in the first round of the boxing match.* 2) kill; get rid of. *He was smoked when they discovered he was a double agent.*

Smoke and mirrors: unrealistic or false projection; fake; to make something look nicer or better than what it really is. *These fancy brochures and models of homes were smoke and mirrors to lure unsuspecting people to place down payments; the homes were never built and the culprits disappeared.*

Smoke out: 1) to stop or eliminate smoking. *This month is smoke out month.* 2) search; find out. *The police finally smoked out the suspect in the wooded area with the help of several search dogs.*

Smoking gun: direct evidence of guilt. *A video tape of the criminal was the smoking gun in the burglary heist.*

Up in smoke: *See,* **Up**.

When/after the smoke clears: when details about a matter become more evident. *We'll have a better idea how to proceed after the smoke clears on the corporate merger.*

Smooth

Smooth operator: an almost undetectable or clean working individual in his or her talent (can be one who is slick or deceptive or even a smart and competent person). *This guy is such a smooth operator that he gets away with a lot before people understand what they really lost.*

Smooth sailing: to have it easy thereafter. *If we can get the contract signed, then it's smooth sailing for us.*

Snafu

Snafu: problem; mess. *What is the snafu all about? Wow, you got yourself into one hell of a snafu.*

Snag

Hit a snag: come across an unexpected obstacle. *Our profits hit a snag during the first quarter of the year, but they should pick up again.*

Snag: to catch. *The fugitive was snagged at the U.S.-Mexican border.*

Snail

Snail mail: mail via the postal service. *Would you like your billing statement sent email or snail mail?*

Snail's pace: moving or progressing slowly, like the pace of a snail. *We are progressing at a snail's pace building this freeway system.*

Snake

Snake in the grass: one who has a concealed and negative motive. *Look out for the last hire; he's a snake in the grass.*

Snap

Snap: 1) lose control emotionally. *He snapped when he learned of her death.* 2) something easily done. *Winning was a snap.* 3) quickly. *The job was done in a snap.*

Snap out of it: recover quickly; come back to (usually used in the imperative). *He couldn't seem to snap out of it after being hit by the ball; he felt dazed for a couple days.*

Snap to it!: get busy. *Same as,* **Shake** a leg. *If we don't snap to it around here, we may find ourselves out of a job.*

Snazzy/Snitzy

Snazzy/Snitzy: high-class. *She wore real snazzy clothes to the prom.*

Snip

Snippy: critical; argumentative. *His snippy attitude is overcome only by his unique talent as an inventor.*

Snotty

Snotty: contemptible; haughty; sarcastic. *She is snotty when she doesn't get her way.*

Snooty

Snooty: 1) detached and not compassionate; to feel that one has a standard that others do not compare; to feel above others. *Sally is warm and personable, but Jane is quite snooty.* 2) a place that is very regal or high class. *This restaurant looks too snooty to me.*

Snow

Snow job: to deceive; cover up; to present something in better light. *When Clark gave me this elaborate excuse for not being able to show up to work yesterday, I knew it was a snow job.*

Snowball's chance in hell: very little opportunity; very unlikely to succeed. *You have a snowball's chance in hell to attend the meeting, and then get to the theater in time to see your child's play.*

Snowed under: overwhelmed, usually with work. *We generally are snowed under with work orders during the Christmas season.*

Snuff

Snuff: to eliminate; to get rid of. *The city tried unsuccessfully to snuff out the rat problems.*

Up to snuff: *See,* **Up** to par/Up to snuff.

Sob

Sob story: tale related for the sole purpose of inspiring pity. *He was excused from work after giving his boss some sob story that his back was hurting.*

Social

Social animal: a person who enjoys going out with others; to party or commensurate with others. *Jack gets along with others because he's a social animal.*

Sock

Knock someone's socks off: *See,* **Knock**.

Sock away: to set money aside; save. *Old Mr. Crotchet had tons of money socked away, but lived like a pauper! Go figure.*

Something

Make something of: create an argumentative issue. *The bully said, "So ya wanna make something of it?"*

Something else: quite extraordinary. *James is something else, I'll tell you!*

Something is up: an interesting or surprising matter that is about to occur soon. *Bob has been very quiet lately; I think something's up.*

Something the cat dragged in: *See,* **Cat**.

Song

For a song: *See,* **For**.

Song and a prayer: *See,* **Have** a prayer.

Song and dance: the use of sweet sounding words aimed to flatter, exert influence, persuade, appease, etc.; a conducive story told in an effort to mislead. *The person gave a song and dance routine about needing bus fare to get home; really, it was a way of getting money from unsuspecting shoppers in the grocery store parking lot.*

Song in one's heart: happy; filled with good feeling. *Harry's got a song in his heart and a spring in his step today.*

Swan song: one's very last performance or final accomplishment; a last act. *His swan song was to die as he did trying to save the old-growth trees from being destroyed.*

Soup

In the soup: in trouble. *That kid has been in the soup from day one!*

Souped up: increased in both power and speed. *Bob put together a souped up car in the old days in Los Angeles that no police officer could catch.*

Space

Breathing space: *See,* **Breathe**.

Space cadet/Space case: airhead; not paying attention; focused elsewhere. *The nitrous oxide leak at the plant turned many of us into space cadets for a while.*

Spaced/Spaced out: not paying attention; in a hypnotic state or attitude; not focused. *We felt a little spaced out after eating grandma's wonderful mushroom soufflé.*

Spare

Spare tire: weight gain around the torso, esp. during middle age. *I never used to have this spare tire when I was younger; I'd better start working out!*

Spark

Spark plug: one who is full of dynamism and hustle in an organization. *This guy is a real spark plug in the organization.*

Spaz

Spaz: a person prone to abnormally emotional behavior. *My brother had a spaz attack when he heard that I damaged his car.*

Speed

Speed: 1) one who always seems to rush around. *Hey, Speed, how goes it?!* 2) a drug or narcotic used to excite the body's nervous system and keep it energized. *The doctor prescribed him speed to keep him from falling asleep on the long flight overseas.*

Speed demon/Speed freak: one who excessively speeds, often toward being reckless. *Jack is such a speed demon on the road.*

Speedy Gonzalez: one who moves fast; to do things very quickly. *This little guy races his tricycle up and down the street like Speedy Gonzalez.*

Up to speed: back to normal. *We won't be up to speed on the boat until we can get new parts for the engine.*

Spill

Spill one's guts: to tell all; to come out with the whole truth. *He spilled his guts about the shooting to his friends.*

Spill the beans: reveal information, either inadvertently or by command. *Jack accidentally spilled the beans about the location of the lost treasure. When pressured to talk, the suspect spilled the beans about the murder.*

Spin

Spin control: exertion of force to keep a situation from getting, or "spinning", out of hand. *This latest rumor will frighten our investors away if we don't put some spin control on it soon.*

Spin doctor: person exerting the force in order to keep a situation from getting out of hand. *We'll get Sheila to confront our investors; she's a great spin doctor.*

Spin one's wheels: activity with no effect or results. *We have been spinning our wheels on the matter and getting nowhere.*

Spit

Spit and polish: sharp and clean; close attention to looking clean and organized. *The cleaning crew did a spit and polish job.*

Spitting image: an almost perfect likeness of someone. *He's a spitting image of his father.*

Splash

Make a splash: cause a stir; attract a lot of attention. *You sure made a splash at the party last night with that moon rock!*

Split

Split: to leave. *This place is boring; let's split!*

Split hairs: argue minutiae on an unimportant subject as if it mattered. *Let's not split hairs on the subject and look to resolve our differences.*

Sponge

Sponge/Sponge off: to impose on the generosity of another. *I was sponging off my parents until I got a job. She sponges off her friends without concern, yet wonders why she is not invited to social gatherings.*

Throw in the sponge: *See,* **Throw**.

Spoon

(Born with a) silver spoon in one's mouth: being raised in financially wealthy surroundings. *He was born with a silver spoon in his mouth, so he did not understand the meaning of hard labor.*

Spoon feed: 1) to feed piecemeal, a little at a time. *Don't spoon feed me the information; just give it to me all at once.* 2) to make it easy for someone. *George was spoon-fed from childhood and rarely had to do any chores himself.*

Spot

Hit the high spots: emphasize only the important or significant spots. *Next time I go to New York, I'm hitting the high spots.*

Hit the spot: to be satisfied or feel satiated. *That hot meal really hit the spot.*

In a bad spot: in a poor or dangerous situation or location. *Between my best friend not speaking to me and being jobless, I was in a bad spot. (also) This is a bad spot in which to wait for a cab.*

Sweet spot: *See,* **Sweet**.

Spout

Up the spout: worthless; a total loss. *My whole investment went up the spout.*

Spread

Middle-age spread: *See,* **Spare** tire.

Spread it on thick: act of being excessive in behavior in order to persuade. *You really spread it on thick in order to get yourself a promotion, didn't you?*

Spread like wildfire: to move rapidly and out of control. *The flu seemed to spread like wildfire around the school.*

Spread oneself thin: distribute one's efforts in too many areas; attempting to do too much. *Don't spread yourself too thin—you might end up in the nuthouse!*

Spring

Spring chicken: young and lively. *Listen, sonny, I'm no spring chicken any more.*

Spring for something: to treat, accommodate or pay for someone's meal or activity. *Let's go out tonight; I'll spring for dinner and a movie.*

Spring (one) loose: set free. *He was sprung loose by the Governor through a pardon after DNA evidence determined his innocence of the crime.*

Spring something on someone: to surprise another with something. *I'll spring the good news about the promotion to the family tomorrow.*

Spunk

Spunk: energy; courage. *Do you have the spunk to walk through that dark alley?*

Square

Back to square one: *See,* **Back**.

Square: a rigidly conventional or unsophisticated person. *Check out the square with the glasses!*

Square deal: honest exchange. *I have made more square deals by just a handshake with trusted partners than with written agreements and attorneys.*

Squeal

Squeal: to betray a friend or secret; snitch. *Martha squealed on me, so I'm not talking to her.*

Squawk

Squawk: to complain; to make irritating noise. *Quit your squawking and clean your room!*

Squawk box: radio or stereo. *We turned the squawk box on to listen to the baseball game.*

Squeeze

Put the squeeze on: to pressure another to do something. *The senior citizens put the squeeze on the mayor for better nursing home facilities.*

Stab

Back stabber/Backstabber: *See,* **Back** stabber.

Stab in the back: to be disloyal; to betray. *If you don't watch out, he'll stab you in the back.*

Stab in the dark: *See,* **Dark**.

Stack

Stack the cards: to arrange in order to cheat; fix. *The cards were stacked in his favor, she could see.*

Stack up: stand in comparison with another. *How do we stack up with the advances made by our rival company?*

Stacked: large breasts. *She was stacked and gorgeous but the gay gentlemen took no heed.*

Stacked deck: a set up to make one lose. *How can you win if you're going up against a stacked deck?*

Stand

Have a leg to stand on: *See,* **Leg**.

Stand one up: to not show up at a pre-arranged time and place; not show at an appointed time with someone. *He stood me up before, but I believe him that he will not stand me up again.*

Stand pat: to retain one's position; refuse to move. *We stand pat on our decision to close the store on account of low business revenue.*

Standing room only: very crowded (refers to the fact that it is so crowded that no seats remain). *We have a full house at the playhouse; it's standing room only.*

Stand-offish/Standoffish: snobbish; reserved. *Diplomacy requires that you lose that standoffish attitude.*

Stank

Stank: stinky; smelly. *Get that stanky dog away from me! What is that stank?*

Star

See stars: sensation of flashing lights, or stars, as being dazed or knocked out. *I'll hit you so hard, you'll be seeing stars!*

Thank one's lucky stars: appreciation for one's good fortune. *I thank my lucky stars for the good life I have lived.*

Start

Start from scratch: *See,* From **Scratch**.

Stash

Stash: 1) to hide. *We had to stash the presents so that the kids would not see them before Christmas morning.* 2) marijuana or drug supply. *John Lennon's stash box was auctioned for over $40,000 in 2002.*

Steady

Go steady: to see or date on a regular basis. *Jack and Jill are going steady now.*

Steal

Steal: a great deal; a bargain. *I got this beautiful sweater for $10! What a steal!*

Steal away: depart quietly or covertly to somewhere; sneak off to. *Let's steal away to the mountains this weekend.*

Steal one's thunder: divert another's power or attention to oneself. *I was getting ready to spring the big surprise on everyone, but Nancy stole my thunder.*

Steal the show: *See,* **Show**.

Steam

Blow off steam/Let off steam: to relieve one's held-up or pent-up feelings (of tenseness) through strenuous activity, loud vocalization, or social interaction. *After a hard day's work, we often blow off steam playing racquetball at the fitness center.*

Get (all) steamed up: become irritated; angry. *My coach got all steamed up when I missed the ball.*

Running out of steam: *See,* **Run**.

Step

Keep in step with: *See,* **Keep**.

Step all over: 1) be disrespectful. *A bad supervisor steps all over the staff without appreciating their work.* 2) be overpowering in every way. *They stepped all over us in tonight's soccer game.*

Step on it: directive to a driver to go faster. *In trying to make time to the airport, we asked the taxi driver to step on it for an extra ten dollars.*

Step on one's toes: to annoy or offend someone. *Be careful how you direct your remarks so that you don't step on anyone's toes.*

Step up to the plate: take something on; to challenge; move forward, onward, or progressively upward. *You have to step up to the plate sometimes and challenge life.*

Stew

Stew in one's own juice(s): suffer from one's own anxieties or anger. *Let her stew in her own juice for a while; she'll get sick of it and come around.*

Stick

Cancer stick: cigarette. *You should lay off those cancer sticks.*

Dirty end of the stick: *See,* **Dirty**.

Faster than you can swing a stick: *See,* **Fast**.

Fiddle sticks: nonsense. *The rumor about the school closing down is fiddle sticks.*

In the sticks: in the rural area. *He lives way over there in the sticks.*

On the stick: quick; alert and competent. *That kid always seems to be on the stick.*

Short end of the stick: *See,* **Short**.

Stick: a very thin person. *Angela, you're a stick! Do you ever eat?*

Stick around: stay; remain nearby. *I was advised to stick around, and perhaps get on the next flight.*

Stick 'em up!: a command to raise one's hands in the air, as during a robbery. *"Stick 'em up!", the bank robber yelled at everyone.*

Stick it: an expression of disgust; a rude interjection to show rejection or insult. *When asked about his criminal past, the rock star told the reporter to "Stick it."*

Stick it out: endure. *If we stick it out through the cold winter, we'll see a beautiful spring.*

Stick one's neck out/Stick out one's neck: expose oneself to great risk and harm; risk one's reputation out of loyalty to another. *When someone sticks their neck out for you, you know they're a true friend.*

Stick out like a sore thumb: very noticeable. *You will stick out like a sore thumb wearing a suit in this place.*

Stick to it: stay on something; keep up with. *Stick to your studies and get good grades.*

Stick to one's guns: *See,* **Gun**.

Sticky fingers: one who is prone to stealing. *He has sticky fingers so keep an eye on him.*

Stiff

Stiff: 1) dead body. *The cadavers for our medical school are stiffs we get from the local morgue.* 2) to cheat or steal. *He stiffed me out of twenty dollars.*

3) stern; disciplined. *Our new science teacher is stiff about making sure we have daily homework assignments.*

Stink

Big stink: a reaction of outrage or protest. *The computer virus created a big stink worldwide.*

Make a stink: to complain or fuss. *Please don't make a stink about this incident to Mom.*

Stinker: person who is devious or troublesome; a handful. [this word is sometimes used affectionately, esp. for children]. *If I see that stinker again, I'll tell him a thing or two! Hi, you little stinker; are you going to play with your toys now?*

Stinks to high heaven: an outrage about something that looks underhanded or is self-dealing; corrupting. *The ability of lobbyists in City Hall to get special deals over the objections of community groups, I think, stinks to high heaven. The company provided its shareholders false information about its revenues for the past year; the whole thing stinks to high heaven.*

Stoke

Stoked: psyched; excited; energized; thrilled. *We are totally stoked about our upcoming snowboarding trip.*

Stone

Cast the first stone: *See,* **Cast**.

Chiseled in stone: *See,* **Chisel**.

Leave no stone unturned: to miss nothing; look everywhere. *Leave no stone unturned; I want that document found.*

Run into a stone wall: *See,* **Run into a brick/stone wall**.

Stone broke: *See,* **Broke**.

Stone cold: 1) without feeling. *He gave her a haunting look with a stone cold stare.* 2) completely; all of. *He has been stone cold sober for 3 years now.*

Stone-hearted: cruel and insensible; without feelings or consideration toward another. *He's a stone-hearted boss, but he rewards his good employees well.*

Stoned: under the influence of a drug, esp. marijuana; high; induced incoherence. *Dude, I'm so stoned.*

Stonewall: to exhibit uncooperative behavior; hold up or delay; stubborn. *The iron foundry has stonewalled union requests for years to provide employees with safe working facilities.*

Stone's throw: very close to; not far away. *We're a stone's throw from the supermarket.*

Written in stone: *See*, **Written**.

Stop

Make a pit stop: *See*, **Make**.

Pull out all the stops: *See*, **Pull**.

Stop and smell the roses: *See*, **Rose**.

Stop short: to cut off just before the ending. *He was stopped short of the goal line as the defensive end tackled him hard. In any oral argument, it is wise to stop short of punching anyone in the face or otherwise committing an assault. The police officer stopped short of giving me a ticket, in sympathy of seeing two crying babies in the back seat of our car.*

Stop your bitching/bitchin': *See*, **Bitch**.

Straight

Give it to me straight/Tell it to me straight: tell the truth. *Don't lie and give it to me straight.*

Straight: conventional or conservative; heterosexual. *Are you straight or gay?*

Straight from the hip: in an honest matter; truthfully. *I like dealing with Benjamin; everything he says and does comes straight from the hip.*

Straight poop: *See*, **Poop**.

Straight shooter: an upright and honorable person; loyal. *You can trust Dan; he's a straight shooter.*

Straight up: liquor with no additions. *He takes his whiskey straight up.*

Straighten up and fly right: correct one's wrongs. *I don't want you showing up to work drunk. This is your last chance to straighten up and fly right.*

Straw

Grasping at straws/Clutching at straws/Pulling at straws: desperate attempt. *You are grasping at straws with that argument.*

Last straw/Final Straw/The straw that broke the camel's back: the final act, of which one can no longer tolerate; the final annoying thing that makes one lose patience. *The straw that broke the camel's back occurred when he failed to show up on time to the court hearing.*

Streak

Streak: a brief run in the nude, done for shock-value. *Every year some fraternity goofball streaks past our front porch.*

Street

On easy street: *See*, **Easy**.

Street smart(s): the ability to survive in the challenging environment of a large city. *I'm sure Debbie will be fine coming home late; she has a lot of street smarts. This job demands one to have a lot of street smarts.*

Stretch

Stretch of the imagination: imaginative effort; something thought to be, but not real (generally used in the negative). *It is by no stretch of the imagination to see that Gerardo will make it big someday.*

STRETCHING THE POINT

Stretch the point: to embellish or not tell the truth about something, which can tend to mislead. *Saying that Dave saved everyone from the fire is stretching the point a bit, knowing that he accidentally started it!*

Strike

Strike a chord: find compatibility or similarity with; harmonize. *Jim struck a chord with Helen 3 months ago, and now they're getting married.*

Strike a sour note: cause unpleasant feelings. *News of the recent mugging in our neighborhood struck a sour note with all the residents.*

Strike it rich: achieve wealth suddenly. *Only a few people in the world strike it rich.*

Strike one's fancy: to appeal to someone. *The magnificent California redwood trees always seem to strike my fancy.*

Two strikes against you: in a precarious situation. *You have two strikes against you, now, so you better behave.*

String

On a string: under one's control. *She has her boyfriend on a string.*

Pull strings: use one's influence. *Can you pull a few strings so I could get a job where you work?*

Pull no strings: use no influence for advantage; pursue a fair-playing field. *This kid is smart; he pulled no strings to get into this fine institution.*

String someone along: to deceive someone over time with false stories. *He had strung her along with thoughts of marriage, only to run off with another woman.*

Strings attached: something obtained, but for a price. *There are strings attached if you want to be part of this deal.*

Strong

Strong as an ox: extremely strong and healthy. *Harvey is strong as an ox but is a gentle person.*

Strong arm: See, **Arm**.

Stubborn

Stubborn as a mule: extremely set in one's ways; resistant. *Mr. Simpson is as stubborn as a mule when someone tries to tell him what to do.*

Stuck

Stuck-up: snobbish; conceited. *She's become stuck-up and rude ever since she moved to a management position.*

Stuff

Hot stuff: See, **Hot**.

Kid's stuff: See, **Kid**.

Know one's stuff: to be very knowledgeable or talented. *She is valuable to the company because she knows her stuff about inventory control.*

Show one's stuff/Strut one's stuff: demonstrate one's talents. *The new applicant was required to show his stuff.*

Stuff it: exclamation of disgust, defiance, contempt or angry retort. *When asked about the drunk driving arrest last night, the famous athlete told the reporter to stuff it.*

Stuff one's face: 1) eat in abundance. *We stuffed our face tonight at the party.* 2) eat speedily. *We had to stuff our faces because the show was ready to begin.*

Stuffed shirt: a pompous, self-satisfied person; arrogant person. *Corporate parties are full of stuffed shirts.*

Stuffy: 1) one who is not very open in feeling or thought; one whose obstinance or rigidity makes others uncomfortable. *The new boss is a bit stuffy, isn't she?* 2) poor ventilation. *Since it is stuffy in here, could we open a window?*

Stump

Stumped: puzzled by a situation. *This difficult problem has me stumped.*

Such

Such is life: one has very little control over events in life; an admission to succumbing to certain challenging moments in life. *We must do the best we can with what we have; such is life.*

Suck

Suck: state of being undesirable; to be bad; an undesirable situation. *This weather really sucks today.*

Suck it up: to endure; be strong; to continue on without complaint. *We were told to suck it up and shut up.*

Suck one in: to convince another by deception or false notions. *He got sucked into buying an expensive watch because he hoped it would give him status.*

Sucker: a person who is easily duped. *There's a sucker born every minute.*

Sucker bet/Sucker's bet: a loser's choice. *Betting on that horse is a sucker bet.*

Sue

Sue someone's pants off: to recover damages through a lawsuit against another person or an entity for all their money or possessions. *If we use this logo, they will sue the pants off us.*

Sup

'Sup: shortened version of "what's up?" *Hey, 'sup, y'all?*

Super

Super duper: great; excellent; thrilling. *That was a super duper show!*

Super jock: a superior athlete. *Super jocks are worth a lot of dough.*

Sure

For sure/"Fer" sure): without a doubt; certainly. *"Do you think I look cool in this outfit?" I asked. "Fer sure", my friend replied.*

Survival

Survival of the fittest: only the most physically able will endure. *It's survival of the fittest, no matter where you go; it's a tough world out there!*

Swallow

Hard to swallow: to not believe. *I find your story hard to swallow.*

Swallow one's pride: retract or bury one's pride; become humble. *I had to swallow my pride and apologize to her, but I'm glad I did it.*

Tough pill to swallow: *See,* **Tough**.

Sweat

By the sweat of one's brow: by hard work. *After 11 years, by the sweat of his brow, our grandfather managed to earn enough money to bring the whole family to America from his native Italy.*

No sweat/Don't sweat it: no trouble. *Mason passed his exams with no sweat. When I thanked him for his help, he replied, "no sweat!"*

Sweat bullets: be troubled or distressed; very apprehensive. *Everyone was sweating bullets waiting for the results of the exam.*

Sweat off: lose weight by sweating. *I can sweat off several pounds in a few days.*

Sweat out: anxiously await the conclusion of a situation. *All the workers' families were sweating out the strike, hoping the work stoppage would end soon.*

Sweep

Clean sweep: *See,* **Make** a clean sweep.

Sweep off one's feet: to inspire classic feelings of passion in the opposite sex. *Jake swept Alice off her feet when he proposed to her.*

Sweep under the carpet/rug: hide; avoid. *The auto accident is an issue I'd rather sweep under the rug. The problems were just swept under the rug, which made the situation worse.*

Sweet

Sweet: great; awesome; wonderful; perfect. *Yeah, Sweet! We're going to the game tonight!*

Sweet on: harbor affectionate feelings for; to like. *I think Joe's a bit sweet on you, Carrie.*

Sweet spot: the best area to make contact with a ball, such as with a golf club, tennis racket, baseball bat, etc., depending on the sport. *When you hit the sweet spot on the ball with my golf club, the ball really flies far.*

Sweet talk: flattery, generally to gain favor of another. *He kept sweet talking her until she finally agreed to go to dinner with him. He somehow sweet talked his way into the deal.*

Sweeten the offer: make an offer even more appealing. *To sweeten the offer, I'll give you your own parking space at work.*

Swim

Sink or swim: *See,* **Sink**.

Swim against the tide: provide much resistance; stubborn. *If you swim against the tide, you're likely to get nowhere.*

Swim with the tide: provide little or no resistance; easygoing. *If you swim with the tide, you're likely to have an easier life.*

Swing

Faster than you can swing a stick: *See,* **Fast**.

In full swing: actively in operation. *The clean-up project around the lake was in full swing this week, with many neighborhood volunteers coming out to help.*

Swing: 1) to be spirited and have fun. *Let's swing, baby!* 2) to rotate sexual partners. *Some couples get bored of the same old routine and want to swing.*

Swing one's weight: to use one's personal power to get something done. *In this competitive industry, you must be able to swing your own weight to survive.*

Swinger: 1) a person who is a spirited socializer; hip. *He's a real swinger for an old guy.* 2) person who enjoys the constant rotation of sexual partners, even if married. *The Smiths, for their conservative appearance, are really swingers!*

Table

On the table: a matter offered or open for discussion. *The matter of health care benefits is on the table for discussion between union and management.*

Turn the table(s): *See,* **Turn**.

Under the table: 1) in secret or confidence. *Many laborers are paid under the table in cash for their work.* 2) being able to drink more than another without getting completely intoxicated. *We drank all of them under the table the other night! I can drink you under the table any day.*

Tacky

Tacky: lacking style or good taste; in bad taste. *Wearing a Hawaiian shirt to Jake's funeral is pretty tacky, but then he would have preferred it that way.*

Tail

Drag one's tail: move slowly; loaf. *Quit dragging your tail and get to work.*

High tail it out of: *See,* **High**.

Make heads or tails of something: *See,* **Make**.

On one's tail: following very closely. *Stay on his tail and make sure he does his job right.*

Tail: to follow. *Tailing too close on the freeway is dangerous driving.*

Tail between one's legs: in defeat; feeling of being subdued. *Mr. James lost the election and went home with his tail between his legs.*

Tail wagging the dog: a deceptively small force, which exerts control over the whole. *Evan seemed like an innocuous mailroom employee, but as it turned out, he was the tail wagging the dog at Finkle & Associates!*

Tailgate: follow another vehicle too closely. *Drivers are seen more often recklessly tailgating other vehicles on the freeway.*

Tailgate party: people in vehicles and trailers who get together prior to a ball game in the ballgame parking lot to enjoy each other's comradery and team loyalty over a barbequed meal. *Are you able to make it to our tailgate party tomorrow at the ballpark in parking lot D?*

Turn tail (and hide): run from or avoid a dangerous situation. *When we heard gunshots, we turned tail immediately.*

Work one's tail off: *See,* **Work**.

Take

Give and take: *See,* **Give**.

I take it: meaning, "I understand this to be...." *I take it that this visit is not a social call.*

On the take: willing to accept bribes or illegal income. *The rumor is that the branch chief is on the take.*

Take a back seat: be in a subordinate position; take a position of lower responsibility. *I'm tired of taking a back seat; I'm sure I could do better elsewhere.*

Take a beating: 1) take a big financial loss. *He took a beating in the stock market.* 2) to suffer physically. *The pod of killer whales took a beating last year when their available food supply of pollard and salmon dwindled significantly.*

Take a breather: *See,* **Breathe**.

Take a crack at something: give something a practical try. *I don't know if I can fix it, but I'll take a crack at it today.*

Take a dim view: view with pessimism or with little regard; observe with low enthusiasm. *Brenda takes a dim view of the mayor's leadership role.*

Take a dump: *See,* **Dump**.

Take a gander: take a look. *I went downtown to take a gander at the holiday decorations.*

Take a hike: get lost; go away. *Take a hike…and don't come back.*

Take a/the hint: realize the hidden meaning; read between the lines. *Mary doesn't smile at Tom anymore; he should take the hint that she doesn't really care for him.*

Take a joke: able to view criticism with humor. *Mr. Smith is a serious individual who cannot take a joke.*

Take a leak: urinate. *He went to take a leak.*

Take a load off: take a break; relax; kick back and be off one's feet. *When you feel tired, take a load off and relax.*

Take a powder: stop what one is doing and relax for a short while; take some time for yourself and rest. *After a tough morning practice, the coach told the players to take a powder for 15 minutes.*

Take a rain check: an offer to postpone an invitation due to changed circumstances that was beyond one's control. *An emergency arose, so would you mind if I took a rain check on dinner tonight?*

Take advantage of: impose on someone. *They all took advantage of good-hearted Sam.*

Take care: stay out of danger; take care of yourself. *Jose signed his email, "Take care, Love, Jose."*

Take charge: assume responsibility. *I'll take charge of everything that goes on in this office.*

Take exception: disagree; dislike. *Jane took exception with Jack for smoking in the car.*

Take five: take a five-minute rest. *Let's take five and relax for a while.*

Take for a ride: *See,* **Ride**.

Take for granted: without appreciation; in assumption. *We easily take for granted the comforts we have in life.*

Take heed: be careful. *Take heed and don't drive under the influence of alcohol.*

Take it easy: be calm; don't get frustrated; approach with care. *Take it easy during your first day on the job.*

Take it hard: react harshly. *Mike took the death of his aunt very hard.*

Take it on the chin: *See,* **Chin**.

Take it or leave it: to accept or reject without any conditions. *I'll give you one thousand dollars for this car, take it or leave it.*

Take no prisoners: have no mercy; fight hard. *Play ball, men, and take no prisoners in this game.*

Take one by surprise: unexpected showing or confrontation; a sudden twist of events that is least expected. *The boaters were taken by surprise when a large wave hit them hard. The opposing team took us by surprise and beat us.*

Take one to the cleaners: 1) procure all or a lot of another person's money, whether competitively, deceptively, or dishonorably. *James was taken to the cleaners by that crackpot investment firm.* 2) lose decisively. *They took us to the cleaners when we played them last year.*

Take one's breath away: *See,* **Breath**.

Take one's hat off to someone: render appreciation toward another. *I take my hat off to Jane for solving the dilemma.*

Take one's time: progress at an even pace; don't hurry. *I'm going to take my time and do it right.*

Take one's licks/lumps: accept responsibility for a bad act. *Mr. Leighton took his licks for leaving the scene of the accident.*

Take pity: have mercy on; feel sorry for. *I take pity on the homeless, and buy them coffee and sandwiches when I can.*

Take root: *See,* **Root**.

Take someone down a peg: reduce someone's self-importance for acting too big. *Someone ought to take that snotty Marie down a peg.*

Take something lying down: go through an unpleasant experience without defending oneself or taking any responsive action. *If he criticizes me again, I won't take it lying down anymore.*

Take something the wrong way: misunderstand. *Helen took Mark's eye wink the wrong way, and thought he was trying to be smart.*

Take the bitter with the sweet: accept the bad along with the good. *Life is a daily lesson in taking the bitter with the sweet.*

Take the bull by the horns: *See,* **Bull**.

Take the cake: 1) with much disrespect. *If that doesn't take the cake to see Bob accept the Padre's praise for the hard work that Claude had done. With* *a salty attitude and the ability to ruin any social gathering, Terry really takes the cake!* 2) to be the best; first prize. *Larry takes the cake in telling the funniest jokes.*

Take the edge off: *See,* **Edge**.

Take the fifth: refers to the Fifth Amendment to the United States Constitution, which protects individuals from self-incrimination in a criminal proceeding. *He took the fifth at the court hearing in regard to the alleged embezzlement of company funds.*

Take the heat: endure punishment or criticism. *In customer service, you have to expect to take the heat sometimes from customers.*

Take the law into one's hands: *See,* **Law**.

Take the load off: relax. *Come on in and take the load off.*

Take the plunge: to commit oneself; to risk it. *He decided to take the plunge and start an espresso business on Main Street.*

Take the pulse of: to try to understand the intent or sentiments of a person or group. *Before I go out there, take the pulse of the crowd to see what they are thinking about.*

Take the rap: suffer punishment or humiliation for something, while others may be culpable. *Dick took the rap for the missing cash that was under his supervision.*

Take the starch out of someone: make one less overbearing; humble someone. *When the clerk got reprimanded for his rudeness, it really took the starch out of him.*

Take the wind out of one's sails: *See,* **Wind**.

Take the words out of someone's mouth: *See,* **Mouth**.

Take to the cleaners: *See,* **Clean**.

Take up a collection: collect money, generally for a certain cause. *When I took up a collection for stray dogs and cats, I got money from nearly everyone.*

Take with a grain of salt: don't believe all you hear; not all you hear is true. *I took his advice with a grain of salt.*

Takeover: assume responsibility or ownership. *The Widget Company engineered a corporate takeover of its main rival.*

Talk

Backtalk: rude or discourteous response. *Don't give me any of your backtalk.*

Double talk: *See,* **Double**.

Money talks: *See,* **Money**.

Sweet talk: *See,* **Sweet**.

Talk big: to try to speak knowledgeably, or at least seemingly so, to make one's self esteem appear important. *Those who talk big tend to look more foolish than intelligent in the eyes of their listeners.*

Talk of the town: what people in town are talking about. *The unsolved murder at the bowling alley 40 years ago is still the talk of the town in this small community.*

Talk one's ear off: to speak incessantly; one who talks and talks, to the point of annoyance. *You know, Mrs. Steminski at the brewery can really talk your ears off.*

Talk out of the side of one's mouth: to speak about something that is untrue or without substantiation. *He tends to speak out of the side of his mouth in order to look impressive.*

Talk shit [expressive]**:** 1) to speak untruths or nonsense. *He talks shit; I wouldn't believe a word he says.* 2) confront a matter through discussion. *We need to talk shit right now, about your financial problems.*

Talk shop/Shop talk: converse about occupational or professional matters; work-related discussion. *The boys in finance usually meet for a beer after work and talk shop. We were just discussing shop talk, and retirement plans.*

Talk someone into it: to convince one to do something. *He talked me into going in on the deal.*

Talk someone out of it: to convince someone not to do something; to dissuade. *He talked me out of it, so I won't be going on the trip.*

Talk trash/Trash talk: to say negative or bad things about something or someone, whether true or not. *The players always talk trash about the other teams.*

Talk turkey: speak plainly or truthfully; get serious. *Ok, let's talk turkey about what it will take for you to join our company.*

Talk up a storm: speak constantly. *He can really talk up a storm. He is well-known for talking up a storm in speeches that can last for hours.*

Tall

Tall order: something seemingly difficult to accomplish. *Going to school and raising a family may seem like a tall order, but you'll find a number of students doing just that.*

Tank

In the tank: 1) in jail. *He's in the tank after getting caught driving while drunk.* 2) in trouble. *You're in the tank for missing your classes today.*

Tanked: 1) drunk. *He's tanked.* 2) to drop a lot; to fall hard; to sink precipitously. *Our stocks tanked today.*

Tar

Tar and feather someone: punish severely (this came from the medieval punishment of literally dipping victims in tar and throwing chicken feathers on them, as a visual indication of guilt). *If I catch that kid scratching my car, I'll tar and feather him!*

Taste

In bad taste/In poor taste/Not in good taste: inappropriate character; unseemly; unbecoming. *It was in poor taste for the studio manager to use foul language in front of the children.*

Leave a bad taste in one's mouth: *See,* **Leave**.

No accounting for taste: having no style; a proverb meaning that the odd preferences exhibited sometimes by others cannot be explained. *Look at the old lady wearing that flashy red dress at the flea market on a hot day; she has no accounting for taste.*

Not in good taste: *See above,* **In bad taste.**

Taste of one's own medicine: where one experiences the damage, inconvenience or harm that he has caused upon another; retaliation. *He had a taste of his own medicine about not being on time when his friend Bob picked him up at the gas station an hour late.*

Tax

Taxin': expensive; charging excessively. *Man, that stuff is taxin'.*

TDY

TDY (temporary duty): official duty outside a military camp or organization. *Joe was on TDY last month.*

Tear

Go on a tear: make a rampage, or go on a partying spree. *The groom went on a tear with his friends the night before his wedding.*

Tear down: destroy something. *We intend to tear down his reputation because we know he's lying.*

Tear into: attack someone or something aggressively. *Violet was so hungry, she literally tore into her sandwich. He tore into her for making embarrassing remarks about him.*

Tear-jerker: an emotionally moving experience that brings tears to one's eyes; something that instigates extreme sadness. *The film about the little boy's hardships was a real tear-jerker.*

Tear one's hair: to be extremely anxious, confused or frustrated. *I'd better leave now, or my parents will be tearing their hair out looking for me.*

Wear and tear: *See,* **Wear**.

Tee

Tee off: upset someone. *Don't tee him off or he'll make us run an extra mile.*

Teed off: extremely upset. *He was teed off that she canceled their date tonight.*

Teensy

Teensy/Teensy weensy: a very small or tiny amount. *We could see teensy weensy spiders crawling on the wall.*

Teeth

By the skin of one's teeth: just barely; very close. *I just made the flight by the skin of my teeth.*

Lying through one's teeth: *See,* **Lying**.

One's teeth into: very occupied with something. *He's had his teeth into that project for a long time.*

Show of teeth: to display a sense of strength. *Countries tend to display a show of teeth in times of confrontation, something very similar to animals snarling at each other.*

Show one's teeth: to display anger. *We showed our teeth to display our displeasure.*

Sink one's teeth into: *See,* **Sink**.

To the teeth: to an extreme degree; full of. *The commando team was armed to the teeth.*

Tooth and nail: with all one's strength and ability. *They fought tooth and nail all the way.*

Tell

Tell it like it is: reveal the truth of a matter; speak plainly. *I tell it like it is. That's why folks respect me.*

Tell on: to disclose information about someone; to reveal. *Dick decided he was going to tell on Jason for stealing postage stamps from the blind kid.*

Tell (one) off: 1) to reprimand severely. *He had to tell off his subordinates for stepping out of line.* 2) to retaliate boldly. *He told them off after being wrongfully accused of stealing the car.*

Term

Bring to term: persuade someone to agree or to submit; make someone surrender. *We were brought to terms on the deal because we needed the product manufactured quickly.*

Come to term(s): arrive at a compromise; reconcile. *We came to terms with the opposition and got most of what we intended in the deal.*

That

That will be the day: that such a day will never come. *That will be the day when you stop playing golf.*

That's all she wrote: that's the bitter end. *When the old car broke down today, we knew, that was all she wrote.*

That's it: 1) one has completed a task; one is finished. *That's it; it's all done.* 2) an exclamation that one will not endure something anymore; an indication of frustration. *That's it! I quit because I've had enough of this job.*

That's the last straw: the last accumulation of negative things that triggers one to capitulate. *The failure to maintain repeat customers was the last straw that put us out of business.*

That's the way the ball bounces/That's the way the cookie crumbles/That's the way the wind blows: that is the way things happen; the randomness of fate. *Oh, well, that's the way the ball bounces sometimes.*

The

The gig is up/The jig is up: the job is finished. *The workers were told by the boss that the gig was up.*

The little boys room: the men's toilet. *Tell me, where is the little boys room?*

The Man upstairs: God. *Many worshippers leave important matters to the Man upstairs.*

The pits: an unbearable place, situation, or person; the worst state of affairs imaginable. *This job is the pits. He is the pits.*

Thick

Blood is thicker than water: *See,* **Blood**.

Lay it on thick/Pour it on thick/Spread it on thick: to exaggerate or embellish; overstate matters; overly patronize. *He really lays it on thick when he talks with the girls. These salesmen really lay it on thick to try to sell you a car.*

Thick as thieves: very close relationship; closely allied. *Those two are as thick as thieves.*

Thick-headed: stubborn; a refusal to listen or to cooperate. *If you would show some respect to him, then maybe he wouldn't act so thick-headed toward you.*

Thick-skinned: insensitive; uncaring. *You have to be fairly thick-skinned to work in the collections department.*

Through thick and thin: *See,* **Through**.

Think

Think a lot of/Think highly of/Think the world of: to greatly admire or respect; to have high regard for someone. *The students think the world of their science teacher.*

Think aloud: speak as one thinks. *In thinking aloud, wouldn't it be better if you parked the car in the garage during the Mardi Gras?*

Think nothing of it: don't mention it; you are welcome. *Jack: Thank you for your good deed. Marty: Oh, think nothing of it.*

Think twice: to make sure of something. *I'll think twice next time before leaving my keys in the car.*

Thought

Food for thought: *See,* **Food**.

Lost in thought: deep in concentration; so concentrated in thought as to be generally unaware of the environment surrounding. *She was so lost in thought about him that she lost her step and fell.*

On second thought: expressing a change of mind or a revision on what was said. *On second thought, I will join you fellows after all.*

Penny for your thoughts: an expression to coax one to tell what he or she is thinking about. *Jack, you look a bit sad; a penny for your thoughts?*

Perish the thought: don't even think about it. *What? Quit school and marry him?! Perish the thought, young lady!*

Train of thought: one's line of concentration; thinking pattern. *I lost my train of thought when the phone rang; now, what was I saying?*

Thread

Hang by a thread: *See,* **Hang**.

Thread: to weave through. *We threaded our way through the holiday shopping crowd.*

Thread the needle: to be able to weave through something in an artful or skillful manner. *He's a great quarterback because he can thread the needle with the football.*

Threads: clothing, generally of higher quality, such as a pair of slacks or a suit. *I bought a new pair of threads today.*

Through

Through and Through: completely; in every aspect. *He's trustworthy as a business partner, through and through.*

Through rose-colored glasses: *See,* **Rose**.

Through the mill: rough time; difficult treatment. *The whole Jameson family has been through the mill with their illnesses and bad luck.*

Through thick and thin: to survive despite all obstacles; to go through good times and bad times. *Through thick and thin, he survived law school. Through thick and thin, their loyalty will keep them together.*

Throw

As far as I can throw him/her: cannot trust a certain person. *I trust him as far as I can throw him.*

Stone's throw: *See,* **Stone**.

Throw a fit: 1. become very angry or upset. *I threw a fit when the dog next door stomped all over my newly planted flowers.* 2. a medical disturbance or seizure where one has an uncontrollable convulsion or spasm. *Being epileptic, he would throw fits unexpectedly.*

Throw a monkey wrench into: to interrupt something from occurring; to cause delay. *The workers strike will throw a monkey wrench in getting enough product to our customers.*

Throw caution to the wind(s): to take a chance; behave rashly. *In throwing caution to the wind, I'll be taking an adventurous detour in my travels to Europe by visiting the Gaza Strip.*

Throw cold water on: to stop something from progressing forward. *Any significant loss of good technicians in the research department will likely throw cold water on any plans to sell the business.*

Throw in for a good measure: additional free item or free weight on top of your regular purchase. *The grocer threw in a few more apples for good measure.*

Throw in the towel or throw in the sponge: give up; quit. *Jack threw in the towel after working twenty years with the company.*

Throw one for a curve: catch someone unprepared; fool or deceive. *Some of the questions on the exam threw me for a curve, but I think I got most of them right.*

Throw one for a loop: *See,* **Knock** for a loop.

Throw one's hat in the ring: a decision to run for political office. *He threw his hat in the ring in his bid to become the next Senator from Oregon.*

Throw one's weight around: to exercise and emphasize one's authority. *Careful how you throw your weight around here without the employees getting annoyed.*

Throw oneself at: in pursuit of love or affection. *He threw himself at her, only to be rudely ignored.*

Throw the book at: punish severely. *The principal threw the book at the rowdy student.*

Throw up: vomit. *On my trip to Tokyo by train, some drunkard threw up right on my lap.*

Thumb

All thumbs: clumsy; awkward; lacking grace or finesse. *That kid is all thumbs.*

Green thumb: one who possesses a skill in gardening. *My next-door neighbor has a green thumb, with a knack for growing beautiful flowers all year round.*

Rule of thumb: *See,* **Rule**.

Stick out like a sore thumb: *See,* **Stick**.

Thumb a ride: *See,* **Ride**.

Thumb one's nose at someone: a gesture of defiance. *We thumbed our noses at the referee for making such a bad call.*

Thumb through: glance rapidly through a document. *I want you to thumb through this document for spelling errors.*

Thumbnail sketch: a brief account or description. *Please give me a thumbnail sketch of the financial plan before I speak with the investors.*

Thumbs down: a signal of disapproval. *All the rank and file gave thumbs down to the idea of a merger.*

Thumbs up: a signal of approval. *Let's give thumbs up for the proposal.*

Under one's thumb: under one's control. *These casinos used to be under the thumb of the underworld.*

Tick

In a tick: instantly; right away (a tick refers to the sound made by a watch or a clock every second). *Okay, I'll be out in a tick.*

What makes someone tick: to inquire how one thinks or operates. *We all wonder what makes him tick.*

Ticked/Ticked off: angry; teed off. *Mary got ticked off when the cook put too much salt in her soup.*

Ticker: one's heart. *My doctor had to repair my ticker with a triple bypass.*

Tickle

Tickle one's fancy: strike a desire for someone or something. *She just tickles my fancy.*

Tickled pink: ecstatic; very pleased; extremely delighted. *We were tickled pink to win first prize.*

Tickled silly: extremely amused; amused with laughter to the point of becoming silly. *The attendees were tickled silly with Jack's endless jokes.*

Tie

Tie into: to go after with force. *The bear tied into the freshly caught salmon with great hunger as if it hadn't eaten for a long time.*

Tie one's hands: to prevent one from doing other things. *These tasks will tie my hands up all day.*

Tie the knot: get married. *Jane and Dick tied the knot during their vacation.*

Tied up: 1) held up. *You should leave soon or else you'll get tied up in traffic.* 2) very busy. *I'm tied up now and unable to see you.*

Tied to mother's apron strings: dominated by mother. *Jack is in his forties, yet he's still tied to his mother's apron strings.*

Tie up loose ends: bring together various items into a reasonable arrangement or conclusion. *I have to tie up some loose ends before I go on my trip.*

Tie up one's shoes: to retire, especially after a long endurance. *He finally tied up his shoes after 35 years with the company.*

Tight

Sit tight: *See,* **Sit**.

Tight: 1) great; awesome; wonderful; perfect. *The classic convertible sports car that won the show looks so tight!* 2) very cool. *In reaction to flying first-class, we all said, "Ooooh, tight!"* 3) close to; in great friendship. *My cousin and I are tight.* 4) frugal; selfish; not generous. *My aunt is real tight with her money.* 5) feeling good; a satisfied state of mind. *Yeah, feeling tight tonight.*

Tight ass [expressive]: 1) very frugal. *He is a tight ass when we go on vacation trips.* 2) one who is morally rigid. *There are too many tight asses in this town.*

Tight corner/Tight spot/Tight squeeze: in a difficult situation. *Thanks for supporting me at the meeting and getting me out of a tight spot with the boss.*

Tight-fisted: frugal; thrifty. *Mr. Dickson is very tight-fisted with his money.*

Tight-lipped: secretive. *Our success depends on everyone being tight-lipped about the program.*

Tighten one's belt: be more frugal; spend less money. *All departments must tighten their belts in order to further reduce expenses.*

Tighten the screws: put the squeeze on; to pressure. *The tax collectors have been tightening the screws on foreign residents.*

Tightwad: a very frugal or cheap person. *Being a tightwad doesn't improve anyone's lot.*

Till

'Till one is blue in the face: to the point of exhaustion; helpless. *I told everyone about it 'till I was blue in the face, but no one listened.*

'Till the cows come home: until the last moment. *We were out last night 'till the cows came home.*

'Till the fat lady sings: not until it's over; nothing is over if further actions exist. *The game isn't over 'till the fat lady sings, so sit down.*

Time

Abreast of the time: up to date. *I want you to keep abreast of the time.*

Against time: a challenge to get something done in a given time. *We're working against time, but we're destined to succeed.*

At one time: in the past. *At one time, I used to high jump.*

At times: sometimes. *At times, I like to play a round of golf.*

Behind the times: not current; out of date. *Your resume is behind the times.*

Between times: occasionally. *Between times, we go to a good eating-place.*

Bide one's time: wait for the right time to act. *He is biding his time to someday acquire that dream house in the hills.*

Big time: *See,* **Big**.

For the time being: temporarily. *For the time being, let's just sit tight.*

From time to time: a period of time. *From time to time, I take a good sleep.*

In good time: at the opportune time. *In good time, we should move to a better neighborhood.*

In no time: right away. *I can fix that motor in no time.*

In the nick of time: at the right moment; just barely. *We got to the bus station in the nick of time.*

Kill time: *See,* **Kill**.

Make time: *See,* **Make**.

Take one's time: *See,* **Take**.

Time of one's life: an exhilarating experience to remember. *I had the time of my life at the show.*

Time is money: time is costly, indicating to another to hurry up; one does not have time to waste. *Time is money, so let's go.*

Time will tell: information will be revealed sooner or later. *I don't know when I'll be able to strike it rich but time will tell.*

Tip

Tip: means, "to insure proper service." *We left an extra large tip for the waiter for his excellent service.*

Tip of the iceberg: what's exposed is only a very small part of a much bigger thing; there is a lot more than what is showing. *The fraud uncovered is only the tip of the iceberg.*

Tip off: information revealed. *The informant tipped off to the police the purported deal in stolen guns.*

Tip the scales: 1) have a determining effect. *What tipped the scales in conducting a criminal investigation against the mortgage company were the deceptive practices reported by customers.* 2) revelation of one's weight, generally in reference to heavier stock. *The baby hippo tipped the scales at 150 kilos, but could eventually grow to over 10 times that weight!*

Tip-top: excellent; the very best. *This wooden vessel is in tip-top shape!*

Tipsy: drunk or unable to stand up straight (term generally but not exclusively referred to a woman). *She began to feel a bit tipsy after taking her medication.*

Tit

Tit for tat: counter action; you do it to me and I'll do it to you. *Blowing leaves in Mr. Robert's yard was a tit for tat by Mr. Jones.*

Tittle tattle: 1) idle gossip. *What sort of tittle tattle is going on along Melrose Avenue?* 2) one who tells on others; to report information about another. *He's a tittle tattle.*

To

To a frazzle: to a ruined or breakdown condition. *He works his subordinates to a frazzle.*

To a "T": exactly. *He got it right to a "T."*

To no avail: without success. *We tried to keep him from leaving, but it was to no avail.*

To the victor belongs the spoils: a proverb meaning that a winner has power over the defeated. *To the victor belongs the spoils, and the one who wins all.*

To whom it may concern: to whomever the matter applies. *My letter of introduction was addressed as, "To whom it may concern."*

Toe

On one's toes/Keep on one's toes: physically and mentally on guard. *You have to be constantly on your toes to succeed around here.*

Step on one's toes: to be bothersome to others; make one angry or displeased. *If you don't want to make enemies, you better not step on anyone's toes.*

Toe the line: to be able to competently handle one's own duties; carry out one's responsibility. *I want all of you to toe the line around here.*

Toe to toe: very close, as in a race. *The horses ran toe to toe until the end, and it required a camera shot to determine the winner.*

Tongue

Cat got your tongue?: *See,* **Cat**.

Forked tongue: *See,* **Fork**.

Hold one's tongue: stop talking. *Hold your tongue when you are with the supervisor.*

On everyone's tongue: everyone talks about it. *The promotion list is on everyone's tongue.*

Tongue-in-cheek: to speak in a joking manner; as a joke. *His remarks were tongue-in-cheek, and were not intended to be disrespectful at all.*

Tongue lashing: attack someone with harsh, critical words. *He got a tongue lashing from his parents for crashing the car.*

Too

Too big for one's britches: *See,* **Big** for one's britches.

Too many chiefs: too many supervisors and not enough workers. *There are too many chiefs in this company.*

Toot

Toot one's (own) horn: bragging about one's accomplishments or greatness. *Jim is very shy; he'd be the last one to toot his own horn.*

Top

Blow one's top: erupt into anger or rage; lose one's temper or composure. *He blew his top at the staff meeting today.*

Off the top of one's head: *See,* **Off**.

On top of the world: glorious feeling due to favorable events. *Jane is sitting on top of the world after her book made the bestseller list.*

Start from the top/Take it from the top: start all over; from the beginning. *Ok, let's start from the top, with everyone following the cue from the percussion section.*

The tops/Top notch: the very best in quality, ability, style, etc. *This hotel is top notch.*

Tip-top: *See,* **Tip**.

Top dog/Top banana: one in control or power; the boss. *He is top dog in this outfit.*

Top of the heap: superior to all others. *It's challenging to get to the top of the heap in any organization, but harder to stay there.*

Top of the line/Top notch: of the best quality. *I like going to that electronics store because they sell top-of-the-line products from major manufacturers. That stereo is top of the line!*

Top this: do better than what is done. *After blowing a bubble measuring 20 centimeters wide with his bubble gum, the kid said to his buddies, "Ok, can anyone top this?"*

Yell at the top of one's lungs: to vocalize most loudly. *We yelled at the top of our lungs each time our soccer team scored a point or made a good play.*

Total

Totaled: wasted; completely destroyed. *He totaled his vehicle after crashing into a tree last night.*

Totally: absolutely. *Jack: "That was one awesome game tonight, wasn't it dude?" Mark: "Totally."*

Touch

Good touch: 1) to have a skilled hand in an activity. *He has a good touch to his work.* 2) a compliment to something well stated or that exhibits noted improvement. *When he mentioned his helpful ideas on the subject, the teacher replied, "Good touch."*

Touch a nerve/Touch a sore spot: sensitive matter that upsets someone. *I touched a sore spot when I mentioned a promotion to my boss.*

Touch and go: 1) uncertain of the results. *It was touch and go for a while with him; we didn't know if he would survive.* 2) a flying practice of momentarily landing on a runway and then suddenly taking off again. *The student pilots practiced touch and go flights today.*

Touch base: be in contact; get together. *Let's touch base later about it. If you have any questions, feel free to touch base with me.*

Touch up: 1) paint and body repair on a vehicle. *My car is in the shop to touch up a few scratches on the left rear quarter panel.* 2) make something look better cosmetically; make-up. *I got a touch up at the make-up counter in the department store.*

Touchy: irritable *As a result of receiving her cholera and tetanus shots, Sue was feeling touchy all day. Don't bother me, please; I'm in a touchy mood.*

Tough

Hang tough: *See,* **Hang**.

Play tough: be highly competitive and aggressive. *Our company president played tough in the proposed merger.*

Tough act to follow: difficult to surpass someone else. *Jane is a tough act to follow.*

Tough break: unavoidable setback; unlucky situation. *It was a tough break for him not to gain acceptance to the college of his choice.*

Tough cookie: a strict or disciplined person. *She is one tough cookie at 96 years old.*

Tough it out: remain firm or unyielding in facing difficulty. *We have to tough it out if we want a winning team.*

Tough pill to swallow: hard to take; painful change. *Laying off employees from the company was a tough pill to swallow for the small community.*

Tough row to hoe: be faced with a difficult task. *We all had a tough row to hoe on the farm after our best worker, Hank, died of a stroke.*

Tough shit: *See,* **Shit**.

Toy

Toy: to fool around with; to harass or agitate. *Don't toy with me, 'less you want to eat a knuckle sandwich.*

Track

(Get) back on track: to assimilate; to normalize; to get back to doing things correctly. *After that great vacation, I need a week to get back on track at work.*

Inside track: *See,* **Have the Inside track.**

Keep track of: stay informed; record what's going on. *For record purposes, you have to keep track of your travel expenses.*

Lose track of: to forget about or to lose sight of (opposite of keep track of). *We lost track of him after college.*

Make tracks: to take off in a hurry. *Simpson made tracks out of here after discovering he was late to the meeting.*

Off track: to wander off one's goal or objective; not appropriate. *What he is doing is way off track.*

On the wrong track: stray from one's purpose or goal. *Jason got on the wrong track early in life.*

On the wrong side of the tracks: in a poor, run-down part of the neighborhood. *My best education came from growing up on the wrong side of the tracks.*

One-track mind: when the mind is focused on one thing, generally in reference to an infatuated yearning for an attractive person. *Ray has a one-track mind, and becomes infatuated with a different girl about once a week in school.*

Track down: pursue or search until found. *We took off immediately to track down the thief.*

Track record: performance over time. *What is the track record of this aircraft in actual air-to-air combat?*

Trap

Bear trap: *See,* **Bear.**

Booby trap: 1) a hidden explosive designed to go off if stepped on. *There are booby traps all over this area.* 2) a concealment or pitfall to an unsuspecting opponent. *This deal is full of booby traps.*

Fall into a trap: *See,* **Fall.**

Shut your trap: be quiet; shut your mouth. *Shut your trap and let him speak.*

Trappings: the physical layout or setup of a place. *There isn't a lot to these trappings, but you're welcome to stay over.*

Trial

Bench trial: *See,* **Bench.**

Jury trial: *See,* **Jury**.

Trial and error: method of trying different things to find a solution. *Did you know that Thomas Edison invented the electric light bulb through trial and error, after conducting thousands of experiments?*

Trick

Dirty trick: *See,* **Dirty**.

Do the trick: *See,* **Do**.

Hat trick: *See,* **Hat**.

Trick: time spent with a prostitute. *She turns more tricks right after each military payday.*

Trick or treat: a custom on the night of Halloween, October 31st, to go house to house asking homeowners, "trick or treat," which is a saying to either request a treat, such as candy, or else a trick would be played on the homeowner (the custom really is to receive a treat, since Halloween is a fairy-tale custom in the United States, and not an occasion for real revenge). *We had a lot of trick or treaters come to our neighborhood this past Halloween.*

Tricks of the trade: expert knowledge not generally shared. *We need him because he knows the tricks of the trade in the business.*

Tricky: risky. *Traveling to that remote region without a guide could be tricky business.*

Trip

Trip/Trip out: to be excessively worried or stressed; to overreact. *We were tripping out about the injured dog in the road. My parents tripped out when they heard I failed my exam.*

Trot

Hot to trot: *See,* **Hot**.

Trot: to go or come to. *Let's trot on over to the café to see who's there.*

Trots: diarrhea. *That turkey dinner last night gave me the trots.*

Trouble

Pour oil over troubled waters: *See,* **Pour**.

Trouble is brewing: trouble is close by. *There will be trouble brewing at the next World Environmental Conference.*

True

Show one's true colors: *See,* **Show**.

True Blue: very loyal or dedicated. *Mr. Smith has been with this organization a long time; he's as true blue as they come.*

True to form: exactly as expected. *Our new hire is true to form.*

Trump

Trump card: hidden ability or maximum effort. *Our trump card is our efficient work force, without which this company could not survive.*

Trumped up charge: a false summons or accusation. *Jason was arrested on trumped up charges, but his lawyers got him off.*

Try

Try: to be a challenge; to stress. *"These are the times that try men's souls." (Thomas Paine writing in the Common Sense newsletter in 1776 about America's fight for independence from British dominance).*

Try one's hand at: try to do something the first time. *I'll try my hand at painting landscapes.*

Try out: 1) test one's fitness. *I tried out for the softball team and made it.* 2) test the quality or fitness of an item. *Why don't you try out the shirt?*

Trying: stressful or annoying. *His bad attitude is really trying on all of us.*

Tube

Boob tube/The tube: television. *Any ball games on the tube tonight?*

Tubing/Tubin': surfing. *Humphrey went tubin' at Malibu Beach.*

Tune

Call the tune: *See,* **Call**.

Change one's tune: to have a different attitude or opinion about something. *He changed his tune about camping in the park after hearing about attacks by black bears.*

Sing a different tune: act differently due to change of attitude. *Senator Jones is singing a different tune about logging after receiving a healthy campaign contribution from the timber industry.*

To the tune of: to the sum, value of, etc. *He sold his home to the tune of $1,000,000.*

Turn

Hairpin turn: *See,* **Hair**.

In turn: in proper order. *Why don't you follow her in turn?*

Out of turn: out of proper order. *Get in line, and don't go out of turn.*

Tables are turned: *See below,* **Turn** *the tables.*

Take turns: in regular or in succession. *Let's take turns on our night shift.*

Turn a blind eye: *See,* **Blind**.

Turn a deaf ear: *See,* **Ear**.

Turn it on: get it rocking; get things into action. *Alright troops, let's turn it on and win this game.*

Turn off: to become disinterested; dislike; boredom. *He's a real turn off when he gets mad.*

Turn on: 1) attractive; someone who excites another. *Her singing turns me on.* 2) deceive; go against; work against. *Hey, I've been 100% loyal; I never turned on you, never.*

Turn on the heat: apply the necessary force. *The boss has turned on the heat to get everything in shape for the next conference.*

Turn one's back: *See,* **Back**.

Turn over a new leaf: do better in spite of past mistakes. *I'm going to turn over a new leaf and be more respectful to others in the office.*

Turn over in one's grave/Turn in one's grave: how one already deceased would likely react, in either shock or anger, to one's action (enough to make them turn around in their grave). *If grandma knew what you were planning to do, she would be turning over in her grave.*

Turn tail: take off at the sign of trouble or danger. *As soon as Dick smelled danger, he turned tail.*

Turn the corner: come across a crucial point; on the way to recovery. *The donated food helped turn the corner in overcoming hunger in many parts of the drought-stricken region.*

Turn the other cheek: to respond non-violently, without retaliation, to insult or injury. *Martin Luther King, Jr., in his quest for non-violence toward equality, told his followers to always turn the other cheek in the face of hate and bigotry.*

Turn the tables/Tables are turned/Turn the tide/Tide has turned: a reversal of events; when a situation changes, for better or worse. *DePaul turned the tables on Marquette in the last seconds of the basketball game by intercepting a pass and dunking the ball for the victory.*

Turn up the heat: put greater pressure on. *The tax collectors have been turning up the heat lately to get business owners to pay their taxes on time.*

Turncoat: traitor. *I wouldn't trust that turncoat.*

Tweak

Tweak: to make small changes to improve on something. *We need to tweak these numbers a bit in the quarterly report so that they are in line with recent sales.*

Twist

Twisted around one's finger: *See,* **Finger**.

Twist in the wind: *See,* **Wind**.

Twist someone's arm: to coerce or persuade someone to do something. *They were trying to twist his arm to get him to vote for their project. We had to do a little arm twisting to get people to support our initiative.*

Two

Two-bit: small time; insignificant. *The deceased was a two-bit hustler who walked these streets for years.*

Two cents: 1) for little or nothing. *I wouldn't give two cents for his advice.* 2) unsolicited advice. *If you want my two cents, I think you should accept the deal.* 3) feeling of worthlessness. *She made everyone feel like two cents at the staff meeting.*

Two-timer: one who has two or more lovers, generally in secret. *Jackson is a two-timer, and everyone knows it.*

Two-way street: success is possible only if two people have a say in it. *Marriage is a two-way street.*

Uncle

Uncle: an expression indicating surrender. *When I wrestled him into a head lock, he yelled, "Uncle," to let him go.*

Uncle Sam: a patriotic, bearded old man, in caricature, who symbolizes the U.S. government. *The states ought to get some money from Uncle Sam to build this freeway.*

Under

Go under the knife: *See,* **Knife**.

Snowed under: *See,* **Snow**.

Under a cloud (of suspicion): *See,* **Cloud**.

Under consideration: to be taken for study prior to a response. *I'll take your suggestions under consideration.*

Under fire: *See,* **Fire**.

Under one's belt: having the experience. *He has ten years under his belt as a tugboat captain.*

Under one's breath: *See,* **Breath**.

Under one's nose: in plain sight; easily seen. *The keys were right under my nose on the shelf in the hallway that I passed by several times.*

Under one's/its own steam: under one's own power; without help. *The ship's engines were in poor shape, yet it crossed the straits and came into port under its own steam.*

Under one's skin: cannot stop thinking about someone, whether out of love, infatuation, anger, hate, or other emotion. *Ever since I started caring for my friend's puppy, he has gotten under my skin and I cannot let him go.*

Under one's thumb: under another's domination. *Jean really has her husband under her thumb.*

Under one's wing: *See,* **Wing**.

Under the hammer: *See,* **Hammer**.

Under the gun: pressed for time. *I'm under the gun to have the report completed by this Friday.*

Under the radar: to be discreet; without being seen or heard; without notice. *We need to stay under the radar to keep the media from finding out about the merger.*

Under the Table/Under the counter: discreet transaction; in secret; illegal activity. *We bought these fireworks under the counter from a friend. Most illegal transactions tend to be cash payments under the table.*

Under the weather: feeling ill; not up to par. *I've been under the weather lately and have not kept up with my daily chores.*

Under the wire: *See,* **Wire**.

Under wraps: to keep secretive; not to be seen or revealed. *The UFO incident is under wraps since it occurred over the military base.*

Underdog: not favored. *We vote for the underdogs who have the spirit and energy to do good in the community.*

Up

An ace up one's sleeve: *See below,* **Up** one's sleeve.

On the up and up: honest and fair dealing. *I guarantee that this deal is on the up and up.*

Own up to: to admit. *He had to own up to the fact that he ate all the cookies.*

Up: feeling good; cheerful. *He has been feeling up ever since he started dating Carol.*

Up a creek (without a paddle): in great trouble no longer under one's control. *Without our technicians, we would be up a creek without a paddle.*

Up a tree: helpless; faced with a difficult situation or choice. *Jason was up a tree when he had to choose between going overseas or quit his job.*

Up against (a wall): 1) nowhere to go; without a choice; no alternatives. *Being up against the wall, financially, we were forced to file for bankruptcy protection.* 2) facing impending and overwhelming force. *Japanese-Americans, up against a wall of racism in 1942, were wrongfully interned in concentration camps without any rights as citizens.*

Up and at 'em: get going; get busy; move it. *Up and at 'em guys...we have a lot of work ahead of us today.*

Up and coming: a future success or star. *He is an up and coming politician who, someday, is expected to be a candidate for the U.S. Senate.*

Up for grabs: available to be taken; first come, first served. *Everything was up for grabs at the liquidation sale.*

Up front: 1) honest and trustworthy. *Mr. Derrick is always up front with his employees.* 2) in advance. *I would like to have payment up front.*

Up in arms: mad; very angry. *The boss was up in arms when the laborers suddenly went on strike for better working conditions.*

Up in the air: 1) undecided; not settled. *We were up in the air about where to go on our vacation.* 2) very angry or excited. *I thought my sailing instructor would shoot straight up in the air when I flipped over the catamaran in the marina; he called it a learning experience.*

Up in the clouds: *See,* **Cloud**.

Up in smoke: to be gone; to wither; fall through. *Our plans to build a waterfront development went up in smoke when the city declared the land to be protected wetlands.*

Up one's alley: what one prefers or excels at. *This assignment requires a lot of field work, which is right up your alley as an archeologist.*

Up one's sleeve: concealed plan. *I can tell by the look in your eye that you have something up your sleeve.*

Up the ante: raise the bet, offer or stakes. *Another bidder in the sale just upped the ante on the corporate assets in bankruptcy.*

Up the gazoo/Up the kazoo: a whole lot of; in excess. *We are out of rain boots, but we are stocked with sandals up the kazoo.*

Up to no good: involved with something bad or unfavorable to others. *Be aware of those loitering in the parking lot; they make a lot of noise and generally are up to no good.*

Up to one's ears/Up to one's eyeballs/Up to one's neck/Up to one's ass (expressive): involved in deeply with; overwhelmed with. *We are up to our neck in work orders, so start hiring at the local union halls.*

Up to par/Up to snuff: 1) feeling in normal health. *I've got the flu and don't feel up to snuff today.* 2) at the usual level; normal. *They had to come up to snuff with the building code.*

Up to the hilt: all the way; to the top; the most. *We filled the gas tanks up to the hilt prior to our trip from LA to San Francisco on the I-5 freeway.*

Up yours [expressive]: a crude and vulgar exclamation of contempt or ridicule (sometimes accompanied with an obscene gesture). *When the guard told the protesters to leave the premises, they responded, "Up yours!"*

Upchuck: to vomit. *The rides got me so dizzy, I had to run to the bathroom and upchuck.*

Uphill battle: a tiring or difficult struggle. *Your father fought an uphill battle to secure civil rights for the oppressed in this country.*

Upper crust/Upscale: the elite; the rich. *He comes from an upper crust family.*

Ups and downs: good periods and bad periods. *Our family went through a lot of ups and downs this past year.*

Uptick: higher level. *There was announced an uptick in the threat level for terror at the border for this week.*

Upset

Upset the applecart: disrupt a plan or ongoing activity. *Keep your peace and don't upset the applecart.*

Vamoose

Vamoose: go away; get lost. *I want you kids to vamoose when our guests arrive.*

Veg

Veg out: take it easy; relax; kick back and do nothing. *We like to veg out and watch the salmon swim up the creek in our neighborhood.*

Vent

Vent: to express, as in one's feelings. *I want you to vent your feelings at this session to help you resolve the problems you are having on the job.*

Vibe

Vibes: feelings; sensations. *I'm getting good vibes about this place.*

Vicious

Vicious circle: unfavorable or bad situation, which keeps repeating; one after another in negative sequence. *Trading violence with violence only creates a vicious circle of blame where both sides suffer.*

Vine

Wither on the vine: unable to complete; to die out; fail to materialize or be completed. *The projects will wither on the vine unless the city decides to provide additional funding.*

VIP

VIP: very important person. *The hotel always has in reserve several suites for any sudden arrivals of VIP's.*

Wack/Whack

Out of whack: *See,* **Out** of kilter.

Wacky/Whacky: crazy; unpredictable. *You may like him, but I think he's wacky.*

Whack: 1) bizarre. *Man, that show was whack!* 2) beat handily; defeat significantly. *We got whacked on the basketball court tonight.* 3) displeasing. *That's whack, man, for your parents to make you do yard work today when the championship tournament is playing on television.* 4) very inebriated, drunk or stoned. *Man, I was whacked after smoking that stuff.* 5) to kill. *An elite hit team of the military whacked the terrorist leader.*

Wait

Lie in wait: to observe in hiding for surprise or attack. *The soldiers were lying in wait for the enemy to cross the river.*

Wait on hand and foot: to serve diligently; do everything possible for someone. *He always has a helper waiting on him hand and foot.*

Wait tables: to serve food. *I wait tables part-time, in between my acting jobs.*

Wait with baited breath: *See,* **Breath**.

Walk

Cake walk: *See,* **Cake**.

Can't walk and chew gum at the same time: to be able to do more than one thing at a time (used generally in the negative). *The guy is so clumsy, he cannot walk and chew gum at the same time.*

Walk a tightrope: be under a watchful or dangerous situation, where any wrong move could cause disaster or complete failure. *We were walking a tightrope all the time and risking a cave-in while trying to rescue the workers who fell into the crevasse.*

Walk all over: 1) defeat overwhelmingly. *In softball today, the Bumblebees walked all over the Yellow Jackets, 18 to 0.* 2) to treat contemptuously; overbearing or arrogant action. *He walks all over her and gives little consideration to her suggestions.*

Walk away from: 1) to survive an accident with little or no injury, and be able to move on one's own volition. *He miraculously was able to walk away from the plane crash.* 2) to leave something. *Please don't get involved;*

just walk away from it. 3) leaving others behind in defeat or loss. *The Chicago Bulls and Michael Jordan met with success in the 1990's, making it seem easy in walking away from the competition.*

Walk in the park: very easy to do; no problem. *He is such a great handyman that building a hot water sink in the basement storage room would be a walk in the park for him.*

Walk on air: feeling of happiness and excitement. *We were walking on air after the Forest Service canceled plans to cut the old-growth forest.*

Walk on eggs: be very careful; proceed cautiously. *We walk on eggs around our temperamental boss.*

Walk the walk, talk the talk: doing what you say you will; backing up one's words. *If you can't walk the walk and talk the talk, then you don't belong in this responsible position.*

Walking encyclopedia: someone who knows a lot; one who is very knowledgeable. *Jack is not only a walking encyclopedia, but a very personable individual as well.*

Walking papers: notice of being fired or dismissed from one's job. *I got my walking papers today.*

Wall

Back to the wall: *See,* **Back**.

Beat one's head against a wall: *See,* **Beat**.

Climb the walls: very frustrated and anxious. *We were climbing the walls waiting to hear the results of our final exams.*

Drive someone up a wall: *See,* **Drive**.

Handwriting is on the wall: *See,* **Hand**.

Like pasting jelly to the wall: will not work; impossible; unable to accomplish. *Doing the job under budget is like pasting jelly to the wall.*

Off the wall: *See,* **Off**.

Push one to the wall: *See,* **Push**.

Run into a brick wall: *See,* **Run**.

Walls have ears: someone may be listening; be careful what you say at the risk of being overheard. *Speak softly because these walls have ears.*

Wall-to-wall: full of; covered with. *I wonder if the wall-to-wall patriotism espoused by many well-meaning leaders under the notion of national security might someday change or dilute our current fundamental rights and freedoms under the Constitution.*

Wash

A wash/It's a wash: come out even; no change. *The whole deal was a wash.*

Come out in the wash: the truth will come forth sooner or later. *It will all come out in the wash.*

Wash one's dirty laundry in public: make one's embarrassing private matter public. *It is interesting to read court documents and see how far parties go in washing each other's dirty linen in public.*

Wash one's hands of: do away with a problem; not becoming involved. *I will not be a part of this scheme; I wash my hands of it.*

Washout: failure; fiasco. *The venture in Mexico was a washout.*

Washed out: 1) without energy. *He was washed out after fighting the floodwaters all night.* 2) to lose out. *Although we were favored to win the tournament, we washed out in the first round of the playoffs.*

Washed up: finished; ruined; failure. *Our technology software company washed up after losing a major government contract.*

Waste

Waste: to destroy. *Waste that cigarette, son; I don't want you smoking anymore.*

Waste of breath/Waste one's breath: talk without results; not worth saying; speak in vain. *It is a waste of breath to get him to change his mind.*

Waste not, want not: efficient use of one's resources helps to save. *I love to eat left overs at home—waste not, want not.*

Wasted: extremely drunk or under the strong influence of drugs. *I got so wasted at the party that it took two days to recover from it.*

Water

Come hell or high water: *See,* **Hell**.

Deep water: *See,* **Deep**.

Doesn't hold water: not suitable; doesn't meet standards; not reasonable. *Your argument doesn't hold water because you have no facts to back it up.*

Head above water: *See,* **Head**.

Ice water in one's veins: *See,* **Ice**.

In hot water: *See,* **Hot**.

Like a Fish out of water/Like a fish to water: *See,* **Fish**.

Like water: in great amounts; freely. *He spent his money like water.*

Like water off a duck's back: to have no consequence; without any effect. *He handled the criticism like water off a duck's back.*

Make one's mouth water: *See,* **Mouth**.

Pour cold water on: to discourage; to cease doing. *A bad manager who does not appreciate hard work pours cold water on my loyal efforts to spend any extra time at work.*

Test the waters: analyze or study something first before going forward. *He is testing the waters with a fundraiser tonight to see if he ought to run as a candidate for the U.S. Senate.*

Treading water: not going anywhere; not progressing or getting better. *I've been treading water with my debts.*

Water down: to weaken; to dilute. *The legislature needs to water down the tax reform bill in order to gain enough votes for passage.*

Watering hole: a bar, nightclub or other establishment where drinks are served. *We usually go to a local watering hole after work.*

Wear

Wear a different hat: be or act completely in another way. *It is a question how he seems to wear a different hat depending upon which audience he is in front of; doesn't such an act catch up with you sooner or later?*

Wear and tear: deterioration and damage done by normal and casual use. *We will not charge for any wear and tear in the apartment, like the carpeting and appliances.*

Wear it on one's sleeve/Wear one's heart on one's sleeve: openly express one's feelings. *He is an open and emotional person who wears his heart on his sleeve.*

Wear out one's welcome: to visit a host's place too long; overextend one's stay. *I love it here at Aunt Betsy's place so much that I fear I may wear out my welcome.*

Wear the pants: the person who has the authority in a household. *Grandpa wears the pants around this house, and no one can do anything without his permission.*

Weed

Grow like a weed: grow fast. *Little Tommy grew like a weed after 4th grade.*

Weed: marijuana. *There are a lot of weed plants that grow wild along the highway during the summer months.*

Weight

Carry a lot of weight: *See,* **Carry**.

Carry one's (own) weight: *See,* **Carry**.

Pull one's weight: using one's own influence to get things done. *If you want things done, you will have to pull your own weight around here.*

Throw one's weight around: *See,* **Throw**.

Wet

All wet: completely wrong; wholly mistaken. *Your idea to drill for oil in this wildlife refuge is all wet.*

Get one's feet wet: get experience; for the first time. *I got my feet wet in radio as a college disc jockey playing late night rock and roll music.*

Wet behind the ears: inexperienced. *Since you are wet behind the ears, we will assign you to a mentor to help you learn the trade.*

Wet blanket: something or someone that prevents others from enjoying life. *The forecast of windy weather put a wet blanket on our outdoors candle party.*

Wet one's whistle: desire to drink, usually alcohol. *After a hard day's work, many workers go to the local tavern to wet their whistle.*

Whack

See above, **Wack.**

What

And what not: and other things. *We were just cleaning the house and what not around the house while you were gone.*

So what (else) is new?: 1) to sarcastically mention about information that is already known. *The headlines talk about conflict in the Middle East. So what else is new?* 2) an expression to inquire with another about any recent and new information. *In meeting his friend for the first time in 3 years, he asked, "So what's new?"*

What are you driving at?: What are you trying to say? *What are you driving at with your questions?*

What gives?/What goes?: what is going on? *What gives on the labor negotiations?*

What in carnation?: a strong, if not frustrated, inquiry about something. *What in carnation are they saying?*

What's eating you?: What is bothering or annoying you? *When he noticed his friend looking upset, he asked him, "What's eating you?"*

What's happening/What's up/Wassup/What up?: a general greeting of "hello." *Hey! Wassup!? Long time no see!*

What's the big idea?: why are you doing that? *What's the big idea telling everyone that I could not show up because I was sick when I was really out of town on business?*

What's the deal?: what's going on? *What's the deal about Mr. Vickers being promoted ahead of Mr. Watkins for vice president?*

What's the use?: why bother? *What's the use trying to convince her on the plan? She already voted against it.*

What the hell?: *See,* **Hell**.

Wheel

At the wheel: in charge. *Who is at the wheel around here?*

Big wheel: important or influential person. *A lot of big wheels will be at the meeting tonight.*

Squeaky wheel (gets the grease): being heard tends to get recognized faster; getting attention. *You have to be aggressive in this business because it is the squeaky wheel that gets the grease.*

Wheeler-dealer: one who is always trying to work a deal for money, especially to make a fast buck; one associated with doing shady transactions. *Jack is a wheeler-dealer, never resting when an opportunity for profit becomes available.*

Wheels: vehicle. *Can I borrow your wheels tonight?*

Whistle

Bells and whistles: *See,* **Bell**.

Blow the whistle/Whistle blower: inform on someone, generally about illegal activity. *It took some brave souls to blow the whistle on management regarding the overcharging of government medical reimbursements.*

Clean as a whistle: *See,* **Clean**.

Wet one's whistle: *See,* **Wet**.

White

White as a ghost: terrified. *I was white as a ghost when footsteps were heard in the basement.*

White elephant: a possession that is hard to get rid of; a possession that is a greater problem than a pleasure; unwanted property hard to sell or dispose of. *With the economic recession hitting this area hard, most of the mansions in the neighborhood have become white elephants.*

White knight: a savior. *An anonymous white knight donated enough funds last night to save the church from a foreclosure sale this Friday.*

White lie: a harmless falsehood intended for polite discretion; innocent social excuse. *She told him a white lie about her family visiting her this weekend so that he would not come by; in reality, she was getting her place ready for his surprise birthday party.*

White sale: a sale on white cloth, such as sheets, towels and the like. *They are having a white sale at all the department stores this weekend!*

Whitewash: an attempt to soften a worse scenario, generally by a government informing the public; to spin a story to soothe the public. *The government whitewash on the corruption in the police force has angered the legislative body, which is looking to conduct an investigation and create new laws on enforcement.*

Whiz

Whiz: 1) very smart. *Jack is a whiz in class.* 2) to depart or go by quickly. *He whizzed out of here when he heard his daughter was ill.*

Whole

Whole ball of wax/Whole nine yards: the complete assortment [originally a belt of machine gun bullets measuring the length of nine yards that was loaded on an aircraft]. *See also,* **Lock,** stock and barrel. *We sold everything at auction; I mean the whole nine yards! There is nothing left.*

Whole enchilada/Whole kit and caboodle/Whole shebang: all things; the entire package. *When they left, they took everything, I mean the whole kit and caboodle.*

Whole new ballgame: *See,* **Ball.**

Whole nine yards: *See above,* **Whole** ball of wax.

Wild

Run wild: grow or behave out of control. *The kids run wild in the field while the parents tend to their gardens.*

Wild goose chase: a futile search, mission or chore. *We went on a wild goose chase looking for little Danny, while all the time he was at grandma's having ice cream.*

Wildcat strike: a strike that is quickly formed by the workers, and generally not sanctioned by a labor union. *The truckers called a wildcat strike to protest the working conditions of the migrant workers.*

Willies

Willies: *Same as,* **The creeps.**

Wimp

Wimp: weak person; wuss; sissy. *He may look like a wimp, but he can kick ass on the futbol field.*

Wind

As the wind blows: following the known trend or public opinion or events. *I'm just moving along as the wind blows.*

Break wind: to pass gas from one's bowels. *We get out of the way whenever Joe breaks wind.*

Get wind of: to receive information on something. *Did you get wind of Bob getting into the Olympic trials on the ski slalom?*

In the teeth of the wind: right in the face of a dangerous situation. *He went to the region in the teeth of the wind to help the poor and starving masses.*

Second wind: 1) a resurgence of energy following the initial period of fatigue, such as when running a long distance. *Runners who run the mile usually get a second wind after about a third of the way.* 2) a renewed feeling of energy following a slowdown or sluggishness. *Studying into the night was tiring, but after catching my second wind I was able to burn the midnight oil.*

Take the wind out of one's sails: do away with one's advantage; to disappoint; to depress, hinder or stop something or someone's action. *When the judge granted the motion to dismiss our lawsuit, it completely took the wind out of our sails. You sure took the wind out of his sails after telling him that he lost the bid to his rival in the industry.*

Test the winds: get feedback; seek a response from an initial action. *The beverage company is testing the winds with its new drink to see how the public likes it.*

That's the way the wind blows: *See,* **That**.

Throw caution to the wind(s): *See,* **Throw**.

Twist in the wind/Dangle in the wind: left alone (generally to suffer in shame); abandoned amidst difficulty. *When he made searing comments about his subordinates, he quickly lost support and was left twisting in the wind.*

Window

Window shopping: looking but not buying. *We bought very little today, and mainly did a lot of window shopping.*

Wing

Clip someone's wings: *See,* **Clip**.

Under one's wing: under one's support or sponsorship. *I took him under my wing ever since he started this job.*

Wing ding: a party; a get-together. *You're invited to a wing ding at my place this weekend.*

Wing it: improvise as you go along; ad lib; act without preparation. *If you forget the script, well, just wing it, stud.*

Wipe

Wipe away: get rid of. *Wipe away that smile and stand at attention, soldier!*

Wipe one's slate clean: do good to overcome a bad record. *Jack did a few days of volunteer work to wipe his slate clean of a prior traffic infraction.*

Wire

Down to the wire: to the very end; to the very last moment that time would allow. *The entire game was very close, all the way down to the wire! We worked right down to the wire to finish the project.*

Get one's wires crossed: to be confused or mistaken about a matter. *Sorry for getting my wires crossed when I jotted the appointment on my calendar under the wrong day.*

Pull wires: use private influence to achieve something. *I had to pull wires to see one of the big wheels in the Mayor's office*

Under the wire: manage to enter or achieve barely on time. *We managed to turn in our application right under the wire.*

Wired: 1) under the influence of an upper drug, such as methamphetamine. *He was so wired and out of control that it took four of us to wrestle him to the ground.* 2) full of energy and zip without drug influence. *John is so wired worrying about losing his job that he is unable to get much sleep; or maybe he's wired on the five cups of coffee he had today.*

Wire-to-wire: too close to call to the end. *The horses ran wire-to-wire to the finish line.*

Wise

Be or get wise to: understand well; get the true facts. *Why don't you get wise to the fact that you are not the boss around here?*

Wise acre: sarcastic or mischievous individual. *Look you little wise acre, you don't know anything about how she feels.*

Wise guy: one who irritates, praises himself, annoys, etc.; sarcastic or obnoxious person. *Why doesn't the boss straighten up that wise guy in the supply office?*

Wise up: get informed; get with the program. *My advise to you is to wise up and get with the program.*

Word to the wise: practical advice. *A word to the wise—respect the environment or else it will unleash its mighty powers against you.*

With

With a grain of salt: *See,* **Salt**.

With a heavy hand: *See,* **Hand**.

With clean hands: doing nothing wrong. *James performed the first six months of his recruit assignment with clean hands. I'm walking out of this mess with clean hands.*

With flying colors: done brilliantly and with ease. *Janet passed the lawyers test with flying colors.*

With no strings attached: without obligation; free. *I got a new car for my graduation with no strings attached.*

Without

Without a hitch: no problem whatsoever. *The crew sailed to Catalina Island through the pitching waves and around the big oil tankers without a hitch.*

Without batting an eye: suddenly; without prior thought. *When Helen fell down she got up and ran without batting an eye.*

Without question/fail: absolutely. *I'll meet you at ten without fail.*

Without rhyme or reason: having no purpose or logic. *There is no rhyme or reason why the new prototype malfunctioned.*

Wits

At the end of one's wits/At my wit's end: unable to use one's mental functions. *It's time to retire since I'm reaching my wit's end.*

Wolf

Cry wolf: *See,* **Cry**.

Wolf in sheep's clothing: something that looks good is actually bad. *The new boss looks kind but he's a wolf in sheep's clothing.*

Wood

Crawl/Come out of the woodwork: to appear or interfere in a bothersome way. *When Jake won the lottery, relatives of every kind seemed to crawl out of the woodwork.*

Knock on wood: *See,* **Knock**.

Neck of the woods: *See,* **Neck**.

Out of the woods: no longer in danger or in trouble. *She was very ill for several days, but she seems to be out of the woods now.*

Wool

All wool and a yard wide: genuine; purebred; real. *Your purpose is all wool and a yard wide.*

Pull the wool over one's eyes: *See,* **Pull**.

Word

A few words: 1) not talkative. *He's a man of few words.* 2) very briefly. *State your case in a few words, counsel.*

By word of mouth: by speaking, not by writing. *They maintained the family history by word of mouth.*

Eat one's words: *See,* **Eat**.

Get a word in: *See,* **Get**.

Have a word with: have a short talk. *I would like to have a word with you.*

Have words with: to argue with. *He had words with his boss.*

In so many words: clearly. *I told him in so many words.*

Keep one's word: *See,* **Keep**.

Mum's the word: do not say or reveal anything; keep quiet. *Mum's the word on this one.*

My word: expression of worry, similar to, "My goodness." *My word, what happened to you?*

Put in a good word for someone: assist in some endeavor. *I put in a good word to one of the professors when my niece entered college.*

Say the word: *See,* **Say**.

Take one's word: believe what one says. *I'll take your word and see the doctor right away. I take him by his word.*

Take the words out of one's mouth: to be thinking in similar fashion with another; intent to say what one was saying. *You took the words out of my mouth about going shopping for new shoes.*

Word to the wise: *See,* **Wise**.

Work

At work: doing one's job. *May I speak to Jim? He's at work right now.*

Get the works/The Works: 1) everything. *He wants the works on his cheeseburger.* 2) get whatever punishment is in store for you. *He got the works for strangling that homeless person.*

In the works: in the planning stage. *Our next submission is in the works.*

Make quick work of: deal with quickly. *He made quick work of the parking problem.*

Out of work: out of a job. *Dick became out of work just last month.*

Piece of work: *See,* **Piece**.

Shoot the works: risk or bet all you have. *Let's shoot the works on the deal, and hope for the best.*

The (whole) works: everything. *I'll bet the whole works on the next deal. He told the barber to give him the whole works, including a haircut, shave, shampoo and head massage.*

Work off: pay a debt by working rather than with money. *I'll work off the hundred dollars I owe you.*

Work one's fingers to the bones: work a lot with great intensity. *I work my fingers to the bone with no appreciation.*

Work one's tail off: work strenuously; exert the hardest effort. *We worked our tails off to get the roof finished before the rainy season started.*

Work one's way through college: hold a part-time job and go to college. *Many students, who don't have the ready cash for tuition, have to work their way through college.*

Work over: subject one to pain and suffering. *The bandit got worked over pretty well by the police.*

World

Come into the world: to be born. *Moe came into the world on the third of June.*

Come up in the world/Move up in the world: one who has done well in life. *A good education and some connections have helped Sam come up in the world.*

For all the world: in every respect; at any cost. *She wouldn't give up tennis for all the world.*

Look at the world with rose-colored glasses/View the world with rose-colored glasses: *See,* **Rose**.

On top of the world: *See,* **Top**.

Out of this world: outstanding; the very best. *The show was out of this world!*

Think the world of: to admire or respect greatly. *I think the world of the Dalai Lama.*

What in the world: *See,* **Earth**.

Worm

Can of worms: *See,* **Can**.

Worm: person who possesses a lack of tack, honesty, or respect for others. *That guy dresses well, but he is a real worm.*

Worm out of: to handle a matter in an artful or otherwise deceptive manner. *You must find a way to worm out of this mess.*

Worn

Worn to a frazzle: nervously exhausted. *We were worn to a frazzle in getting the flowers on the float before the start of the parade.*

Worth

Not worth a damn: *See,* **Damn**.

Not worth a hill of beans: *See,* **Not**.

Worth its weight in gold: of great value. *These ancient artifacts are worth their weight in gold.*

Worth one's while: to merit consideration of one's time or effort. *It would be worth your while to spend a few extra days here and travel around the country.*

Wrap

Wrap it up: to finish up what one is doing. *Ok, let's wrap it up for today.*

Wrapped around one's finger: *See,* **Finger**.

Wrapped up: obsessively consumed. *We were wrapped up in a heated discussion about the death penalty.*

Write

Write-in: vote for a person not listed on the ballot by writing the name in. *John Simmons was a write-in for the county clerk position.*

Write off: absorb a loss in accounting; cancel a debt. *The company had to write off the debt since it was uncollectible.*

Write one up: to cite; to report on someone. *Are you gonna write me up, sheriff?*

Write the book: authority on a subject. *He wrote the book on Amazon crocodiles.*

Written

Written all over: obvious in meaning or understanding; showing obvious signs. *He had guilt written all over his face.*

Written in stone: to remain in place; not to be easily changed. *These by-laws are written in stone, and can only be changed by the founders of the company.*

Wrong

In the wrong: not right or true; not on the side of justice. *Dick was in the wrong for making a U-turn on a one-way street.*

Wrong side of the bed: not feeling up to par; having a grouchy day. *Looks like you got up on the wrong side of the bed today.*

Wuss

Wuss/Wussy: weak person; sissy; wimp. *He may be big, but he's a wuss if you challenge him.*

X marks the spot: to indicate an exact spot. *I would like you to move the picnic table right here. X marks the spot.*

X out: cross out or delete from a prepared text. *Why don't you x-out the second line, initial it, and I'll sign the document?*

X-rated: adult entertainment material; not recommended for viewing by minors. *The movie was X-rated.*

Yack/Yak

Yack: to talk and talk (sometimes to the point of annoyance); useless chatter. *She kept on yacking away about the poor service at the restaurant.*

Yackety-yak/Yakitty-yak: *Same as,* **Yack**.

Yap

Yap: mouth. *Shut your yap and pay attention, soldier!*

Yard

Bone yard: *See,* **Bone**.

Whole nine yards: *See,* **Whole**.

Yeah

Hell yeah: *See,* **Hell**.

Yeah right: an expression of doubt or disbelief. *He thinks the boss is going to give us a pay raise. Yeah right.*

Yo

Yo: a saying to get one's attention; to say, "hey." *Yo, is anyone home? Yo…wassup?*

Yo-yo: mentally erratic; not very intelligent; awkward, etc. *We saw this yo-yo running naked through the streets today.*

Yoo-hoo

Yoo-hoo: a greeting. *Yoo-hoo, is anyone there?*

You

You all/Y'all: referring to two or more people. (Folksy southern American English) *Now, y'all come next Sunday and enjoy our cook out.*

You bet your boots: definitely. *Are you coming to the dance next weekend? Oh, yes, you bet your boots I am.*

You better believe it: absolutely right; you can be assured. *You better believe it we're going to succeed.*

You can say that again: agree wholeheartedly. *Jack: Yesterday was the rainiest day I've seen in ages. Marianne: You can say that again!*

You can't have your cake and eat it too: you can't have it both ways; you have to choose one or the other. *Ken wanted to date both of them, but knew that he couldn't have his cake and eat it too.*

You can't take it with you: You can't take your possessions with you when you die. *Don't be a miser; you know you can't take all of this with you.*

You can't teach an old dog new tricks: a proverb meaning that old people have difficulty in registering new learning while struggling to maintain the knowledge they already possess.

You can't win 'em all: one cannot come out ahead all the time; you win some, you lose some. (A phrase generally used to comfort someone). *When the Yankees lost the 2001 world championship playoffs, you could almost hear Yogi Berra say, "Well, you can't win 'em all, son."*

You could cut it with a knife: *See,* **Cut**.

You don't say: A phrase denoting surprise when hearing about something (similar to the phrase, "Is that so?"). *Marianne: "Joe went to Jordan last week to search for religious sites." Bob: "You don't say?"*

You-ee: a U-turn. *I got a traffic ticket today doing a you-ee on Beverly Drive.*

You get what you pay for: If you paid less for it, it is probably because it is inferior in quality. *This cheap furniture fell apart within the first year. Well, it seems that you get what you pay for.*

You lost me: not understand what someone said (an indication to repeat it or interpret it another way). *You lost me; could you repeat it again?*

You never had it so good: everything could not be better. *Little kitty, you never had it so good after I took you away from the streets, and adopted you into my home and family.*

Yours truly: a phrase referring to "I" or "me." *The one who was stuck with the bill at the restaurant was yours truly.*

Yuck

Yuck: exclamation of disgust or surprise. *When the girls spotted little Kevin picking his nose, they yelled, "Yuck!"*

Yucky: bad. *This candy tastes pretty yucky.*

Yum

Yum-yum/Yummy: an exclamation of pleasure or something to eat. *That veal was yummy; I'll take another serving.*

Z

Zap

Zapped: 1) tired; exhausted; burned out. *I'm really zapped from the week-long hiking trip in the mountains.* 2) beaten; overtaken. *He zapped us real good in the chess tournament last week.*

Zero

Zero: a total nothing (in character); a complete deadbeat. *That guy is a real zero not to appreciate the assistance he got from others who saved his house from the flood.*

Zero in on something: concentrate directly; to find. *"I want you to zero in on this subject matter and understand it before you meet the scientists."*

Zilch

Zilch: amount to nothing. *That car is worth zilch after you banged it up.*

Zillion

Zillion: a very large amount. *With his talent, he's worth a zillion bucks.*

Zip

Zip: 1) travel quickly to. *Why don't we zip over to Jake's Café for lunch?* 2) to know nothing. *He knew zip about the program, yet they put him in charge.*

Zip it/Zip your lip: be quiet. *Zip your lip around here!*

Zippity-do/Zippity-doo: a somewhat sarcastic show of concern or attention, when the person really does not care. *Well, zippity-doo, look who showed up at the party tonight.*

Zit

Zit: pimple. *It was bad timing to get zits on my face, a day before my first date with Sheila.*

Zone

In the zone: feeling of strong competence and confidence; when things are happening just right; everything about one's work is going exceptionally well. *He was in the zone when he won the gold medal in the ski slalom.*

Zone out: to not be paying attention; detracted or disassociated. *I was so zoned out at school today, with so much on my mind.*

Zonk

Zonk out: fall asleep; be unaware of the surroundings, either asleep or unconscious. *I drank two cups of coffee before the meeting so that I wouldn't zonk out.*

Zonked: so extremely inebriated or tired that one has blurred senses. *I was zonked and unable to stay awake.*

Zoo

Zoo: a disorderly and confused situation. *It's a zoo around here with all these little kids; childcare is certainly a challenging occupation.*

Numerals

180

Do a 180: 1) change one's mind completely the other way; do an about face on a decision. *The mayor did a 180 on the monorail project after he discovered how much business it would bring to the downtown area.* 2) to turn in the opposite direction (by turning 180 degrees). *We did a 180 back to the house after realizing that we forgot our fishing gear. His car did a 180 when trying to turn on the slippery road.*

24/7

24/7: all the time; around the clock, 24 hours a day, 7 days a week. *This place is open 24/7.*

4-1-1

4-1-1: information; what's the deal? *What's the 4-1-1?*

5-0

5-0: police. *Heads up, 5-0 is just around the corner.*

86

86: to abort. *I want you to 86 that deal first if you want any additional funding.*

9/11

9/11: the day terrorists attacked the United States on September 11, 2001, and killed over 3,000 innocent people. *Many businesses suffered economically after 9/11.*

9 to 5

9 to 5: work hours of the regular worker, from 9 a.m. to 5 p.m. *This 9 to 5 stuff gets to be a real drag.*

ABOUT THE AUTHORS

Joseph Melillo taught conversational English in Japan for over 25 years to students who were willing to learn outside the English class. He compiled a notebook of American slang terms that he taught in those classes, which became the basis for this publication. After high school, he attended the School of Professional Arts in New York City. He developed a professional background in advertising design, illustrative techniques and cartooning. He also attended the University of Maryland where he obtained his bachelor of arts degree in government and politics. Joseph was born in Teora, Italy, and immigrated to the United States at the age of 11.

His son, **Edward M. Melillo**, completely revised the notebook of American slang, and updated the book with many more contemporary slang terms. He attended UCLA where he received his bachelor of arts degree in economics, attended DePaul University College of Law in Chicago, Illinois for his juris doctor degree, and attended the University of Washington Law School under the LLM tax law program. He currently practices law in the State of Washington.